# A-level Study Guide

# General Studies

Anthony Batchelor

Gareth Davies

Edward Little

Revision Express

## Acknowledgements

We are grateful to the following for permission to reproduce copyright material:

Guardian Newspapers Limited for an extract from 'Great Divide As Census Reveals Two Nations Growing Far Apart' by Jamie Doward, Tom Reilly and Mary Graham published in The Observer, 23 November 2003 © Tom Reilly 2003; the OECD/IEA for the table on page 17; the United Nations for the population graph on page 17; the Parliamentary Office of Science and Technology for the graph on page 58; the British Election Study 2001 for the table on page 79; and HMSO for the use of *Social Trends 33* Crown Copyright data in the social sciences section.

In some instances we have been unable to trace owners of copyright material, and we would appreciate any information that would enable us to do so.

Series Consultants: Geoff Black and Stuart Wall

**Pearson Education Limited**

Edinburgh Gate, Harlow

Essex CM20 2JE, England

*and Associated Companies throughout the world*

www.pearsoned.co.uk

© Pearson Education Limited 2005

The rights of Anthony Batchelor, Gareth Davies and Edward Little to be identified as authors of this work have been asserted by them in accordance with the Copyright, Designs and Patents Act 1988.

**British Library Cataloguing in Publication Data**

A catalogue entry for this title is available from the British Library.

ISBN-10: 1-4058-2364-X

ISBN-13: 978-1-4058-2364-7

First published 2005

Second Impression 2006

10 9 8 7 6 5 4 3 2

09 08 07 06

Set by 35 in Univers, Cheltenham

Printed by Ashford Colour Press, Gosport, Hants

# Characteristics of the sciences

Science tries to explain how the Universe works – there's nothing like being ambitious!

Scientists propose and test **explanations** for their observations. The explanations should be as simple as possible. The simpler the explanation, the more powerful and general it is likely to be.

Science is vast, and divided into branches, based on the subject matter – physics, chemistry, biology, biochemistry and so on. In principle all branches depend on experiments, but for some, such as astronomy and cosmology, experiments consist of making predictions that certain objects exist, in particular places. Experimenters then search for the objects, or even the effects of the objects. Because there were irregularities in the orbits of Saturn and Uranus, the existence and position of other planets further out in the solar system was predicted, and ultimately confirmed by astronomers.

## Exam themes

→ Different branches of science

→ The content of different branches of science

→ The relationship between science and technology

→ How science develops and the nature of a revolution

→ Know about three scientific revolutions

→ Inductive reasoning in science

→ The importance of experiments in science

→ The achievements of three different scientists

## Topic checklist

○ AS  ● A2

| | AQA A | AQA B | EDEXCEL | OCR |
|---|---|---|---|---|
| The Earth and the Universe | ○● | ● | ○ | ○● |
| Is medicine science? | ○● | ● | ○ | ○● |
| What is the world made of? | ○● | ● | ○ | ○● |

# The Earth and the Universe

**Checkpoint 1**

What do these mean: universe, star, galaxy and planet?

**Action point**

Find out when and by whom the telescope was invented.

**Examiner's secrets**

Always make it clear that you understand the similarities and differences between 'science' and 'technology'.

**The jargon**

The system with the sun and everything else circling the Earth is the **geocentric** model.

Where the Earth and planets circle the sun, it is called the **heliocentric** model.

From the beginning, we have wondered about our place in nature, that is, apart from our need to feed and protect ourselves. So what is 'out there' has always been a subject of speculation, and explanations of how the Universe came to be the way it is have always been bones of contention. Such ideas continue to fascinate and perplex us.

## The Earth and its place in the Universe

→ Since the invention of powerful telescopes and the use of space travel, observation has led most people to have a reasonably common view of the relationship between the Earth and the various bodies in the sky. It was not always so, and our modern view derives from the work of **Nicholas Copernicus** in the 16th century. Up to then, ideas of the universe were very diverse, and often determined by the dominant religious views of the society at the time.

→ Early societies assumed that the place they lived in was a centre of some kind. Up in the sky were strange, but apparently regular, phenomena, and below their feet was unknown territory. If you have no reason to question it, the easiest assumption is that your part of the world is stable and central, and that the sun rises in the east and moves overhead to set in the west. The moon too has a regular motion that can be explained if you assume it revolves around the Earth. The other small bodies appear at night and, if you observe them carefully and for long enough, some appear to move through the sky, although not always in a regular pattern. What could one make of all this?

→ Why was it important to know and understand these patterns? Two practical reasons are readily apparent – the use of heavenly bodies for finding your way about, particularly at sea; and the prediction of important earthly events such as the tides, the flooding of large rivers and the timing of seasons. Mystical reasons included fortune telling (astrology) and religious ceremonies.

→ **Ptolemy** (around AD 130) made an attempt at a consistent description, trying to pull together all observations on the sun, moon, planets and stars into a scheme whereby future positions of these bodies could be predicted. In his scheme all the bodies moved in or on clear spheres that surrounded the Earth. To explain why these bodies did not all follow even curved paths in the sky, he thought the bodies circled while they went round the Earth, in loops called epicycles. The Ptolemaic system was not a scientific revolution – it systematised what was already believed about the arrangement of the universe, and whenever the calculations did not match the observations, more epicycles were added to the paths of the stars and planets.

## The heliocentric revolution

→ With time, however, more and more anomalies were found, and Copernicus (around 1500) realised that perhaps the whole basis of Ptolemy's model was wrong. A Greek mathematician, **Aristarchus** (around 300 BC), had suggested that the sun and stars were fixed and that the Earth circled round the sun. He used geometric methods successfully to calculate the relative sizes of the Earth, sun and moon, and the distances between them. His theory was not widely accepted at the time since it conflicted with deeply held religious views of the universe, and with the formidable reputation of Aristotle. Copernicus realised that Aristarchus' idea of a heliocentric universe made more sense. Careful observations and calculations led him to change the view of the universe held by most people, although it took a long time for it to become completely accepted. Only when Newton (around 1650) was able to provide sound physical reasons did the relationships between stars, planets and other astronomical bodies become clear.

→ We should credit Copernicus with this scientific revolution; indeed we might regard him as the first to make science in its modern sense a part of human culture. Others contributed to this particular change – Tycho Brahe, Galileo Galilei and Isaac Newton, most notably – but Copernicus literally changed people's view of the world. It is this dramatic turnabout that we call a '**scientific revolution**'. Such changes are not common, obviously, but we are interested in them because they can be so important in the longer-term effects that they have on our culture and our daily lives. Also, if we understand how science can change, we understand more about how our civilisation might change.

## How science develops  ●●●

→ **Thomas Kuhn** was a historian who has greatly influenced our thinking about developments in science. He tried to explain how science proceeds by using current theories about a topic, until some things are just impossible to understand. He called this **normal science**. This situation may last for a long time, until someone comes up with a radically different way of looking at it that appears to solve many of its impossibilities. Then we get a **paradigm shift**, and scientists then start working on all the implications of this change. This state of affairs may last for a similar length of time, and so on. There are some interesting implications of this process – for example, scientists whose work has been based on a theory or theories that might have to be modified or thrown out are sometimes reluctant to make the change. Conversely, scientists who believe they have a radical new theory sometimes think that others will not listen to them because of the weight of authority from those holding the classical view.

**Exam preparation**                                          answers: page 10

1  [AS] Astronomers made two critical observations – very large groups of stars (galaxies) are moving away from each other; and those furthest away are moving fastest. How did these observations give scientists a different understanding of the universe?   (4 minutes)

2  [AS] Discuss why scientific progress sometimes leaps ahead and is sometimes static.   (45 minutes)

**Check the net**

Who was Aristotle? Why was he important?
Search for 'Aristotle'

**Checkpoint 2**

In how many ways is the word 'revolution' used?

**The jargon**

A paradigm is best thought of as a model or set of models which provides the best agreed understanding of how things work.

**Links**

See page 186: Science and culture.

# Is medicine science?

Medicine for many centuries was a pretty inexact technology. The ways in which the body functions, even in its simpler aspects, took a long time to discover. It is difficult for us to realise the problems in questioning the beliefs of authorities that have held the fort for thousands of years. Even though observations are easy to make, overturning this authority is not a simple matter.

## The circulation of the blood

→ The fact that blood circulates around the body is a commonplace to us, but it was not always so. The most influential Greek physician of his time was **Galen**, around AD 150–200. His understanding of the working of the human body held sway for 1500 years. He made many experimental observations of human and animal bodies and, through very competent dissection, knew a great deal about anatomy. He knew, for example, that arteries contained blood (before his studies, people thought they contained air) and that they pulsed with the heart. He knew the structure of the venous system but did not come to understand that blood circulates in arteries and veins through the heart. This was mainly due to his understanding of the physiology of the body. He thought that the liver converted digested food into venous blood and infused it with '*pneuma*' or *living spirit*. The blood was then distributed through the body by the liver pushing it back and forth through the veins. Blood with impurities was sent to the lungs, where they were eliminated. Some blood passed through small pores, which he believed must exist although they were invisible, between the ventricles of the heart to receive *vital spirit* from the air. *Animal spirit* was generated in the brain and was passed through the arteries. Galen's beliefs on blood dominated medicine until the 16th century.

## William Harvey (1578–1657)

→ Harvey was rather more scientific in his approach. Like Galen, he knew that blood spurted out from the main artery from the heart. He calculated that for each heartbeat, about 60cm³ of blood left the heart. In one hour, therefore, about 260 litres of blood left the heart. This was far more blood than the body contained; indeed, it was three times the weight of the body. Harvey couldn't believe that the body made blood in these amounts so quickly and realised that the simplest explanation was that the same blood was being pumped round and round the body. He examined the heart and blood vessels of humans and many different kinds of mammals and noted that there were structures in the heart and blood vessels that behaved as valves, letting the blood pass in only one direction. One simple demonstration was to push a thin rod into a vein – it would only go in one direction, towards the heart. He carried out a famous experiment on the veins of the upper part of his arm. He tied a cord around his upper arm, just tight enough to prevent the blood from

**The jargon**

**Anatomy** is the study of the structure of the body, often achieved through dissection; **physiology** is the study of the processes going on in the body; **biochemistry** is the study of the chemical reactions in the processes.

**Checkpoint 1**

Why is the circulation of the blood so important in understanding how the body functions?

**Checkpoint 2**

If Galen's ideas about blood were correct, what would have been the results of Harvey's experiment on his arm?

flowing through the veins back into his heart – but allowing blood to enter the arm through the arteries, which are deeper in the flesh. Below the cord, the veins swelled up; above it, they remained empty. This showed that the blood could be entering the arm only through the arteries. By carefully stroking the blood out of a short length of vein, Harvey showed that it could fill up only when blood was allowed to enter it from the end that was furthest away from the heart. You can see the same thing if you stroke a large vein on the back of your hand, towards your fingers. The vein stays empty until you reach a branch, when the blood flows in from the branch – towards your body.

## Science and belief ●●●

→ Harvey's discovery completely changed our understanding of how the body works. The puzzle is that, although Galen's observational and technical skills were equal to Harvey's, why did he not make the same leap in understanding? His problem was his philosophical beliefs. Galen was heavily committed to the idea of the soul as described by **Plato**. Plato conceived of three parts of the human soul – the appetites (hunger, thirst), the emotional (appetites of feeling) and the rational. Galen believed that the bodily systems had to conform to these concepts, and thence moulded his observations to his beliefs.

→ While we may think that science progresses through coldly rational and objective processes, beliefs have always played a significant part in the ease with which new discoveries and insights come about. Harvey's demonstration that part of the body behaved like a machine could be taken as evidence for a mechanistic view of the workings (physiology) of all living things. Modern biology adopts such a view because it has produced results in the form of useful hypotheses and working theories that have improved medical treatments. A belief in vital spirits, held by Archimedes, Plato and Galen, was relatively unsuccessful in doing so. There is a modern parallel in the widespread beliefs in 'alternative medicine'. Some alternative medical treatments, such as acupuncture, pressure points and reflexology, postulate energy fields or lines in the body, none of which can be measured by any scientific instrument. No scientific study has shown that the treatments they support actually work, but this is unlikely to inhibit believers.

**The jargon**

Something is **rational** if it is completely logical (based on reason); it is **objective** if it is based on evidence that can be independently confirmed.

**Checkpoint 3**

If the body is like a machine, does this mean that it has been manufactured?

**Action point**

Why is alternative medicine popular?

[AS] Describe the scientific methods you might use to determine whether a newborn baby has a hole in the wall between the two ventricles of the heart.

(10 minutes)

# What is the world made of?

Understanding the nature of matter is obviously a very important part of comprehending the world. Ideas that do not seem sensible to start with turn out to be true, and even when we have digested those, along come the physicists with even more unsettling ideas.

## Atomic theory

→ We take atoms for granted. The particulate nature of matter is now familiar to us – even though it defies our normal senses. The idea that an object such as a rock or a bucket of water really consists of a thin fog of tiny balls in a lot of space takes a bit of believing – especially if the rock descends swiftly on your head. The concept goes way back to the classical Greek philosophers **Leuchippus** and **Democritus** (around 400 BC). However the ideas of these first atomists were regarded as odd for 2000 years, because Aristotle, whose reputation was immense, did not believe in atoms. The early Christian church absorbed Aristotelian views and followers of Democritus' ideas were in a small minority. **Robert Boyle** (1660s) wrote about matter composed of 'corpuscles' since believing in 'atoms' would have been considered irreligious. It is significant that Boyle was one of a new breed of scientific thinkers who adopted a more experimental approach to problems. However, it is not sufficient to have a good hypothesis to explain some part of the world – you need to support it with observations based on predictions from your hypothesis.

→ **John Dalton** (early 1800s) provided really solid evidence for the existence of atoms. Although most of his ideas were not original, he was able to provide support through painstaking and accurate experiments. The French chemist **Lavoisier** had done exceptional groundwork in careful measurements and experiments on the chemistry of combustion.

→ **Lavoisier** lived during the French Revolution (late 18th century). His revolutionary countrymen executed him: the reason given at his trial was that 'The Republic has no need of intellectuals'.

→ Dalton was able to take such ideas further by combining different elements in different ways to make new substances, but making very careful note of the weights involved. These may seem rather dry assertions, especially compared with Newton's ideas on motion and forces, or the heliocentric universe, but they were basic ideas that enabled chemists to work in a systematic way to discover new elements, to make new chemical compounds and discover new forms of manufacture of useful products. All of these contributed to the Industrial Revolution.

→ Dalton's Atomic Theory:
1. chemical elements are made of atoms
2. the atoms of an element are identical in their masses
3. atoms of different elements have different masses
4. atoms only combine in small, whole number ratios such as 1:1, 1:2, 2:3 etc.

---

**Checkpoint 1**

What is the difference between a **hypothesis** and a **theory**? Give an example of each.

**Checkpoint 2**

How does atomic theory qualify as a **scientific revolution**?

He believed that atoms could not be created, destroyed or changed in their chemical nature.

## Splitting the atom  ●●●

→ The early atomists thought that the atom was a something that could not be broken or divided any further – indeed, that is what the word means in classical Greek. As is well known by just about everyone nowadays, atoms are not the solid particles that Dalton and others theorised, but they are formed of smaller particles still. This discovery was made about 100 years ago, mainly through the work of **Ernest Rutherford**. He studied the radiation from the radioactive elements and discovered that some of this radiation was formed of particles. In a classic experiment, he fired alpha particles at a thin gold foil and was surprised to find that most of the particles went through, some of them spreading out as they did so, but a few bounced back. From this he was able to show that gold atoms consist of a lot of empty space, with most of their mass in a central nucleus. This crucial experiment changed the nature of both physics and chemistry and led the way, eventually, to weapons of unimaginable power.

## Yet more fundamental particles  ●●●

→ Studies of nuclear physics have shown that mass and energy are different aspects of the same thing, and in a sense one can be changed into the other. This is one outcome of the famous equation of **Einstein** – $e = mc^2$, where e is energy, m is mass, and c represents the speed of light in a vacuum. A little calculation will show you that only a small mass can convert into an enormous amount of energy, the basis of the nuclear bomb.

→ For the first half of the 20th century, there were thought to be just a few fundamental atomic particles – the neutron, proton, electron and a number of others formed in the process of nuclear decay. Subsequently, developments in theoretical physics showed that some of these particles were composed of combinations of even smaller particles called quarks. More recently, theoretical physicists have suggested that a much smaller object – a 'string', consisting of vibration energy – could provide the basis for bringing together all the forces in physics to provide a simpler and more powerful explanation of nature.

→ Studies of the nature of matter are closely linked to the origin and future of the universe itself, since the astronomers and physicists studying the events around the Big Bang have to take into account the way matter and energy interact under very strange conditions.

**Check the net**

Find out why Einstein and Bohr disagreed about the nature of the atom. Search for 'Einstein', 'Bohr' and 'quantum'.

**Links**

Science, technology and ethics.

**Links**

How do scientific ideas change the nature of society?

---

**Exam preparation**  answer: page 11

[A2] Why is it important to carry out expensive research into nuclear physics?

(45 minutes)

# Answers
## Characteristics of the sciences

### The Earth and the universe

#### Checkpoints

1 Universe – everything we can observe; star – a large body in which nuclear processes create heat and light; galaxy – a vast collection of stars; planet – a body that orbits a star.

2 Revolution means many, but related, things – check the dictionary for rotation, overturning, violent overthrow (e.g. the Russian Revolution) and turnover of thought. Scientific revolutions involve a complete change of thinking, from one point of view to something different. It is helpful in this context to compare it with 'evolution'. Evolution means gradual change, slow and steady, and the theory of evolution is itself an example of a revolution in biology.

#### Exam preparation

1 This question expects you to have some basic science **knowledge**, namely, that galaxies are distant, very large and moving relative to other galaxies, and that the universe is currently thought to have started with an immense explosion. The observations provided are consistent with the **theory** that galaxies are spreading out, and with the idea that those furthest away were thrown out earlier by the Big Bang, and have had time therefore to accelerate to greater velocities. If the universe were 'stationary' then these observations would be much more difficult to explain.

2 For this type of question you would be expected to produce a few **examples** of scientific advance, so it would be worth jotting a few of these down to begin with. You may want to consider some of the big ideas – because the question seems to imply them – such as gravitation, atomic theory, atomic structure, evolution. The question is in the form of an **assertion**, and you are asked to suggest possible **explanations** for the assertion – that there is an uneven rate of scientific progress. First, do you think the assertion is true? You might argue that it is self-evidently true – but it depends on the specific meaning attached to 'uneven'. It is worth clarifying this meaning. In this case it is best to assume that the assertion is true. The **command verb** is 'discuss'. In this examination we assume that this means to describe two or more possible explanations, then **evaluate** which one of these is likely to be the best explanation. What possible explanations are there? Let's list some ideas. If you find this difficult to do, then go back to look at your initial list of examples – something will jog your thoughts on the topic.

- If it is true, that science advances by revolutionary jumps, this presumably means that the jump is a radical change in theory. This change has to be absorbed by all the scientists involved.
- The radical change may need to be followed through in lots of details. This could take a long time.
- Lots of scientists find it a difficult idea to accept, since it flies in the face of what they have been taught. They will lag behind and slow the pace of acceptance, and may even put blocks on the advance.
- There may need to be more experiments whose outcomes support the theory; or there is a need to carry out critical tests of the theory.

Try to expand a little on each of these with reference to one or more scientific advances. Make it clear whether you are **speculating** – and therefore your evidence is in the form of **belief** on your part – or if you are sure that there is other (**objective**) evidence for what you say. Make this explicit. Also make it clear when you are **deferring to authority**. You may also want to argue with an **analogy** – 'scientific advance is like a game of Chinese whispers, because no one wants to appear to be stepping out of line'. Make it clear that you understand what an analogy is and be careful, because analogies are rarely very good explanations of events. Finally, you need to draw your thoughts together to form a conclusion. The question doesn't actually ask you for one – but you will complete a better essay by saying how **justified** your explanations are, and whether some are stronger, or more objectively based, than others.

### Is medicine science?

#### Checkpoints

1 This draws on your understanding of biology. From first principles – food is digested and absorbed in one place in the body, so too is oxygen. Cells and tissues in other parts of the body need food and oxygen to live; therefore, there has to be a system of transport. Cells and tissues produce waste products which need to be taken away and removed from the body, or changed, so there needs to be another system to do that. It seems simpler and more efficient to have one system to do both tasks, so a blood system fits the bill. You may also point out the double blood circulation in mammals – blood goes in separate loops to the body and the lungs, passing twice through the heart in one circuit round the whole body.

2 Galen's theory was that blood in the veins flowed back and forth, pushed by the liver. Harvey would have seen nothing happening in his demonstration; each vein would have appeared to contain blood on either side of where he placed his finger. Presumably too, valves would not have been apparent as knots or swellings in the veins, because if the blood was going back and forth, the valves would have obstructed the flow in one direction, preventing completely any ebb and flow effect.

3 The assumption of modern medicine is that most of the body seems to work in a machine-like way. Whether or not this is totally true, the observation has led to the belief that if any part of the body is like a machine, then it must have been made that way, by somebody or something. It is fundamental to modern biology however, that living things and systems have developed according to the theory of evolution. This theory gives a rational and comprehensible explanation for the origin of structures and working of living things, which does not depend on a designer. All can be explained through the power of

natural selection. Not everyone believes this, but all biological scientists find the explanation convincing, and well supported by evidence. An opposing idea relies on the use of **argument by analogy** – watches are complex machines, all of which have been designed and built by watchmakers; the body is a complex machine, so somebody must have designed it.

### Exam preparation

You need to think from first principles. What would be the effect of having a hole between the ventricles? At every beat of the heart, blood will pass through the hole and mix with blood on the other side. This means that blood that is full of oxygen from the lungs is mixed up with blood lacking in oxygen from the rest of the body. Some of this blood will go to the lungs to take up oxygen; most will be pumped round the body. Since this blood contains less than its maximum amount of oxygen, the body muscles and cells will be deprived. The blood will also not be a healthy red colour, so the baby is likely to be bluish, and this could be a symptom. The heart is not working correctly so the blood flowing through it will slosh about in a different way, so listening to the heart sounds with a stethoscope could provide more clues. An ultrasound scanner could provide an image of the heart but might not be clear enough to see a small hole. Answering a question like this demands some clear thinking from basic science knowledge.

## What is the world made of?

### Checkpoints

1 Hypotheses are suggestions that have not yet been tested. For example, 'Writing with a coloured pen causes more spelling mistakes'. Scientific theories are relationships that have been tested (by experiments) but can still be falsified by experiment – for example, 'the force exerted by a body is the product of its mass and its acceleration'. This is one of Newton's laws, part of his theory of force and motion. Scientists may use 'theory' to cover several interlinking laws or relationships – such as the theory of gravitation.
2 Atomic theory was a complete change from Aristotle's long-held theory of matter – that all substances were made up from mixtures of the primal substances: earth, water, fire and air. Although an atomistic theory of matter was also an old classical idea, the most influential thinkers did not support it. Dalton's work showed that the idea of atoms was a vastly superior theory, which easily explained his experimental observations on combining substances.

### Exam preparation

Scientific research today is costly no matter which branch of science we are looking at. The question is asking you to **justify** a point of view – that expensive research in nuclear physics should be supported, because it is important. In planning for this essay, then, you will need to **list points for and against**. It would probably be a good thing to start by explaining two things: your idea of what **nuclear physics** is all about; and what you consider to be **expensive**. If you haven't any idea about nuclear physics, then choosing the question is probably not a good idea. On the other hand, you don't have to be a nuclear scientist to know that this branch of physics is the study of the nucleus of the atom and the particles inside this nucleus. You will also probably know that in order to study these particles it is necessary to smash the atoms up in very large machines that use a lot of energy. The result of the work will be a greater understanding of the composition of matter, possibly an insight into the release and everyday use of nuclear energy, and possibly the development of destructive forms of energy for use in bombs. **List** all this in your plan, and make **bullet points**. Note that 'expensive' is a relative term – you probably won't know the exact amounts involved, nor do you need to. You can plead ignorance, but say something about the size and scale of the laboratories necessary and the (electrical) energy required. You may want to conclude that for a small nation such research could not be the best use of its resources. **For** could include: study of energy production, with commercial and social benefits; basic research into the nature of matter, not knowing quite where this might lead us; evidence that nuclear research in the past has led to many benefits – energy and medical. **Against** could include: money could be better used for more everyday uses of direct benefit to citizens' lives; potential dangers in building nuclear bombs, ethics of this. A lateral point is that the research is so expensive that it is often an international enterprise, with the advantage of openness that this brings. These points must be weighed up before you draw a **conclusion**.

# Databank

Some scientists and technologists of note, in no special order or importance:

**Isaac Newton** – possibly the most influential scientist of all time. Produced three Laws of Motion and the Theory of Gravitation (1669–87), which enable scientists to make sense of the motion of all bodies. His theories were subsequently modified by Einstein.

**James Clerk Maxwell** – produced equations that explained the behaviour of and relationship between electricity and magnetism (1864). His work predicted the existence of electromagnetic radiation, then unknown.

**Ada Byron, Countess of Lovelace** – mathematician and co-worker on the calculating machine of Charles Babbage (1842–3).

**Albert Einstein** – made fundamental discoveries in physics – explanation of Brownian motion; theories of space–time; relativity; tried but failed to produce a theory linking all the forces of nature (gravitational; strong nuclear; weak nuclear and electromagnetic) – for which we are still waiting.

**Bertrand Russell** – primarily a logician, who attempted to construct a complete system of mathematics (*Principia Mathematica*) with AN Whitehead. His work in logical and analytical philosophy made the ground rules for the subject. Also a notable campaigner for peace.

**Kurt Gödel** – a brilliant mathematician who showed (1931) that you cannot create a complete system of mathematics – there will always be some propositions that cannot be proved using the rules of the system.

**Werner von Braun** – pioneer of rocketry and passionate advocate of space travel; leader of the team who developed the V2 rockets for Germany in the 1940s. After the war and emigration to USA, became the director of the Marshall Space Flight Center.

**JJ Thomson** – discovered the electron (1897).

**Ernest Rutherford –** showed that the atom contained a nucleus (1911).

**Niels Bohr** – made further discoveries on the structure of the atom (1914).

**Max Planck –** suggested (1900) that radiation was emitted in packets called quanta.

**Werner Heisenberg –** a founder of the important but difficult subject of quantum mechanics; author of the Uncertainty Principle (1925–7) that states that it is impossible to measure both the position and momentum of a subatomic particle, such as the electron, at the same instant. This has had profound implications for physics.

**Francis Crick and James Watson** – first proposed the double helix structure for DNA, building on the X ray analysis work of Rosalind Franklin and Maurice Wilkins.

**Dorothy Hodgkin** – Nobel Laureate in Chemistry for outstanding work in the X-ray analysis of biological molecules.

**Christian Barnard** – a South African surgeon, famous for carrying out the first successful heart transplant (1967).

**George Washington Carver** – born into slavery (1864), became a leading agriculturalist and teacher, changing commercial practice in southern states of America.

**Richard Dawkins** – evolutionary biologist and proponent of the 'selfish gene' idea. Outstanding teacher of biological ideas.

**Barbara McClintock** – distinguished researcher into the behaviour of genes in chromosomes (1950).

## Some useful terms

**Hypothesis** – A tentative explanation, which has not yet been tested, is called a hypothesis.

**Experiment** – If a hypothesis has been tested by experiment, usually several times, other scientists will generally accept it as **a theory**. Scientific theories should make reliable predictions about the workings of nature; they are valid theories as long as the predictions hold in all testable circumstances. A critical experiment can destroy a theory. For example, the Michelson-Morley experiment showed that light travels at the same velocity in any direction. This completely overturned the theory that light travelled in a hypothetical substance called the ether, even though the experimenters believed in that theory.

**Theories** are the bedrock of science. Confusingly, the word 'theory' is also used in an everyday way – 'but it's only a theory' – to indicate one of several untested explanations. A scientific theory is usually the best explanation we have, and should always be supported by evidence from experiments.

# Revision checklist
*helps you check what you still need to do*

## By the end of this chapter you should be able to:

| | | | |
|---|---|---|---|
| 1 | Use all the information in Databank, above, with confidence | Confident | Not confident. **Revise** pages 12, 24 |
| 2 | Understand the nature of different types of science | Confident | Not confident. **Revise** pages 6, 9 |
| 3 | Describe the nature of their content | Confident | Not confident. **Revise** pages 6, 9 |
| 4 | Distinguish between science and technology | Confident | Not confident. **Revise** pages 6, 56–58 |
| 5 | Explain briefly how science develops | Confident | Not confident. **Revise** page 5 |
| 6 | Describe briefly three scientific revolutions | Confident | Not confident. **Revise** pages 4, 7, 8, 10 |
| 7 | Explain three examples of inductive reasoning in science | Confident | Not confident. **Revise** pages 24, 30, 78 |
| 8 | Explain the importance of experiments in science | Confident | Not confident. **Revise** pages 12, 24, 25 |
| 9 | State briefly the achievements of three scientists | Confident | Not confident. **Revise** pages 6, 9, 20, 24, 31, 48 |

# The nature of scientific objectivity and the question of progress

Science is said to be an **objective** study. Although scientists, like everyone else, have beliefs and opinions that are not necessarily open to test, in carrying out their scientific work they should be prepared to consider evidence that may overturn their accepted theories. On the other hand, if they wish to challenge a theory, then they must be prepared to demonstrate how the theory does not explain certain observations, and those observations must be repeatable by other scientists. This is, of course, an ideal that is not always realised.

Science is also said to demonstrate '**progress**' – new scientific theories are more powerful than older theories and, as a result, humankind is in a better state than it was before. But we often ask, as time goes on, do things become better or worse for everyone?

## Exam themes

→ Ideas on the origins of the universe

→ History of some important aspects of science

→ Sources and forms of energy

→ Distribution of the Earth's resources

→ Greenhouse gases and global warming

→ Fertility control

→ Genetic modification and biotechnology

→ Nature of experimental procedures

→ Ideas of progress in science

## Topic checklist

○ AS   ● A2

| | AQA A | AQA B | EDEXCEL | OCR |
|---|---|---|---|---|
| Science and change | ○● | ○● | ○● | ○ |
| Energy and civilisation | ○● | ○● | ○● | ● |
| Climate change | ○● | ○● | ○● | ○ |

# Science and change

Whatever we do can have unpredictable results. This is no less true of scientific progress than it is of social and cultural development. We might expect scientists and technologists to be wary of change, in view of our past experiences, but in our wish to solve a problem or become more prosperous, it is not always straight-forward to predict and warn of all the potential consequences, and even more difficult to persuade others.

## Science and change

→ Does having a scientific explanation that works every time you test mean that the explanation is now a fundamental truth? The truth is that it is always possible that a theory can be overturned (or falsified) by some experiment or set of circumstances. If this happens, a new theory or modification of the old will be needed. The outcome is that science is **never** finished or complete, even though you may find some optimists who believe that there is a 'theory of everything'.

→ The fact that there is something called 'time' means that the universe is constantly changing. Or you might say that because you can detect change, this is evidence for a property of the universe called 'time'. Science is dependent on the phenomenon of **causality**, where some event is a result of another – and if this always happens then the prior event is said to cause the later.

## Evolution and natural selection

→ Evolution is a very important idea; the word means 'change', and in everyday language it is used to mean a smooth and gradual change, often in contrast with the more explosive 'revolution'. Much of science is involved in the study of change – astronomy, chemistry and physics are all concerned with evolution in the physical universe; biology deals with the changes evident in living things, who show growth, change over time and cyclical activities. The numbers and types of organisms have also changed over time through the process.

→ Biological evolution is readily observable – although some refuse to believe that the living organisms we see today are different to those that have lived before, or that present-day organisms are changing, sometimes quite quickly, in response to changes in their environment.

→ The mechanism of evolution is more debatable and there have been many scientific theories about it. The most plausible and widely accepted theory is that of natural selection.

→ How natural selection works:
  → Organisms have more offspring than will survive
  → Food supplies/resources are always limited
  → Therefore there will be competition for survival
  → Offspring vary
  → Offspring with useful variations will be better equipped to survive
  → Therefore those variations will be passed on to their offspring
  → If anything changes, different variations will prove to be better for survival
  → In time, organisms with new variations will be recognised as new species.

### Checkpoint 1

Write a brief definition of the terms: **causation**; **correlation** and **coincidence**.

### Checkpoint 2

Briefly list the major biological discoveries of each of the following:
Charles Darwin;
Alfred Wallace;
Jane Goodall.

→ Evolution gave biology a tremendous boost because living things could be studied in the same way as physical and chemical phenomena; there was no longer any need to presume that a 'life force' or other undetectable energy supported or brought about changes in them.

## Inheritance and genetic modification ●●●

→ Inheritance is a key factor in evolution – and evolution was never a totally satisfactory theory until a sound theory of genetics was put forward. Mendel, and those who succeeded him, right through to the workers on the Human Genome Project, provided the nuts and bolts of evolutionary change. Thanks to them we have the possibility of genetic modification (engineering), which has already contributed to human health, for example, through the bulk production of human insulin for the treatment of diabetes. Ultimately, scientists hope to remedy defective genes by replacing them with functional versions. It is also hoped to produce special tissues from stem cells to replace, for example, heart muscle or nerve cells that have stopped working properly. Some doctors have even suggested that there is no limit to the normal life span as a result of these developments.

→ Genetic modification has potential benefits and risks:

| Benefits | Risks |
|---|---|
| Remedy mutations in genes | Changes may have unforeseen consequences |
| Improve human capabilities, by design | Changing people's genes 'for the better' is unethical |
| Help body to repair itself, potentially for ever | What happens to people's personality if they can become immortal? |
| Make people healthier and therefore happier | Will the population increase even further? |

→ How can you stop science and medicine making changes in response to everyone's desire to live without illness and to have healthy children?

→ All of these changes are regarded as 'progress', but there is always a flip side – what are the ethical, moral, economic and political issues that arise from developments in medicine?

→ If you were the parent of a sick child, would you seek out the best way of curing the illness, no matter what the long-term consequences might be, or the ethical implications of what needs to be done? For example, if the remedy lay in an organ transplant, and you had the resources, would you hesitate to purchase illegally a kidney from a poor Indian labourer? Scientists, politicians and religious believers could all have different approaches to this problem. What if you are such a parent, a scientist and a Christian?

**Checkpoint 3**

Name three other important developments in medicine in the last 70 years.

**Links**

Links to page 196.

**Exam preparation**                                          answers: page 20

1   [AS] List three benefits and three risks from planting genetically modified crops in the UK.   (5 minutes)

2   [A2] Describe the scientific, social and ethical issues arising from the Human Genome Project.   (30 minutes)

# Energy and civilisation

The basic requirements of human life – food and shelter – can be considered under the umbrella of energy requirements. Technology and scientific developments have led to great improvements in the transfer of energy from resources to machines serving human purposes. However, there are great inequalities in the distribution of resources and the quality of life

## Energy and civilisation ●●●

→ The history of civilisation can be seen as the history of the use and transfer of energy. The more 'advanced' the society, the more energy it needs. We are beginning to realise the importance of conserving energy sources and using more renewable resources. We have changed from small groups of hunter-gatherers to an agricultural economy, where animals are used as labour and energy comes in the form of food for the human labouring machine. We used organic fuels, such as wood, for heating, lighting and cooking.

→ Early man found ways to improve his capacity for transferring energy (a measure of the adaptability of an organism). For weapons, throwing spears became augmented by the use of bows and arrows, stones by catapults and slings. Lifting and shifting became easier with crowbars, wheels and pulleys. Sails, as well as oars, moved boats. Wind and watermills were very useful devices for heavy and time-consuming tasks such as grinding corn.

→ The Industrial Revolution came about largely because of inventions for transferring and applying energy produced by steam engines to burdensome tasks, such as weaving and spinning. When suitable engines were designed, transport of humans and goods was transformed.

## Energy requirements for rising populations ●●●

→ We have become much more aware of the availability and use of energy resources as the world has become more populated and technology has enabled economic development. If we compare the amount of energy available in different regions, it is clear there are huge differences. The amount of energy available per head to developed nations is vastly different to the poorest.

→ Where is this leading? Is it just energy that we need to be concerned about? What about room for living? The world population has been predicted to grow phenomenally, but with great differences between the less and more developed countries. If the demands for energy for less developed countries increase to those of the more developed countries, several sets of problems are inevitable: will there be sufficient energy resources to cope?

→ What about the pollution from the use of this energy? Will there be increasing international tensions in the distribution of energy reserves?

## Sustainable development ●●●

→ There will be technological developments, not least in renewable energy, which will change the nature of these problems. Another

**Checkpoint 1**

Using animal and human muscle, the ancient Egyptians built enormous stone pyramids. Why did they do this?

**Links**

Pages 58, 106: Transport and the need for transport systems.

**Checkpoint 2**

Work out the energy supply per head for the regions. Explain why the electricity generation and consumption of oil products are so different in North America and Africa.

| Region | Total Primary Energy Supply  Millions of tonnes of oil cquivalent | Electricity generation   GWh | Oil products consumption   Thousand tonnes | Population    Millions |
|---|---|---|---|---|
| World | 10 000 | 15 000 000 | 3 500 000 | 6 200 |
| OECD North America | 2 700 | 4 700 000 | 1 000 000 | 417 |
| OECD Europe | 1 800 | 3 200 000 | 700 000 | 511 |
| Africa | 500 | 460 000 | 120 000 | 821 |

Source – OECD/IEA, 2001, IEA statistics 2001: http:www.iea.org.Textbase/stats/index.asp

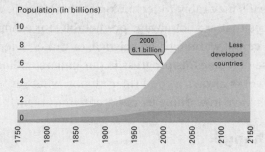

Source: United Nations, *World Population Prospects, The 1998 Revision*; and estimates by the Population Reference Bureau.

concept has been developed – **sustainability** – to provide the means for economic development without compromising the needs of future generations.

→ Sustainability originated in forestry as a system that aimed at not felling more trees than were able to regrow. **Sustainable development** implies a **fair distribution of resources**. It also implies the protection of natural resources in the ecological system. The use of the word **development** rather than **growth** is significant, indicating that improvement in quality and not just quantity is important.

## Energy consumption and environmental change ●●●

→ Developed countries with under 20% of the world population and a consumption of about 75% of the world's mineral resources and fossil fuels are thought mainly responsible for global environmental damage. Fundamental changes of production and consumption structures as well as self-limitation of consumption in industrialised countries are considered essential to prevent ecological disaster. We don't know if the changes we have already set in motion are irreversible.

**Links**

Globalisation, pages 56 and 86.

**Links**

See also page 120: The global economy.

**Checkpoint 3**

What organisations could help us limit consumption in industrialised countries? What are the roles of scientists and technologists?

**Exam preparation**                                    answers: page 21

1  [AS] List the environmental issues arising from the use of nuclear power stations.   (5 minutes)
2  [AS] What problems come from the exploitation of 'alternative' sources of energy, such as wind, tidal, solar and geothermal?   (30 minutes)

# Climate change

Weather is notoriously unpredictable. The importance of weather to our daily lives has produced an industry of weather forecasting, challenging scientists' ability to model the atmosphere. Human activity alters the climate, and it is a major problem for science to show how such changes can be controlled and possibly reversed.

## Science and survival ●●○

→ The mere existence of living organisms ensures that the world is constantly changing, never mind the astronomical (asteroid or meteorite collisions) and geological events (volcanic eruptions, earthquakes) that affect the world from time to time. Scientific discovery leads inevitably to technological innovation, with consequences that are not always predictable, for example, climate change and global warming. Can science, or rather scientists, help us predict these outcomes? Is progress in our understanding of the world and how it works always a good thing? If not, what responsibilities do scientists have in warning us of potential problems?

## Climate change ●●○

→ This is a controversial subject, not least because there are many vested interests. If all the gloomy predictions are correct then humankind has a miserable future unless drastic commercial and economic changes are made, all of which has considerable political overtones.

→ Measuring techniques and computing power have all improved enormously in the last 20 years.

→ The **Intergovernmental Panel on Climate Change (IPCC)** is composed of scientists from many nations and publishes reports summarising the situation with information that has the broadest base of agreement. The findings are not reassuring and show that the balance is towards warming brought about by the greenhouse gases (halocarbons, $N_2O$, $CH_4$ and $CO_2$), although there is a counterbalancing effect of air particles that reflect some thermal energy back into space. Here are some findings of the IPCC report for 2001:

  → The global average surface temperature has increased over the 20th century by about 0.6 °C.

  → Snow cover and ice extent have decreased.

  → Global average sea level has risen and ocean heat content has increased.

  → Emissions of greenhouse gases and aerosols due to human activities continue to alter the atmosphere in ways that are expected to affect the climate.

  → Concentrations of atmospheric greenhouse gases and their effect on warming have continued to increase as a result of human activities.

  → There is new and stronger evidence that most of the warming observed over the last 50 years is attributable to human activities.

**Action point**

How frequent are:
- meteorite, comet or asteroid collisions?
- major earthquakes?
- volcanic eruptions?

**Checkpoint 1**

How trustworthy are scientists in providing evidence?

→ Global average temperature and sea level are projected to rise under all projections.

## How sure can we be of this?

→ A subject as complex as this requires everyone to be as clear as possible about the facts presented. The most reliable information is likely to come from large reputable international organisations, although you cannot be completely certain of that.

→ What are scientists completely agreed about? The IPCC conclusions above are the most commonly accepted observations and predictions.

→ What is open to debate? Basically the rate and the ultimate size of warming. The uncertainty is because the interaction of the variables is very difficult to work out. The theories that scientists use are not completely tested, and predictions are based on computer modelling. Also controversial are predictions about the effect on ocean levels, local climate and the consequent changes in the ecology of organisms. Added to this uncertainty is the fact that changes in these features bring about changes in the causes of the warming; in other words, the whole situation is highly dynamic.

→ Many experts are concerned that the changes we are noticing cannot be undone whatever we do. A few think that the change will accelerate and produce intolerable conditions. Others believe that the change is well within the 'normal' variation in climate, and that we should not be too concerned about it.

→ The public is interested in Doomsday scenarios – from tsunamis to asteroid collisions. Such events have occurred, even in the very recent past. The problem is that they are on such a scale that we are unlikely to be able to do anything to prevent them. Even earthquakes with very small effects and minor volcanic eruptions involve vast energy changes equivalent to millions of nuclear explosions. The best we can hope to do is to try to predict when they might happen and move people out of the way. The most consoling thought could be that during 4 billion years, there has been no catastrophe that has eliminated life from the Earth, even though some events might have changed its evolution.

→ People have had profound effects on the environment wherever they have passed the hunter-gatherer stage. Man, for example, has managed the whole of the English landscape for possibly thousands of years, yet it is capable of reverting to forest or moor in a short time. However, globalisation and the demand for more energy may make reversion less likely.

**Checkpoint 2**

How can we persuade any particular country that it should reduce gas emissions from burning fossil fuels?

**Links**

Globalisation; sustainability, pages 56, 189.

**Exam preparation**                                           answers: page 21

1   [AS] Why is it so difficult to forecast the weather?   (10 minutes)
2   [A2] Is it right for developed countries to expect less developed countries to reduce their greenhouse gas emissions at the same rate as themselves?

(20 minutes)

# Answers
## The nature of scientific objectivity and

## Science and change

### Checkpoints

1  **Causation** refers to the philosophical idea that if one event always precedes another, and if the second event never occurs without the first, then the first event is said to **cause** the other. **Correlation** is a statistical concept – if two events happen together, more than just by chance, they are said to be **correlated**. It is possible that one of a pair of correlated events causes another, but it is more likely that two correlated events have a **common cause**. Two events may happen by **coincidence**, meaning they occurred together just by chance. It is quite easy to believe that two things 'just couldn't be coincidence', where in fact coincidences are much more likely than you might think.

2  **Charles Darwin –** best known for showing how the idea of evolution explained the range and variety of living things and, most importantly, for showing how a simple mechanism makes species change. **Alfred Russell Wallace** shares the distinction of proposing the theory of evolution by natural selection with Darwin, and his contribution to Darwin's thought was considerable. Like Darwin, he spent several years studying living organisms in tropical regions, as well as writing studies of island life and explaining the distribution of different groups of animals and plants in South-East Asia. **Jane Goodall** studied chimpanzees in the African wild and produced many thought-provoking ideas on their behaviour. Most important was her discovery that these animals were not just 'primitive' apes but they had forms of behaviour and a structure to their society that was far more complex than had ever been imagined.

3  This cannot be totally objective, but the most significant (i.e. have saved more lives) medical developments in the last 70 years are probably antibiotics, immunology and vaccination, and body imaging. The first antibiotic discovered was penicillin, and since then many antibiotics, specific to particular disease-causing organisms have been found. Immunology has given us amazing protection against diseases which have been terrible scourges of mankind – poliomyelitis, smallpox, diphtheria, measles, tetanus – the list is very long. Body imaging – which includes the use of X-rays, ultrasound, magnetic resonance imaging (MRI), computer tomography (CT) scans – has revolutionised the diagnosis of disease by enabling the observation of virtually all body structures. Moreover, modern techniques carry far less risk of damage than the X-rays of old.

### Exam preparation

1  Benefits are: producing crops that are better adapted to the climatic conditions; that have useful economic features, such as longer ripening time; that have greater resistance to particular pests; that can be herbicide resistant (so that weeds in the crop can be killed without damage to the crop). Risks are: potential risk of pollen contamination of non-GM crops nearby; possible spread of GM plants into the environment, with unknown consequences; possible harmful effects on the health of people eating GM foods (although there is no evidence yet of such a possibility).

2  This question asks only for a **description** of the issues, not an evaluation of them, and therefore only tests the knowledge objective. Give a brief introduction to show that you understand the HGP. The key points would be: international effort; working out the base sequence of human DNA; and determining the base sequences of different genes. Scientific – issues are about the interpretation of the data obtained, since the amount of information is enormous; and linking genes to their functions, which is not easy; replication of the genes if they are to be used in any therapeutic procedures. Social – issues are about the resources devoted to the work; the usefulness to public health programmes; the availability of treatments derived from the HGP; the economic consequences of any developments. Ethical – issues are about the use to which the knowledge is put; whether some people, or countries should have more access to the data than others; was the data acquired ethically and who has rights to the knowledge gained? You need to describe as many of these issues as possible, in only a few lines.

## Energy and civilisation

### Checkpoints

1  The pyramids were giant tombs for the rulers (pharaohs) of Egypt around 5000 years ago. Until the 20th century, the pyramids were the largest buildings on the planet. Because the pharaohs were believed to be gods, they were given such tombs, each one of which took 20 years or more for thousands of workers to complete.

2  Energy supply per head for World (in tonnes of oil equivalent = 1.613; OECD N America = 6.47; OECD Europe = 3.52; Africa = 0.61. This crude comparison shows the level of difference – 10 times more in the richest, as compared with the poorest regions. There are several, rather obvious, reasons for the differences in electricity generation and oil products usage in North America and Africa – use of cars, types of industry, agricultural economics; communications and so on. If you calculate the differences **per head of population** they are even more significant.

3  There are two types of organisation to tackle this – governmental or non-governmental. Governments may set out to limit consumption, say, of materials that have to be imported (such as oil), or that may generate long-term problems (e.g. tobacco), but will always have a conflict of interest since the sale of such materials usually creates tax revenue. Non-governmental bodies may be more altruistic, but more narrow in their focus. Scientists' roles might be to provide solutions through more scientific discoveries; technologists by improved solutions to problems of society and its habits of consumption.

# the question of progress

## Exam preparation

1 Location (away from centres of population); access in remote areas; disposal of nuclear waste; accidental release of radioactive materials; accidents (e.g. Chernobyl). You may have to explain the nature of the risk for some types of question.

2 We tend to think that only traditional forms of energy production (oil, gas, coal, hydroelectricity) present us with problems, but any process that is transferring energy will have some knock-on consequences. **Wind** – the use of wind is limited by variable weather conditions, so that placing of wind turbines has to be in exposed (i.e. very visible) areas, in areas of natural beauty, at sea where they may interfere with shipping; turbines can also be noisy, and they may also be dangerous to birds and other flying wildlife. **Tidal** schemes are large and expensive; they can only generate when the tide is flowing; they may cause silting and sedimentation in the area. **Solar** energy comes in the thermal form, which may be inefficient to collect, and can be difficult to store; and the photovoltaic – turning light into electricity – with only small amounts of energy involved, it is limited by the amount of sunlight, which is notoriously variable. **Geothermal** energy, from hot springs in areas of volcanic activity, or from warm rocks below the surface of the earth, is limited because it is only available in certain areas.

## Climate change

### Checkpoints

1 This is easy to answer in theory, because science can only progress if the observations and experiments made by scientists are open to scrutiny by other scientists. Openness to scrutiny, peer review – i.e. the necessity for getting your work examined by other scientists before it is published – all should mean that the work is genuine and repeatable. Most scientists are trustworthy, but they are also human, with all that implies. So there have been (and will always be) cases of fraud; however, examples of bias are much more frequent.

2 With great difficulty! If the activity is essential to a nation's economy it is unlikely to be sympathetic. So bribery might be the answer – a richer nation might subsidise another, or a collective approach from several. Sanctions – such as refusing to trade, or blocking imports and exports – are notoriously difficult to maintain. In the long run, only self-interest and education are likely to have any effect.

## Exam preparation

1 For a start, there are so many variables – temperature, pressure, air movements, clouds and other atmospheric phenomena – and a change in one affects all the others, in a highly dynamic state. Forecasting is relatively successful for short times ahead – because it assumes that movements of air will continue a little longer in the way they have just done. This can be done with a computer, and meteorologists use some of the most powerful computers built. Longer than a few days is more difficult, but the larger computers are making better forecasts all the time. The real problem is when you try to forecast for weeks or months ahead. There are substantial economic reasons for weather forecasting – if cold or hot weather can be predicted then appropriate food, clothing and energy requirements can be identified. Travel is greatly affected by weather. So it isn't just the traditional British grumble, after all.

2 The Kyoto Protocol set limits and targets for the reduction of carbon dioxide emissions but not all countries signed up to them. The distribution of energy sources is not even and richer countries can buy oil, coal and gas in line with the expansion of demand for energy. Developing countries argue that developed countries produced the increase in gases that we see now and, therefore, why should they be penalised for historical decisions by rich countries? If this argument is accepted then richer countries should make bigger reductions, relatively.

Richer countries argue that they are already introducing cleaner forms of energy production and that the greatest improvements would come from cleaner and more efficient use of non-renewable resources by developing countries. Thus, developing countries should make bigger relative reductions. Some richer countries want to pay poorer countries for their share of emission reduction. The whole business is more complicated because carbon emissions come from changes in forestation and agriculture, not just industrial processes. If you get a question like this, you must draw up some reasonable propositions – facts about the situation, even if they are simple and you are uncertain of their validity. Then develop a coherent argument leading to a justified conclusion.

# Databank

**Genetic modification** means changing the genetic make-up of an organism. Plant and animal breeders, over thousands of years, have produced genetically modified organisms by selecting individuals with desirable characteristics and breeding them. In time, they produced, for example, all the varieties of dog. Today, 'GM' is taken to mean the direct transfer of a gene into an individual, so that the result is less open to chance and can be done relatively quickly.

**Gene therapy** is a medical treatment that is so far more a dream than actuality. For individuals with genes that don't work as they should, as in cystic fibrosis, it is hoped to put the 'correct' gene into the nuclei of cells in the lung, and therefore provide a perfect cure. There are some encouraging results, however, but it is not going to be easy.

**Evolutionary psychology** is a branch of biology that tries to explain all human behaviour in evolutionary terms. For example, explaining how looking after your relatives better than strangers is understandable because you are helping to preserve genes that you have in common with them for the future. It is controversial because much of it is speculative, although it can make predictions that can be tested, some of which are supportive.

**Creationism** is a belief that a god or divine being has specially created all organisms. It is peculiar to those who hold, for example, that the Bible is a literal and exact description of the origin of the world and everything in it. Creationists go to great lengths to deny, for example, the validity of fossils and the determination of the age of the Earth using chemistry and physics. Not all religious believers are creationists – many accept that evolution has occurred as biologists have shown. Creationists, such as those in many parts of the USA, insist that 'Creation Science' and 'Intelligent Design' should be taught in schools as an acceptable alternative to evolution, but they require total belief in something which is not demonstrable using scientific methods, so they cannot possibly be classed as science.

**Intelligent Design** is a belief that because living organisms appear to be 'designed', there must be a designer. Believers in ID cannot bring themselves to accept that natural selection could possibly bring about structures as complicated and apparently 'designed' as the mammalian eye, for example. This is not a problem to biologists, who, on the other hand, do not claim to have solved every evolutionary problem. The vertebrate eye is a complex structure, but what intelligent designer would have let light pass through a layer of nerve cells before it hits the receptors? This does not happen in the octopus eye, which is as complex as the vertebrate's. Evolution has far more convincing explanations for these things.

**The Three Laws of Thermodynamics** are said to be the most important scientific laws for anyone to understand. They deal with the energy in the universe and completely govern the ways in which we can control and transfer energy from one place to another. The scientist and author CP Snow had an excellent way of remembering them:

1 You cannot win (you cannot get something for nothing, because matter and energy are conserved).
2 You cannot break even (you cannot return to the same energy state, because there is always an increase in disorder; entropy always increases).
3 You cannot get out of the game (because absolute zero is unattainable).

It is probably not worth your while learning the mathematical expressions of these laws, unless you are a physicist!

**Environmentalism** is an influential concept. Make sure you understand the political as well as the scientific use of the word. Dangers in environment policies lie in assumptions that it is possible to keep the world exactly as it is or was – in other words, ignoring the inevitability of change.

# Revision checklist
## *helps you check what you still need to do*

### By the end of this chapter you should be able to:

| | | |
|---|---|---|
| 1 Use all the information in Databank, above, with confidence | Confident | Not confident. **Revise** page 22 |
| 2 Understand some ideas on the origins of the universe | Confident | Not confident. **Revise** pages 4, 5, 9 |
| 3 Know the history of some important aspects of science | Confident | Not confident. **Revise** pages 4–9, 30 |
| 4 Know the sources and forms of energy | Confident | Not confident. **Revise** pages 20, 22 |
| 5 Know about the distribution of the Earth's resources | Confident | Not confident. **Revise** pages 16, 17 |
| 6 Know about greenhouse gases and global warming | Confident | Not confident. **Revise** pages 18, 19 |
| 7 Understand some issues about fertility control | Confident | Not confident. **Revise** pages 51, 52 |
| 8 Know about genetic modification and biotechnology | Confident | Not confident. **Revise** pages 14, 15, 20 |
| 9 Understand the nature of experimental procedures | Confident | Not confident. **Revise** pages 12, 24 |
| 10 Understand ideas about progress in science | Confident | Not confident. **Revise** page 196 |

# Understanding of scientific methods, principles, criteria and their application

All the specifications expect an understanding of the way in which scientists work. Much of this should be familiar from GCSE science courses. Those courses focus on the basic content of biology, chemistry, physics and the earth sciences. In General Studies you are expected to have some knowledge and understanding of modern developments in the sciences, particularly those that have effects on our daily lives or are at the forefront of human understanding.

## Exam themes

→ Nature of scientific investigation

→ What is an experiment?

→ Recent developments in science

→ How do we investigate difficult subjects such as human behaviour and matters that seem to be beyond reason?

## Topic checklist

○ AS ● A2

| | AQA A | AQA B | EDEXCEL | OCR |
|---|---|---|---|---|
| What is scientific method? | ○● | | ○● | ○ |
| Why are we superstitious? | ○● | ○ | ○● | ○ |
| Why is genetics important to us all? | ○● | ○ | ○● | ○● |

# What is scientific method?

> *"The great tragedy of Science – the slaying of a beautiful hypothesis by an ugly fact."*
>
> Thomas Huxley

**Checkpoint 1**

Where does the word **science** come from?

**The Jargon**

**Induction** is a form of reasoning where you make generalisations from your observations.

**Checkpoint 2**

How does **deduction** differ from **induction**?

**Link**

See also page 68: Social and natural sciences: differences in issues and methodologies.

Without realising it, we are involved in scientific investigation, evaluations and procedures almost every day of our lives. There is nothing particularly mysterious about the way in which scientists work, although some of the concepts they deal with may be complex and difficult to follow. Science that affects our well-being is always going to be a focus of attention.

## Scientific explanation

→ Science is about explaining how the world works. Scientific **theories** are explanations of different aspects of nature, and scientists try to make the theories as simple as possible but also to explain as much as possible. If a scientific theory helps us **predict** what is going to happen, or helps us understand why some things happen and others don't, then we are likely to go on accepting it. If, however, predictions are not fulfilled, or there are several competing theories, then we need to carry out experiments in order to improve or replace our theories. **Scientific method** is no more than designing and carrying out **experiments**. Of course, theories have to come from somewhere, usually from the minds of people who observe a lot and ask questions about why things happen. Scientific method is also said to be reasoning by **induction**.

## Scientific experiments

→ Some people react with apprehension at the mention of an 'experiment'. It sounds as thought it will be something very unpleasant at the worst, or difficult to understand at the best. However, it is nothing more than a test of an idea, a scientific explanation or **theory**.

→ Scurvy is a serious debilitating disease that kills if not remedied. When the world was largely explored by boat, scurvy was the main danger during long voyages. James Lind showed, **by experiment**, that scurvy had a simple cause and could easily be remedied, in *A Treatise of the Scurvy*, 1753.

→ Lind took a **sample** of similar scurvy sufferers:

*On the 20th May, 1747, I took twelve patients in the scurvy on board the* Salisbury *at sea. Their cases were as similar as I could have them. They all in general had putrid gums, the spots and lassitude, with weakness of their knees. They lay together in one place, being a proper apartment for the sick in the fore-hold; and had one diet in common to all.*

→ He then divided this group into six pairs and gave them different extras. For example:

*Two of these were ordered each a quart of cyder a day . . . Two others took two spoonfuls of vinegar three times a day upon an empty stomach.*

→ The crucial pair was given:

*. . . two oranges and one lemon every day. These they eat with greediness at different times upon an empty stomach. They continued*

*but six days under this course, having consumed the quantity that could be spared.*

→ He recorded that:

*the consequence was that the most sudden and visible good effects were perceived from the use of the oranges and lemons; one of those who had taken them being at the end of six days fit for duty*

and ultimately made more tests of his theory that scurvy is a disease caused by a deficiency of something contained in oranges and lemons.

## Features and types of experiments ●●●

→ Experiments broadly fall into two types. In the first, scientists can make observations (measurements) of different **variables** and then show whether there are **correlations** between them. For example, data on the number, per day, of cigarettes smoked and the occurrence of lung cancer show a significant correlation. Further research shows that other possible variables do not show such a correlation – the conclusion is that smoking is a main, but not the only, **cause** of lung cancer.

→ The other kind of experiment is where the scientist **changes** one variable – for example, changing the potential difference across a wire – and **measures the effect** this has on another, for example, the current in it. If there is a relationship then this may represent a successful test of a theory (in this case, that electrical energy can be transferred in a predictable way along a wire).

→ The concept of a variable is particularly important in science. Experimental variables are of two kinds – **independent** and **dependent**. The independent variable is the one that the investigator changes deliberately. For example, James Lind changed the diet of his unfortunate seamen. The dependent variable is what changes as a result – in the seamen's case, whether they recovered from scurvy or not.

→ Carrying out experiments is a skilful manipulation of variables. Physicists and chemists are often able to control an independent variable, and demonstrate a mathematical relationship with a dependent variable. For example, Newton's Second Law of Motion ($F = ma$) shows the relationship between two independent variables – the **mass (m)** of and the **force (F)** exerted on an object – and the dependent variable, the **acceleration (a)** experienced by that object.

→ Making correlations is more characteristic of the biology and earth sciences, mainly because it is not always possible to change the independent variables in just the way one would wish. Scientists often stress the importance of repeating measurements, because it is often difficult to control the independent variable in the way needed. Also, the sample must be big enough so that the results you get are unlikely to have arisen by chance.

**Checkpoint 3**

Why would it be very difficult to carry out an experiment like Lind's today?

**Links**

Check on the way in which research in the **social sciences** is carried out, page 68.

**Checkpoint 4**

Why do all scientists need to have an understanding of **statistics**?

**Exam preparation**                                                   answers: page 30

1   [AS] How would you set about finding whether the food you eat has been genetically modified?   (10 minutes)

2   [A2] Some scientists suggest that genetically modified food is beneficial. How is this possible?   (40 minutes)

# Why are we superstitious?

Science does not provide complete explanations of every phenomenon. Our expectation of scientists is, however, to provide us with the best possible rational explanations of phenomena at the time – not just to satisfy our curiosity, but because the explanations may be useful in the future. It is customary to distinguish between phenomena that can be explained by generally agreed scientific theories, and those that cannot. The latter might be of many different kinds, as discussed here.

## Science and non-science

→ Scientific theories are applied to newly observed phenomena in the hope of explaining them. An explanation should allow us to make predictions about similar events. Some events await generally accepted scientific explanations – they might be religious, or very rare, or unique to an individual, or there is no satisfactory theory for a common event. Look at the different questions we can ask.

→ 'Why does the sun rise every morning?' 'Why' questions can usually be of two sorts – one answer could be 'because the Earth is rotating on its own axis once every 24 hours, and this means that each spot on the Earth will come to face the sun once a day, giving the appearance of the sun coming up over the eastern horizon'. However, and this is well known to young children, you can carry on asking 'why' questions – 'Why does the Earth rotate?' – with the implication that there is some fundamental reason for all events. 'How does the Earth rotate round the sun?' is a better question for a scientist. 'Why' implies a philosophical or belief-based answer.

## Searching for answers

→ Sometimes a question may be deceptively simple – 'Why did X die?' We may be able to provide a scientific explanation – 'X had lung cancer that could not be cured'; 'X smoked heavily since being a teenager, and this is a strong contributory factor in lung cancer.' But we cannot easily answer the anguished relative who says, 'I know lots of people who have smoked heavily but who have not developed lung cancer, so why did X have to get it?' This question implies that there must be some **undetected** reason for this **particular** person developing the disease. A scientist in this situation would point out that this is an example of a random event, which the sufferer has made more likely by his or her own behaviour. Any other explanation lies in the realm of philosophy – you may be a believer in **determinism**, which says that there is a specific cause for all events, or in a **religious** or **superstitious** explanation

→ There are respectable forms of belief, the many religious faiths that ask followers to accept unusual events or possibilities such as an afterlife in heaven or hell. Some scientists find it possible to work objectively in their field, yet accept that there are many things for which they have no explanation except in religious belief. Others do not accept there is a need for religious belief.

**Checkpoint 1**

List the different ways in which we use the word **theory**.

**Action point**

George was asked by his teacher why he could see a flash of lightning before hearing the crash of thunder. 'Because our eyes are in front of our ears!'
Do you think this is a reasonable answer?

**Links**

Check that you understand the meaning of **agnosticism** and **atheism**.

## Coincidence

→ Coincidences abound in our daily life and are often used to challenge scientific explanation. Most people assume that when two events occur together some form of supernatural force might be at work. Why should your friend or partner suddenly start thinking about someone that you haven't seen for some time at the same time as you? Why should you bump into a distant relative, who you haven't seen for years, on holiday on the other side of the world? You notice that we are posing these as 'why' questions – because the event is unusual we tend to believe that something or someone is there, pulling the strings to make it happen. The simplest explanation, that it is just a chance happening, becomes acceptable if we think of all the times we are thinking of someone, or travelling somewhere, and **not** finding such a coincidence.

→ Probability and statistics can help us with surprising results. If you want to be **certain** of getting two people with the same birth date in one room, you will need to gather 367 individuals together. If you are satisfied with a 50/50 chance of this event then you need gather only 23. Since 50/50 events are, by definition, quite frequent, then carrying out the test will often give you a positive result – something that is always nice for a party trick!

## Horoscopes

→ Horoscopes are simple examples of general statements from which the readers make up specific examples for themselves. They are classic examples of **confirmation bias**, in which you look for evidence that supports a belief and ignore that which does not. Astrology has a long history and supporters claim that individually prepared horoscopes are accurate assessments of your character and predictors of future events. There is no evidence at all for this claim, even though some weak correlations have been produced for birth sign and features such as athleticism. Correlations never prove causation – they may **suggest** a cause but separate confirmation is required.

## Conspiracy theories

→ Almost every news item produces a crop of these – there is an insatiable desire for people to believe that events are never what they seem. They range from the bizarre – that astronauts never landed on the moon – to the more bizarre – all world political events are part of an evil takeover of the world by an anti-Christ. Some are scientific and often faintly plausible – such as the idea that the everlasting light bulb has been invented but the patent is owned by manufacturers who stand to lose money if it was ever made and sold.

---

**Action point**

Is it coincidence or correlation that the incidence of house burglary in a town increased in the months after the opening of a large car boot sale every week?

---

**Exam preparation**                          answer: pages 30–31

[AS] Explain the difference between scientific investigation and common sense. How would you show a possible relationship between lung cancer and smoking?   (25 minutes)

# Why is genetics important to us all?

The discovery of the chemical basis for genetics through the structure of the DNA molecule, the subsequent working out of the details of the genetic code and following that the elucidation of the code sequence for human DNA (the Human Genome Project) were landmark events for biology and medicine. Entangled in this scientific story are many personal stories about scientists and their motivation.

## The structure of DNA

→ Darwin was able to show that simple, measurable processes in nature could account for the evolution of the amazing diversity of life. He knew, however, that a full explanation of the way in which features could be handed down the generations was critical to his theory. But it took another hundred years before it was shown that there was a simple chemical mechanism that explained how chemicals in cells could affect bodily characteristics and how these characteristics could be passed from parents to offspring. The fact that the nucleus of cells contains an unusual chemical was known in the 1930s, and that this chemical was acidic was known for many years because microscopists used basic dyes to stain and show up the nucleus. The acid was known to be a large molecule, probably a chain structure. In the 1940s **Erwin Chargaff** found that although nucleic acid from different organisms varied widely in the amounts of adenine, thymine, cytosine and guanine forming part of the molecule, for every adenine there was a thymine, and for every cytosine a guanine.

→ It was believed that discovering the peculiar structure of nucleic acid (DNA) would be very significant in understanding genetics. As a result, a race involving several groups of scientists developed – **Linus Pauling**, **James Watson** and **Francis Crick**, **Maurice Wilkins** and **Rosalind Franklin**. Pauling was already a very famous and prolific chemist who had shown that proteins consisted of folded chains of amino acids, and he was first to suggest that DNA might consist of helical chains. In 1952 he published a structure for DNA consisting of three chains. In a now classic story of mild intrigue, Watson and Crick realised that Pauling's model did not fit with the evidence from X-ray analysis of DNA crystals produced by Wilkins and Franklin. They came to the correct insight that there were two chains, linked by the adenine-thymine and cytosine-guanine pairs and, worried that Pauling would realise his error, quickly published a short paper in 1953. In it, they wrote, '*It has not escaped our notice that the specific pairing we have postulated immediately suggests a possible copying mechanism for the genetic material.*' And so it proved to be.

→ Pauling was awarded the Nobel Prize for Chemistry in 1954, and for Peace in 1962. Watson, Crick and Wilkins received the Nobel Prize for Medicine in 1962, but Rosalind Franklin sadly died from cancer in 1958 and could therefore not be awarded a Laureate.

**Checkpoint 1**

What theories explaining life on Earth were available before Darwin proposed the theory of evolution?

**Checkpoint 2**

What significant development in evolution did **Mendel** make? Why did his work not have any influence until the early 1900s?

**Check the net**

Search for 'Nobel Prize' and find out the criteria for winning the prizes. Find out the names and discoveries of recent science winners.

## Cracking the code

→ In the forty years since the discovery of the structure of DNA, the basic nature of the genetic code – that three base pairs, or triplets, form the coded instruction for putting a specific amino acid into a protein chain; which triplets code for which amino acid, and the basic mechanisms for making proteins in the cell – was worked out in the 1960s. Rapid progress in techniques for working out the triplet sequences for particular genes took place in the 1980s, which led the way to sequencing the whole human genome, completed in most aspects in 2002. We are now on the verge of working out in detail how all the genes produce the effects they do, with the ultimate aim of providing tools for dealing with all major health problems.

## Science and society

→ The breakthroughs to the genetic code contain many pointers about the way in which scientists work and how discoveries are made.

→ The revelation of the genetic code involved several very difficult areas of science. Biochemical methods identified the chemical components of DNA; chemical analysis enabled Chargaff to quantify the amounts of the bases; X-ray diffraction analysis of crystallised DNA led to an understanding of the three-dimensional form of the molecule. Watson and Crick had to draw all these pieces of evidence together to form a coherent picture. That picture contained an even more powerful hypothesis about how genes actually work, which set research tasks for thousands of scientists in the years to come.

→ Scientists need resources to carry out their research – and this means they have to justify their work to those who provide the funds. Much research is now collaborative, which raises issues of efficiency and bureaucracy.

→ Begun in 1990 in the US, the Human Genome Project originally was planned to last 15 years, but rapid technological advances and international cooperation have accelerated the completion date to 2003. The main aim of the project was to identify all the genes in human DNA, but it also has to consider the ethical, legal and social issues that may arise. In 1998 Craig Venter founded Celera Genomics as a private business and announced that Celera, using slightly different methods, would decode the human genome faster and more economically than the publicly funded consortium of scientists.

**Exam preparation**                                    answer: page 31

[A2] 'We solve human health problems, but often at a high cost.' Evaluate this assertion, with reference to at least two examples.   (50 minutes)

# Answers
## Understanding of scientific methods, principles, criteria and their application

### What is scientific method?

**Checkpoints**

1 The Latin word *scientia* meant all knowledge, and kept that meaning until the 18th century. Nowadays we use science in a more limited sense – the knowledge gained from observations and experiments.

2 **Deduction** is reasoning by the strict rules of logic. It works from premises to conclusions that are true if the premises are true. You can think of it as arguing from the general to the particular – all birds have wings; sparrows are birds; therefore sparrows have wings. **Induction** is the form of reasoning most used by scientists, and argues from the particular to the general – sparrows have wings; other birds have wings; therefore sparrows must be birds. The conclusion is not necessarily true for all things with wings (butterflies have wings but are not birds) but is possible, and open to test by more observations or experiments. This is a simplification of philosophy and logic, but it is sufficient for you to understand how science can use both **inductive** and **deductive reasoning**.

3 It would be impossible to carry out Lind's experiments today, because they would be regarded as **unethical**. The sailors were already very ill, and subjecting some of them to further peculiar diets would not be acceptable to any experimenter. Lind apparently persisted with diets that produced worse symptoms, when one of his treatments quickly had a clearly beneficial effect. It would not have been possible to experiment on animals in this case, because their responses to vitamin deficiency are often very different to humans.

4 Scientists need to have an understanding of mathematics, not least because measuring and calculating quantities needs to be accurate. Much of theoretical physics is mathematical (and overlaps with applied mathematics). Statistics is a special branch of mathematics, dealing with **chance**, **probability** and **correlation**. Since scientists are trying to generalise from the particular, they need to know how confident they can be when they only have a few experimental results. Could these results be produced by chance? Statistics will tell them whether they need to do more experiments, and also get the most out of the results they have already obtained.

**Exam preparation**

1 You first need to explain very clearly what 'genetically modified' means – a food plant that has had genes added to it in order to make it resistant to herbicides, for example, so that it can be sprayed with weed-killer without harm. The weeds will be killed, and the GM crop can grow without competition, with a consequently bigger yield. You could ask questions of the food supplier – in the EU labelling is required and is quite specific. A simple answer to the question would be to look at the labels. In order to gain good marks you would have to comment on what the labels might tell you. However, it is possible that the question is looking for a more scientific answer – which is also very much harder. For a short answer like this, you would need to outline briefly an experiment that would detect a difference in the DNA of the suspect food and its 'natural' relative. You would gain marks if you described briefly the principles of such an experiment – you could **not** be expected to give actual details. For example – extract and sequence the DNA from the food and compare the sequence from a non-GM sample. If the modifying gene is known, it may be possible to identify this by the sequence. If the food is a seed, grow it and compare its response to weed-killer with that of non-GM and other GM samples. Since the question is ambiguous, you will gain marks from tackling all aspects of it – so briefly dealing with both aspects is a good thing, if you make sure the examiner knows what you have done.

2 This question also has social and economic implications that you would be expected to consider. These are more straightforward but do require some thought. The term 'beneficial' could refer to the 'health' aspects of the food. This could be relevant, for example, if the crop has been modified to provide, say, a vitamin or nutrient that is not otherwise available in the diet. Alternatively, beneficial could refer to the possibility of growing the plant in situations normally unsuitable – for example, if it were able to survive drying out more – thus enabling farmers to grow it to the benefit of themselves and the local population who now have more food. You may be able to provide actual **evidence** – such as examples of the economy or otherwise gained by growing GM crops, or the improved nutrition available in some parts of the world. You can also give your opinion (in other words you will be **subjective**) if you believe GM food is being foisted on the world just because it allows giant multi-national food producers to make more money. **Always** make sure that you distinguish between **facts** and **opinion**, and remember that some people often present opinions as though they are facts. The question asks you to speculate – you can do this without specific knowledge. You could argue that the foods might be of special use to developing countries or that they should not be grown at all until we have better understanding of the longer-term effects.

### Why are we superstitious?

**Checkpoints**

1 You should be totally familiar with the scientific use of **theory**. It is an explanation for some aspect of the universe, and has a higher status than a **hypothesis** because it should have been tested experimentally. People use it in an everyday sense to mean something that is **not proven** ('It's only a theory'; 'Well, theoretically, it should work like this'), which is all right as long as we understand that this is not the scientific use of the term.

**Exam preparation**

You need to explain how a scientific investigation **differs** from common sense. This is rather difficult since there is no universally agreed definition of 'common sense'. To scientists, presumably common sense is the way in which they ought to work – it would not be sensible to do otherwise. To the person in the street, it could mean anything – things are common sense if they are 'obviously' true. To one person it might be obvious that smoking causes lung cancer. Smoke is a damaging substance – it makes you cough and splutter; therefore, it is more than likely that it will damage your lungs. Lung cancer is serious damage to your lungs, so more smoking will cause more serious damage. Simple. Another person argues with that by saying that they have known lots of people who don't smoke, yet contracted lung cancer. Even more convincing, they say, we know lots of people who have smoked for years and haven't got lung cancer. So using common sense helps you argue both ways. A scientific investigation is the **only** way in which these conflicting arguments can be resolved. You then need to show how such an investigation might be set up or, if you are familiar with the original research, how that was done. Important points are: examining **matched** groups (for sex, health history, type of smoking, age when smoking started); use people for whom you have a reliable history; eliminate other variables, such as exposure to other people's smoke (you may be able to allow for this in the samples you have set up); use large enough samples so that the results are very unlikely to be produced by chance.

## Why is genetics important to us all?

### Checkpoints

1 Before Darwin (pre 1850s), people, including scientists, thought that God created the range of living organisms on the Earth. It was very difficult to see how the complexity of life could have been produced in any other way. Geology was a young science, although it was becoming accepted that rock strata were laid down over a very long time, and not in the very short periods worked out by some theologians. Fossils were a problem – and some people believed that they had been placed in the rocks by the devil to lead humans astray. The French biologist **Lamarck** believed that living things had changed from simple to complex, but proposed that they did so by a process of internal effort, and changes brought about by the environment.

2 Mendel carried out breeding experiments with plants and discovered two significant things – that inheritance was brought about by particles in cells, and that these particles behaved in predictable ways. The particles are what we now call genes, although he never used the word. He realised that his work might be significant for Darwin's theory – it gave an explanation for how characteristics can be passed from parents to children. It is possible that Darwin read it, but there is no evidence that it influenced his thinking.

### Exam preparation

The statement suggests that solutions to problems often create more, but different, problems. In relation to health, one example might be – we solve the problem of infant mortality from common diseases, only to produce problems of over-population. You need to choose two examples – the specification you are following may require knowledge of particular developments, so check these first. Otherwise you are relying on general knowledge and GCSE Science. Improvements in general health have come about through:
- Water supply and sanitation
- Vaccination and immunisation
- Greater understanding of diet, particularly of vitamins and minerals
- Wider availability of medical services
- Antibiotics
- Sterilisation and antisepsis techniques
- Safe sex routines
- Birth control methods (but controversial)

Costs associated with these could be:
- Increases in population, leading to food shortages
- Rapid evolution of disease-causing organisms in response to over-use of antibiotics
- Breakdown of some structures in society, such as the family
- Damage to the environment through over-population
- Greater demand for energy and consequent pressure on the environment

You should be able to link these together. Since you are asked to **evaluate** the statement, you must consider it from as many points of view as possible, and **draw a conclusion** – does the balance of evidence you have produced lead you to agree with it, or not?

# Databank

**Sir Francis Bacon (1561–1626)** was a highly influential thinker who tried to describe the ideal ways of investigating the world. He believed that 'knowledge is power' and, by producing new inventions and discoveries, it pushed human beings to a better future. His contribution to scientific method was to suggest that we make observations from which we can produce generalisations (one form of induction), and that more observations make for better generalisations.

**Gregor Mendel** carried out breeding experiments in plants that are models of painstaking analysis. His results were notable because he used statistical methods to make sense of patterns in the results. It was generally believed that characteristics of the parents were 'blended', or mixed together, in the children. This blend was mixed together when those children had children and so on. Mendel showed that some characteristics could separate out from the mixture in later generations – the characters behaved as though they were produced by distinct particles.

**Nuclear physics experiments** – some experiments are truly mind-boggling. Ray Davis began an experiment in 1968 that changed the basis of nuclear physics. He built a huge tank in a mine, filled it with 100 000 gallons of cleaning fluid. He surrounded it with an array of detectors to pick up the flashes when particles called solar neutrinos, which are produced by the nuclear reactions in the sun, collided with particles in the cleaning fluid. On the basis of the current theories, he and his co-worker, John Bahcall, expected, out of the billions of neutrinos passing through the tank, to detect about 10 neutrinos a week. Remarkably, they did detect neutrinos, but only about a third of those expected. This was a real puzzle and critics thought there must be flaws in his set-up. However he persevered and his results were eventually explained by changing some basic assumptions. The whole theory behind the standard model of nuclear particles had to be changed.

**Parapsychology.** Many people believe that things can happen through the 'power of the mind'. Unfortunately the more such claims are examined, the less substance is revealed. The first problem to be overcome is the possibility of trickery. Stage magicians are very knowledgeable about the way in which you can be deceived, but let you know that they are using tricks. One, James Randi, has spent much of his life exposing fraud of this kind, and offering a very large reward to anyone claiming to have these powers demonstrating them under closely controlled conditions. Others are less scrupulous. Thousands of these experiments have been carried out in university psychology departments, as projects for students, but without reaching very satisfactory outcomes. A few experiments have shown a statistically significant result, but they have not shown the result when repeated. Some experiments give a small significant response when a 'believer' carries out the experiment, which cannot be confirmed by exactly the same experiment carried out by a 'non-believer'. So far, nothing of practical significance has come out of many experiments.

**Experiments on animals.** This is a very emotional area. It is perfectly acceptable to hold, on the basis of your ethical beliefs, that experiments on animals are wrong and should not be carried out. Some scientists hold this view. However, if you hold this belief, you must also accept that the solution to many medical problems will not be found, certainly not in the near future. Anti-vivisectionists have begun to claim that results obtained from research on animals are not applicable to humans – this, however, is just untrue.

# Revision checklist
*helps you check what you still need to do*

## By the end of this chapter you should be able to:

| | | | |
|---|---|---|---|
| 1 | Use all the information in Databank, above, with confidence | Confident | Not confident. **Revise** page 32 |
| 2 | Explain the nature of scientific investigation | Confident | Not confident. **Revise** pages 24, 25 |
| 3 | Explain what experiments are and why they are so important in science | Confident | Not confident. **Revise** pages 12, 24, 25 |
| 4 | Describe some recent developments in science | Confident | Not confident. **Revise** pages 18, 19, 28, 29 |
| 5 | Explain how we investigate difficult subjects such as human behaviour and matters that seem to be beyond reason | Confident | Not confident. **Revise** pages 26, 27 |

# Moral responsibility: the social, ethical and environmental implications of scientific discoveries and technological development

You need to understand the basis for **moral reasoning** and the principles of **ethics** for this section of the specification. Scientists and technologists' work is essentially objective – solving their problems depends on **deductive and inductive** thinking about observations of nature. However, scientific discoveries always raise the question of whether the results of research should be applied or not. This is self-evident in many medical applications – IVF, transplants, cloning and genetic modification are topical cases, but similar consideration has to be given to major technical projects, such as dams or nuclear power plants, where there may be risks to the general population, either to their health or their quality of life. Often these considerations are complex and involved. To illustrate these problems and some of the principles that must be used, three scenarios are presented here – weapons of mass destruction, 'designer' babies and cosmetic surgery. For each we have tried to present the basic facts about the problem, then looked at the moral and ethical issues that arise (you may be able to suggest more) and how you might arrive at a decision. Another aspect is the question of whether any particular scientific or technical problem **should** be solved before any other, or even at all. That involves an understanding of the **relativity of morals**, **utilitarianism**, and possibly even **logical positivism**.

## Exam themes

→ Moral responsibilities of scientists and technologists

→ Implications of new inventions, developments and techniques

→ Ethical questions in genetics, including cloning and genetic modification

→ Environmental effects of modern technology

→ Controversy in science and technology, for example over mobile phones

→ The enhancement of the human body

## Topic checklist

○ AS  ● A2

| | AQA A | AQA B | EDEXCEL | OCR |
|---|---|---|---|---|
| Weapons of mass destruction | ○● | ○● | ○● | ● |
| Playing at God | ○● | ● | ○● | ○ |
| Cosmetic surgery | ○● | ○ | ○● | ○ |

# Weapons of mass destruction

It has probably occurred to you to wonder why any scientist or technologist would wish to develop any weapons, let alone those that might be used to slaughter indiscriminately. They are much the same morally as the rest of us, and probably possessed of the same wide range of ethical standards. So if you can recruit soldiers to use such weapons, why not scientists and technologists to make them more destructive?

## Weapons of mass destruction ●●●

→ This is a new name for several forms of warfare that in the past have been thought of as 'unnatural' – chemicals, such as poison gas; nuclear bombs; biological weapons, involving deadly diseases and poisons derived from living things. 'Terrorists' might use all of these weapons, as well as ordinary guns and bombs. The linking features are that fighters who may not identify themselves as conventional soldiers may use the weapons indiscriminately against soldiers and civilians. How are scientists and technologists involved in producing or using them? What are their responsibilities in doing so since the development of such weapons now necessitates scientific research and technological expertise?

## Chemical warfare

→ Chemical warfare was used on the battlefields of the First World War, and more recently in Kurdish Iraq. It depends on chemicals that are relatively easy to manufacture, but are difficult to handle successfully. Mustard gas in the First World War frequently affected as many of those who used it as their enemy. Chemicals are the key component of flame-throwers, widely used by all sides in the Second World War, and napalm bombs were used against the Communist guerrillas in Vietnam. The relative lack of accuracy in use means that these weapons can have terrible consequences for civilians.

## Biological warfare

→ Use of living organisms and materials produced by them constitutes biological warfare. Pathogenic organisms and the toxic substances they produce may be turned into weapons by putting them into conventional shells and missiles. There are major problems in protecting your own soldiers against their effects. Scientific input is essential because the growth, enhancement and extraction of agents from the organisms are very specialised.

## Nuclear warfare

→ The effects of nuclear weapons are well known, and the knowledge needed to produce such devices is available in many countries. The difficulties facing anyone who wants to produce a device are technical – extracting and accumulating sufficient raw materials – rather than scientific.

**Checkpoint 1**

In what ways are weapons of mass destruction different from 'ordinary' weapons?

**Checkpoint 2**

What is the Nuclear Non-Proliferation Treaty?

→ Scientists are a key in all weapons research; they solve the highly technical problems involved. They may be able to invent weapons based on new developments in science – a classic example is the atom bomb. In view of this, scientists carry a special burden of responsibility. Some scientists find it unacceptable to work on weapons; others believe that if they are able to invent better weapons, or defences against weapons developed by other countries, their use by their own nation would be only for peaceful or peace-keeping purposes. In this way they move into the personal, moral and political areas.

## Responsibilities of scientists

→ Scientists:
  → understand the technical problems better than the average politician or citizen, and knowledge brings responsibility with it;
  → can provide technical advice and assistance in solving the incidental problems that may emerge;
  → can warn of possible dangers that may arise;
  → form an international community that crosses natural boundaries, so they are well placed to take a global view.

→ There are many examples of scientists whose knowledge brought them moral dilemmas. Nils Bohr, in occupied Denmark, and Werner Heisenberg, working in Germany, met in Copenhagen in 1941 possibly to discuss the implications for weapons research of their contribution to fundamental physics. Because of some basic mistakes in Heisenberg's mathematics, Germany did not come close to developing an atomic bomb, but it is also possible that Heisenberg deliberately failed to correct the errors.

→ In 1939 Leo Szilard, a Hungarian scientist in England, alerted President Roosevelt to the possibility of producing an awesome device, the atom bomb. In 1945, when Szilard heard the first bombs were being made, he – with others – tried unsuccessfully to persuade the President to test the bomb openly before the Japanese and representatives of other countries. They would be given the opportunity to realise its power and surrender before it was used to kill anyone. That this initiative failed is not a failure of scientists alone; it is that of politicians, military, civil servants, scientists, indeed everyone.

→ There are, of course, other examples of scientists who see their responsibilities only to their employer or solely to their country, and are uncritical of what they are asked to do. Cruel research on prisoners in concentration camps by Nazi doctors led to some advances in human physiology. It is difficult for most of us to understand how they could do this, and there has been general agreement never to make use of this work.

---

**Action point**

What is the difference between a **scientific** problem and an **ethical** problem?

**Action point**

Find out the discoveries in physics made by Bohr and Heisenberg.

---

**Exam preparation**                                        answers: page 40

1  [A2] Effective nuclear deterrence depends on only a few countries having nuclear weapons. Briefly explain this view.   (10 minutes)

2  [AS] What moral problems face scientists who work on the development of conventional weapons, such as guns and hand-grenades?   (10 minutes)

# Playing at God

Ethical issues become much more difficult to resolve when everyone seems to be trying to do their best to produce healthy children and happy parents. We need to consider issues that affect society as well as individuals, and potential long-term effects for everyone.

## Playing at God with the designer baby

→ 'Designer babies' are those whose genes have been preselected in some way, in other words, not in the chance way in which genes come together in the normal reproductive process. However, no baby's genes are entirely randomly selected from the population at large. The genes can only be a combination of those available from the sperm and egg of the parents and, to that extent, they have been selected since the parents selected each other to bear their children. Because the word 'design' is used, we are presuming that **someone** is making informed choices about the genetic make-up of the baby, and we might ask 'who' and 'why?' There are many reasons why parents may wish to determine their children's genotypes:
  → desire to have children who are brighter
  → desire to have children who are sportier
  → desire to have children who look beautiful
  → desire to have children of a particular sex
  → where there is a risk of an inherited disease
  → where a baby may have potential for 'helping' others (for example, by acting as a donor of stem cells).

→ One objection to this research is the belief that it is wrong to change or interfere with a natural event. The objection could be religious, if based on the belief that only a deity should have the power to select the features of a child and that God alone exercises the ability to 'design' the baby. The objection could be precautionary – since you cannot know all the consequences of the process of generating a particular genotype, you cannot be sure that the outcomes will all be good, so it is better not to try.

→ Attempts to determine the genetic make-up of individuals have a contentious history. **Francis Galton** in the late 19th century believed it would be possible to encourage parents with 'good' characteristics to have more children, and pass on their characteristics to future generations, founding the **eugenics** movement. Hitler, in Nazi Germany, wanted to create a master race and encouraged men and women of favoured physical types to produce children. In more recent times, sperm banks for the use of mothers who wished to have children with fathers who were highly intelligent or in some way exceptional are readily available. The movement has generally been unsuccessful in achieving notional genetic improvement of the population, not least because of the phenomenon of **regression**. Randomly choosing sperm or eggs of parents who are exceptional is only likely to produce children whose characteristics are between those of the parents and the mean for the population. This is because the characteristics are generally determined by several genes, and can be readily demonstrated mathematically.

**Action point**

Find out the meaning of IVF, stem cells, embryo, sex chromosomes, and how the sex of a baby is determined.

**The jargon**

The **genotype** is the full set of genes in an individual.
**Genetics** is the scientific study of inheritance.

**Checkpoint 1**

Why is eugenics so popular with authoritarian regimes?

→ Medical advances now mean that there are more techniques available to produce children with genotypes that are at least partly known. Some regard the fact of prenatal diagnosis of genetic problems in the foetus as evidence that eugenics is already being practised. It satisfies the needs of individuals, both for themselves and as parents, because they would like to have children who are free of genetic diseases, and potentially in the future they will want to have children who are intelligent. As and when the technology allows them to do this, people will take it up.

→ However, in the UK, attempts to determine the genetic composition of children are tightly controlled. Society is concerned about medium and long-term consequences and the government has set up a regulatory body – the Human Fertilisation and Embryology Authority (HFEA). After consultation it has recently recommended that parents should not be allowed to specify the sex of their children, except if there is a likelihood of a sex-linked inherited disease. The recommendation has the support of the majority of the general public. Reasons for it are:

→ belief by many people that the baby is a 'gift', which should not be interfered with;

→ belief that it is wrong on social grounds;

→ concern over potential psychological damage to the child if the technique is not successful and a child of the 'wrong' sex is born.

Reasons put forward to support being able to choose the sex of your child are:

→ ensuring that it does not have a high chance of inheriting sex-linked abnormalities such as haemophilia (the only reason accepted by HFEA and the public);

→ ensuring a gender balance in the family;

→ 'replacing' a child who has died, so that the family is, in gender terms, as it was before the tragedy.

→ The scientific techniques are not perfect but there is every reason to suppose that they will get better. Some British parents have already exploited the fact that some countries allow parents to determine the sex of their baby. An important point is that this is not just a scientific matter, and the recommendation has been made on social grounds.

**Check the net**

Review the activities of the HFEA at http://www.hfea.gov.uk

**Checkpoint 2**

Why would a **government** want to set up a regulatory body such as the HFEA?

**Exam preparation**                                                        answer: pages 40–41

[A2] 'The applications of modern genetics can do great harm as well as enormous good'. By use of appropriate examples, discuss what controls should be placed on applied genetics.   (45 minutes)

# Cosmetic surgery

In this scenario we look at the moral dilemmas facing scientists in relation to human problems, some of which are clear candidates for medical treatment, and others that some people would regard as trivial or self-indulgent.

## Cosmetic surgery ●●●

→ Plastic surgery is the general name for methods of repairing damage to the human body. It would seem to be obviously worthwhile, for example, to deal with burns, injuries from conflict and terrible accidents. Cosmetic surgery is done for aesthetic reasons, although it is traditionally performed by trained plastic surgeons. There is a wide range of conditions that might call for plastic surgery, for many different reasons. What about differences evident from birth – birthmarks, shortened limbs, hare-lip, webbing between toes or fingers, or the extreme case of conjoined twins? Some conditions, where they affect the normal functioning of the body, are no different to problems such as a hole in the heart and there would be little argument about whether they should be corrected or repaired or not. Others are debatable, not least from the point of view of those affected. For example, some people with a hearing malfunction that can be corrected by surgery feel that they do not wish to have it because they have adapted to being deaf and would be out of place with those who have always had their hearing.

→ Some people whose bodies are different from the rest of the population say that the problem is not for themselves, but for the public, many of whom find it difficult to deal with those differences. In other words, the general public should accept great physical differences in the same way that they have learnt to accept those with problems of vision, hearing and the nervous system.

## Fashion statements

→ There will always be those who want to change their appearance. Age, fashion and vanity provide spurs to cosmetic surgery. In the latest trend in New York, women are having their toes shortened in order to fit into the latest fashionable narrow shoes.

→ Who controls the providers of cosmetic surgery? Is it just a matter for the normal professionalism of doctors and surgeons?

→ Does payment for surgery that is purely to improve appearance or conform to fashion really divert resources from patients with urgent medical needs? Or does the additional research that is needed ultimately benefit everyone? Does the private patient subsidise the general public in the long run?

**Check the net**

Read about the British Association of Plastic Surgeons at http://www.baps.co.uk.

**Checkpoint 1**

List the reasons why it might be necessary to regulate the activity of cosmetic surgeons.

**Links**

Moral codes and society.

→ Fashions for tattooing and body piercing lead subsequently to patients who want them changed or removed. Who has to put things right if they go wrong? Should this be a potential extra burden on the NHS? Much cosmetic surgery can enormously improve the patient's quality of life and should be available under the National Health Service. Treatment can be economically worthwhile and may also aid in the rehabilitation of offenders.

## International issues

→ There are international and economic issues – for example, there has been a dramatic increase in British medical patients flying to South Africa for surgery instead of waiting months for state-funded treatment at home. They are paying cash for heart operations, cancer treatments and cosmetic surgery. The journey works out cheaper than seeking private care in Britain, partly due to the exchange rate. How does this relate to the resources available for the healthcare of the South African population?

→ The scientific and medical aspects of these questions are perhaps less complex. The technical skills, knowledge and resources necessary to remove a self-inflicted tattoo are pretty much the same as removing a disfiguring birthmark. Research on skin grafts would benefit plastic surgery generally. Problems for doctors are largely those of deciding priorities in allocating limited resources.

## Animal research

→ Another dimension is the use of animals in medical research. Many surgical procedures and the drugs used in treatments have been developed using animals. The subject arouses strong feelings, but in any question where you are asked to evaluate the position you must consider all sides of the problem.

→ Testing cosmetic products on animals doesn't fall into the area of cosmetic surgery, but this is an emotive subject from which cosmetics manufacturers are now careful to distance themselves.

**Checkpoint 2**

Make a simple cost/benefit analysis for cosmetic surgery (see 'Relationship between technology, science, culture (past and/or present) and ideology').

**Check the net**

Two different views on animal experiments can be found at http://www.simr.org.uk/ and http://www.buav.org/f_home.html.

**Exam preparation**  answer: page 41

[A2] How can the use of National Health Service resources for cosmetic purposes be justified? (20 minutes)

# Answers

## Moral responsibility: the social, ethical and environmental implications of scientific

### Weapons of mass destruction

#### Checkpoints

1 Basically because they are more indiscriminate. Ordinary military weapons usually have a very specific function – the rifle, machine gun, mortar, artillery, all are intended for military targets – soldiers, armies or vehicles. While they can, of course, injure or kill civilians, that is not their main purpose. WMD are intended to kill anyone, including civilians, and by so doing, to spread fear and anxiety. Nuclear weapons, and chemical and biological agents are therefore WMD. There is much play on words – it is difficult to discover where the phrase WMD came from, but it is now associated with international terrorism.

2 A United Nations initiative, opened in 1968 and now signed by 187 countries, including the 5 countries officially recognised as having nuclear weapons. Its objective is 'to prevent the spread of nuclear weapons and weapons technology, to promote co-operation in the peaceful uses of nuclear energy and to further the goal of achieving nuclear disarmament and general and complete disarmament'.

#### Exam preparation

1 Think through this question logically. Start with the situation with one country possessing nuclear weapons. That country can feel secure, since any threat to it can be prevented with massive force. This situation lasted for a very short time after the Second World War, with America and its ally the UK, until Russia carried out their own tests and produced an atomic bomb. These countries opposed each other ideologically and territorially, but while their nuclear capability was reasonably balanced, they maintained an uneasy stalemate. If other countries then acquire nuclear weapons, the balance of force may become lop-sided, or the new nuclear power may just wish to act on its own. This was the situation when China built its first bomb in the 1950s, followed by France. The situation was more or less stable until the 1990s when India and Pakistan joined the club. With few nuclear powers, no one wished to be the first to use the weapons, for fear of retaliation by the others. A difficult question is why would any state want to use a nuclear bomb when the effects are unlikely to be local and could affect the attacker as badly as the attacked? The short answer is that with more holders of nuclear weaponry, the greater the chance of it being used either accidentally or by an ill-considered decision or, worse still, by a terrorist or extremist faction. Therefore, with more nuclear powers, the greater the chance that a nuclear weapon will be used, and hence the deterrent value is much less.

2 A moral position can be taken by anyone who has particular beliefs. So, a scientist who believes that it is absolutely wrong to kill another human is not likely to be working in an armaments research laboratory. However, not many people fall into this special category, and many scientists, in common with the rest of the public, have a conditional view of killing another – that is, it may be morally acceptable in certain circumstances – when one's life or that of others is threatened, or to prevent the chance of that threat. On that basis, a scientist can feel justified in working on weapons, or creating new ones, if they are clearly for military or security use. However, not all weapons have quite such clear-cut uses. Landmines, for example, were developed for use against soldiers, but since technology has made them almost undetectable, they are a continuing threat to civilians, particularly children, in areas where they were used in huge numbers. A scientist might, however, work on methods to counteract the use of landmines, and feel morally justified. Moral dilemmas might arise for scientists working on antidotes to poison gases. In order to test them, the gases must be produced – and therefore might be used.

### Playing at God

#### Checkpoints

1 This depends on the nature of the authoritarian regime. The Nazis believed in a view of their race (the Aryans) that was largely an invention by Hitler. A belief that this race was exemplified in a particular body form and colouring led to extraordinary 'breeding' programmes. Such regimes may also see the control of marriages and the restriction or promotion of the number of children as desirable. It is also a way of demonstrating the state's power over individuals and some regimes see that as acceptable.

2 The HFEA is a non-departmental Government body that regulates and inspects all UK clinics providing IVF, donor insemination or the storage of eggs, sperm or embryos. The HFEA also licenses and monitors all human embryo research being conducted in the UK. The Government has set up the HFEA to regulate these things because of the amount of public controversy that would be caused if it were not doing so. All HFEA responsibilities are seen as controversial by one group or another, but the HFEA is able to consider those views at a distance from government, who might be seen as being partisan.

#### Exam preparation

In this question you are asked to provide examples. The best thing is to start by listing these, others may occur to you as you are writing. Note that the question is not just about **human** or **medical** genetics. Examples of applied genetics therefore come from all applications: genetic modification of crop plants; hybridisation of crops and food animals; cloning of farm animals; production of microorganisms with desirable features; genetic testing and pharmacology (pharmacogenomics); protein functions (proteomics); genetic counselling; human genome project (HGP); gene therapy. Many of these are complex and, at the moment, highly experimental techniques, but you would not be expected to show wide or specialist knowledge of them. If you only know a few – don't panic, because the question is about the **controls** that should be put on applied genetics

# discoveries and technological development

procedures. Why should any of them need to be controlled? Think in general terms – they may damage the environment/wildlife/human health/human wealth; they may be unethical because they may conflict with the beliefs of individuals/groups/society as a whole; they may create long-term problems for society. Once you have created some categories, think of the example that goes with it. Thus – damage to the environment may be caused by growing herbicide-resistant GM crops if farmers need to spray herbicides to get rid of weeds. In time, perhaps, more herbicide will be needed, potentially causing chemically polluted soil. Therefore, the sowing of GM crops may need to be controlled, and limited in certain places. Long-term problems for society could be caused by allowing all parents to choose the sex of their children; therefore, the practice may need to be limited or controlled. Write about as many such examples as you can think of, but make sure you have time to make a final summing up and a conclusion. You may come up with an optimistic view – that very few controls are needed because geneticists, farmers and doctors are all responsible people and don't do risky things; or you may lack confidence in the free operation of geneticists, farmers and businesses, because they will only consider fame and/or profit. You would need to support your conclusion by reference to the examples you have chosen. You may think that existing controls are quite sufficient, in which case, show why by reference to your examples.

## Cosmetic surgery

### Checkpoints

1 It is necessary because: people are very keen to improve their appearance, and may therefore be easily persuaded to have treatments that may be unnecessary, or may have a poor chance of success. Cosmetic surgery is likely to be expensive, and practitioners might recommend operations that are the most expensive, rather than producing cheaply the simplest or best results. Regulation is sometimes a very good thing for the cosmetic surgeons themselves – they will know that the public's view of their work is not being prejudiced by the few who do the job badly, as long as regulation prevents such people working.

2 Something to consider is whether the surgery is 'necessary' or not, and this will not always be clear-cut. Costs – training of surgeons is long and expensive; nursing support before and after an operation may be expensive; equipment and drugs may be expensive. Benefits – the individual may now be able to have a job that was previously not possible; the individual may feel much happier/contented; health services may be used less in the long term because individual is healthier/happier. Are the benefits only for the individual, or are they good for society as a whole?

### Exam preparation

You can structure the answer to this on the cost benefit analysis in Checkpoint 2. The basic issue to resolve is whether the proposed cosmetic procedures are solely to satisfy the personal preferences of the patient – and you must discuss how you could decide this – or if the procedure is **necessary** to give a patient a satisfactory quality of life. You need to come to a conclusion, but this is likely to be a conditional one, because there will always be cases which fall into a grey area.

# Databank

**Landmines** are anti-personnel devices, originally devised to prevent enemy soldiers from crossing ground between the lines of opposing armies. They were also designed to stop vehicles, and were thus quite large, but buried in the ground. They could be found by metal (mine) detectors relatively easily. Since the development of new materials, plastic mines have been developed which are small and very difficult to detect. Such mines have been laid in hundreds of thousands in all theatres of war in recent years, but are difficult to clear. The result is, after the conflict, many accidents to civilians, especially children. The International Campaign to Ban Landmines began in 1991, and has now been signed by all but 46 countries. Checkout **http://www.icbl.org/**.

**Clones.** A clone is an exact genetic replica of an organism. Most strawberry plants are clones – they are produced by growing runners from another plant. With most plants, and some animals, it is possible to take a cell or two from the plant and produce replicas. Cloning mammals is much more difficult and involves removing the nucleus from an unfertilized egg and replacing it with the nucleus from a body cell. This can, with difficulty, grow as though it was a normal fertilised egg. The cloned offspring is identical in genetic make-up to the owner of the body cell. The possibility of doing this to humans has raised much controversy. One objection – that the clone will be an exact copy of the original and therefore we could be surrounded by lots of 'identical' copies of our cells – is not valid. Clones would grow to be as different as identical twins, who are obviously unique individuals, and probably more so. Don't forget that the environment has an effect on the way we develop. The real problem is the danger that there will be faults in body functioning, and many attempts to produce clones have resulted in damaged embryos.

**Part of the ethical code of the International Society of Aesthetic Plastic Surgery**
Members will:
- Strive always to improve medical skills and make available to patients and colleagues the benefits of professional knowledge.
- Practice methods of healing on a scientific basis and not associate professionally with anyone who does not uphold this principle.
- Strive to protect the public and the profession against physicians who are incompetent or have a low moral character.
- Expose illegal or unethical conduct of fellow members of the profession.
- Refrain from soliciting patients.
- Never reveal the confidence entrusted in the course of medical attendance or deficiencies found in patients, unless required to do so by law.

**Performance enhancement in sport** is a well-publicised ethical problem. There are literally thousands of food supplements available to athletes, or anyone, to help their bodies perform better. Information is available at **http://www.pponline.co.uk/**. Some additives are deemed to be 'unfair' and are banned by many sports.

**Communication masts.** Disputes over putting mobile phone and radio masts near schools or homes start because it is claimed the radio waves and microwaves used by these devices affect our health. Concern about the effect of mobile phones on users led companies to measure the radiation produced and see if heavy users were affected. The results failed to show any short-term effects, but no one really knows what 20 or more years intensive use might do. The effect of radiation from masts is also not thought to be dangerous, but the issue raises questions about the ethics of putting such devices close to homes.

# Revision checklist

*helps you check what you still need to do*

## By the end of this chapter you should be able to:

| | | | |
|---|---|---|---|
| 1 | Use all the information in Databank, above, with confidence | Confident | Not confident. **Revise** page 42 |
| 2 | Describe the moral responsibilities of scientists and technologists | Confident | Not confident. **Revise** pages 34, 35, 40 |
| 3 | Comment on the implications of new inventions and techniques | Confident | Not confident. **Revise** pages 40, 41 |
| 4 | Answer ethical questions in genetics | Confident | Not confident. **Revise** pages 36, 37 |
| 5 | Describe the environmental effects of some modern technology | Confident | Not confident. **Revise** pages 18, 19 |
| 6 | Comment on a controversy in science and technology | Confident | Not confident. **Revise** pages 34, 35 |
| 7 | Comment on the enhancement of the body | Confident | Not confident. **Revise** pages 38, 39 |

All specifications include references to the ability of students to use simple arithmetical, algebraic and geometrical methods, such as should have been gained for GCSE mathematics. It is not possible in this guide to revise the whole of this material and it is expected that candidates are able to demonstrate the ability to extract and manipulate numerical data from tables, charts and graphs, and generally show a facility with arithmetical manipulations, including the intelligent use of a calculator. This is also particularly relevant to work in the social sciences – and there is work provided in this field later in the guide.

The special topics in this section assume knowledge of percentages, rates, mode, mean, median and substitution in equations.

## Exam themes

→ Simple probability involving combinations of independent events

→ Statistical measures and diagrams

→ Sampling and basic statistics

→ Exponential growth and decay

→ Basic arithmetic and algebraic formulae

→ Graphs and their interpretation

## Topic checklist

| ○ AS ● A2 | AQA A | AQA B | EDEXCEL | OCR |
|---|---|---|---|---|
| Sudden infant deaths | ○● | ● | ○● | ○● |
| Measles, mumps and rubella | ○● | ● | ○● | ○● |
| Population growth | ○● | ● | ○● | ○● |

# Sudden infant deaths

We use more mathematics in our daily life than we realise – and it is nowhere more important to understand some basic mathematical concepts as in probability. This is because sometimes the answers to our problems are nothing like the ones we expect. It is possible for experts to be mistaken – sometimes with disastrous results.

*"When a distinguished but elderly scientist states that something is possible, he is almost certainly right. When he states that something is impossible, he is very probably wrong."*

Arthur C. Clarke

## Probability

→ This is a subject that often confuses people. It plays an important part in human affairs, from the trivial, such as Lottery draws and betting odds, to the highly significant, as in risks to life and limb. It is very important in biology, particularly genetics. Everyone knows that an egg becomes a boy or girl, depending on whether it is fertilised by a sperm carrying either a Y or an X chromosome. Equal numbers of Y- and X-carrying sperm are formed and therefore we expect that equal numbers of boys and girls will be born. This is nearly the case, but in fact the ratio is about 105 boys to 100 girls, and it varies slightly around the world. Let's assume the ratio is 1:1.

→ A common myth is that if one mother has a sequence of boys, the next baby is more likely to be a girl (to 'even things up'). On the other hand, one might expect another boy, because the mother is a 'boy-producing' mother. In both cases we need to be careful. There is good reason to believe that the fertilisation of an egg is not affected by any previous fertilisations, i.e. it is an **independent** event. What is the chance of the next baby being a boy, if the previous two babies were boys? Simple – 1 in 2, the same as for any fertilisation. It isn't really as simple as this, because we are ignoring possibilities like differential deaths of very young embryos in the womb.

→ More difficult is working out the chances of getting a family of, say, two boys. How many possible families are there? Three, of course: 2 boys, 1 boy and 1 girl, 2 girls. Therefore the chance of getting a family of two boys should be 1 in 3. But this is not so. Look at the problem differently – the first baby is either a boy or a girl, so the chance of a boy is 1 in 2 (a probability of 0.5). The probability of the second baby being a boy is also 0.5. The chances of both being boys is therefore half that of one boy, i.e. chances of 1 in 4 (a probability of 0.25). We have simply multiplied the two chances together, because the events are independent. The reason it is different to our first calculation is that there are **two** ways of producing a mixed family – a boy first, or a girl first. Therefore there are four kinds of family – 2 boys, boy + girl, girl + boy, 2 girls, and the chances of a family of two boys is thus 1 in 4 (a probability of 0.25).

## Infant deaths

→ There have been several headline cases where very young children have died in perplexing circumstances. Sally Clark, a 34-year-old mother, was convicted in 1999 of the murder of her two sons –

Christopher, who died at the age of 11 weeks in December 1996, and Harry, who died at the age of 8 weeks in January 1998. Both the children had been previously healthy; they died suddenly in her care. Post mortem examinations of both children showed abnormal findings. An appeal against her conviction eventually succeeded, mainly because her husband discovered in the records that one baby was suffering from an infection which could well have contributed to his death, although this evidence was never produced in court. Influential statistical information was produced in the trial and at appeal. Some of this evidence suggested that the chances of two such deaths in one family were so small as to be totally unlikely; therefore, someone must have killed them.

→ What is the chance of a baby dying from SIDS (sudden infant death syndrome)? We need to have information on the occurrence of such deaths, from medical records, for the population. Does this chance vary with the background of the family? Yes it does, but we depend on the detailed records of deaths of babies in different kinds of family. What are the chances of two babies from one family dying of SIDS? If we assume that the two deaths are **independent** events, then the occurrence of both events happening can be calculated by multiplying the separate probabilities of each death together. In the case of Sally Clark, the chance of a baby dying is 1 in 8543. So, **on the face of it**, the chance of two of her children dying in this way is 1 in 73 000 000. If this were true, there would be one pair of deaths in this way in every 200 years. However, we know that a second such death occurs much more frequently than this, under no suspicious circumstances. We need statistics on the number of families with two SIDS deaths. The two deaths are **not independent** events. There are all sorts of factors that mean that if one such death in a family has occurred, it is more likely that a second will. Of course, such events are very rare.

**Action point**

Evidence in court is often provided by **expert witnesses**. Find out how these witnesses can be called and used.

**Checkpoint 2**

In a drawer containing 3 pairs of black and 3 pairs of blue socks, how many socks do you need to pull out at random to be sure of having a pair the same colour?

**Exam preparation**                                          answer: page 50

[A2] 'There are three sorts of lies – lies, damned lies and statistics' (B Disraeli). How far do you agree with this view?   (45 minutes)

# Measles, mumps and rubella

We are, in general, not very good at assessing risks. Partly this is because of our wish to know things **for certain** and partly because some of the concepts are not intuitive and depend sometimes on simple but tension-building mathematics. It is very important for us all to care about risks, not least because we can be fooled easily – with damaging consequences to our pockets, our emotions and our health.

## Who is trying to manipulate us?

It is a common belief that 'you can prove **anything** with statistics'. This is clearly untrue, but it is possible for numbers, tables, charts and graphs to be presented in very deceptive ways. You need to be very watchful. Frequent tricks are:

→ The **selective axis.** This clip shows a steep and presumably optimistic rise in value, return on investment or anything. But it means nothing if the axes are unlabelled, particularly if they are uncalibrated.

→ **Two dimensions are better than one.** The large bag of money is 1.5 times the height of the small bag – and therefore is intended to represent £1500 against £1000. But what message does the picture give you? The visual effect is greater because the bag has grown by 1.5 times the width as well.

→ **Keep your sample small.** It is vital in scientific work that you work out how many repetitions or how many observations you need to make in order to show that your positive results are not just due to chance. This is why the adverts of the kind where '9 out of 10 golfers use Blastoff drivers' are so misleading. Were only ten asked?

→ **Lose your control.** Controls are important in scientific experiments. Years ago, a medical business developed a vaccine for poliomyelitis. They vaccinated a large (500) sample of children, and had a matched control group that was not vaccinated. There was an epidemic of polio in the town – and the vaccine was declared a success because none of the vaccinated children developed the disease. However, nor did any of the control group.

→ **Spurious correlations.** It is a well-known fact that the distribution of births in Scandinavia is closely correlated with nesting storks. So is it irrelevant that storks tend to nest on the roofs of houses?

## Which is worse – vaccination or the disease?

→ Vaccines have reduced the health risks to children since the discovery of the smallpox vaccination around 200 years ago. Medicine has not had a better success story, except perhaps for antibiotics. Use of the smallpox vaccination led to the declaration by the WHO in 1980 that smallpox had been eradicated as a naturally occurring disease, although samples of the virus have been retained

**Checkpoint 1**

When assessing risks we rely on information from various sources. How do you decide what to believe?

**Checkpoint 2**

What reasons would we have for retaining stocks of live smallpox virus?

in various laboratories for possible use as a biological weapon, or for research in the future.

→ However, vaccination itself carries risks. In the recent concern over terrorist threats of biological warfare, mass vaccination against smallpox has been considered. The possibility of rare but potentially serious side effects is the main drawback to widespread smallpox vaccination. In the USA it has been estimated that 2.7 deaths per million could result. If 60% of Americans were vaccinated, that would mean nearly 500 deaths, even if smallpox never reappears. In the circumstances of terrorist attack, it is most unlikely that the public would object to a programme of vaccination. The public would probably put down the 2.7 deaths per million from the vaccination to an unfortunate side effect, and regard the protection of the vast majority, especially medical staff, as paramount.

## Measles, mumps and rubella (MMR)  ●●●

→ This vaccination has caused much controversy recently. Measles causes 50–60% of the estimated million deaths worldwide per year attributable to vaccine-preventable diseases of childhood. Measles may be responsible for more child deaths than any other single agent because of complications from pneumonia, diarrhoea and malnutrition. Measles is also the major cause of preventable blindness in the world. Mumps is a potentially distressing illness with some particularly unpleasant side effects in adults. Rubella is a mild disease in children and adults but has serious consequences for an unborn baby if contracted by the pregnant mother.

→ Countries with programmes use a triple vaccine administered to babies at about 7–12 months and again before the child goes to school. This reduces the number of vaccinations from 6 to 2. About 1 in 100 000 have severe allergic reactions straight after any immunisation. If the child is treated quickly, he or she will recover fully. People giving immunisations are trained to deal with allergic reactions.

→ One researcher suggested a link between the measles vaccine or vaccines containing measles (such as MMR) and inflammatory bowel disease or autism. Autism, a disorder causing behavioural and language problems, was well known long before MMR was ever used in this country. Autism is diagnosed more often now than in the past and the increases in the cases of autism occurred before MMR was introduced. Parents often first notice the signs of autism around the time MMR is usually given, but this does not necessarily mean that one causes the other.

→ As a result of this assertion, which has not been confirmed or supported by any other medical group, national or international, some parents have demanded to have separate vaccinations for the three diseases or, worse, decided to have no vaccinations at all.

**Links**

Argue the ethical position of any group opposed to invasive medical treatment.

**Checkpoint 3**

What benefit does a country with mass vaccination gain?

---

**Exam preparation**                                   answer: pages 50–51

[AS] In modern society we worry far too much about the risks of new inventions. How far do you agree or disagree with this opinion?   (30 minutes)

# Population growth

Among the many problems of humanity, the fluctuating and usually increasing number of people is always present. Science and technology benefit us most obviously in the way that we are able to feed ourselves and look after our health and welfare. All of which translates into increasing numbers. On the other hand, numbers which decrease rapidly are also of importance.

## How do numbers grow?

→ **Fibonacci** was an Italian mathematician, living around AD 1200. He wrote about interesting problems based on 'real-life' situations. His most famous is the rabbit problem: *A certain man put a pair of rabbits in a place surrounded by a wall. How many pairs of rabbits can be produced from that pair in a year if every month each pair begets a new pair which from the second month on becomes productive?* You can work this out easily if you write down how many pairs there are in month 1, month 2 and so on. What will happen after several years, if you assume that the rabbits are immortal?

→ Numbers that increase **exponentially** become large very quickly indeed. Put in 1 on a calculator and multiply by 2 repeatedly – how long before your result goes off the display? The only rule you have used is that one individual becomes two. There are living organisms that behave this way – bacteria, for example. What would be the difference if each individual could become 4?

→ The difference between **linear** relationships and others is easily appreciated if the graphs are drawn. **A** shows a population that is becoming bigger at an increasing rate; **B** shows a steady increase.

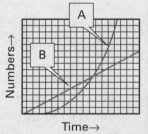

→ **Thomas Malthus** (1766–1805) was a social philosopher who was impressed by some simple mathematics. In a very influential essay he made some basic assumptions:

  → First, that food is necessary to the existence of man.
  → Second, that the passion between the sexes is necessary and will remain nearly in its present state (in other words, many babies will be produced!)

On the basis of these, he noted *'that the power of population is indefinitely greater than the power in the earth to produce subsistence for man. Population, when unchecked, increases in a geometrical ratio. Subsistence increases only in an arithmetical ratio. A slight acquaintance with numbers will show the immensity of the first power in comparison of the second.'* His conclusion was that humanity would be faced with mass starvation unless something was done to resist human powers of reproduction.

→ Forty years later, Malthus's essay was read by **Charles Darwin**, who suddenly realised that here was a possible explanation for the evolution of organisms – if more living things are born than are going to survive, then the more vigorous will be the ones to do so. He used

**Checkpoint 1**

Write down the rule or equation used to work out the number of rabbits for each month.

**Action point**

List three situations where numbers increase exponentially, and three where they rise in a linear way.

a vivid example of growth in exponential fashion – *'The elephant is reckoned to be the slowest breeder of all known animals; if we assume that it begins breeding when 30 years old, and goes on breeding till 90 years old, bringing forth six young in the interval, and surviving till one hundred years old; if so then, after a period of from 740 to 750 years there would be nearly nineteen million elephants alive descended from the first pair.'*

→ In fact, Malthus's very bleak prediction has not yet materialised. Although there are famines in many parts of the world, and the population has increased enormously, technology has increased food production by more than a simple arithmetic ratio in the last 200 years. The problems of food supply are those of local climate, ease of distribution and politics, rather than agriculture.

→ Many biological growth curves start off by showing exponential growth, but later level off, for all sorts of reasons – a population stabilises, probably in balance with its food supply.

## Exponential decrease

→ An example where numbers decrease rapidly at first and then slowly level off is in radioactive decay. The nuclei of the atoms of some elements break down, releasing radiation, becoming different atoms. It is impossible to say when a particular atom will break down. However, in a certain time, half the atoms will decay, and this time is characteristic, the **half-life** of the isotope of the element. Some isotopes have very short half-lives, e.g. iodine 123 has a half-life of 13 hours; but that of carbon 14 is very long at 5730 years. This is important to know when we are trying to dispose of radioactive materials produced in nuclear reactors. Radioactive isotopes are used in medicine to track the course of materials or blood in the body, because they can be detected using a counter, or show up on X-ray pictures. In this case, a very short half-life is an advantage, because the patient is not exposed to radiation for longer than necessary.

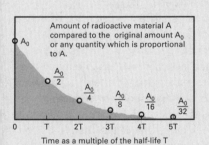

Amount of radioactive material $A$ compared to the original amount $A_0$ or any quantity which is proportional to $A$.

Time as a multiple of the half-life $T$

**Checkpoint 2**

If a radioactive isotope has a half-life of 48 hours, how long will it take for its radioactivity to decrease to 1/16 of the initial amount?

---

**Exam preparation**                                    answers: page 51

1  [AS] Explain how a nuclear chain reaction causes the explosion of an atomic bomb.   (5 minutes)

2  [A2] Do politicians or scientists have the greatest influence on limiting the size of the human population? Explain how you came to your conclusion.

(30 minutes)

# Answers
## Mathematical reasoning and its application

## Sudden infant deaths

### Checkpoints

1 There are 8 possible families: BBB, BBG, BGB, BGG, GBB, GBG, GGB, GGG. The probability of a family of three boys is 1/8 (or $0.5 \times 0.5 \times 0.5$). The probability of two boys and one girl is 3/8.

2 The first sock must be blue or black; the second is also either blue or black. So you could have a pair with the first two socks, but the probability of that will be 0.5, not 1.0 or certainty. The third sock will be either blue or black, but you will already have at least one blue or black sock in your hand, therefore you **must** have a matching pair after pulling out **three** socks.

### Exam preparation

In questions like this you should comment on the source, if you have any knowledge of it. In this case you may only know that Disraeli was a Victorian politician, but that would allow you to comment on why a politician might want to make a disparaging, rhetorical remark about statistics. No matter if you don't know. The remark **is** rhetorical, and therefore you could guess that a politician might have made it. The implication is that statistical information is totally unreliable and unbelievable. Is this reasonable? You need to clarify what you understand by **statistics**. Two meanings are covered here – the study and use of numerical information, and the data. You are now in a position to comment on the **validity** of the statement, and you would be justified in being critical. Use other common quotes, such as 'You can prove anything with statistics', and discuss whether this is a fair criticism of the use of data. Use examples – '9 out of 10 housepersons prefer X to any other household detergent'. This is misuse of a statistical context – you don't know whether more than 10 people were asked, nor how they were selected, nor how they were tested for their preferences. Bring in examples of statistics that are clearly useful, such as census data. Used properly, they serve human needs – what housing and civil amenities will be needed in the next 50 years? What about sports statistics? Another use of this branch of mathematics is to decide if the results of experiments could have been produced by chance, and therefore are used as a matter of course by scientists and technologists. You would be justified in ending your essay with some rhetoric of your own – 'Who is more likely to lie through their teeth – statisticians or p*********s?'

## Measles, mumps and rubella

### Checkpoints

1 The short answer must be 'With great difficulty!' This doesn't get you far; so most people believe sources that have proved to be reliable in the past. A crucial question to ask is whether a source has a **vested interest** in the information it is providing. For example, can you be sure of getting the facts on the safety of a product from the manufacturer? You would prefer to get independent confirmation from a consumer watchdog, or know that the product had been made to a national safety standard.

2 It is possible that the disease has not been eradicated, or that an unknown organisation or individual has kept live stock for their own purposes. If so, and the virus escapes or is released, then we might need to produce vaccine, or identify the virus for research purposes. To keep stocks constitutes a risk, and whoever does so needs to maintain them securely for obvious reasons.

3 Benefits to an individual child are obvious, and the tiny known risks of vaccination are far less than the risks from the disease itself. There is a political benefit from showing that the government cares about the health of its citizens, especially children. There is also the cost of the disease in treatment, disruption to life and to business through time off work and the provision of support services that is avoided by the relatively cheap mass vaccination programme. The only snag is that there is a minimum proportion of the population that must be vaccinated to provide 'herd immunity'. This is where members of a community who are not immune to a disease are still protected from it provided sufficient numbers of people in that community are immune. This is because when enough people are immune to a certain disease, it has little opportunity to spread and so find a non-immune person. Herd immunity only applies to diseases that are caught from other people. For measles this proportion is 95%.

### Exam preparation

The opinion needs to be examined carefully. It is a good idea to list some modern inventions, especially those where you think you have some knowledge of how society might worry about risks from them. Examples might be mobile phones, the computer, nuclear power stations, and cloning. You need to describe the risks from your examples, and then make some kind of assessment of how much worry this causes 'modern society'. For each invention, we assume that it has been produced in order to make society better in some way, so you could say that the invention begins by **reducing** worry. So mobile phones were invented to allow people to contact others and be contacted without the need to be near a landline phone. Various wireless devices such as CB radio, police and emergency systems preceded them. They required fairly heavy equipment and were mostly used in vehicles. There has always been a core of people concerned about the amount of wireless radiation in the environment and the bad effects it might have on the body. It did not take long before fears were expressed about the safety of radiation-using equipment that could be held against the side of the head for long periods. When these ideas became newsworthy, the public expressed worries – but, significantly, bought and used the phones in ever-increasing numbers. So this leads you to suggest that **some parts** of modern society worry a lot about the effects of mobile phones, for different reasons. Newspapers use these stories because they make the paper exciting to read, and some groups of people worry because they are natural worriers.

However, this worry cannot be too bad, because out of it comes restraint and caution in situations where there might well be cause for concern. Phone manufacturers were quick to start research into the effects of radiation, and to make sure that their phones reduced it as much as possible, once they realised that sales might be affected. Consideration of one or two examples in this way should lead you to a conclusion – for example, that we **should** worry a lot because modern technology is very powerful and has a habit of springing nasty surprises.

## Population growth

### Checkpoints

1 Make a table of several months (M), and under each add up the pairs of rabbits (R):

| M | 0 | 1 | 2 | 3 | 4 | 5 | 6 | 7 |
|---|---|---|---|---|---|---|---|---|
| R | 1 | 1 | 2 | 3 | 5 | 8 | 13 | 21 |

From this you can see that the number in any one month is equal to the sum of the pairs in the previous two months or $R_M = R_{M-1} + R_{M-2}$ This is the best-known example of a **Fibonacci series**, and you can see that it increases very rapidly.

2 This is also best seen as a table

| Time | 0 | 48 | 96 | 144 | 192 | 240 |
|---|---|---|---|---|---|---|
| Rad | 1 | 1/2 | 1/4 | 1/8 | 1/16 | 1/32 |

So – 192 hours or 8 days.

### Exam preparation

1 You should know that an atomic bomb contains an isotope of uranium. The nuclei of its atoms break down (fission) when hit by neutrons, releasing some energy and more neutrons. If these neutrons hit other nuclei, these will undergo fission, releasing yet more energy and neutrons. If the piece of uranium is small, many neutrons escape and the uranium stays intact. Above a certain size (the critical mass), however, neutrons are much more likely to hit more nuclei, and release energy. This will happen very quickly, and the energy release is so great that the uranium and anything near it is vaporised violently. The chain reaction in the bomb is started by crashing two small pieces of uranium together, so that they exceed the critical mass.

2 This is a highly speculative and provocative question. A glib answer might be that **everybody** has an influence on the size of the population, since they are likely to be reproductive and want to have families and children. The question, however, prompts you to think about the different ways in which politics and science influence our lives. **Politicians** deal with everyday problems of society and can have very different ideologies – democratic, socialist, communist, fascist, and so on. Depending on their ideals, they may see changes in population in very different ways – some seek to stabilise or even reduce the population because the country has insufficient resources. Another country, with a particular religious outlook, may set out to increase the population of believers as that increases the power of that religion. Think of other examples. **Scientists** try to explain human reproduction – and medical researchers try to find ways of dealing with illnesses or problems with reproduction. They have been successful in increasing fertility through IVF and other techniques, and in enabling reproductive restraint through contraception, physical and hormonal. It isn't immediately obvious how to measure the effects on population of these various activities. A safe conclusion would be that it is impossible to disentangle the influences – after all, the dispersal of contraceptives to a rapidly increasing population is almost certainly a political action after a scientific discovery.

# Databank

**Independent events.** Throwing dice is a classic case of independent events. There is no obvious reason why the second or subsequent throws of dice should be influenced by the first throw. So the chance of getting a 6 on the first throw is 1 in 6 (1/6 or a probability of 0.16666). The chance of getting a 6 on the next throw is exactly the same. The chance of getting two sixes in a row, or two sixes with a throw of two dice, is clearly small – the product of the two chances – 1/6 × 1/6 = 1/36, or 0.02777. If the dice are biased – heavier on one side than another – this makes no difference to our method of calculation, although the chances of getting a particular number may not be quite 1/6.

**Dependent events.** If the probability of an event is changed by a previous event, the events are said to be dependent. Take a pack of cards and draw a card. What is the probability of it being a red card? – 0.5. Without replacing the card, draw another card – what is the probability of it being a red card? Not 0.5, because you now have 51 cards, of which either 25 are red and 26 are black, or 25 are black and 26 are red. So the probability of drawing another red is 25/51 = 0.49 if the first card was red or 0.51 if the first was black. The two draws are **dependent**.

**Significance.** Many results in science are close to expectation, but not always exactly so. If you think a die might be biased, you would look for some numbers coming up more frequently than others. But how do you tell if there is a bias? You know that in any sequence of throws you are **unlikely** to get the **ideal** distribution of each number. What you need to be able to work out is the probability of getting that distribution – the actual order doesn't matter. If what you throw differs from the expected one, you then have to work out if this difference is **significant**. Generally speaking, the convention is that if the result you get would have been expected less than 1 time in 20 (0.05 probability), it is regarded as significant.

**Everyday risks.** '*The greatest hazard in life is to risk nothing.*' We are not good at judging levels of risk, and we are mistaken if we believe that anything in life is risk free.

**Limits to human population growth.** World population will stop growing when the birth rate equals the death rate; no one knows whether this will happen. Birth and death rates should reach equilibrium a few years after couples average two children each. This is the **replacement level fertility**, because couples replace themselves in the population. The **total fertility rate** refers to the average number of children per woman. When the total fertility rate is 2.1 children per family, the children replace the parents when they die. The 0.1 child accounts for child mortality, because some children die before they grow up to have their own children. Therefore, the value for replacement level fertility could be higher in a country where mortality is higher.

# Revision checklist
*helps you check what you still need to do*

## By the end of this chapter you should be able to:

| | | | |
|---|---|---|---|
| 1 | Use all the information in Databank, above, with confidence | Confident | Not confident. **Revise** page 52 |
| 2 | Work out simple probabilities involving combinations of independent events | Confident | Not confident. **Revise** pages 44, 50, 52 |
| 3 | Use simple statistical measures and diagrams | Confident | Not confident. **Revise** pages 46, 48 |
| 4 | Understand the need for good sampling | Confident | Not confident. **Revise** pages 44, 45, 46 |
| 5 | Describe exponential growth and decay | Confident | Not confident. **Revise** pages 49, 51 |
| 6 | Use basic arithmetic and algebraic formulae | Confident | Not confident. **Revise** pages 106, 110, 111 |
| 7 | Interpret different forms of graph | Confident | Not confident. **Revise** page 48 |

# Relationship between technology, science, culture (past and/or present) and ideology

You are expected to understand how science and technology are both part of our culture and at the same time define it. Much of this topic is more relevant to A2 candidates, as there is a need to link social, cultural, scientific and technological issues, and it demands a more synoptic view of things. AS candidates must expect to have questions on single aspects of the topics listed below.

## Exam themes

→ The effects of changes in the availability of resources

→ The effects of different forms of communication

→ The effects of using different forms of transport, private and public

→ The concept of sustainability

→ The impact of globalisation

→ The importance of science and technology in relation to national wealth

## Topic checklist

| ○ AS ● A2 | AQA A | AQA B | EDEXCEL | OCR |
|---|---|---|---|---|
| Computers and culture | ● | ● | ○● | ● |
| Technology and globalisation | ○● | ● | ○● | ● |
| Science, technology and transport | ○● | ○● | ○● | ○● |

# Computers and culture

The technology developed by a culture has a great influence on the nature of that culture. The culture adopted by society greatly affects the technology used. This is a sort of chicken-and-egg situation, and the points we make will often depend on our point of view – as a technologist, scientist, philosopher, theologian, artist, critic or just plain old person in the street. Some people say that technology will always destroy, or at best change, our culture, others that our technology is totally limited by our culture. Computerisation is a technological change in point.

## Computers and culture ●●●

→ Sociologists and anthropologists describe cultures and the ways in which they develop in terms that are linked with the technologies they use – for example, hunter-gathering, agricultural and industrial revolutions. History tells us about the technological changes that brought about the Industrial Revolution. Most people believe we are living through another revolution – the **information revolution**, with the computer as its most important tool.

→ Computers are in essence only glorified calculating machines – they can only carry out simple mathematical operations on 0s and 1s. It is the speed with which they do this, and the ways in which the mathematical operations can be combined, that turns them into machines which can apparently talk to us, control complex processes, store and send vast amounts of information and, some people believe, might even acquire characters and identities equivalent to our own. Computers have changed information for us in the same way that printing changed the availability of books in the 1550s, and cheap mass-produced paperback books of the mid 1900s. The significance of books cannot be underestimated, not least because they were the petrol for the engine of mass education in the UK from the 1850s on. Computers are changing the way we regard the presentation of information, but certainly won't do away with books. Computers give us incredible power to search and ferret out information, but only if it is stored digitally and provided we have the equipment and the energy source to do so. The Internet is totally dependent on machines, but it is a highly flexible thing and survives having pieces added or taken away.

→ Today there is much concern about the damaging effects that technologies may have on our culture. Can we put aside the idea that our 'culture' is something distinct from information technology? Almost everyone is touched by it – from cradle to grave, peasant to prince, and scientist to scientologist. More information means more food for arguments, more questioning, more ways to understand and more to misunderstand.

→ How do computers influence our society? The way in which information is stored digitally, rather than in analogue forms, has a profound effect on the ease with which it is stored, copied and retrieved. But this is only the tip of the iceberg – for example, we

**Link**

Energy and development of society.

**Action point**

Sample any newspaper for stories involving computers or computerisation and assess the spin put on the story.

**Checkpoint 1**

List the positive and negative effects that use of a computer might have on the work of:
a scientist; an artist; a church leader; a store manager.

have new forms of recreation, which may not be totally different to previous games, but which could lead to forms of gaming where the participants cannot be sure whether they are dealing with real or simulated events. Online multi-user gaming might lead to a situation where a gamer has an opponent in the sights of a rifle. How does he know that there isn't a real rifle and body at the other end of his electronic system in another part of the world?

→ Should we be really worried by the advance of computerisation? A little cost/benefit analysis might help. Not so long ago it was predicted that technology would give all of us easy lives, with short working weeks, more leisure time and the resources to use it. Has this happened?

**Checkpoint 2**

What ethical issues might arise in simulations? You might think of games, but staff training is increasingly carried out with computer simulations.

| Benefit | Neutral | Cost |
|---|---|---|
| Clerical tasks are made easier for everyone – for example, the production of well-presented written material | Tasks may be changed, but a workforce is still needed | Office jobs become redefined – no need for specially trained secretaries and copy typists, so there might be redundancies |
| Speed of working is seen as a key to success, and computers make it possible, for example, to produce a report and despatch it overnight | Working fast may reduce the quality of the work, and hence there is no benefit | Pace of life becomes intolerable for some – increased health/stress problems |
| Efficiency of working leading to less error, for example, in numerical matters | Errors will always be present in computer systems, because humans program them | Increased expectations of workforce, who may resent the challenges |
| Collecting information is very much easier. More data can be shared, so that citizens know more about their society | Waste of resources on uncritical gathering of information, but system capacities are now vast | Big Brother problems – citizens feel that nothing in life is private |
| Analysing information can be done more quickly and powerfully. Support for human reasoning | Increased amounts of data, but it may not be relevant to the particular problem | Information may only be accessible to those with adequate resources – reinforces gaps between social classes and less-developed countries. [See globalisation] |
| Communicating information is far more rapid and flexible | | Changes in the form and technical nature of work make extra demands of training and staff development |
| Potential for preventing crime – improving and speeding up forensic analysis; tracking and identifying goods and people | | Potential for crime, through access to banking systems; fraud; identity theft; child grooming and pornography |
| Control of other forms of technology | | Loss of human control – potential for accidents |

**Examiner's secrets**

If you have a topic which has many aspects to evaluate, you might find producing a table of benefits and costs helpful to your analysis.

**Exam preparation**                                answers: page 60

1   [A2] How do recent developments in communications affect business and industry?   (40 minutes)

2   [AS] List the ways in which modern computers are at present useful in the home. Suggest a new future use for a home computer.   (5 minutes)

# Technology and globalisation

The computer affects the way traditional business works, and at the same time opens up trade to new customers. This is mainly due to the Internet, but this development was envisaged well before the Internet was invented. Science and technology are affecting the world in very new ways.

## Technology and globalisation ●●●

→ In 1962, a Canadian professor, Marshall McLuhan, suggested that the invention of printing completely determined the Western culture. He predicted that electronic media would transform culture and values in society, because they reduced or removed barriers to communication. In this way we all become part of the **global village**.

→ The Internet, the collection of linked computers, and the World Wide Web, the software that controls it, are now familiar. People all over the world can communicate easily, and some call the process whereby we become hooked up **globalisation**. In wealthy countries this has been quickly appreciated as a way of increasing markets for products and services and, unsurprisingly, by developing countries as a completely new way of gaining access to services and information.

→ This has been made possible by scientific and technical innovation – computing and communication – as well as a cheap infrastructure for communications – the telephone system.

→ While globalisation is seen by many businesses, economists and politicians as a good thing, this is not the case for everyone. The situation is made more difficult by the different ways in which **globalisation** is defined. Most narrowly, it refers to international access to the WWW; more broadly, to the potential impact on the health and wealth of everyone, by reducing barriers to trade and

**Links**

Culture and the mass media.

**Check the web**

A site concerned with the opportunities for international web applications is: http://www.globalisation.com/. The World Bank Group promotes globalisation: http://www.worldbank.org/. An organisation critical of globalisation is: http://www.ifg.org/

| Points for globalisation | Points against globalisation |
|---|---|
| The Internet provides convenient and cheap ways of communicating with home and family from anywhere in the world | It allows powerful companies and organisations to become even more powerful, since they have the resources to exploit the opportunities |
| Developing countries can reach wider markets for their goods and services – particularly tourism | It increases the gaps between the rich and poor nations |
| Academic users can find information and communicate with experts anywhere | Organisations can move information-based operations from one country to another very easily, creating instability and economic upheavals |
| The usefulness of the medium promotes the expansion of infrastructures – e.g. the mobile and satellite phone in places where there are few landlines | The values and culture projected by the Internet are mostly Western and the language is English. Other countries see this as imperialism |
| Importing advanced technology allows developing countries to jump over industrial development stages and raise income levels | Because we are moving from an industrial to an information age, more advantages are gained by those countries which have undergone the 'information revolution' |

the flow of information. Therefore, supporting or criticising it will depend on the definition you adopt.

→ Those who support or disapprove of globalisation assess the economic differences between countries – the poverty gap – differently. You can measure a country's wealth in many ways. For example, the UN Development Report (1999) measures wealth in US$. If the value of the US$ changes relative to other currencies (the exchange rate), it is possible that wealth can become greater if the dollar weakens against that country's currency, with no actual change in the 'real' wealth. The World Bank prices things that can be bought using the local currency. In this way the actual purchasing power of the currency is better assessed. Therefore, a currency may devalue against the US$, but since most products inside a country are paid for by local currency, they do not fall in price because the US$ appreciates.

→ Supporters of globalisation refer to evidence that suggests that global inequalities are decreasing. For example, the World Bank shows that in 1980, Americans earned 12.5 times as much as the Chinese, per capita. By 1999, they were only earning 7.4 times as much. The countries that are getting poorer are those that are not open to world trade, notably many nations in Africa.

→ By lowering their barriers to trade and investment, poorer nations have increased employment and national income because labour and capital shifts from importing industries to competitive export industries. Companies moving to developing countries bring higher wages and better working conditions compared with those in local companies. Others believe that the gap between the rich and poor countries is increasing. The United Nations 1999 Development Report finds that over the past ten years, the number of people earning $1 a day or less has remained static at 1.2 billion while the number earning less than $2 a day has increased from 2.55 billion to 2.8 billion people.

## The poverty gap  ●●●

→ The gap in incomes between the 20% of the richest and the poorest countries has grown from 30 to 1 in 1960 to 82 to 1 in 1995

→ By the late 1990s the fifth of the world's people living in the highest-income countries had:
  → 86% of world gross domestic product – the bottom fifth 1%.
  → 82% of world export markets – the bottom fifth 1%.
  → 68% of foreign direct investment – the bottom fifth 1%.
  → 74% of world telephone lines, today's basic means of communication – the bottom fifth 1.5%.

→ Some say that the increasing gap is the inevitable result of market forces since they give the rich the power to add further to their wealth. Hence, large corporations invest in poor countries only because they can make greater profits from low wage levels or because they can get access to their natural resources.

---

**Exam preparation**                                      answer: page 60

[A2] Discuss how scientists and technologists have contributed to globalisation.   (20 minutes)

---

**Checkpoint 1**

How can we reduce the poverty gap?

**Examiner's secrets**

If you answer a question where you think there may be several interpretations of a word, *always* state what you understand by it. If other meanings are relevant, give them as well.
This will show that you have *interpreted* the question and will gain you marks.

**Links**

Employment and social conditions. In particular, see also page 190: The global economy.

57

# Science, technology and transport

Civilisation, beyond the stage of the hunter-gatherer, developed through the capacity of human beings to move themselves and their goods. Survival required the exploration of new areas, the discovery of new raw materials, and obtaining adequate food supplies. Ways and means of transport both define and limit society.

## A transport of delight

→ There are many reasons why we need transportation systems. We travel to and from work, and for leisure and recreation. We also need to move goods for manufacturing, food and, in the worst case scenario, the military and emergency services. Most of us live our lives in one small area; with everything we needed close at hand. Some of us travel to search for and exploit new resources. We may have to extend our frontiers, into space, if resources are no longer available on Earth.

→ Some futurologists believe that, as more powerful and intrusive electronic communications become more part of our lives, there will be no need for us to travel in order to work or entertain ourselves. Even so, there will be stuff that has to come to us. In modern families, members isolate themselves in their rooms, yet rely on machines to carry them, cushioned from the environment, to places they need to go. Contrast this with the youthful desire for excitement and travel during gap years.

→ Transport of the kind we expect to use these days is dependent on the latest technology, and it is highly energy-dependent. It raises many economic, political, social and scientific issues. The major scientific and technological issues are to do with **sustainability and the environment**.

### Transport policies

→ The UK government's *Strategy for Sustainable Development* (DoE, 1994) defined sustainable transport policy as one which:
  → strikes a balance between economic development and protecting environment and quality of life;
  → provides economic and social needs for access;
  → takes measures to reduce environmental impact;
  → ensures users pay the full social and environmental cost of their transport decisions.

→ What beliefs and facts lead to the production of such a policy? With greater, more flexible forms of communication it might be argued that there is less need for people to travel, particularly to work. There are inevitable pressures, however, from increases in:

From a summary of a 110-page report available from the Parliamentary Office of Science and Technology, November 1995

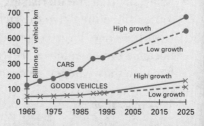

Figure 1 National road traffic forecasts

→ population, although in the UK it is reasonably stable;

→ individual prosperity, which is dependent on national prosperity. This brings more vehicles on to, and in some cases off, the road. More people want to travel, by car, plane and boat, for both business and leisure.

## Environmental problems

→ One of the greatest dangers to the environment is the physical damage from the presence of people. More travel using petrol and diesel engines means more greenhouse gases, hence degradation of the atmosphere and ultimately the climate. Science may be able to help through the development of improved and competitive alternative fuels – such as hydrogen cells and bio-fuels – and improved energy storage in batteries. However, the full cost of all these developments is difficult to work out – hydrogen cells may be cleaner when they burn hydrogen, but hydrogen is a greenhouse gas, as well as being potentially explosive and difficult to contain. Also, hydrogen gas has to be produced by electrolysis, using lots of electricity, which has to be generated somehow.

→ Supporters of **green** movements want to provide improved public transport, such as buses and trains, in the belief that it is more energy efficient, frees up road space and is safer. Comparisons are quite difficult to make, but in principle this could improve matters. We could use our bodies more, by walking or using bicycles.

→ A difficult factor in all these decisions is human nature. A car is under your control and its possession is closely linked to status. One can hardly blame the newly wealthy in China wanting a car, after riding cycles for so long, but the consequences for the environment in a country with crowded cities are not difficult to imagine.

→ Can science produce better long-term answers? Apart from developing and improving existing technology, it is difficult to see how. A **new** form of travel would have to involve some fundamental changes in the laws of physics. After all, if we can send sufficient information about an object so that it can be recreated anywhere the signal can be received, for example through a fax machine, why not about people? However, that does raise the problem of what to do with the originals!

**Checkpoint 2**

List the benefits and costs of a policy of rationing individuals to one air flight per year.

**Link**

See also page 86: Europe, globalism and internationalism.

**Check the net**

The following sites illustrate different views of the issues of transport and the environment. They also have links to other sites. What do they have in common?
http://www.thisislocallondon.co.uk/links/links/linksgreen/.
http://www.sweltrac.org.uk/default.htm.

**Exam preparation**                                     answers: page 61

1  [A2] Describe the problems faced by the travelling public in the UK. How could science and technology solve these problems?  (40 minutes)

3  [AS] Globalisation reduces the need for transport. How far do you agree with this opinion?  (20 minutes)

# Answers
## Relationship between technology, science,

## Computers and culture

### Checkpoints

1 The best thing here is to produce a table for each example, as this is really a brainstorming exercise. It is probably easy to find positive effects, e.g. the scientist – enable accurate and **quick** calculations; use of computer models; storage of information; easy communication with other scientists. However negative effects are less easy to predict, e.g. scientists might overlook errors in calculations if the program has bugs; spread of information is so quick that it is very difficult to claim that you had the idea first – therefore you might be more secretive. Some of these points would apply to the other occupations.

2 This is quite tricky – make sure you know what an **ethical** issue is. Since it is something that is believed, and may be different for different people and societies, it may apply to some and not others. You might consider that humiliating someone, by demonstrating failure to complete an online task, is not ethical, because it hurts someone's feelings. On the other hand, you might feel that it is quite ethical because the exercise is not a 'real' one, and it helps the person improve their skills or knowledge. You could take a positive view – the simulation might be something that is completed in private, and therefore your mistakes are not made public. Since we all learn by making mistakes and then correcting them, this could be a very efficient learning process, carried out ethically because no one else knows how well you are performing.

### Exam preparation

1 You must first define what you mean by 'recent developments'. These are open to interpretation, but you are entitled to use your own definition. To help your answer, you might take 'recent' to mean within the last 50 years. This gives you reasonable scope, and provided you have stated this clearly, the examiner will allow you credit. You are taking 50 years ago to mean a relatively recent time in the history of civilisation. If you take 10 years then you are making life more difficult for yourself. Now think of actual developments in communication – what has happened since 1950? Radio, TV and landline telephones were all in use then – but satellites (used to globalise TV and radio communications), the Internet and mobile phone networks are recent. You should take a couple of paragraphs to explain these developments. You might also make a case for the importance of personal, face-to-face communications, and therefore the need for global mobility for some workers. Now clarify what you understand by 'business and industry'. It may seem that everyone knows what these words mean, but you help yourself if you list the features and think around the meaning of the words. What are the differences between 'business' and 'industry'? Does communication have anything to do with the differences? Industry could be taken to mean production processes, business the process in which production, marketing and sales are

managed. Different forms of communication would be needed, and you can create several arguments to show how these relate to the nature of business and industry. An obvious example to expand would be the increase in Internet shopping and banking. This essay allows you to draw several conclusions – it is important that you do so.

2 Entertainment; managing a business at home; home office applications – letters, notes etc.; email; home shopping and researching bargains; controlling household electrical devices. A possible new use might be as a home security device or control centre. This is probably not an original, completely new use, but you would be credited with any plausible recent device. No examiner expects you to show innovative skills in 5 minutes of an AS examination!

## Technology and globalisation

### Checkpoint

1 This is not easy! You could argue that the efforts of one, or a few individuals, are likely to have no effect at all, so that an individual needs to be part of an organisation or a communal effort. One well-known example is the Fairtrade initiative, supported by many supermarkets and charities. International organisations have been set up to try to reduce the exploitation of cheap labour. Some developing countries have crippling debts with richer countries, carrying ever-increasing interest, which they are unlikely ever to repay. There are organisations that campaign to cancel these debts.

### Exam preparation

In the introduction to this question you need to explain what is meant by 'globalisation'. We have dealt with that in this article, so you need to put it all into your own words. You also need to describe the outcomes of the work of scientists and technologists. On the basis of these explanations, you could argue forcefully that globalisation would have been impossible without technology – the printing press and the Internet. Technology is dependent on the discoveries of science. You could also argue that science and technology are in turn enhanced by globalisation, since ideas, techniques and inventions are disseminated quickly and at low cost to the whole planet.

## Science, technology and transport

### Checkpoints

1 This is a simple exercise, but valid none-the-less, since it gets you thinking about the general principles and objectives of transportation. Land, water and air are probably the easiest first divisions to be made. For each type it might help to consider the energy source for motion – this is a scientific section, after all. For example – on water, first transport might have been down a river (gravitational potential energy), on a lake (human muscle and differences in air pressure) or on the sea. Invention of

# culture (past and/or present) and ideology

oars allowed better deployment of muscle, sails enhanced the use of wind; later, the invention of steam engines, the internal combustion engine and jet engines allowed faster and more predictable motion on water. Recent inventions are rockets and transport into space (some forecasters speculate that journey times to very distant countries could be greatly decreased by a rocket flight out of the atmosphere), and linear magnetic induction motors for high-speed trains. You could also comment on personal rather than mass transport – escalators, elevators, walkways – and the varieties of road transport.

2 This idea arose because of worries about the effect of the increase in flights and the emissions of engines on the atmosphere. Therefore, benefits would be mainly social and long-term environmental – reduction of emissions, global warming, noise pollution, land blight by flight paths and airports. Costs would be social and political – reduction of personal freedom, increase in costs of flights, probability that flights are only available to the very rich. Some indeterminate effects might come from the interruption to business meetings, but it might be argued that the availability of phone, Internet and video-conferencing would get round these problems.

## Exam preparation

1 This needs to be considered by type of transport. The travelling public use roads (for buses, coaches and cars), water (for ferries), and railways. Deal with the problems of each – since they are not related. Define the priorities of the travelling public – they want, presumably, cheap, safe, fast and reliable means of getting to work or going on holiday. For example, there are many news stories about problems on roads – congestion is a serious issue, with obvious causes but less obvious solutions. Science and technology have been used to help implement the congestion charge in London – they have provided means of issuing charges, detecting avoidance, recording offences and issuing fines. The effect has been a measured reduction in congestion and an improvement in journey times and punctuality of public transport.

2 Once again, be sure that you explain what you understand by globalisation – see above. Once you have done so, it is comparatively straightforward to explain how the need for transport, of people at least, has reduced. On the other hand, there is probably an increased expectation for moving goods and raw materials around, because manufacturers will seek the locations with lowest labour costs, once transportation costs have been allowed for. A more speculative idea could be that globalisation has brought the more interesting features of the world to more people, and they wish to see them for themselves. Granted, this is a recreational reason, but it is almost certainly a very significant factor in the huge increase in international air travel in the last 20 years.

# Databank

**Science, technology and culture.** New genres of literature have grown up. Fifty years ago the science fiction writer **Isaac Asimov** explored the possible uses of robots – machines containing computers – using the 'Laws of Robotics' to explore the ethical and practical problems that might arise. **William Gibson** is credited with using the idea of **cyberspace** and the possibility of living in **virtual** worlds. Computerisation has profoundly affected the **film industry**, not just in the use of the technology for computer generated and manipulated images but also in story lines – such as *The Matrix*.

**Personal music players** have revolutionised the ways in which music is distributed and paid for. Digital music files can be easily exchanged between computers and other devices, including the Internet. This raises questions about copyright and the payment to the creators of music (or any other published material). If plagiarism is so easy, will it be worth anyone creating anything, except for the glory?

**Environmental impact of air travel.** Everyone wants to fly away – it is quick and glamorous. But at what cost?

- increased number of terminals and runways
- increased noise, over wide area
- increased atmospheric pollution from exhausts, at high altitudes, with no real alternatives
- air safety – excellent at the moment but risks increase with more traffic.

**Women and science.** It has been said, controversially, that the physical sciences have been dominated by males, because the topics are impersonal and technical, and that biological and medical science are the aspects of science most favoured by females, because they are related to people. It is easy to show that more males have made published contributions to science overall, but that things have changed in the last 50 years. Whether or not women have contributed equally to science is related more to social issues than whether they are constitutionally unsuited to the subjects. If women have to bear children and bring up families, the time and effort necessary to follow any kind of academic work is bound to be more limited.

# Revision checklist
*helps you check what you still need to do*

## By the end of this chapter you should be able to:

| | | |
|---|---|---|
| 1 Use all the information in Databank, above, with confidence | Confident | Not confident. **Revise** page 62 |
| 2 Describe the effects of changes in the availability of resources | Confident | Not confident. **Revise** pages 16, 17, 58, 59 |
| 3 Describe the effects of different forms of communication | Confident | Not confident. **Revise** pages 54, 55 |
| 4 Explain the effects of using different forms of transport, private and public | Confident | Not confident. **Revise** pages 58, 59, 106, 107 |
| 5 Understand the concept of sustainability | Confident | Not confident. **Revise** pages 17, 58 |
| 6 Describe the impact of globalisation | Confident | Not confident. **Revise** pages 56, 57, 60, 86, 189 |
| 7 Evaluate the importance of science and technology in relation to national wealth | Confident | Not confident. **Revise** pages 16, 17, 56, 57 |

# Studying society

All the specifications study society and the social sciences. *Social sciences* is a term that refers to elements of sociology, economics, politics, law, geography and psychology. Each of these disciplines will often ask very different questions about a particular issue – and it is therefore not a bit surprising that they come up with different answers and policy recommendations. Understanding the methods social science uses to develop answers to these different questions involves the study of different *methodologies*.

The different Boards ask questions covering largely the same ranges of topics. Candidates may be asked to write essays, to interpret material from texts, to work on statistical information and assess its meaning and significance or to choose a correct answer from multiple options. The precise requirements of coursework, too, will vary – though the knowledge and skills you need for success in the examinations or if you choose a coursework option are largely the same.

## Exam themes

→ How is the UK changing?

→ Why do societies change over time?

→ Is society increasingly secular and has the significance of religion changed?

→ What is multiculturalism?

→ Is equality natural or do we have to take specific actions to achieve it?

→ Discrimination between individuals in society

→ How do social scientists conduct research?

→ Are the research findings of social scientists as reliable as those of natural scientists?

## Topic checklist

○ AS ● A2

| | AQA A | AQA B | EDEXCEL | OCR |
|---|---|---|---|---|
| Socialisation, culture and multiculturalism | ○● | ○● | ○● | ○● |
| Ideology, equality and discrimination | ○● | ○● | ○● | ○● |
| Social and natural sciences: differences in issues and methodologies | ○● | ○● | ○● | ○● |

# Socialisation, culture and multiculturalism

From generation to generation, some values change yet others stay the same. Throughout our lives we are influenced by what happens around us. The young are influenced by family, school, friends and the media. As adults, we are influenced by work, friendships and our experiences – this is socialisation; it is how we learn the culture of our society or about the subculture of a group loyal to a particular religion, interest, community or lifestyle. Increasingly multiculturalism occurs in the UK – not subcultures, each existing separately, but a mixture of cultures coexisting alongside each other, each valuing the distinctiveness of the others.

## The changing UK ●●●

Fifty or sixty years ago (i) wages were lower and people did their best to avoid debt, (ii) wealth was less evenly divided, (iii) more people went to church, (iv) fewer women went to work, (v) most children left school at 15, (vi) youth culture was in its infancy, (vii) more people identified themselves as working or middle class, (viii) social deference was common and people expected to obey authority, (ix) many fewer ethnic minorities resided in the UK, (x) people generally died much younger, (xi) the welfare state was in its infancy, (xii) as was television, (xiii) few people owned cars or had telephones in their homes, (xiv) pressure groups made little impact and (xv) over three-quarters of the population expected to vote in general elections, (xvi) largely choosing between two parties – Labour and Conservative.

### The pressures for change

Change often occurs not because someone decides it would be a good idea but as a result of lots of independent individual choices:

→ Increased wealth, education and opportunity have made many people more ambitious for themselves and their families.
→ The status quo is less accepted. Traditional values such as church attendance, acceptance of authority and social deference are challenged.
→ Easier communication – cars, mobile phones and the Internet – widened people's horizons and expectations.
→ Jobs for life and sticking to the same jobs as our parents, living in the same communities and sharing their attitudes are less likely to occur.
→ The traditional belief in marriage as a life-long commitment was often replaced by cohabitation and divorce or single parenthood.
→ A more tolerant society and changes in the law meant some people have openly adopted gay, lesbian or celibate lifestyles.
→ People are increasingly aware of national and global influences and are interested in the lifestyles and attitudes of people in other countries.
→ Commuting to work hundreds of miles a day by car or rail or air is increasingly common.

**Checkpoint 1**

What is the difference between culture and socialisation?

**Checkpoint 2**

Identify two other political parties which now attract significant support.

**Checkpoint 3**

What is social deference? Give an example.

**Check the net**

Look at the ONS website for the latest data on the family:
http://www.statistics.gov.uk.

**Action point**

Think about how you or your friends become aware of the lifestyles, attitudes and interests of others. Which influence is greatest – meeting people from other countries, chatting to people overseas in call centres, Internet and chat rooms, or food and clothes styles learned about through travel?

## The changing culture

The culture of the UK – our values, attitudes and beliefs – is increasingly paradoxical:

→ Being richer has made us more materialist – some see this as greed and selfishness, yet we give more to charity and the country is widely involved in humanitarian giving throughout the world.
→ In spite of our wealth, we are more willing to take on debt.
→ Church attendances are down – yet there is growing interest in and observance of Muslim, Buddhist and other beliefs.
→ Interest in parties and elections is down, yet our willingness to join pressure group campaigns has never been higher.
→ We value new technologies and scientific advances, yet we are sceptical about many scientific claims in relation to health or food.
→ The welfare state has increased expectations, yet rising education standards give us increased confidence to do things for ourselves – finding jobs, buying pensions, healthcare and our own homes.
→ We are part of society but increasingly think and act as individuals with the right to make our own choices – and expect others to do the same.

## The importance of knowing and understanding each other

To live together in harmony, we need to know and understand each other – celebrating, not distrusting, differences:

→ When communities have little or no contact – e.g. Protestant and Catholic communities in Northern Ireland – enmities, hatreds and violence can arise since people neither know nor understand each other.
→ Similarly, riots arose among Asian and white youths in northern cities such as Oldham, Burnley and Blackburn – exacerbated by the fact that the youths concerned attended largely different schools – the Asians going to comprehensives and the whites to denominational C of E or RC schools.
→ *Knowing and understanding each other* means that urban myths about this group being advantaged over that are quickly seen as false – many people in both groups are equally poor or disadvantaged and most face the same problems of daily living, regardless of the extremist propaganda circulated by the BNP.
→ Daily living in cities with a high level of multiculturalism, such as Leicester and Birmingham, suggests that harmonious coexistence can be achieved, as is conspicuously seen in festivals such as the annual Notting Hill Carnival.

**Examiner's secrets**

When you introduce general points such as these, always try to back them up with examples.

**Link**

See also page 126: The nature and importance of culture.

**Jargon**

A multicultural community is a community made up of people from different cultural or ethnic groups; multiculturalism involves the interactions between people from these different cultures or ethnicities.

**Checkpoint 4**

Name one paramilitary organisation supporting each of the Protestant and Catholic communities in Northern Ireland during the violence since 1970.

**Checkpoint 5**

What does BNP stand for? Why is it described as 'extremist'?

---

**Exam preparation**                     answers: page 70

1 How far do you agree that the biggest influence on our socialisation is our schooling? (30 minutes)
2 'We should do all we can to avoid multiculturalism – it is simply unnatural.' How far do you agree? (30 minutes)

# Ideology, equality and discrimination

An ideology is a way of looking at things – Marxists see things in terms of a ruling and a working class while a New Right advocate would focus more on individualism, the nuclear family and market forces. Not everyone regards everyone else as their equal – some people prefer to think in terms of *equality of opportunity*. History reveals much discrimination – Nazis discriminating against Jews, Jews against Arabs, Chinese against Tibetans. In the UK we recognise human rights and understand the importance of inclusiveness, but are we certain that no one is ever discriminated against by reason of age, gender, race, religion or disability?

**Checkpoint 1**

Why are disputes between followers of different religions so divisive?

**Checkpoint 2**

What do you understand by inclusiveness? Give an example.

**Checkpoint 3**

Identify two cases where the European Court of Human Rights upheld the rights of a UK citizen against the UK government.

**Examiner's secrets**

Always put inverted commas around terms to which you are giving a specialist meaning.

**Jargon**

A meritocracy involves decision making in government, councils, business and the professions by an elite of the most capable, intelligent and educated people.

**Watch out!**

Many of these rights depend on people having sufficient money to support particular activities. Without money a theoretical right often means little!

## Equality as a right

The Universal Declaration of Human Rights asserts human rights to which people in every country are entitled as human beings. In Europe this is augmented by the Convention on Human Rights agreed by the Council of Europe in 1951 and backed up by the adjudications of the European Court of Human Rights in Strasbourg ever since. In 1998 the Human Rights Act made the Convention enforceable in the UK courts. Every UK citizen is equal because she or he has the same rights.

## Equality in practice

In practice, equality often means little. Unlike the poor, high-income earners can afford to buy services – health insurance, healthcare or to send their children to fee-paying schools. So unless publicly funded services are available for all and universally good, inequality is inevitable, for example:

→ Some people lack the ability, skill, talent or determination to set ambitious goals for themselves and succeed.

→ Those who are poor often have an unbalanced diet, experience significant illnesses and they die earlier than others.

→ In many areas there is a 'postcode lottery' for healthcare and certain drugs to combat serious illness are not universally available.

→ Many accused people do not have the same access to the best lawyers as those who can afford to hire anyone they choose.

→ Some state schools are very good, others are satisfactory and a few are poor – so all children do not receive a uniformly good education.

## Equality of opportunity

While equality is available in theory, but sometimes not in practice, it is more possible to guarantee *equality of opportunity* – (i) entitlement to exercise human and legal rights, (ii) receive an education, (iii) receive healthcare, (iv) have a job, (v) own a house, (vi) get married, (vii) become a parent, (viii) drive a car, (ix) go where we want, (x) vote in elections (as long as we are not a member of the House of Lords or an alien), (xi) serve on a jury (as long as we are aged under 70). The Education Act 1944, which gave all pupils access to grammar school education based on ability and regardless of their parents' income, was seen as a step towards equality of opportunity and the growth of a meritocracy – an aim which comprehensive schools and sixth form colleges endeavour to continue.

Rich people have more opportunities than poorer people. Since 1945 living standards have improved and many benefits have been introduced.

## Government actions to limit discrimination ●●●

It is impossible to know whether a person has been denied a job for reasons of age, gender, sexual orientation, disability or race rather than merit – we need to avoid stereotyping people according to arbitrarily chosen characteristics and judge them fairly on their merits. By establishing clear guidelines and good practice, the past 30 years have seen considerable progress in making society more equal. Legislation to increase equal opportunities and the establishment of public bodies charged to promote good practice includes:

→ *Disability Discrimination Act 1995* established the Disability Rights Commission to support those who complained of discrimination in terms of, for example, access to shops or public buildings or employment;

→ *Equal Pay Act 1970*, guaranteeing equal pay for equal work – the position has improved since the Act was passed, though even in 2003 women still receive barely 80% of what men are paid for doing identical work.

→ *Minimum Wage Act 1998* sets a floor on wage levels, though this does not always benefit casual workers exploited by gangmasters who often employ illegal immigrants – if all immigrants were 'legal', gangmasters would not be able to exploit them or deny them rights such as health and safety at work.

→ *Race Relations Act 1975* established the Commission for Racial Equality which supports those seeking good practice or who feel their rights have not been fully met. Unemployment is often still much higher among black people than whites even when they share the same qualifications.

→ *Sex Discrimination Act 1975* establishes guidelines for fair employment practices and gives those who are treated unfairly on grounds of gender or sexual orientation the support of the Equal Opportunities Commission.

→ The UK government has announced it expects (i) to appoint a Commission for Equality and Human Rights (CEHR), which will bring together the work of three existing equality commissions – the Commission for Racial Equality, the Equal Opportunities Commission and the Disability Rights Commission and (ii) to outlaw ageist discrimination (this will take effect in 2006).

**Exam preparation**                                   answers: pages 70–71

1  What is the difference between equality and equality of opportunity?
(5 minutes)

2  Suggest three ways in which we can avoid stereotyping people.   (5 minutes)

3  What is the difference between an economic migrant and an asylum seeker?   (5 minutes)

4  How far do you agree that discrimination cannot be outlawed by legislation?   (30 minutes)

**Jargon**

A direct tax is progressive because people with a higher income pay more than those on lower incomes – so progressive taxation reflects ability to pay.

**Speed learning**

Remember these laws with a mnemonic: D-E-M-I-Ra-S.

**Jargon**

*Gangmasters* organise casual workers, such as fruit-pickers, employing them for low wages and often exploiting economic migrants or asylum seekers who are not fully aware of their rights

**Examiner's secrets**

Examiners always welcome answers where a candidate has taken the trouble to cite laws or cases accurately.

**Checkpoint 4**

How has the role of women changed in recent years?

**Check the web**

You will be better placed to discuss organisations such as these if you look at their websites and find one good example of what each organisation has done recently – a target met, a case won, a new initiative launched.

# Social and natural sciences: differences in issues

Social sciences are concerned with society – how well individuals and communities work together; they include the disciplines of economics, geography, law, sociology, politics and psychology. By contrast, natural sciences study the natural world of astronomy, biology, chemistry, geology and physics, where generally relationships are more long-standing and predictable and theories involving atom-splitting or boiling water or gravity are more open to test. The matters of concern to social and natural scientists differ and so also do the questions they ask and the methodologies they must employ to find answers. We then have to assess the reliability of the answers provided.

## The different perspectives of natural and social scientists

In explaining natural sciences, eventually one answer is usually agreed upon – if physicists can agree on how gravity works, then it is unlikely that a biologist or chemist will advance a different explanation. Social science differs because the ways different disciplines look at a particular problem will yield different answers because the questions themselves will differ. For example, if we think of **unemployment**:

→ *sociology* would be interested in the impact on a community if a coal mine or a steel mill or a fishing port were to lose many or all of the jobs;
→ *law* will want to be sure workers are given their legal rights – and they know that in areas of high unemployment, poverty tends to increase and with it crime;
→ *geography* will ask where most unemployment occurs, how diminishing industries could be revived or replaced, the importance of transport links and the location of essential raw materials or skilled labour;
→ *economics* looks at how employers make profits, cut costs and increase the productivity of workers – workers who cannot be afforded cannot be employed;
→ *politics* asks how key decisions were made and by whom, if alternative options were fully considered, how job losses could be averted and what the impact of job losses might be on voting behaviour;
→ *psychology* thinks about the impact of job losses on individuals themselves – losing a job can lead to depression, loss of confidence and, in extreme cases, even suicide.

## The different methods of natural and social scientists

Social and natural sciences do ask different questions about different phenomena and therefore it is not surprising they adopt different methods:

→ Scientific method (*empirical* or *inductive* method) involves observation, the development of an initial hypothesis, further observation, testing and experimentation leading to the formation of a theory which is open to falsification.

**Speed learning**

Remember these six disciplines by using a mnemonic: So-L-G-E-P-P.

**Checkpoint 1**

State three ways in which the answers to such questions would assist a government in its policy making.

**Examiner's secrets**

Always give different points of view, e.g.: compare the perspectives of natural and social scientists or contrast the questions sociologists or psychologists ask with what interests geographers or politics specialists – and then compare their different answers!

# and methodologies

→ *Deduction* may occasionally be used in solving a particular question. If we know that a circle has 360° and that one segment accounts for 147°, then we can be confident that the remaining segment is 213°. The conclusion has to be correct if the premise is correct.

→ This can work satisfactorily for natural scientists but it is less reliable for social scientists where premises are more likely to be a generalisation, e.g. (i) most people sent to prison re-offend or (ii) children from broken homes are more likely to commit crimes than those from stable nuclear families – these are little more than tendencies and will not be true in all circumstances. Therefore, the conclusion reached from such analysis will be at best possible and never certain.

→ Much of the data gathered by a natural scientist will involve investigations undertaken for a specific purpose – *primary data* – and involve weighing samples or measuring the results of a particular experiment – *quantitative* methods.

→ To understand attitudes, perceptions and lifestyles, social scientists often also use such *quantitative* methods, for instance census information or surveys based on samples of the population which are usually reliable to within 2% or 3%, e.g. leisure interests, miles travelled to work each week, hours typically worked in a week, voting intentions, etc.

→ Social scientists can undertake only limited experimentation (i.e. in psychology and sometimes sociology) since to experiment on human beings would be unethical and therefore much evidence gathered by social scientists involves use of *secondary* data – information from participant observation, records of parishes, schools and employers, reports in mass media, diaries and autobiographies – such evidence is largely regarded as *qualitative* data.

→ The danger from using such sources is that they may contain implicit *values* which compromise the objectivity of the social scientist.

## Differences in the findings of natural and social scientists

Social scientists often conduct interviews (and are careful to avoid bias); they know there is a danger that if people know they are being watched, they will behave differently (Hawthorne effect), and if they are being watched covertly, there may be a danger of observer bias. The conclusions reached will rarely ever have the certainty of a natural scientist's investigation into a boiling point or forces of gravity. Yet the covert *participant observation* of BBC reporter Mark Daly in the BBC programme *The Secret Policeman* in October 2003 achieved evidence of racism that was devastating in its impact.

Measuring attitudes is less precise than boiling points but can have just as much – or even greater – significance.

---

**Exam preparation**                                                answers: page 71

1   What is the difference between quantitative and qualitative methods?
                                                                    (5 minutes)
2   Suggest three ways in which the methods of natural and social scientists differ.   (5 minutes)
3   'Anything but scientific.' How true is this assessment of the methods used by social scientists?   (30 minutes)

**Checkpoint 2**

What is the difference between the inductive and deductive methods?

**Examiner's secrets**

Make sure you understand social science methods such as (i) use of facts and opinions, (ii) qualitative and quantitative information, (iii) inductive and deductive arguments, (iv) primary and secondary data. Make sure you can illustrate your answers with examples when you need to.

**Check the net**

A quick means of accessing local and national journals is to go to: http://www.wrx.zen.co.uk/alltnews.htm.

**Checkpoint 3**

What is the Hawthorne effect?

**Quote**

Haralambos and Holborn say, 'Researchers may decide to be covert participant observers, where the fact that they are a researcher is not revealed . . . An obvious advantage . . . is that the groups being studied are not likely to change their behaviour as a result'. (p. 1008, *Sociology Themes and Perspectives*, 5th edn, Collins)

# Answers
## Studying society

## Socialisation, culture and multiculturalism

### Checkpoints

1 *Culture* is the values and beliefs of a society, whereas *socialisation* is the process by which people learn those values and beliefs during their lifetime experiences.

2 In the 2001 general election, Liberal Democrats secured 18.3% of the votes and 52 seats; Scottish Nationalists obtained 1.8% of the UK vote and 5 seats.

3 Deference is the practice of looking up to those who hold positions of authority or privilege.

4 The Ulster Volunteer Force (UVF) supported the Protestant and Unionist communities while the Provisional IRA supported the Catholic and Nationalist communities during the violence since 1970.

5 BNP stands for British National Party. It is described as 'extremist' because it challenges consensus support for the UK as a multicultural community and pursues far-right policies of extreme British (white-only) nationalism.

### Exam preparation

1 School experiences undoubtedly affect the way we relate to others, our perception of our own abilities and our attitudes to rules, learning, discipline and authority. However, socialisation is a life-long experience – in childhood we are influenced not just by school experiences but also by parents, family and friends, as well as people we look up to such as pop stars or sports personalities. Later in life our relationships will develop our values; also, self-image and beliefs will be affected by our experiences at work, including any role we have in organisations such as trade unions or political parties or leisure interests and friendships we develop.

2 Ever since the Vikings attacked our Celtic and Anglo-Saxon predecessors, Britain has been a multicultural society. For years we took our culture to the furthest corners of the Empire and it would be hypocritical to think people from different countries, faiths or backgrounds did not properly have a place in our country. Trying to represent multiculturalism as unnatural is close to stereotyping people according to their outward or superficial appearances rather than recognising their worth and how they can contribute to society.

## Ideology, equality and discrimination

### Checkpoints

1 Divisions between religions are so powerful because they are deeply rooted in history – the Holocaust saw the persecution of Jews just as some people nowadays see Jews as persecuting Palestinians; in the Middle Ages bloody power struggles were fought between Protestant and Catholic monarchs for the crown; Catholic Ireland regarded itself as oppressed by Protestants following the Battle of the Boyne, 1690, and earlier still there were heroic struggles between Christian crusaders and the Muslim world.

2 Inclusiveness seeks to prevent individuals or social groups from becoming or expecting to be isolated or separated. A good example is the emphasis now given to educating youngsters with special needs in mainstream schools.

3 (i) In *Golder v UK 1975* the ECHR ruled against the UK government after a prisoner was denied access to a solicitor, breaching fair trial provisions.
(ii) In *Republic of Ireland v UK 1978* the ECHR ruled against the UK government after IRA suspects were interrogated in a degrading manner.

4 Compared to 1983, when there were just 23, there are now 119 women MPs. In the last three years alone the number of women directors of FTSE-100 companies has increased by about 30%, though there still are some firms with no women holding directorships at all.

### Exam preparation

1 *Equality* means people are treated equally – all work the same hours or are paid the same wage; *equality of opportunity* – giving everyone an equal chance to apply for a job or take GCSEs or be coached for the local football team – is usually an excuse for treating people differently when they do not perform with the same level of success.

2 People must be judged objectively, not according to subjective stereotypes – so, using examples from job recruitment, all applicants should be matched against objective criteria stated in a job description and person specification, not assessed subjectively: (i) if the person specification says a person must be able to work with spreadsheets and databases, all applicants' skills undertaking such work can be tested; (ii) if it also requires an ability to produce accounts, candidates can be asked to demonstrate whether they have such skills or experience; (iii) if the job description requires people to work every other Saturday morning, people can be asked whether or not they are able and willing to do this on a regular basis.

3 An asylum seeker is someone seeking refuge from persecution in another country; an economic migrant is someone who wishes to settle in a country not because they are being persecuted elsewhere but because they want to improve their economic position. When Ugandan Asians were expelled by President Idi Amin in 1972, many came to the UK and not only improved their own economic situation but also contributed greatly to the wealth of the UK. Given the low birth rate, the government is to welcome young, fit, well-qualified economic migrants into this country and when they pay tax and contribute to society we shall all benefit.

4 As anti-discrimination laws have been passed, more people have become aware of good practice and have wished to pursue it, so such laws do have a powerful educative effect. Work by the Commission for Racial Equality has ensured candidates from ethnic minorities are much more fairly judged by prospective employers – and monitoring the ethnic minority profile of employees is an important part of quality assurance procedures in many

large companies. Similarly, the gender balance of employees has changed; slowly more women are breaching the *glass ceiling* and being appointed to senior positions as judges or school headteachers or college principals or members of government – some may still be excluded unfairly but all who appoint applicants for such positions now know they must be able to demonstrate objectively, if challenged, how and why a successful candidate was the most suitable for the post.

## Social and natural sciences: differences in issues and methodologies

### Checkpoints

1 The answers would help the government plan its response, e.g. how to support the local community: (i) seeking alternative jobs that could be developed there, (ii) developing strategies to deter increased crime – perhaps by increasing a police presence and (iii) alerting medical services to the need to support those who might suffer from depression and think of suicide as a response to their problems.

2 An inductive method makes observations and develops a general theory as a result of what is observed; a deductive method starts with a general premise which is believed to be true and applies it to particular circumstances or events.

3 The *Hawthorne effect* suggests that observing workers doing their work causes them to behave differently – e.g. working more quickly, more slowly or with fewer distractions or greater care – and thus questions the reliability of any conclusions reached from the observations.

### Exam preparation

1 While quantitative methods are based on the analysis of numerical data, qualitative methods involve collection of facts, beliefs and opinions which are descriptive rather than numerical.

2 (i) Natural scientists can conduct experiments (e.g. on animals) and repeat them many times over; this would be potentially unethical for social scientists since they cannot conduct experimentation on human beings if it may have anything other than a short-term effect.
(ii) The nature of the social sciences means that sometimes the data they study is less appropriately measured in quantitative terms than is the case with natural sciences – e.g. it would not be reliable to try to assess the amount of racism evident at a football match simply by counting racist calls from the crowd.
(iii) Often social scientists will use overt or covert participant observation to study how people behave in certain situations in contrast to how they say they behave in questionnaires, etc. This method is rarely if ever used by natural scientists because the topics they study and the questions they aim to answer are so different.

3 If social science were a haphazard set of opinions promoted on a subjective basis, the claim that social science methods are *anything but scientific* might be confirmed. However, there is evidence that social scientists go to great lengths to ensure the data on which they reach conclusions is accurate – if this were not so, the reliability of their recommendations would be questionable. Because the questions asked by social scientists are different from the concerns of natural scientists, the methods by which they get answers and reach conclusions may differ – but that doesn't mean they are any less scientific. Social scientists will be just as concerned as natural scientists to ensure their evidence is accurate and their conclusions are value-free, avoiding observer bias. Because actions in society are often driven by values, social scientists cannot behave as if they did not exist – they understand, though, that explanations for behaviour require explicit not implicit (i) factual evidence; (ii) statement of theory and (iii) statement of values.

# Databank

**CEHR** – Commission for Equality and Human Rights: new organisation intended to bring together the work of three existing equality commissions dealing with Racial Equality, Equal Opportunities and Disability Rights.

**community** – group of people with a strong shared link which may be where they live or where they work or what they are interested in – e.g. IT or football.

**culture/subculture** – culture is the values and beliefs of a society; where a subgroup, such as a religious movement, has a different way of regarding the world, this is regarded as a subculture.

**discrimination** – act of treating people differently, e.g. in employment: discrimination based on age, gender, race or disability is not acceptable in society.

**fact/belief/opinion** – *facts* are statements supported by verifiable evidence; *beliefs* are considered true by those who hold them – e.g. a member of the Church of England would believe statements in the Bible; *opinions* may or may not be true or supported by evidence and may therefore be subjective.

**ideology** – distinctive way of looking at issues which may reflect the perspective of a particular group – e.g. Marxists, feminists, racists.

**meritocracy** – society in which the most educated/able are in charge rather than those with, for example, aristocratic backgrounds or inherited wealth.

**multicultural society** – society in which people with diverse cultural backgrounds coexist together.

**power/authority** – power involves achieving a particular outcome (X making Y do something), authority is the *right* of X (as a teacher, parent, police officer, etc.) to make Y do something – which Y may or may not do.

**progressive/regressive taxation** – taxation in which the rate of tax rises with income (reflecting *ability to pay*) is progressive; where the share of income taken is higher for the poor than the wealthy, this is a regressive tax (e.g. airport tax – a £20 charge may be 10% of the income of someone earning £200 per week but only 1% for someone on £2 000 per week).

**quantitative/qualitative data** – information based on number – e.g. exam results or birth or death rates or soccer league tables – is *quantitative* because it involves counting and measurement or calculation; recording a series of events, keeping a diary, quoting what people say would all be *qualitative* data which provides an important but different form of evidence.

**social deference** – looking up to/respecting another, e.g. a parent or someone in authority or a famous person.

**socialisation** – the lifelong process of life in our families or at school or with our peers or at work through which we learn the values of our culture and our place within it.

**social science** – social scientists sometimes disagree because they have different values – for example, *are individuals more or less important than the society itself?* Social scientists are from different disciplines and therefore ask different questions. For example, **economics** studies how income and wealth are created and distributed and how resources are allocated; to increase demand in the economy at times of high unemployment, economists favour paying benefits (transfer payments) to poorer people to stimulate demand and keep the rest of us in work; **geography** examines the physical characteristics of the planet including the spatial distribution of resources and the settlement patterns and use of the resources by human beings; **law** establishes rules and order so that society can operate with certainty; **sociology** looks at society itself – e.g. importance of families or religion or education – not at the individuals who make up the society. **Politics** is the study of how disagreements may be resolved and links closely to **government**, the processes by which legitimate decisions are made, while **psychology** has the different perspective of understanding how the world is perceived by an individual and what influences those perceptions.

# Revision checklist
*helps you check what you still need to do*

## By the end of this chapter you should be able to:

| | | |
|---|---|---|
| 1 Use all the information in Databank, above, with confidence | Confident | Not confident. **Revise** page 72 |
| 2 Explain how the UK is changing | Confident | Not confident. **Revise** pages 64, 65 |
| 3 Show how and why societies change over time | Confident | Not confident. **Revise** pages 64, 65, 108 |
| 4 Consider whether society is now more secular and whether the significance of religion has changed | Confident | Not confident. **Revise** pages 64, 65, 104 |
| 5 Discuss multiculturalism and its impact | Confident | Not confident. **Revise** pages 65, 67 |
| 6 Show whether equality is natural or if specific actions need to be taken to achieve it | Confident | Not confident. **Revise** pages 66, 67, 70 |
| 7 Explain how discrimination affects individuals in society | Confident | Not confident. **Revise** pages 67, 70, 130 |
| 8 Say how social scientists conduct research | Confident | Not confident. **Revise** pages 68, 69 |
| 9 Consider whether the research findings of social scientists are as reliable as those of natural scientists | Confident | Not confident. **Revise** pages 68, 69 |

# Citizenship and democracy

Increasingly, the importance of discussing and understanding our rights and responsibilities as citizens is coming to be understood – thanks largely to the inclusion of Citizenship in the National Curriculum up to Key Stage 4. Democracy is not something that can be left to others. Confident, engaged and empowered citizens can make a real difference to the communities where they live.

Often they will be active in local organisations such as political parties and pressure groups. These organisations are important for helping people become informed about events, issues and choices for their communities. They can also be the organisations through which people campaign for change.

Many decisions at local, national and international level depend on who wins elections and the types of electoral system in use. In the UK in recent years, greater use has been made of referendums and devolved assemblies, and elected mayors have been introduced and, for many elections, new ways and systems of voting have been put in place.

## Exam themes

→ The rights and responsibilities of citizens

→ How informed citizens become effective citizens

→ Classifying political ideas

→ Party programmes, leaders and ideologies

→ Pluralism and pressure groups

→ Different forms of democracy

→ The changing electoral system

→ Patterns of voter choices at the ballot box

## Topic checklist

| ○ AS  ● A2 | AQA A | AQA B | EDEXCEL | OCR |
|---|---|---|---|---|
| Rights and responsibilities: citizens at work | ○● | ○● | ○● | ○● |
| Pluralism in action: political parties | ○● | ○● | ○● | ○● |
| Democracy, voting and elections | ○● | ○● | ○● | ○● |

# Rights and responsibilities: citizens at work

Democracy depends on participation and active citizenship. Effective citizens are informed, empowered citizens who know their rights and how to exert them and who diligently fulfil their duties as citizens. Good government depends on citizens remaining alert, informed and engaged – to understand how the system works, how we can make a difference, how we can work together to improve things.

**Link**

See also page 198: Can citizens of the world 'walk by on the other side'?

**Checkpoint 1**

What human rights do all UK citizens enjoy?

**Watch out!**

Make sure you understand the difference between legal rights (which can be enforced) and human rights (which in some countries sometimes seem to be more like ambitions).

> *"No arts, no letters, no society, and which is worst of all, continual fear and danger of violent death, and the life of man solitary, poor, nasty, brutish, and short."*
>
> Thomas Hobbes, Leviathan

**Checkpoint 2**

Name an organisation which helps people find out about their rights and helps to ensure they get them.

## Rights and responsibilities

Recently it has been recognised that people need to understand the rights and responsibilities of citizenship. The two go together.

→ To enjoy the protection of society, we need to be law-abiding ourselves.

→ To benefit from living in a democratic society, we need to keep ourselves well informed, *expect* to participate and be listened to and to vote in elections.

→ We need to express our viewpoints openly and engage with debates about how things can be improved – *leaving it to others* is not acceptable.

→ To enjoy all the rights to which we are entitled as citizens, we have to treat others with consideration and not behave antisocially.

→ To enjoy public services, we need to pay taxes and heed the advice from the medics on health hazards or from teachers on how to progress.

Those who enjoy their rights but ignore their responsibilities find their freedoms curtailed – people who terrorise a locality will receive an antisocial behaviour order. Those sentenced to an extended period in prison lose the right to vote.

## Rule of law

Being an effective citizen is to make full use of our rights. If we dislike a proposed planning development, we can express our objections and the planners have to listen to our points. If we dislike proposals for the constituencies which elect MPs, we can object and the Boundary Commission has to take our objections into account. If we buy faulty goods in a shop, the law gives us rights to get our money back or have the goods replaced. Often the Benefits Agency make mistakes over the benefits they pay to claimants – yet some people lack the confidence or knowledge about how to claim what they are entitled to. No one in the UK is above the law. But many people don't yet understand their rights well enough to exert them fully.

## Information is power

→ Unless we *know about* plans for our school, our workplace, our community, we stand little chance of influencing them.

→ In recent years, information has become much more *available and accessible* – especially using interactive media and the Internet.

→ Many people react to new ideas by *protesting* against the closure of a school or post office or the building of a road or a new housing estate; to be effective, such activities need to occur early on – long before a council has endorsed it or binding legal contracts have been signed.

→ Organising a petition or protest may make people feel good but such actions are unlikely to be successful unless many people take part and the events are part of a *well-planned, intensive* campaign.

→ Sometimes decision makers say people are 'not interested' yet when people feel their views are being *taken seriously*, they become very interested indeed.

## What are the hallmarks of a successful campaign?

To influence things, citizens need to know about a few simple but important rules.

→ Don't be afraid to put forward *positive* ideas.

→ Get informed and involved early on – many councils now give local people the right to attend and express their own opinions.

→ Know 'who does what' – if you have a problem on an environmental health issue, talk to an environmental health officer; don't talk to a school governor about something school governors cannot decide or to a councillor about matters outside council control. However, governors or councillors and other local opinion leaders *can* help just by giving public support to your campaign.

→ Campaigners may need to influence local MPs or councillors, parliamentary or council candidates who hope to be successful in the future, political parties, pressure groups, community organisations, local businesses and the local media.

→ Find out where a proposal has come from and why – there may be better ways of solving the problem.

→ Talk to people – they are often willing to modify proposals if asked and often welcome your interest and engagement if you get involved soon enough.

→ Citizenship is about understanding how decision-making systems 'work' so effective inputs can be made.

---

**Examiner's secrets**

Try to find an example of your own to back points you want to include in an exam answer. If everyone taking the exam in your class has the same example, examiners will be less impressed than if your example is different, the result of your own research and therefore evidence of your commitment and understanding.

**Examiner's secrets**

If you are talking about a citizen's wish to put forward ideas, always give examples, e.g. how to influence the sports played at your school or the uniform you wear, the times of buses in the evening, the times your local council holds meetings or car parking charges.

**Checkpoint 3**

How would you know where or when your local council was meeting or what was to be discussed?

**Example**

Lots of people in the community often come up with good ideas but then don't make people aware of them, e.g. putting the local post office in the village hall or pub, a different route for a road, building houses on land with disused buildings rather than on open countryside or changing the route of a local bus service.

---

**Exam preparation**                                   answers: page 80

1  What is the difference between rights and responsibilities?  (5 minutes)

2  Give three reasons why some protests against new proposals are ineffective.  (10 minutes)

3  Suggest three reasons why the government decided to make Citizenship a compulsory part of the national curriculum.  (15 minutes)

4  To what extent do you agree that an informed citizen is an effective citizen?  (30 minutes)

# Pluralism in action: political parties

Pluralism – people and organisations working together to achieve shared goals – is strong in a liberal democracy such as the UK, where we are not dominated by an autocratic monarch or dictator. Freedom of speech and movement means people can freely argue for changes they favour through political parties or pressure groups. In the past 50 years, both political parties and pressure groups have seen major changes.

## Left and right

Political parties and ideas are often classified on a 'left' to 'right' scale.

A **left**-wing party would probably favour:

+ a large role for government
+ much state ownership
+ relatively high taxation
+ considerable regulation
+ emphasis on internationalism, equality and fraternity

By contrast a **right**-wing party would want to see:

+ a smaller role for government
+ low taxes
+ individuals becoming more self-reliant
+ little or no state ownership
+ market forces at work
+ free scope for capitalism
+ emphasis on patriotism or nationalism

**Checkpoint 1**

On a horizontal left–right scale, how would you locate the British National Party, the Communist Party, Conservatives, Labour and Liberal Democrats?

## Problems of classification

If you discuss politics in terms of left or right, you must show an awareness of the following difficulties.

→ Such analysis can be very confusing because in some ways extreme right-wing fascist states or left-wing communist states had much in common. Their lack of belief in human rights, the repression of their people and their authoritarianism would make living in such states a very similar experience.

→ Such states often regard the continuance of the regime as being more important than the quality of life for their people.

→ An alternative approach is to measure parties and beliefs on an **authoritarian–libertarian** scale, reflecting the freedom allowed to their people.

**Checkpoint 2**

Give an example of a right-wing fascist state and an autocratic left-wing Communist state.

**Example**

An **authoritarian–libertarian** scale would indicate where a state should be placed in terms of the amount of regulation or repression experienced by its citizens (authoritarian) or whether people were allowed to speak out freely, enjoyed freedom of movement and had few if any restrictions placed on their enjoyment of human rights.

## The roots of the parties

→ As more people gained the right to vote, the Conservative Party was formed to ensure Conservative MPs were re-elected.

→ Labour and other parties formed since have grown from popular movements to elect MPs and are more influenced by rank-and-file members.

→ This explains why supporters of the Conservative Party are more deferential to their MPs than Labour, Liberal Democrat, Scottish or Welsh Nationalist MPs.

→ These differences are greatest in the ways the parties choose their leaders and the influence the MPs have over policy when the party is not in government.

**Action point**

Go to your local library or town hall and look up the results in the constituency where you live for recent elections. How many parties contested the seat – and did the same party always win?

## Policies and leaders

Policies change all the time. As parties hunt for vote-winning policies and consult opinion pollsters and focus groups, the differences between them are much less clear, consistent and predictable than previously.

The post-war leaders making the greatest impact have been:

→ **Conservative** – Winston Churchill (PM 1940–45 and 1951–55) and Margaret Thatcher (PM 1979–90).
→ **Labour** – Clement Attlee (PM 1945–51), Harold Wilson (PM 1964–70 and 1974–76) and Tony Blair (PM 1997– ).
→ **Liberal Democrats** – Jo Grimond prevented the death of the old Liberal Party in the 1950s; the two LD leaders since the party's formation (amalgamation of Liberals and SDP) are Paddy Ashdown (1988–99) and Charles Kennedy (1999– ).

## The changing political system

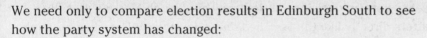

We need only to compare election results in Edinburgh South to see how the party system has changed:

| *1955 General Election* | | *2001 General Election* | |
|---|---|---|---|
| **Conservative** | **68%** | **Labour** | **46%** |
| Labour | 32% | Liberal Democrat | 27% |
| | | Conservative | 17% |
| | | Scottish Nationalist | 10% |
| | | Scottish Socialist | 2% |
| | | Independent | 1% |
| Conservative majority | 36% | Labour majority | 19% |

Key features during this 46-year period – derived from the example – were:

→ A significant decline of Conservative support in Scotland, Wales and urban areas.
→ Nationwide support for Labour in urban and rural, and middle- and working-class areas.
→ Liberal Democrats nominating candidates in virtually all constituencies and winning around 50 seats instead of 5 or 6.
→ Establishment of nationalist parties throughout Scotland and Wales.
→ Nomination of many candidates from minor parties such as Greens and Scottish Socialists or Independents.

A new trend has emerged for people to join pressure groups rather than political parties and to campaign through them for the specific causes they wish to support. Groups such as the Royal Society for the Protection of Birds saw their membership rise from 98 000 in 1971 to 1 020 000 in 2001 and Greenpeace grew from 30 000 to 221 000.

---

**Exam preparation**                                                    answers: page 81

1  What is the difference between left and right? (5 minutes)
2  What is the difference between libertarian and authoritarian? (5 minutes)
3  More people now stand for Parliament because more people are now interested in politics. To what extent and in what ways do you agree?

(30 minutes)

---

**Check the net**

Go to the Labour, Liberal Democrat and Conservative Party websites and find out (i) how the party leader is elected, (ii) how the parties make policy, and (iii) what their policies are on key issues: http://www.labour.org.uk; http://www.libdems.org.uk; http://www.conservatives.org.uk.

**Action point**

Decide on a few policies which interest you and research them on the party website. Or phone the MP's office and the contact points for other parties and compare the answers.

**Checkpoint 3**

Identify two major achievements of each of the party leaders mentioned in this section.

**Links**

For more coverage of voting behaviour, see also the section 'Democracy, voting and elections'.

**Example**

There were 1 409 candidates for 630 seats in 1955 compared to 3 133 candidates for 659 seats in 2001.

**Checkpoint 4**

What is the difference between a political party and a pressure group?

**Checkpoint 5**

What other kinds of pressure groups are there? What decides how successful a pressure group will be?

**Links**

See also the section on protest and persuasion in 'Political institutions at work in the UK'.

# Democracy, voting and elections

In the 21st century there are many instances of both direct and indirect democracy. In some elections we now use *proportional representation* or the *supplementary vote* instead of the *first-past-the-post* system. All-postal-vote elections or text voting increasingly occur. With elections for the European Parliament, Westminster, devolved parliaments or assemblies, directly elected mayors and local authorities, some people now fear voters are suffering fatigue and overload, leading to low turnouts. Declining *partisan identification* and low turnouts make election results seem more volatile, with increasingly uncertain outcomes.

## Direct democracy

Democracy involves *majority rule*. So in small villages, local residents meet to vote on decisions periodically at a Parish Meeting. Deciding matters directly like this is called *direct democracy*. The same principle applies when a *referendum* is held.

The first national referendum was held in 1975 to decide whether the UK should remain in the European Union (as it is now called) and they are now usually used before significant constitutional changes are introduced.

## Representative (or indirect) democracy

→ With over 40 million people entitled to vote in this country, most decisions are made through elected representatives – MPs or councillors.

→ A general election must be held at least once every five years to elect MPs, representing 659 constituencies – each with about 70 000 electors.

→ Turnout has fallen from 80% of the electorate in the 1950s to 59% in 2001 in some urban constituencies, such as Liverpool Riverside where turnout tumbled to 34%.

→ Low turnouts are dangerous; they signal disengagement from the political system – leaving it to others; this can give control of things to extremists.

→ The Electoral Commission has been set up to look at new ways of voting – by post, by text, in supermarkets or at weekends.

## Voters and parliaments

→ Every UK citizen over 18 (except members of the House of Lords, long-term prisoners or anyone declared insane) is entitled to vote if they have made sure their name is on the electoral register. Turnouts in all-postal ballots are often much higher than when people have to go to polling stations to vote.

→ There is a campaign at present to lower the voting age to 16.

→ All women gained the right to vote in 1928 (over-30s gained the vote in 1918).

→ In 2001 87% of voters over 65 voted but barely 52% of under-35s. Results were thus distorted towards the wishes of the elderly!

→ There are 659 MPs in the Westminster Parliament and elections must be held within 5 years of the previous general election.

**Checkpoint 1**

What is partisan identification? Why is it important?

**Examples**

In 1998, Wales voted in favour of having an Assembly – but only by 50.3% to 49.7% on a turnout of 50%. The margin was wider when the idea of having a Mayor of London was approved by 72% to 28% but on an even lower turnout of 34%.

**Watch out!**

In exams candidates often confuse the electorate (those who are entitled to vote) with the voters (the people who do actually vote).

**Check the net**

Look at the Electoral Commission website to get a better idea of the work it does: http://www.electoralcommission.gov.uk.

**Checkpoint 2**

Think of one reason for and one reason against lowering the voting age to 16.

**Checkpoint 3**

Why do you think UKIP and the Green party have MEPs in the European Parliament but no MPs in the House of Commons?

→ The European Parliament is elected by proportional representation, with elections every five years.

## The changing electoral system

Although the first-past-the-post system applies in Parliamentary and Council elections, *proportional representation* applies for elections to the Scottish and European Parliaments and the Northern Ireland and Welsh Assemblies.

→ Proportional representation means that 20% of the votes should give a party 20% of the seats.
→ Critics say the first-past-the-post system distorts the wishes of voters – in the 2001 election, Labour gained 41% of the votes but 62% of seats in Parliament.
→ Mayoral elections use the *supplementary* vote, with voters expressing a second preference if the winner gains less than 50% of votes cast.

## Changing voting behaviour

Working-class people used to vote Labour and middle-class people Conservative – but in recent years *partisan dealignment* has occurred, with fewer people automatically voting for a party – these trends still occur but less so nowadays.

→ Over 40% of voters admitted to a strong *partisan identification* in 1964 but by 2001 the figure had dropped to below 15%.
→ Many people now cast their vote on the basis of a particular *issue* about which they are particularly concerned – e.g. animal rights, abortion, taxation or pensions.
→ *Tactical* voting is growing. In a first-past-the-post election, increasing numbers of people seem to be voting *for* the candidate who has the best chance of *defeating* the party or candidate they like *least*.
→ Many people also vote on which *party leader* they like best or dislike least, how they view the *past performance* of the government or how they have fared in *economic terms* in the period *preceding* the election or hope to fare (i.e. in instrumental terms) *after* the election. There are now significant variations in voting patterns between men and women and different age groups:

| % | men | women | 18–24 | 25–34 | 35–44 | 45–54 | 55–64 | 65+ |
|---|---|---|---|---|---|---|---|---|
| Labour | 49 | 46 | 43 | 53 | 51 | 45 | 45 | 48 |
| Conservative | 27 | 29 | 17 | 23 | 24 | 25 | 35 | 36 |
| Lib Dem | 18 | 21 | 36 | 19 | 19 | 25 | 17 | 13 |

Source: 2001 *British Election Study* reported in *Politics Review*, September 2002.

### Check the net

Have a look at the Stoke-on-Trent City Council website to get the full figures for their interesting mayoral election and see how the supplementary vote system works: http://www.stoke.gov.uk.

### Link

See also page 193: The relationship between needs, interests and opinions.

### Jargon

Partisan identification is the long-term sense of loyalty that voters feel to a particular party.

### Example

In Kingston and Surbiton in 1997, Ed Davey (Lib Dem) was elected 56 votes ahead of the Conservative, while Labour polled 12 811 in third place; in 2001, when the Conservatives campaigned to regain the seat, the Lib Dems squeezed the Labour vote down to 4 302, resulting in Ed Davey's re-election by 15 676.

### Checkpoint 4

What differences do you notice in the profiles of party support among different age groups?

---

### Exam preparation                    answers: page 81

1 What is the difference between proportional representation and first-past-the-post? (5 minutes)
2 How has turnout at elections changed in recent years? (5 minutes)
3 What are the reasons for and against making greater use of direct democracy? (30 minutes)

# Answers
## Citizenship and democracy

## Rights and responsibilities: citizens at work

### Checkpoints

1 Human rights (also *legal rights* because they are included in the Human Rights Act 1998 (effective in 2000)) include:
Article 2 – the right to life;
Article 3 – the prohibition of inhuman and degrading treatment;
Article 5 – the right to liberty;
Article 6 – the right to a fair hearing;
Article 8 – the right to a private family life.
2 Citizens' Advice Bureau.
3 Notices of Council meetings are published outside civic buildings. Councils will provide local residents with dates of meetings if requested. Agendas are available a few days before the meeting.

### Exam preparation

1 A right is something an individual is fully entitled to do – e.g. freedom of speech; a responsibility is the other side of the coin – e.g. freedom of speech must be used responsibly and not to incite, for example, racial or religious hatred.
2 (i) Some protests are aimed at the wrong people. If a multinational company decides to close a factory, that is their decision – protesting to a councillor or your MP or a trade union may make you feel good, but the decision will be the company's.
(ii) Some protests have no effect because the decisions are already made. If a local park has been sold for development as an industrial estate, with the contracts signed and the planning permission given, protestors will have missed the boat.
(iii) Pressure groups are most effective when they are regarded by government or a council as *insider* groups for their expertise. *Outsider* groups are not listened to in the same way and often the only thing they can do is to protest, march or demonstrate. Things may not change until new MPs or councillors have been elected.
3 (i) Many young people say they are not interested in politics but when pressed it is clear they are very interested in some issues but do not know how to make a difference – the Citizenship agenda aims to empower them by giving them the information they need.
(ii) Citizenship is a good way to attack racism and homophobic bullying – mentoring and peer mediation schemes can help many young people gain a positive self-image, helping both themselves and others in the process.
(iii) Participation in elections has fallen in recent years and Citizenship shows everyone how they can make a difference and become engaged; this will be important if the voting age is reduced to 16.
4 The better informed a citizen is, the more likely is she or he to be effective – a citizen who is well informed would know when the deadlines were for consultation exercises and make sure she or he submitted well-argued representations in good time and encouraged friends to do the same. Well-informed citizens are likely to have the *confidence* to take action, raise issues, ask questions and make an impression if they are reported in the media. But there are other attributes people require to be *most* effective. A person needs to have the time and inclination to find things out. A person needs to have good communication skills if they are to persuade or mobilise others. People also need self-assurance to use information to the best effect.

## Pluralism in action: political parties

### Checkpoints

1 Probably the order would be from left to right – Communist, Labour, Liberal Democrat, Conservative, BNP, though in view of some of their social welfare policies and stance on the Iraq War, some people believe Liberal Democrats are to the left of Labour.
2 An example of a right-wing fascist state could be Spain under Franco and an example of an autocratic left-wing Communist state could be the Soviet Union under Stalin or modern-day China.
3 Winston Churchill – wartime leader; led the first post-war Conservative government and thereby re-established the operation of the two-party system which saw rival parties alternating in power.
Margaret Thatcher – as first woman PM, she became a role model for women; had a major impact on politics because she challenged the status quo with conviction politics and adopted New Right attitudes.
Clement Attlee – first Labour PM with a big majority; introduced radical reforms to rebuild post-war Britain including much nationalisation and welfare state reforms, including the establishment of the NHS.
Harold Wilson – won back power for Labour in 1964 after 13 years of Conservative rule; tried to continue Attlee's social justice agenda but did not succeed in making Labour the natural party of government.
Tony Blair – won back power for *New* Labour after 18 years of Conservatives in power – though his approach was more managerialist than ideological; wanted to improve public services but earned the scepticism of the Labour movement because of the Iraq War.
Jo Grimond – arrested the decline of Liberal support from 1918 to 1955; adopted radical policies which led to increased party membership and support with Liberals contesting 300+ UK constituencies.
Paddy Ashdown – first leader of the Liberal Democrats (merged SDP and Liberals); his energetic *action man* image proved popular, though some LDs disliked his desire for close links with Labour.
Charles Kennedy – detached LDs from links with Labour, taking a strong stance against the Iraq War; saw LDs increase MPs in by-elections at Romsey and Brent East and the 2001 general election.

**4** Political parties generally contest seats on local councils and for parliaments, whereas pressure groups aim to influence public opinion and those in power – some pressure groups have close links to political parties (e.g. trade unions and Labour).

**5** Apart from *environmental* pressure groups, there are *trade unions* and also groups aiming to improve the lifestyles of *vulnerable* people, e.g. Child Poverty Action Group, Shelter and Age Concern; there are also *conscience* groups such as Liberty and Amnesty International.

### Exam preparation

**1** The left believes in far more state involvement in ownership and regulation than the right, which wants a big and largely unregulated private sector.

**2** A libertarian believes people should be free to make their own choices and lifestyles with little or no intervention from the state; an authoritarian believes in much greater control and intervention by the state.

**3** At a superficial level more candidates could equal greater interest. But a better explanation is that whereas the Labour and Conservative parties of the 1950s and 1960s were *broad churches* or coalitions, which could accommodate lots of party differences, Margaret Thatcher's conviction politics saw people being less willing to compromise so those who favour right-wing policies now break away and join the BNP or UKIP rather than staying inside the Conservative party. Instead of remaining inside Labour or the LDs, environmentalists back the Greens. The greater support for pressure groups and individual causes may explain why more people do want to vote for a candidate who supports attitudes and values exactly the same as their own.

## Democracy, voting and elections

### Checkpoints

**1** Partisan identification is the strength of an individual's long-term identification with a particular political party –

this is generally now much weaker than 20 or 30 years ago.

**2** FOR: Giving young people the responsibility of voting would make them consider policy issues at an earlier age, especially now the Citizenship curriculum exists and many young people are better informed than their parents. AGAINST: Young people do not have a broad enough experience of life to be able to judge many of the issues.

**3** Green and UKIP supporters may have turned out more enthusiastically than other voters for the European Parliament elections than the elections for Westminster when turnouts were 30% and 60% respectively. Remember, European elections are conducted under a form of proportional representation, which aims to give each party approximately the same share of seats as it obtains votes, while MPs are elected using the first-past-the-post system, which may give victory to a party with fewer votes than its main rival – as in 1951 and February 1974.

**4** Labour support is more evenly spread across all age groups than other parties. The LDs are strongest among young voters; the Conservatives among the oldest voters.

### Exam preparation

**1** PR aims to give each party about the same proportion of seats as it receives votes whereas a first-past-the-post system will produce an individual winner in every constituency but there is absolutely no guarantee of proportionality or even of the party with most votes winning most seats.

**2** Turnout in all elections has declined in recent years.

**3** When an issue divides political parties (e.g. whether devolved assemblies should be established in Scotland and Wales or whether the UK should join the Euro), a referendum allows people to indicate which options they prefer. Referendums are particularly useful to decide changes in the way we govern ourselves, e.g. regional government, elected mayors, etc. The argument against is that most people don't pay attention to the detailed arguments and such decisions are best left to MPs.

# Databank

**Abstention/differential abstention** – not voting. Sometimes this is seen as a way of expressing opposition but it could also be a sign of declining confidence in the democracy. Differential abstention is when more of one party or candidate's supporters abstain than those of other parties or candidates. Did Sam Nixon fail to reach the 2003 *Pop Idol* final because more of his supporters thought he was certain to get into the final and so did not bother to vote?

**Beveridge, William** – architect of the Beveridge Report; Liberal MP in 1940s and Director of the London School of Economics.

**by-election/general election** – a general election for the Westminster Parliament must be held at least once every five years; by-elections occur if an MP or councillor resigns and a replacement person is elected.

**citizen** – member of society with rights and responsibilities and a full entitlement to participate.

**devolved assembly** – assembly, such as the Scottish Parliament or the Welsh Assembly, operating powers *devolved* or granted by UK Parliament which could, in theory, be withdrawn – e.g. Northern Ireland Assembly.

**direct/indirect democracy** – democracy involves a commitment to *majority rule*; in direct democracy, people decide things for themselves in parish or other meetings or through referendums; indirect democracy (sometimes called *representative* democracy) involves the election of a small number of representatives, e.g. MPs or councillors, to take decisions for the majority of people.

**Electoral Commission** – body which updates the elections system and methods by which we vote, ensuring financing rules are obeyed and that there is fairness in referendums and between parties.

**first-past-the-post** voting system – this means the party with most votes in a constituency wins. If five candidates stand and all get 10 000 votes except one who gets 10 001, the winner effectively has only slightly over 20% of votes. This system causes the distortion which gave Labour 40.7% of the votes in the 2001 general election but 62.5% of the seats but does have the advantage of being easy to vote, count and understand.

**Freedom of information** – *information is power*, so if the principle of *freedom of information* is accepted, this strengthens the capacity of citizens to participate effectively, become engaged and therefore empowered. Without information, individuals are less able to influence events or hold people accountable.

**pluralism** – decision making by a plurality of people or organisations. In the *conventional pluralism* of the 1950s and 1960s, decision making was seen as a battle between rival forces, in some ways like a rugby scrum.

**proportional representation** – voting system designed to give a party same share of seats in Parliament as it receives votes, e.g. Scottish Parliament.

**public sector/private sector** – public sector comprises activities and organisations directly funded by local, regional or national government; private sector comprises activities undertaken by businesses or voluntary bodies. Margaret Thatcher's view was that *anything the public sector can do, the private sector can do better.*

**referendum** – form of direct democracy – vote in which public decide a particular issue, e.g. whether the UK should adopt the Euro currency.

**turnout** – proportion of the electorate voting – turnout has dropped significantly in the past 50 years, possibly because 'spin' means the differences between the parties are now less easy to identify.

# Revision checklist
*helps you check what you still need to do*

## By the end of this chapter you should be able to:

| | | | |
|---|---|---|---|
| 1 | Use all the information in Databank, above, with confidence | Confident | Not confident. **Revise** page 82 |
| 2 | Explain the rights and responsibilities of citizens | Confident | Not confident. **Revise** page 74 |
| 3 | Show how informed citizens become effective citizens | Confident | Not confident. **Revise** pages 74, 75 |
| 4 | Consider how political ideas may be classified | Confident | Not confident. **Revise** pages 76, 77 |
| 5 | Discuss party programmes and ideologies and the achievements of party leaders | Confident | Not confident. **Revise** pages 77, 80 |
| 6 | Show how pluralism embraces both political parties and pressure groups | Confident | Not confident. **Revise** pages 77, 80, 82 |
| 7 | Explain the nature and implications of different forms of democracy | Confident | Not confident. **Revise** page 78 |
| 8 | Describe and explain the changing electoral system | Confident | Not confident. **Revise** pages 79, 81 |
| 9 | Identify patterns of voter choices at the ballot box | Confident | Not confident. **Revise** pages 79, 81 |

# Debates about public policy: decision making

The foundations of public policy rest on the research findings of social scientists, the institutions (and personnel within them who prescribe the options and make the choices) and the global environment within which they all work. These institutions and figures comprise the main bodies forming both the government of the UK – Parliament, Government, Prime Minister, Cabinet, Civil Service and the agencies – and the European Union – Commission, Parliament, Council of Ministers, Court of Justice.

The choices eventually made will to some extent be compromises between what can be afforded, what shortfalls in provision are identified to exist, and whether certain services should be provided by the EU, government or councils, by the private sector, by a mixture of these or by individuals for themselves and their families.

As the UK emerged from war, no areas of public policy provoked more debate – both in terms of ends and means – than the management of the economy and the welfare state. Does a welfare state promote *dependence*? Should it offer *universal* provision or simply a *safety net*? Are such matters properly the role of government or of the *individuals* themselves? Whatever we *want*, what can we afford?

## Exam themes

→ The Prime Minister, Government and Parliament

→ Institutions of government and processes of politics

→ Globalism and internationalism

→ Role and purpose of the EU

→ Europe of Nations or United States of Europe?

→ The economy in post-war UK

→ The structure of the workforce

→ The aspirations of the welfare state – slaying the *giant evils*

→ Problems of welfare provision – cost, need, equity and choice

## Topic checklist

| ○ AS  ● A2 | AQA A | AQA B | EDEXCEL | OCR |
|---|---|---|---|---|
| Political institutions at work in the UK | ○● | ○● | ○● | ○● |
| Europe, globalism and internationalism | ○● | ○● | ○● | ○● |
| Post-war Britain | ○● | ○● | ○● | ○● |
| The welfare state and its problems | ○● | ○● | ○● | ○● |

# Political institutions at work in the UK

A UK Prime Minister takes office not because he or she has been directly elected but because his or her party controls most seats in the House of Commons. Yet sometimes the machinery of government – the civil service and the agencies – fail to deliver the outcomes the Prime Minister has promised and which the electorate expects.

## The power of the Prime Minister ●●●

Prime Ministers have a lot of power as long as they have a united party behind them – if disunity makes the majority uncertain, the Prime Minister suddenly becomes vulnerable, as John Major found in 1995–7. Prime Ministers 'hire or fire' the 100 or so ministers who form the government including the 20 or so senior figures who form the Cabinet. The Prime Minister is the public face of the government, decides its priorities, acts as a world statesman and determines the programme announced at the State Opening of Parliament in November each year by HM The Queen.

## Parliament and legislation ●●●

The sovereignty of Parliament becomes most evident once a party's majority seems about to disappear:

→ If a Prime Minister (PM) loses a vote of confidence in Parliament, as Labour PM James Callaghan did in 1979, he and his government will resign and, probably, this will be followed by a general election.
→ Select committees scrutinise government policy and EU legislation – a select committee of 10 or 12 MPs shadows most of the main departments of government, chaired by a senior backbench MP.
→ MPs can ask questions, put down motions for debate, draw attention to issues which concern them, meet ministers or refer cases of maladministration to the Parliamentary Commissioner for Administration or 'ombudsman'.

Most government-sponsored Bills are passed but only a few of those put forward by backbench MPs or peers are successful.

## The work of government and the agencies ●●●

→ Choosing ministers who can deal with particular policy proposals effectively is a test of any Prime Minister – especially key appointments such as Foreign Secretary, Home Secretary and Chancellor of the Exchequer.
→ Senior ministers comprise the Cabinet and are expected to vote together on all policy matters; if they cannot do this, they are expected to resign. With the support of senior civil servants, the main work of most ministers is to:
  → promote new legislation
  → negotiate budgets with the Treasury
  → deal with policy issues as they arise
  → run their departments
  → answer questions
  → speak for and represent the government

---

**Example**

A Prime Minister who loses party support will resign, as Margaret Thatcher did in 1990.

**Check the net**

Go to the Parliament website, http://www.parliament.uk, and find out the date and topic of the most recent question asked or speech made by your MP.

**Action point**

To understand the legislative process, track a Bill going through Parliament – use the Parliament website, find out when the Commons debate the bill and record the debate from the Parliament Channel (508 Digital). If you choose a Bill a local MP is interested in, they will probably provide information.

**Watch out!**

Make sure you understand the simple but important difference between standing committees in the House of Commons, which go through bills after second reading with a fine-tooth comb to sort out problems or disagreements, and select committees, which exist for longer periods to check up on particular aspects of policy.

Day-to-day matters are mostly dealt with by semi-independent executive *agencies* such as the Benefits Agency or DVLA – up to 200 of which have been established to implement policy at arm's length from government.

## The devolved assemblies ●●●

The election of the Blair government was quickly followed by referendums which approved the setting up of the Welsh Assembly and the Scottish Parliament, elected by proportional representation. This voting system meant that in both countries Labour could not govern alone and formed coalitions with the Liberal Democrats.

The devolved assemblies have made a truly democratic input into Welsh and Scottish affairs that might have been missing if matters had been left to the Welsh and Scottish Offices, their ministers and civil servants.

## Protest and persuasion ●●●

Pressure groups are best understood in terms of Wyn Grant's classification of *insider* groups, on which the government relies for technical advice, and *outsider* groups, which have no automatic hearing in Whitehall ministries and must seek to influence government by winning over public opinion through marches, demonstrations, civil disobedience and direct action.

→ Generally speaking, *civil disobedience* can be effective – it helped suffragettes gain the vote for women over 30 and the *direct action* of refusing to pay the poll tax in the early 1990s certainly led to its demise, but *violence for its own sake*, as in the anti-capitalism riots on May Days or protests at G8 meetings of world leaders, appears to be largely ineffective and often counter-productive.

→ All governments want to stay in office and to help them do so they keep an eye on their standing in the opinion polls. Nothing will concentrate the mind of government leaders more than falling poll ratings or poor election results. Often government defeats in by-elections (as in 2003 when Labour lost Brent East to the Lib Dems) will lead to a ministerial reshuffle or new policies!

→ The key factor for a party in government is the economy. If people feel financially secure, many will support the party; if they feel vulnerable and believe another party could do better, they may well protest and switch their vote.

**Examples**

The Benefits Agency deals with social and welfare benefits, the Prisons Agency deals with prison matters and the Driver and Vehicle Licensing Agency deals with driver and vehicle records.

**Check the net**

Look at the Welsh Assembly and Scottish Parliament websites. Notice how they try to engage Scottish and Welsh people in contributing to decisions: http://www.wales.gov.uk/index.htm; http://www.scottish.parliament.uk/.

**Checkpoint 1**

Identify one insider group and one outsider group.

**Checkpoint 2**

What is the difference between a local election and a by-election?

**Checkpoint 3**

Identify two typical differences between a left-wing party and a right-wing party.

---

**Exam preparation**                                    answers: page 92

1  List four key functions of Parliament.   (5 minutes)
2  What factors determine how powerful a Prime Minister will be?
                                                        (10 minutes)
3  How far do you agree that the advantages of proportional representation are outweighed by the disadvantages?   (30 minutes)

# Europe, globalism and internationalism

We all need to understand how global forces affect public policy. Like the French, who are no less French because France is in the EU, most UK citizens are proud of their identity but sometimes appear uncertain how EU institutions can help to bring about commonly shared goals.

**Link**

See also page 189: Proud cultures and globalisation.

## Increasing globalism and the inevitability of internationalism

Global forces mean no country can now isolate itself from the rest of the world.

→ Global warming means that cutting down or setting fire to a forest in one country may cause devastating effects elsewhere in the world.
→ Firms which pollute the atmosphere may be miles away from the forests which are depleted by acid rain or the communities whose health suffers as a result.

**Checkpoint 1**

Can you think of three other multinational companies?

→ Multinational companies such as Microsoft, Adidas and Ford thrive on the capitalist principle of seeking profit wherever they can – manufacturing goods such as cars, computers, trainers or sweatshirts where raw materials and labour are cheap and selling them in countries where they can add the biggest mark-up.
→ International trade means that inflation in the US or a collapse in investor confidence or increases in interest rates in Asia will have an immediate impact in Europe.

**Example**

The UK had no influence over the causes of acid rain from central Europe before but, as an EU member, we now help to create policies which will prevent harmful industrial emissions causing such problems in the future.

Such problems mean that countries must work collectively. International cooperation and bodies such as the United Nations, the World Bank, the World Trade Organisation and world summits on the environment, such as those held in Rio de Janeiro, Kyoto and Johannesburg, mean that goals can be set for the future. Globalism inevitably diminishes *sovereignty*; however, by working together, countries can gain *autonomy* – influence over what happens in other countries.

## From Common Market to European Union (EU)

**Example**

Before, we had no influence over the levels of humanitarian aid other European countries provided for *less economically developed countries* but now we can influence EU policy on such matters and make a real difference.

The Common Market was formed in 1957 by countries such as France, Germany and Italy, with the UK joining in 1970. In 2004 the membership rose from 15 countries to 25, bringing the EU's population to some 500 million. The EU is a single market, with citizens having the right to reside or work or trade anywhere in the EU area.

## The organisation and functions of the European Union

The four main bodies in the EU are:

→ The *European Parliament*, which meets in Strasbourg – its members are elected democratically from the member countries. The Parliament acts as a consultative body, agrees the budget and confirms the appointment of the Commission.
→ The *European Commission*. Members are senior political figures from each member country. The Commission is the permanent

bureaucracy of the EU and is situated in Brussels; it proposes policies and implements laws once they have been agreed.

→ EU laws are passed not by the European Parliament but by the *Council of Ministers*, with the relevant minister from each country present. Some laws require unanimous agreement, others are passed by a majority of votes.

→ The *European Court of Justice (ECJ)* in Luxembourg comprises justices appointed by each country and it enforces EU law; its rulings take precedence over the laws of individual countries if there is a conflict.

## The single market and the euro

The EU currency, the euro, has been created to support the single market. European leaders believed that apart from abolishing tariffs they needed a common currency. Most EU member countries now benefit by not having to convert, for example, French francs into German deutschmarks or Spanish pesetas every time a deal is done. The existence of a single currency means that buyers and sellers know what they will respectively pay and receive as a result of a transaction.

## The European Central Bank and its interest rates

A problem for the Euro-zone is that one rate of interest is set by the European Central Bank which applies in all member countries. The problem for Europe is that some countries may be experiencing rapid economic expansion, which could justify a higher rate (e.g. Ireland), while other countries may be experiencing depression and high unemployment (e.g. Germany), which could justify a lower rate.

## Policy agendas

If the single market is to operate as one market rather than a different market in 25 countries, the *transport* and *communications* infrastructures will need to be improved and harmonised, as will the efficiency of *food* producers and the development of *greener* policies for *energy generation* and production of *manufactured* goods. Public opinion in the wealthier parts of the EU may complain about cash injections to raise incomes, living standards and improve production methods in poorer states.

Perhaps the two biggest issues facing the EU are (i) encouraging *fair trade* and reaching a fair accommodation with *less economically developed countries* to give them access to EU countries and to avoid damaging their markets with subsidised food exports and (ii) working more energetically towards *local agenda 21* targets, set to reduce global warming at the Rio de Janeiro environmental summit in 1992.

**Check the net**

Have a look at the EU website for the MFPs from your region; at the same time, see what are the party loyalties of all the present MEPs and which countries they come from – http://europa.eu.int/.

**Watch out!**

Don't confuse the ECJ with the entirely separate European Court of Human Rights which adjudicates on matters arising from the European Convention on Human Rights, established by the Council of Europe, not the EU.

**Checkpoint 2**

What would be the effect if a French exporter sells a €200 product to a British firm when £1 = €2 but the purchaser finds the exchange rate has changed to £1 = €1 when the time comes to pay?

**Checkpoint 3**

What are the advantages of having one single market rather than 25 or more separate markets?

**Example**

In the long term, raising incomes in poorer countries is an excellent investment because the more prosperous such countries become, the more will they be able to contribute to the EU budget and the more goods and services they will come to acquire from countries such as the UK, Sweden, Ireland, France or Germany.

**Link**

See also page 191: Is environmentalism a scientific or political issue?

| Exam preparation | answers: page 92 |
|---|---|

1 What are the main decision-making bodies of the EU? List the main function of each. (5 minutes)

2 What is the difference between free trade and fair trade? (5 minutes)

3 Why does globalism reduce the power of individual countries to control their own affairs? (15 minutes)

4 How far do you agree that the UK gains nothing by being a member of the EU? (30 minutes)

# Post-war Britain

The post-war recovery of the UK in 1945 was dominated by two thinkers – John Maynard Keynes and William Beveridge. Keynes developed the whole idea of *macroeconomic theory* and Beveridge identified five *giant evils* to be slain – poverty, ignorance, idleness, sickness and squalor.

## Macro- and microeconomic theory

→ During the 1930s many economists believed that in times of economic depression it might be necessary for firms to dismiss workers or reduce wages, but all would naturally improve in the end. It was not seen as the duty of government to intervene even if millions became unemployed.

→ This view was challenged by Keynes who urged that the nation's economy could not be run on the same basis as a family or a business trying to pay its way. He argued that at such times government spending needed to increase to boost demand.

→ This approach justified the post-war spending programmes of Labour and Conservative governments alike, rebuilding the country's homes and jobs.

## The prescription offered by Keynes and Beveridge in 1945

Keynes recognised that balancing budgets during a depression was wrong and that government spending could stimulate the economy, encouraging the new Labour government to rebuild homes and nationalise and improve industry. Post-war recovery depended on government investment in manufacturing, services, roads, houses, schools, power supplies and water since individuals and businesses were not able to finance rebuilding immediately after the war. This approach to the economy emphasised the need for full employment and Keynes supported the Beveridge commitments to:

→ fight *poverty* with what we now think of as social security;
→ fight *ignorance* with much improved education provision for all;
→ fight *idleness* with a commitment to full employment;
→ fight *sickness* with a National Health Service free at the time of use; and
→ fight *squalor*, replacing war-damaged houses and slums with modern homes.

**But how far should the state be involved in the 21st century?**
The 1945–51 Labour government embarked on a large-scale nationalisation programme, taking over industries as diverse as coal, steel, telephones, gas and electricity, as well as establishing the NHS. But by the 1980s the New Right were very critical of the *nanny state* and the *dependency* culture. This led to a large-scale privatisation programme by the Thatcher governments of the 1980s; previously loss-making operations had large amounts of debt written off by government so they could be sold off – but often the new privatised companies failed to make the long-term investments necessary to improve services.

---

**Jargon**

Instead of each firm cutting wages/prices hoping to survive (*microeconomic* theory), Keynes argued that the health of the economy depended on taking a broader view (*macroeconomic* theory – looking at the whole economy).

---

**Speed learning**

Make up a mnemonic from the first letter of the five evils Beveridge wanted to slay to help you remember them, e.g. S-I-S-P-I.

---

**Jargon**

The *New Right* refers to conservatives who believe in individualism – each person being responsible for meeting her or his own needs – and they favour minimal intervention by government, believe restrictions on competition should be removed and would use market forces to allocate resources in society.

The Blair government introduced the *New Deal* under which benefits are payable only in return for working or going on training programmes; childcare support is now offered to help parents go to work and earn money.

### Arguments for and against means-tested benefits

A continuing debate is over *means testing*, which people – particularly the elderly – resent as an intrusion into their private affairs. Many *means-tested benefits* are so complex that many poor people who most need support, such as pensioners, never claim it. People who support means-tested benefits claim that more can be paid to those who need it if nothing is paid to better off people; also, they say means testing gives greatest support to those with the greatest needs.

## Government budgets and the economic cycle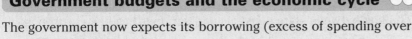

The government now expects its borrowing (excess of spending over revenues received) to increase when the economic cycle has a downturn (unemployment rising) and to largely pay off accumulated government debts when things improve, with employment rising, new businesses being formed and tax revenues increasing.

### Boosting the workforce

Post-war Britain welcomed many people from Commonwealth countries, such as the West Indies, India and Pakistan, to come and work and study here – and often the new arrivals did jobs others did not choose to do.

→ Many of these new Britons have established themselves here and their families make an important contribution to all parts of the UK economy.

→ In 2003 David Blunkett openly questioned whether, given the low birthrate and the ageing population, it was not now time to welcome more economic migrants to the country. Young economic migrants from other countries would change the ratio of workers to pensioners to the advantage of everyone; also, economic migrants are often the most qualified, talented and ambitious people – architects, doctors, teachers, entrepreneurs – who could add to the GDP of the UK if they became *bona fide* members of UK society.

→ Opponents say that encouraging economic migrants to settle here could generate short-term costs to help them establish themselves – e.g. providing housing and demands on schools or colleges; it could also cause resentment if people believe the new arrivals are 'stealing' homes or jobs.

> *"There is no such thing as society . . . There are individual men and women, and there are families. And no government can do anything except through people, and people must look to themselves first."*
>
> Margaret Thatcher, *Woman's Own*, October 1987

**Examiner's secrets**

Examiners like to see arguments in your answers, but make sure you always back them with strong examples; don't forget to give both sides of an argument and always reach a clear conclusion.

**Watch out!**

Candidates sometimes say benefits paid to the unemployed take money that could otherwise be spent on the NHS as if government can call on a set amount of money – their capacity to borrow for the short term means this is a mistake. Transfer payments to the unemployed are a key element of keeping demand in the economy strong.

**Checkpoint 1**

Why did the UK ask many people from Commonwealth countries to come and work here – and why do you think the people decided to come to live here?

**Exam preparation**                                                             answers: pages 92–93

1   What were the five giant evils Lord Beveridge believed the welfare state should conquer?   (5 minutes)

2   'It was a mistake to privatise the nationalised industries.' How far do you agree?   (30 minutes)

# The welfare state and its problems

Living standards improved after the war so some argued that people should be self-reliant and provide increasingly for themselves. Yet in fact so many people now expect government to provide a *safety net*, it has become clear that lifelong support, *from the cradle to the grave*, cannot be afforded if taxes are to be kept low.

## Pensions

The desire to give the elderly a reasonable income in retirement so they can keep dignified living standards is a goal of the welfare state. But, as the proportion of the retired dependent population to working population has grown, this has become more difficult to sustain, especially when low taxation is a widely shared goal.

→ The link between state pensions and earnings has been broken, so pensions are now linked to inflation – i.e. cost of living increases. Consequently, state pensions represented 27.5% of national earnings in 1974, but this figure had fallen to 16.2% by 2002.

→ Few people have purchased private pensions – with disappointing results.

→ Short of encouraging more births to augment the working population in twenty years' time or encouraging more economic migrants to settle in the country, the only possible solution involves delaying retirement until workers reach 70 or 75 instead of 60 or 65 – yet most people apparently want to retire earlier, not later.

→ There are now so many over-60s that the government realises it must not offend the *grey power* of older voters in case they vote against it.

## Education

Education is the biggest single tool for achieving both equality and equality of opportunity, yet there are still concerns over the barriers families encounter in seeking the best education for their children.

→ In 2004 in England, all three- and four-year-olds are entitled to a free part-time pre-school (or nursery education) place.

→ Between 1945 and 1970 there was a *tripartite* state system of selective grammar schools (11+ exam), secondary modern schools and technical schools, which focussed on developing skills. Now most pupils attend *state* comprehensive schools, as grammar schools and technical schools have been largely phased out.

→ Only about 4% of children attended fee-paying *private* or independent schools, such as Eton, Harrow, Winchester or Roedean, though, since 1970, numbers have increased to about 6%.

→ The Blair government wants most pupils to stay at school till they are 18 and for 50% of school leavers to attend university. Rising costs have made this difficult to achieve as student grants have been replaced by loans and top-up fees. Some say top-up fees will deter pupils from *poorer* families from applying to HE. Those who argue

**Checkpoint 1**

Why does the proportion of retired people to working population matter?

**Check the net**

Look at the age structure of the population in the 2001 census: http://www.statistics.gov.uk.

that grants should be restored say that graduates get better jobs and pay far more tax during their lifetimes.

## Full employment and unemployment ●●●

Different governments approach the goal of full employment in different ways but all governments understand that unemployment is an expensive blight on the economy to be eliminated and a major disaster for the individuals concerned.

→ After 1945, UK governments were committed to achieve full employment through employment in state industries, support for private sector businesses and by pursuing pro-employment monetary and fiscal policies.

→ This commitment was weakened when the Thatcher government said its main goal of economic policy would be low inflation – it said that *if inflation was low, the UK would be competitive and full employment would be the result.*

→ The New Right (i.e. 'supply side') policies advocated cutting unnecessary jobs in nationalised industries (which were then often privatised) and led to the collapse of many businesses and the loss of millions of jobs.

→ The Blair government has sought to (i) improve productivity through better training, (ii) increase access to work through schemes such as the New Deal and Welfare to Work, and (iii) attract jobs and businesses to the UK. Its big spending on public services has also increased numbers of jobs significantly.

## Health ●●●

Nowhere is the dilemma of how far the state or the individual is responsible for welfare sharper than in the area of health:

→ Aneurin Bevan, who introduced the NHS in 1948, resigned when the Attlee government introduced prescription charges – regarding the move as a betrayal.

→ The NHS has struggled to meet the rising costs of new hospitals, new equipment, new doctors and nurses and to pay for costly new drug therapies.

→ Many patients have opted for private care, sometimes funded by the NHS in private UK hospitals or hospitals overseas or sometimes funded privately through health insurance.

→ To speed up improvements *public private finance* (PPF or PPI) initiatives have seen the NHS lease back private sector funded equipment and premises.

> **Checkpoint 2**
>
> If the Thatcher government no longer emphasised controlling inflation, does this mean it no longer wished to achieve full employment?

> **Check the net**
>
> Look at the 10 Downing Street website and find out the current level of unemployment in the UK. In which regions of the UK is unemployment highest and lowest?

> **Example**
>
> According to the Office of the Deputy Prime Minister, the number of households in England will increase from 16 m in 1971 to a projected 24 m in 2021 with the number of *married couple* households expected to fall from 71% to 38% and *single person* households rising from 19% to 35%.

---

**Exam preparation**                                    answers: page 93

1   What are the main elements of the welfare state? Name two problems faced by the welfare state in the 21st century.   (5 minutes)

2   Examine the argument that the views of the New Right have been damaging to the welfare state.   (30 minutes)

# Answers
## Debates about public policy: decision making

## Political institutions at work in the UK

### Checkpoints

1 Which groups are *insiders* and *outsiders* depends on the party in power – during a Labour government, *trade unions* would be insider groups, while anti-hunt campaigners such as the *Countryside Alliance* would be an outsider group.

2 A local election is to fill one or more seats on a council; a by-election is an extra election to fill a vacancy if an MP or councillor dies or resigns.

3 A left-wing party may support nationalisation or other forms of public ownership, whereas a right wing party is likely to favour denationalisation or privatisation.

### Exam preparation

1 Parliament is responsible for (i) passing new legislation; (ii) agreeing tax levels and public expenditure; (iii) scrutinising government decisions and EU law, holding the government accountable for its actions; (iv) addressing the needs of citizens.

2 The power of a Prime Minister will depend on (i) his or her popularity with the nation at large – few people are willing to make trouble for a popular PM; (ii) the size of majority backing the PM in the House of Commons; (iii) the extent to which the PM's party is united in backing him or her; (iv) how far there is unity between those who oppose the PM.

3 The first-past-the-post system is used for Westminster and council elections; elections for the European Parliament, Scottish Parliament, Welsh Assembly and Northern Ireland Assembly are conducted by various forms of proportional representation (PR). PR aims to give a party with 25% of the votes 25% of the seats, which is seen as fair. By contrast, there is no guarantee of any proportionality between seats and votes when the first-past-the-post system is used; e.g. in Cumbria in 2001 Labour received 39% of votes and the Conservatives 40% but Labour was rewarded with 4 seats and the Conservatives only 2. Opponents of PR say coalitions are more likely to arise (e.g. Scottish Parliament) and that this undermines the single party basis of government which is valued in the UK.

## Europe, globalism and internationalism

### Checkpoints

1 Three other multinational companies are Prudential, HSBC and BP.

2 If a French exporter sells a €200 product to a UK firm when £1 = €2 the British firm will expect to pay £100 but if the exchange rate changes to £1 = €1 when it comes to pay, the British firm will have to pay £200.

3 One market for an estimated 500 million people will mean *economies of scale* can be achieved and the advantages of large-scale production achieved for businesses as long as communication and transport links are strong and reliable. One market will mean that no one buyer or seller will dominate the single market and therefore all participants should enjoy keen prices and the benefits of competition.

### Exam preparation

1 The main decision-making bodies of the EU are: (i) Council of Ministers – agrees legislation; (ii) Commission – develops and proposes new policies, implements decisions; (iii) European Court of Justice – adjudicates on possible breaches of EU law; (iv) European Parliament – democratic, consultative body which agrees budget and approves appointment of the Commission.

2 The difference between free trade and fair trade is that while free trade involves trade without tariffs, fair trade is about ensuring producers in LEDCs receive a fair return.

3 Globalism means little can happen in any part of the world without affecting other parts. Imports from countries with high inflation mean the price rises will also affect the UK when we buy their goods. Globalism also means countries do not have control over matters such as acid rain; it is caused in central Europe but can devastate forests in northern Europe, just as greenhouse gases caused in Asia can change water levels and climate many, many miles away.

4 To say that the UK gains nothing from EU membership is absurd since our trade with the EU would be much less if we were outside the tariff-free zone. Although the UK pays more money into the EU budget than it receives back, this is not surprising since the UK is one of the richest and largest countries (in terms of population) in the EU – so we should expect to pay more than poorer or smaller countries. To complain of this is to adopt a very short-term view. As these other countries become economically stronger they are likely to want to trade with the UK and this will be to our gain.

## Post-war Britain

### Checkpoint

1 The UK sought additional workers as post-war reconstruction got underway – many of the new arrivals took jobs as bus or train drivers or conductors or in the NHS or other public services. Many Commonwealth citizens came to the UK because they or their families had served in the armed forces during the Second World War.

### Exam preparation

1 The giant evils were ignorance, poverty, sickness, idleness and squalor.

2 Many people argued that it was a mistake to privatise the nationalised industries when they saw the accidents and poor timekeeping on the railways. It was generally agreed that the privatisation of British Rail, with different firms running trains on lines operated by Railtrack, was a recipe

for confusion. It was argued that even when they had been nationalised, there was insufficient modernisation. Those who favoured privatisation claimed state-run companies had no incentive to adopt the values of an 'enterprise ethic' and that the spur of competition would be good for them. In reality, since they existed to make profits for shareholders, they only invested in change when they absolutely had to – continuing the neglect of services (e.g. water) experienced in the public sector.

## The welfare state and its problems

### Checkpoints

1 Look at the following simplified example to understand how and why the proportion of retired people to working population matters. Pensions for retired people are funded in Week 2 from the national insurance contributions received from existing workers in Week 1. If the average pension is £100 and there are twice as many workers as pensioners, the average load on each worker is £50 per week; if this changes to a position where there are equal numbers of retired people and workers, then the average burden on each worker is £100.

2 The Thatcher government said full employment could not be achieved in the long term by subsidising jobs or creating unproductive jobs in industries which were not really needed. It thought that if inflation was low in the UK, our goods would be competitive with those from other countries and therefore demand would rise for good-value UK goods, ensuring there would be jobs for all as a result. Now, we understand that even when productivity is increased in the UK, other economies with lower labour costs (e.g. India) may still be able to undercut us.

### Exam preparation

1 The welfare state embraces health, housing, education, full employment and social security. (i) Some of the biggest problems are in health – shortage of doctors, hospitals and rising costs of treatments – leading to waiting lists and escalating budgets. Targets set to bring down waiting lists mean that often simple, easy, non-life-threatening conditions are treated before more serious, costly and lengthy cases. (ii) The second problem area is pensions – increased longevity means that as more of the population retire, this throws a greater burden on the remaining workforce which is smaller because of low birthrates.

2 Public services in the 1960s and 1970s were thought wasteful, ineffective and very bureaucratic, with officials working at their own speed and to their own satisfaction. The New Right wanted such services to be shaken up, made more accountable and to feel the disciplines of market forces. They wanted to see inputs and outputs measured so it could be seen just how productive the public sector was and Margaret Thatcher's view was clearly that *anything the public sector can do, the private sector can do better*. The New Right's approach meant that many hospitals no longer ran their own cleaning or laundry services and many other services were often outsourced too – admin, IT, personnel management, etc. The New Right encouraged the sale of council housing to tenants or private landlords and also saw greater private sector involvement as many schools or school services – e.g. catering or cleaning – were also outsourced. Putting welfare state services on a more businesslike basis is clearly desirable if the new arrangements actually work – however, many people fear such changes take away the public service ethic which was valued and used to exist in these services.

# Databank

**asylum seekers/economic migrants** – those fleeing from danger are asylum seekers, long welcomed by the UK; economic migrants are enterprising people who aim to move to countries such as the UK/USA to better themselves; they pay a lot of taxes and often add to the wealth/prosperity of the country in which they settle.

**costs/prices/profits** – costs include wages, electricity and raw materials used to make a product or create a service; profit is the difference between the price paid by the buyer and the costs met by the seller; generally, prices reflect the equilibrium of demand and supply.

**demand/supply** – demand is the amount of a good or service which will be purchased over a given period at a particular price (if price goes up, generally demand will fall); supply is the amount of the good or service suppliers will bring to the market over a given period at a particular price (if price goes up, generally supply will rise).

**demand/cost inflation** – inflation is *rising prices*; if prices rise because of increased costs (e.g. wages, fuel, raw materials, rate of interest paid on borrowing), this is known as *cost* or *wage inflation*. If prices rise because of a scarcity of supply in relation to the quantities demanded, this will create an 'auction effect' known as *price* or *demand* inflation.

**European Union** – in May 2004 the 15 member countries (Austria, Belgium, Denmark, Finland, France, Germany, Greece, Ireland, Italy, Luxembourg, Netherlands, Portugal, Spain, Sweden, UK) were joined by a further 10 (Cyprus, Czech Republic, Estonia, Hungary, Latvia, Lithuania, Malta, Poland, Slovakia, Slovenia).

**executive agencies** – bodies such as the Passport Agency or the Benefits Agency which carry out specific policies of government once agreed.

**Keynes, John Maynard** – economist who identified the importance of macroeconomic policies.

**market** – any area over which buyers and sellers are in communication.

**merger** – when two companies combine.

**monopoly** – when a good or service is available from one seller only; this may lead to prices being higher than they would be if competitors existed.

**multiplier** – idea introduced by Keynes suggesting that instead of cutting wages and prices at times of unemployment, the appropriate action was to stimulate aggregate demand through government spending – funded by borrowing if necessary; the multiplier is the number of times by which an increase in income exceeds the initial investment which caused it; thus, increasing government spending on roads, railways, benefits and public services is a good way to combat unemployment or an economic slump.

**New Right/individualism** – Thatcherite attitude to society which believed in individualism (i.e. people looking after themselves) and rejected the desirability of a large public sector in favour of market forces.

**single market** – market of 25 EU countries within which people from member countries can travel, work and trade as they wish without tariff barriers.

**trade union** – organisations which campaign to improve rights, pay and conditions enjoyed by workers.

**wages/labour costs** – a worker's weekly wage tells us she or he is paid, say, £200 before tax; if the worker produces 400 units per week, labour cost per unit is 50p; higher wages can be justified if productivity rises.

# Revision checklist
*helps you check what you still need to do*

## By the end of this chapter you should be able to:

| | | | |
|---|---|---|---|
| 1 | Use all the information in Databank, above, with confidence | Confident | Not confident. **Revise** page 84 |
| 2 | Explain the relationships between the work of the Prime Minister, Government and Parliament | Confident | Not confident. **Revise** pages 84, 85, 92 |
| 3 | Show how the institutions of government relate to the processes of politics | Confident | Not confident. **Revise** pages 84, 85, 187, 198 |
| 4 | Consider the nature and impact of globalism and internationalism | Confident | Not confident. **Revise** pages 86, 87, 92, 187, 189 |
| 5 | Discuss the roles and purposes of the European Union | Confident | Not confident. **Revise** pages 86, 87 |
| 6 | Understand the debate about the future of Europe, i.e. Europe of Nations or United States of Europe | Confident | Not confident. **Revise** pages 86, 87 |
| 7 | Explain the changing economy in post-war Britain | Confident | Not confident. **Revise** pages 88, 89, 93 |
| 8 | Describe and explain the aspirations of the welfare state – slaying the *giant evils* of *poverty, idleness, sickness, ignorance* and *squalor* | Confident | Not confident. **Revise** pages 90, 93 |
| 9 | Identify the problems of welfare provision – cost, need, equity and choice | Confident | Not confident. **Revise** pages 90, 93 |

# Law, culture and ethics

When law and prevailing moral values are the same, society will work well, but when they drift apart, difficulties can arise. If a law is passed based on moral beliefs which are not widely shared, such laws will be *oppressive* to some individuals. Dissenters may be seen as deviants. *Do such people have the right to be different?* If one person's morals are not widely shared, does society have the right to designate the practice of their beliefs as a crime? Should *all* deviance be punishable? The passing of the Human Rights Act 1998 means that where UK law conflicts with declared rights, government and the courts have a dilemma to resolve.

When cases go to court, are we confident 'the system' ensures defendants are fairly treated – as we would wish to be treated if we were in such a position. And if people are guilty of breaking the law, what issues should be at the back of our minds when penalties are being decided?

## Exam themes

→ Law and morality
→ How should society respond to deviance?
→ Absolute and relative standards of morality
→ What is the rule of law?
→ Legal aid and equal access to justice
→ Judges and juries
→ What is a crime?
→ How should criminals be treated?
→ What rights do victims possess?

## Topic checklist

○ AS  ● A2

| | AQA A | AQA B | EDEXCEL | OCR |
|---|---|---|---|---|
| Morality, deviance and rights | ○● | ○● | ○● | ○● |
| Courts, justice and the rule of law | ○● | ○● | ○● | ○● |
| Crime and punishment | ○● | ○● | ○● | ○● |

# Morality, deviance and rights

### Example

Thomas Hobbes spoke of *a war of every man against every man.*

### Checkpoint 1

Apart from Hobbes, name one other theorist who supported the idea of a social contract as a basis for organising society.

### Example

Drinking alcohol is unacceptable in Saudi Arabia but perfectly acceptable in the UK; various religions emphasise particular and very different practices which are not shared by others – male or female circumcision, particular forms of dress, eating or not eating particular foods, different roles in society for men and women.

### Action point

If the law insists on sexual relations not starting before age 16, think about what practical steps can be taken if up to 40% of younger teenagers are already enjoying such relationships among themselves. Are such laws justifiable or enforceable?

*"There is no society known where . . . criminality is not found . . . No people exist whose morality is not daily infringed upon. We must therefore call crime necessary and declare that it cannot be non-existent, that the fundamental conditions of social organization . . . logically imply it."*

Emile Durkheim, *Suicide*

Human rights mean we cannot overlook the beliefs and wishes of minorities – to be deviant from mainstream values does not have to mean a person should be regarded as a criminal. Sometimes those from a particular religion pursue perfectly acceptable practices; but some beliefs held by others may be less acceptable – and it is the legislators who make the laws and the judges who enforce them who need to establish such boundaries.

### Why can't any individual do exactly as she or he pleases?

Without rules and rulers, society is disorderly. So the culture and ethics of a society – its values, beliefs and moral concerns – are quickly developed into moral codes which then become laws. Hobbes believed a *social contract* existed between society and rulers who ruled only as long as they could keep order. In that way, people can own property, buy and sell goods and run their lives on an organised basis, safe from the danger of robbery or attack.

## Morality

Make sure you understand the important distinctions which follow:

→ *Morality* is the moral code for a society, sometimes referred to as a *shared value system*. Some people see this as fixed and *absolute*, saying it is always wrong to break the moral code for a society, e.g. killing or eating people, stealing their property, taking drugs, sex before marriage.

→ Others see moral values in *relative* terms because they *differ* according to the country where you live or the religion to which you belong.

→ There is also debate about the changeability of moral codes *over time* – gay sex or cohabiting outside marriage happened in 19th century England but perhaps less frequently or less openly than now.

→ Channel 4 ran a series in 2003 about the sexual activities of up to 40% of 13–15-year-olds among themselves and argued that the age of consent should be reduced from 16 to 12.

→ It used to be an unwritten rule that husbands were older than wives but by 2004 24% of husbands were younger – sometimes by more than six years.

## Deviance

*Deviance* is the practice of not following the moral code of your society – breaking its *consensual rules* – sex is natural and healthy but not if one person forces themselves on another. In this example, breaking such rules would also mean you broke the law and could be accused of raping the other person – with the possibility of a long prison sentence if found guilty. Deviance does not always involve breaking the law and deviants do not need to be seen as criminals – for example, some people like swimming naked in the sea and on certain beaches this is accepted unless their actions threaten or harm society.

## Rights

→ *Rights* exist for citizens in every country. Some people speak of *natural rights* in which we all treat each other as we would ourselves wish to be treated – in this sense, rights are an extension of *conscience*.

→ We all have *legal* rights – e.g. to own property and *universal* rights as human beings. In the UK the rights stated in the European Convention on Human Rights have largely been incorporated into the Human Rights Act 1998.

→ In a multicultural society, where people from different religions and cultures live in close proximity, statements of *human rights* help to define where or when the law will or will not require particular uniform behaviour.

## Law and morality

Law becomes oppressive if it sets in stone moral values which are no longer widely shared. From time to time Parliament recognises the need to address issues which have previously been taken for granted. In the 1960s, Parliament saw it was time to introduce new *conscience* legislation, removing criminality from suicide (but not euthanasia) and gay sex, widening the availability of divorce and abortion.

### Do *right* and *wrong* represent an absolute or relative standard?

→ Murder is seen as wrong in all countries – here moral codes and national laws exactly overlap – though the issue becomes blurred when the legalisation of euthanasia in some countries enters the discussion.

→ But there are many other instances of some practices being seen as unlawful in one country and acceptable in others: think of issues such as abortion and divorce and you will find widespread differences between different religions and different countries.

→ Differences also occur in our responses to crime – in the UK we think it wrong to subject those found guilty to amputation of limbs or corporal punishment or capital punishment, yet amputation occurs in some countries, corporal punishment is considered right in Malaysia and Singapore and capital punishment is used in the USA and China.

→ There is clearly no worldwide view of right and wrong, so there cannot be an absolute standard.

**Action point**

Have a look at the rights set out in the Human Rights Act and consider how an individual who feels she or he is being denied such rights could remedy the position.

**Examiner's secrets**

Always be as specific as possible – if you are going to talk about topics such as abortion or divorce, try to quote the legislation – Abortion Act 1967 and Divorce Reform Act 1969.

**Link**

See also page 195: How and when should people be punished?

**Checkpoint 2**

Explain the difference between an absolute and a relative moral standard.

**Watch out!**

Don't confuse corporal and capital punishment: corporal punishment is a sentence of caning (or something similar), capital punishment involves a death sentence – hanging, lethal injection or death in an electric chair.

---

**Exam preparation**                               answers: page 102

1   Why is it not possible for the same laws and punishments to apply in every country?   (5 minutes)

2   How do we gain an understanding of the moral values of our society?
                                                        (5 minutes)

3   How far do you agree that people should not be punished if they commit an offence with good motives or for reasons of conscience?   (30 minutes)

# Courts, justice and the rule of law

The rule of law means that no one is above or beyond the law and all of society is regulated by laws. Courts exist to decide innocence or guilt and determine appropriate penalties for offenders irrespective of whether they are the richest or poorest in the land. Some people believe that, although justice is said to be impartial, the rich get better treatment than the poor.

## The rule of law ●●●

The law applies to everyone and it comes from a variety of sources, such as:

1 Laws approved by Parliament, which have been given the Royal Assent.
2 European laws, which take precedence over UK law if there is a conflict.
3 Common law, which has grown up since the Norman Conquest.
4 Case law, based on precedent.
5 Statutory interpretation – delegated legislation.

### Civil law and criminal law
There are two types of law:

→ *Criminal* laws (leading to fines, prison or other punishments). After investigations by the police, it is the Crown Prosecution Service (CPS) which decides whether there is enough evidence to bring criminal charges.
→ *Civil* laws (action taken by an individual to determine responsibilities or obtain damages). Civil law usually involves breaches of contract, tort, family law, employment law or company law.

### What is justice: civil litigation or regulation?
→ Greater use of civil litigation arose as a result of the 1980s New Right agenda to reduce regulation – e.g. allowing firms to self-certify they had complied with safety rules, knowing they would have to pay heavy compensation later if their self-certification proved inadequate.
→ Civil cases sometimes involve victims of smoking-related diseases sueing manufacturers for not warning them about the dangers of smoking. In future if we find that GM foods or mobile phone masts or beefburgers present long-term health dangers, people may bring civil cases against those responsible.

*Is this justice – or would we be better off denying choice and insisting that all foods or technology should be banned until we can be 100% sure they are safe?*

### A day in court
We need to understand the key roles of different people in a court:

→ *Solicitors* work mostly in private practice, write wills, organise the sale of properties from one person to another, brief barristers to represent clients in serious cases and themselves appear in lower courts.
→ *Barristers* are specialist advocates who appear as prosecution or defence lawyers generally in the Crown Court and higher courts. They give written opinions of law and may draft specialist documents.

---

**Check the net**

Use the search engine on your computer to find one clear example of a law from each type of source.

---

**Checkpoint 1**

Which of the following would involve civil law and which criminal law: (i) cutting the parachute of a sky diver causing her death; (ii) breaking the windows of a shop selling animal-fur coats; (iii) next door neighbours arguing about the boundary between their properties?

---

**Checkpoint 2**

Is civil legal liability a reasonable alternative to regulation?

---

*Magistrates and Judges* preside over courts. They include:

→ *Lay magistrates*, who serve part-time, have local knowledge, receive some training but are not legally qualified. They can be criticised as being middle class and middle aged, having little understanding of young people, the working class or ethnic minorities. Some people claim they are biased against the accused and pay too much attention to their legally qualified clerk.

→ *District judges*, who do broadly the same work as lay magistrates in larger courts; they are legally qualified.

→ *Judges* in Crown Courts and higher courts are usually barristers with experience. They are often affluent, elderly, middle class, male, white and conservative. Judges now retire at 70, appointments are more open and of late more women and lawyers from ethnic minorities have become judges.

## Decisions of the courts    ●●●

→ Who wins a case is decided in most higher courts by a *jury* of 12 people selected randomly. Judges prefer juries to reach decisions unanimously but majority verdicts are allowed if the split of opinion is 10–2 or 11–1.

→ The Blair government's attempts to reduce the role of juries have run into considerable resistance from Parliament and also public opinion.

→ Courts decide not only which side wins but also they evaluate motives or circumstances; e.g. if a person dies, did the accused intend them to die, did the accused contribute to the reasons for their death or was the presence of the accused at the death entirely unrelated or accidental?

→ Partly because (i) DNA techniques and medical science have improved and (ii) some expert witnesses 'got it wrong' and (iii) because of police over-enthusiasm to get a conviction, which later proved to be unjustified, many *miscarriages of justice* have been brought to light and innocent people released after years of wrongful incarceration.

## Is there equal access to justice?    ●●●

Help to meet legal costs has been much restricted with severe means testing, which arguably denies justice to everyone except those far below any known poverty line or those in the millionaire class. A Legal Services Commission (LSC) runs two schemes – the Community Legal Service for civil cases and the Criminal Defence Service which provides advice and representation for people on criminal charges. Personal injury claims are now not funded and must be pursued under *no win, no fee* agreements. Even where cases are funded by the LSC, the best barristers are often not used because they are the most expensive.

**Checkpoint 3**

Identify two similarities and two differences between solicitors and barristers.

**Checkpoint 4**

Do you think magistrates find 75% of accused people guilty because they *are* guilty or because of some bias in the system?

**Checkpoint 5**

Give two reasons why the Blair government wanted to replace juries with judges.

**Example**

The wrongful conviction (and subsequent release) of Sally Clark for murdering her two young sons.

**Check the net**

Have a look at the Legal Services Commission website and see whether you think the 'rules' are fair or restrictive – http://www.legalservices.gov.uk/.

**Action point**

Think about adverts you have seen on television offering cash payouts to accident victims – what benefits and what dangers can you see in such a system?

**Exam preparation**                        answers: pages 102–103

1   Is the distinction between barristers and solicitors justifiable?   (5 minutes)

2   Identify one reason for supporting 'no win, no fee' agreements and one reason for opposing such arrangements.   (5 minutes)

3   How far do you agree that everyone receives justice in the UK?   (30 minutes)

# Crime and punishment

What is crime? How can we reduce crime? How should we treat those found guilty of committing crime? Is sending people to prison an appropriate solution?

## Patterns of crime ●●●

*Social Trends* (33) reported thus:

→ *Crime rates.* In 2001/02, 5.5 million crimes were recorded by the police in England and Wales, 7% more than in the previous year. About 60% of these crimes involved burglary, theft or handling stolen goods, nearly a third of which involved thefts of or from vehicles.

→ *Offenders.* In 2001, 467 000 people were cautioned for, or found guilty of, an indictable offence in England and Wales, 8 000 fewer than in 2000.

  → Men commit more crimes than women. In 2001, 167 per 10 000 men were found guilty of, or cautioned for, an indictable offence, compared with a rate of 37 per 10 000 women.

  → The peak ages for offending were 18 for males and 15 for females. A small number of offenders are responsible for a high number of offences. Often, offending patterns of behaviour are established at an early age.

→ *Victims* Some individuals and households are more at risk than others of being on the receiving end of crime: 28% of those questioned by the British Crime Survey in 2001/02 said they had been the victim of a crime in the previous year. The most at risk group was aged between 16 and 24, who were six times more likely to suffer some sort of vehicle theft, and four times more likely to fall victim to burglary, than those aged 75 and over. The type of housing in which people live can affect their likelihood of experiencing burglary. The risk of private renters being burgled is twice that of owner-occupiers.

→ *Police and court action.* In 2001, 323 000 people were sentenced for indictable offences in England and Wales. Those sentenced for motoring offences were the most likely to be fined (46%).

→ By 2004, the prison population figure had risen to 75 000, of whom 80% were adult males, 14% were young male offenders, 5.3% were adult female offenders and 0.7% were young female offenders.

→ *Resources.* Police officer numbers in England and Wales reached record levels with 129 603 officers in March 2002. This was the largest increase for 26 years – nearly 4 000 officers up on 2001.

## Does prison work? What are the alternatives to custody? ●●●

Prison undoubtedly works to some extent – by locking up the most dangerous convicted people, society is protected from them. However, many prisoners soon return, suggesting that any training given to inmates is not sufficient to change their behaviour once released. It could be argued that more intensive and better education and training should be given – literacy levels among prisoners are low and many

**Check the net**

Look at the Office for National Statistics website to find the latest information published on crime – http://www.statistics.gov.uk.

**Checkpoint 1**

Suggest two reasons why young people are more likely to be victims of crime than older people.

**Checkpoint 2**

What is an indictable offence? Give an example.

**Example**

In England and Wales the overall *detection rate* for crimes recorded by the police in 2001/02 was 23% – the 94% clear-up rate for drug offences may reflect on the proportion of such offences which are reported; for violence against the person, rape and forgery/fraud, the detection rates were 58%, 42% and 28%; for most other crimes the detection rates were below 18%.

**Check the net**

Look at the Prison Service website to see how many people are in prison today – http://www.hmprisonservice.gov.uk/statistics.

**Check the net**

Look at the reports of HM Chief Inspector of Prisons at http://www.homeoffice.gov.uk to see the criticisms made of inadequate training given to prisoners to give them better life skills to succeed outside prison.

prisoners learn more about committing crime than reading, writing or job skills. Changing a prisoner's habits requires professional inputs, e.g. challenging counselling, as at HMP Grendon. In recent years, the treatment of young offenders has changed, with many new non-custodial orders being introduced, such as supervision orders and anti-social behaviour orders.

## If you commit crime . . .

→ Some people recommend longer and harsher sentences to deter crime, but if those responsible for 77% of crimes are never apprehended, they are never likely to be punished unless detection rates can be greatly improved!

→ To get people to abandon crime, we must focus on the behaviour rather than possible punishments. *Empathetic* techniques, getting a person to think themselves into someone else's position, can change behaviour.

## Why do criminals commit crime? ●●●

→ Different law-breaking is explained in different ways. The motives of speeding motorists and the reasons for their offending behaviour will, in many cases, be different from those who steal other people's property, engage in violence or use drugs or commit sex offences.

→ Some crime may be justified in the minds of those who commit it by relative poverty and the culture of crime.

→ If law enforcement is thought weak and there is little or no police presence, wrongdoers may think they are in little danger of being caught.

→ Punishment may be for revenge or retribution, deterrence or reformation.

### Victims and offenders

In some countries, decisions about the punishment are largely in the hands of a victim. Although some victims focus mainly on retribution, some want to help the wrongdoer be rehabilitated. Where offenders meet victims this can have a big effect, causing them to avoid future wrongdoing. Victims can be compensated in the UK via the Criminal Injuries Compensation Authority.

answers: page 103

### Exam preparation

1 Explain the difference between deterrence and retribution. (5 minutes)

2 Give two reasons why rehabilitation may be the most effective strategy for dealing with criminal behaviour. (15 minutes)

3 How far do you agree that UK law pays insufficient attention to the needs of victims? (30 minutes)

---

**Example**

Where inmates must be serving a sentence that will allow a stay of at least 24 months; prisoners have to choose to go to Grendon themselves, they must have a genuine desire to change and to work at changing, and they must also be committed to staying free from drugs while in therapy.

**Checkpoint 3**

What are anti-social behaviour orders? Explain how they work.

**Jargon**

*Revenge or retribution* is punishment for its own sake. *Deterrence* aims to deter the individual from repeating her or his offence or setting an example to others so they will not suffer the kind of penalty imposed on wrongdoers. *Reformation or rehabilitation* helps a wrongdoer avoid crime in future, teaching them to read and write or how to get and keep a job.

*"There is one, and only one, thing in modern society more hideous than crime — namely, repressive justice."*

Simone Weil, *Human Personality*

**Check the net**

For up-to-date information on the ways victims can be compensated, see the Criminal Injuries Compensation Authority website at http://www.cica.gov.uk.

# Answers
## Law, culture and ethics

### Morality, deviance and rights

#### Checkpoints

1 John Locke or Jean-Jacques Rousseau.
2 An absolute standard applies in all circumstances, whereas a relative moral standard probably differs between cultures or is modified over time.

#### Exam preparation

1 Laws need to reflect moral values in societies. If moral values differ, laws cannot be the same. In Western countries, noted for their tolerant attitudes, laws criminalising adultery or drinking alcohol would be seen as a breach of human rights. Elsewhere, such laws might fit well with moral values and be acceptable to the population.

2 We gain an understanding of the moral values of our society at home from our families, at school from learning about RE, PSHE and Citizenship, at church and from media programmes or publications. Moral values will be reflected in how we treat others and how we expect them to treat us.

3 The doctrine of the *rule of law* expects the law to apply to everyone on all occasions and in all circumstances. If circumstances arise which cause someone to break the law – a life or death car journey to take a sick person to hospital – the driver will still be guilty of breaking the law if charged, though she or he may have mitigation to put forward when punishment is being decided. Arguments supporting theft of food by a hungry person are much weaker – we live in a welfare state and there is no reason for people to have to steal to be fed; citizenship is partly about teaching people how to obtain rights and benefits.

   Those who justify lawbreaking sometimes speak as though theft from Tesco's is a victim-less crime. Shoplifting is morally wrong, can erode profits for companies and may cause job cuts and lesser dividends for shareholders who may need the income to sustain their own lives. Sometimes people break the law as civil disobedience. The suffragettes did this to gain votes for women in the early 1900s; similar direct action was undertaken by poll tax protesters who refused to pay the poll tax, and those opposing the construction of new airport runways or motorways. We may understand such reasons – but people have still broken the law and there is no reason why they should not be punished for doing so. Having a *good reason* does not provide an excuse.

### Courts, justice and the rule of law

#### Checkpoints

1 (i) Cutting the parachute of a sky diver, causing her death, would be murder – **criminal** case; (ii) breaking the windows of a shop selling animal-fur coats would be a **civil** case since the shopowner would be seeking compensation – unless there were also **criminal** charges of criminal damage – could therefore involve two cases;

(iii) next door neighbours arguing about the boundary between their properties is a **civil** case.

2 If a firm certifies that it followed all safety procedures in relation to its work – e.g. maintaining railway tracks and signalling – but then an accident occurs as a result of some of that work proving defective then civil litigation will not bring back to life any people who are killed or reduce the pain or suffering of bereaved relatives or those who experience injury; any financial penalty imposed on the company may not hit them particularly hard either if they have taken the precaution of insuring themselves against such claims. Before 1979, a different culture applied in which the work of many contractors was checked by others.

3 Solicitors and barristers are legally qualified and both have the right to become a judge – though it is less usual for a solicitor to do so. Normally solicitors interface with individual clients whereas barristers are introduced to a case and a client by a solicitor, rather than initial direct contact. Barristers belong to, and are regulated by, Inns of Court and solicitors by the Law Society.

4 Some people found guilty by magistrates may not be represented by a solicitor. It is often suggested that middle-class magistrates are unfairly biased against young or working-class defendants because they do not understand the values of their youth or working-class culture.

5 The government seems to believe that juries may acquit defendants (i) even if they believe them to be guilty if they disapprove of the law they are charged with breaking or (ii) if the matters they are asked to determine are extremely complex and perhaps beyond their understanding – as in serious fraud cases.

#### Exam preparation

1 Some solicitors never appear in court; others spend most of their time appearing in court, and the same is true of some barristers. Solicitors spend much time giving advice to their clients and barristers spend a lot of time writing legal opinions requested by solicitors. Previously solicitors could not become judges but this is now possible, though it occurs relatively rarely. If there was a single unified profession, different members would specialise, as now. But, if the two roles remained separate it would be true to say that solicitor partnerships provide a good generalist legal advice and practice system for clients, while it is generally barristers who appear in higher courts and interpret more complex areas of law and precedent.

2 FOR: 'No win, no fee' agreements mean that a complainant can take a case to court without any burden on the taxpayer or the legal aid scheme since the legal firm doing the work will probably not take the case unless there is a good chance of success, in which case it will be awarded costs. AGAINST: Because a complainant has nothing to lose, they may exaggerate the details of a claim and cause expense to the person or firm being claimed against.

3 It is true that the rule of law applies to all and it is true that if we are caught speeding, a speed camera will pick

up any speeding vehicle no matter who is driving it. But many victims of crime feel they have not received justice because such a small proportion of crimes are ever solved and, often, offenders are neither identified nor convicted and punished. Justice is available to all in the sense that all who are charged experience the same judicial process, whether they are a Lord Archer or a Jonathan Aitken or a common thief, and those found guilty can appeal against the verdict or sentence or both. Unfortunately, many miscarriages of justice arise because people are not adequately defended when their case is first heard. In civil matters it is much more difficult to see how justice can be available to all since the costs are prohibitive and legal aid is available only to the very, very poor. Apart from millionaires, who can afford to bring or defend cases, justice is available to others only if they take out legal expenses insurance.

## Crime and punishment

### Checkpoints

1 Those aged between 16 and 24 are likely to suffer some sort of vehicle theft – either losing goods from within a vehicle or the vehicle itself – perhaps because they are about more than older cohorts of drivers and if their vehicles are older they may be easier to break into. Since rented property occupiers are more likely to experience burglary than owner-occupiers, 16–24s are vulnerable because those who do not live with their parents will probably be renting. Youngsters who go out and about to football matches or clubbing may be more exposed to violence than those who pursue more sedate pastimes.

2 An indictable offence is an offence which can only be tried at a Crown Court, e.g. rape.

3 ASBOs were introduced by the Crime and Disorder Act 1998. They are civil orders designed to protect the public from anti-social behaviour. They are not designed as a punishment for the offender. ASBOs involve local people in the collection of evidence and in helping to enforce breaches. Anti-social behaviour is classed as *behaviour which causes or is likely to cause harassment, alarm or distress to one or more people not in the same household as the perpetrator*. Orders can be made against anyone over the age of 10.

### Exam preparation

1 Retribution and deterrence both involve punishing a person, but the reasons for doing so differ – someone supporting *retribution* probably believes a wrongdoer should be punished simply because he has done wrong, whereas someone thinking in terms of *deterrence* wants to make an example of the wrongdoer so neither the wrongdoer nor anyone else who becomes aware of her or his punishment will dare commit the same offence in future.

2 (i) Simply overcoming a drug addiction may be enough if the need to steal to get money to buy drugs is no longer there – but the offender may not gain a job, unless they have been taught to read and write.
(ii) To hold down a job, an offender may need to gain or update skills to do things for which an employer would wish to pay them. A prison sentence can provide a chance to gain skills unless the prisoner is simply locked up in a cell learning nothing.

3 In some Middle East countries, whether an offender is executed or has limbs amputated is decided by the victim. In some Western countries, victims have the right to address a court before sentence. The UK does not go as far as these countries, though some victims believe we should. There is no greater need for victims than for the person who victimised them to be caught and punished – this can be seen as an act of closure, especially in cases where the offender meets the victim to apologise to her or him. The argument against major involvement of victims in determining sentences is that victims are not impartial – and the impartiality of the justice people receive is a major feature of the UK judicial system. Some victims might be too forgiving; some may be too vengeful.

# Databank

**ABSO** – anti-social behaviour orders were established by the Crime and Disorder Act 1998. They are civil orders which aim to protect the public from anti-social behaviour.

**British Crime Survey** – annual survey of crime based on a survey of public opinion rather than crimes reported to the police; suggests much crime is never reported.

**conscience** – when Parliament discusses moral issues, such as suicide, MPs are allowed to vote freely, without instructions from their party, because it is thought wrong to make them go against their moral values; but the rest of us are expected to obey laws – disagreeing with a law is no reason or excuse for disobeying it.

**deterrence/rehabilitation/retribution** – different approaches to **punishment**; a **deterrent** is designed to put the offender off future offending and to set an example to others – yet if those guilty of about 80% of offences are never caught, many criminals may feel there is a good chance they will therefore avoid punishment. **Rehabilitation** is giving convicted people training – reading, writing, job skills, get them off drugs – so they have a better chance of being law-abiding in future. **Retribution** is punishment for its own sake – the price offenders must pay for breaking society's rules.

**deviance** – deviating from normal moral values; no law says young men cannot marry much older women but 50 years ago this was seen by some as deviant because it was very unusual; today it is seen as less unusual and is probably no longer an example of deviance.

**euthanasia** – significant numbers of terminally ill people seek help from friends and family to end their lives – yet to give such help is against the law. A case which attracted publicity was that of Diane Pretty, who suffered from motor neurone disease; the European Court of Human Rights ruled that her husband could not be given immunity from prosecution if he helped to kill her. However, in 2003 three members of a House of Lords committee that agreed on a complete ban on euthanasia 10 years ago have changed their views and now support the right for a patient, terminally ill and close to death, to be helped to die, if they are mentally competent. **This is a good example of how moral values change.**

**Human Rights Act 1998** – a UK law which means people can seek the rights given by the European Convention on Human Rights in UK courts rather than having to go to the European Court of Human Rights in Strasbourg.

**mitigation** – reasons offered in a court as to why the behaviour of a guilty person should be treated leniently.

**no win, no fee** – legal aid is no longer available if we wish to win compensation for accidents, etc. We are now expected to enter *conditional fee agreements* with solicors, who help us take such cases through the civil courts – if the claim is unsuccessful, the litigant will not be charged a fee by the solicitor; the alternative is to buy legal expenses insurance so we can bring a claim and the costs will be met by the assurance company.

**secular** – non-religious; for example, in countries such as France it is becoming less acceptable for people to adopt the distinctive dress of a particular religion because of the secular nature of the French state; in the UK, which has an established religion, we do not try to prevent people from wearing particular dress, e.g. a turban.

**Supreme Court** – In 2004 the government proposed that the House of Lords should no longer form the most senior court in the country and that their judicial powers should pass to a new Supreme Court.

# Revision checklist
*helps you check what you still need to do*

## By the end of this chapter you should be able to:

| | | | |
|---|---|---|---|
| 1 | Use all the information in Databank, above, with confidence | Confident | Not confident. **Revise** page 104 |
| 2 | Explain the differences between law and morality | Confident | Not confident. **Revise** pages 96, 97, 102, 195 |
| 3 | Show how society does or should (in your view) respond to deviance | Confident | Not confident. **Revise** pages 96, 195 |
| 4 | Consider the difference between absolute and relative standards of morality | Confident | Not confident. **Revise** page 97 |
| 5 | Understand the nature and implications of the rule of law | Confident | Not confident. **Revise** pages 98, 99, 102, 103 |
| 6 | Consider how legal aid operates and how far access to justice in the UK is genuinely equal | Confident | Not confident. **Revise** pages 99, 102 |
| 7 | Explain the roles of judges and juries | Confident | Not confident. **Revise** pages 99, 102 |
| 8 | Describe the nature of crime, including the patterns of offences and offenders | Confident | Not confident. **Revise** pages 100, 103 |
| 9 | Examine the ways in which criminals are or should (in your view) be treated | Confident | Not confident. **Revise** pages 100, 101, 103, 195 |
| 10 | Consider the perspectives and rights of victims | Confident | Not confident. **Revise** pages 101, 103 |

# Objectivity in the social sciences 1: society and application of number

*Is social science any more than people's opinions dressed up as science?* We partly answered this question in *Social and natural sciences – differences in issues and methodologies*.

But this section goes further in exploring three things:

1 How does society change – particularly, where we live and work and the significance of changing patterns of family life?

2 In reaching conclusions, what is the relative importance of facts, opinions and beliefs?

3 What sorts of insights can *application of number* add to our understandings?

By the end of this section you should feel more confident about how social scientists examine information, analyse it and reach conclusions.

## Exam themes

→ Commuting and congestion

→ Migration patterns

→ Social mobility

→ Changing patterns of work

→ Social engineering, equality and inequality

→ Declining birth and marriage rates

→ Increasing divorce and longevity

→ Thinking and analytical skills – facts, opinions and belief

→ Application of number and the social sciences:

   – addition and subtraction, multiplication and division

   – percentages, mean, median and mode

## Topic checklist

| ○ AS ● A2 | AQA A | AQA B | EDEXCEL | OCR |
| --- | --- | --- | --- | --- |
| The mobile society | ○● | ○● | ○● | ○● |
| Pressures for social change | ○● | ○● | ○● | ○● |
| The changing family | ○● | ○● | ○● | ○● |

# The mobile society

In the modern world, people are as likely to commute across the Channel or across the Atlantic to work as they are to live and work in the same town all their lives. Not only do more people now commute further to work but some people also move with their families from one country to another to achieve the lifestyles they desire.

## Patterns of commuting

→ In the 21st century, even with all the new electronic communications, high-income earners make 10 or 12 times as many business trips and 5 times as many commuting trips as low-income earners.

*Passenger transport, by mode*

| Great Britain | | | Billion passenger kilometres | | | |
|---|---|---|---|---|---|---|
| | 1961 | 1971 | 1981 | 1991 | 1996 | 2001 |
| Cars, vans & taxis | 157 | 313 | 394 | 582 | 606 | 624 |
| Bus & coach | 76 | 60 | 48 | 44 | 44 | 46 |
| Motorcycle/bicycle | 22 | 8 | 15 | 11 | 8 | 9 |
| Rail | 39 | 35 | 34 | 39 | 39 | 47 |
| Air | 1 | 2 | 3 | 5 | 6 | 8 |
| **All types of travel** | **295** | **419** | **495** | **681** | **703** | **734** |

*Social Trends*, 33.
Crown copyright material is reproduced with the permission of the Controller of HMSO.

→ If asked to identify the main changes in transport patterns between 1961 and 2001, what would you say? Could you give any possible reasons to explain the changes you noticed? Were these the changes and reasons you came up with?

| *Change* | *Reason* |
|---|---|
| Big rise in cars, vans and taxis | Increase in number of commuter and other journeys |
| Decline in bus, coach and cycle journeys | Fewer services in many areas as more people now own cars and travel greater distances |
| Slow increase in rail travel | Congestion on roads makes rail an attractive option where convenient services exist |
| Slow but steady increase in air travel | More regional services now offer competitively priced travel for business users |

## Commuting and congestion

→ Between 1999 and 2001 27% of all car journeys and 33% of bus, coach and rail journeys by males were commuting between home and work or journeys for business; the figures for women are 15% and 26%. Such commuting – and related tasks such as dropping off and collecting children before or after work – has led to a significant increase in congestion.

---

**Examiner's secrets**

Make sure you can differentiate between a *fact* (verifiable objective statement), a *belief* (may or may not be true but believed to be true, even without empirical evidence) and an *opinion* (subjective statement giving a view which may (not) be supported by evidence), and recognise facts, opinions or beliefs as you see them.

**Checkpoint 1**

In which type of travel was the percentage change greatest? What does this show us about the significance of percentages?

**Example**

In 2003, London (where the journey time to work averaged 40 mins for men and 35 mins for women) introduced a congestion charge of £5 for each vehicle entering a central area – encouraging more commuters to share cars or use public transport; other cities are now expected to adopt this approach.

→ Elsewhere commuter journey times were lower, though averages may be misleading since a few people may travel hundreds of miles while many others may travel less than a mile.

→ How should transport improvements be funded?
*Should* vehicle licenses be abolished and extra tax placed on fuel so people pay according to the mileage travelled?
*Should* all tax from vehicles or fuel be spent only on transport improvements?
*Should* more private motorways (e.g. M6 Toll) be constructed to relieve pressure on existing main routes with payments by motorists to private developers?
*Should* government keep the country moving by funding new roads from taxation or government borrowing without imposing additional tolls?

## Migration patterns ●●●

→ There is growing understanding in the UK of the view expressed by Lord Skidelsky that, on the whole, immigrants are good for countries – they jolt them up, introduce new skills and do jobs others don't want to.

→ All EU citizens can travel freely between member countries and settle in any EU country. Any EU citizen from the other 24 countries can move to the UK, just as UK citizens don't need anyone's permission to move to Malta or Spain, France or Italy – though entitlements to benefits in the country people move to may be restricted initially.

→ Many people in less economically developed countries wish to live in the UK and the government has said a limited number of **economic migrants** will be welcomed to boost the working population.

→ In 2001, the UK came eighth for the number of asylum seekers received (1.5 per 1 000 population) compared to 3.7 for Austria, which was top of the table, and 0.2 for Spain and Italy, which came 13th and 14th.

Perhaps one day migration patterns will arouse less controversy – just as there is little comment if a family moves from Kent to Leeds or from York to Dorset.

**Checkpoint 2**

Identify an example of a fact and an opinion on this page.

**Examples**

Attempts to improve public transport have been successful (e.g. increased usage of buses in London) but slow to be implemented, as constructing or extending metro systems (as in Birmingham and Manchester) or improving rail links has proved to be slow, disruptive and expensive (e.g. West Coast route between London and Glasgow).

**Action point**

In December 2003, government adviser Professor David Begg suggested that quite soon tolls of up to 16p a mile would be commonplace on UK roads – does current evidence back up this idea?

**Links**

See also Databank on page 94.

**Check the net**

A fuller breakdown of immigration and emigration can be found at http://www.statistics.gov.uk.

**Checkpoint 3**

The net inflow of migrants was 153 500 in 2002. What would the figure have been if the inflow and outflow of British citizens is excluded from the figures?

---

**Exam preparation**                              answers: page 112

1  Calculate the percentage increase in inflow of immigrants to the UK between 1996 and 2002 using the data included above.  (5 minutes)

2  Give and explain three reasons why the number of journeys travelled in the UK has increased from 295 billion passenger kilometres (bpk) in 1961 to 735 bpk.  (15 minutes)

3  Evaluate the view that 'the UK is a little island that is now full – we have no room for new arrivals, no matter how good their reasons for wanting to come' and point out alternative arguments which could lead to a different conclusion. You should indicate in your answer which view you believe to be the stronger.  (30 minutes)

# Pressures for social change

> *"Society is indeed a contract . . . it becomes a partnership not only between those who are living, but between those who are living, those who are dead and those who are to be born."*
>
> Edmund Burke, *Reflections on the Revolution in France*

21st-century Britain is socially divided, but there is evidence of social mobility – up and down. Work patterns are changing – few people taking a job at 20 feel it will be their *job for life*. As people achieve higher qualifications, people's goals broaden. There is less discrimination than previously, yet inequality may be greater

## Divided Britain

*The Observer* (23 November 2003, p. 7) highlighted the inequalities in modern Britain by dividing society into five groups:

→ *wealthy achievers* – 25% of population; £50 000 income with savings;
→ *urban prosperous* – 15% of population; e.g. single graduates with no mortgage;
→ *comfortably off* – 27% of population; middle income owner-occupiers;
→ *moderate means* – 15% of population; blue-collar, few savings, avoid debt;
→ *hard pressed* – 22% of population; generally in rented accommodation; many are single-parent families on tight budgets with few if any savings.

## Social mobility

Social mobility reflects the fortunes of different age and class groups. Measuring it helps us see how far we have progressed towards achieving equality of opportunity, social cohesion and inclusion.

→ Studies by Heath and Payne revealed that many fathers do see their sons in higher occupational classes than themselves – for example, while 12% of Class 3 fathers saw their sons in the same class as themselves, 48% now considered their sons to be in Class 1 or Class 2, yet others believe their sons are now located in a lower occupational class than themselves.
→ In 2001, the Performance and Innovation Unit pointed out that (i) earnings mobility in Britain has declined over the past 20–25 years and (ii) where sons get better jobs than their working-class fathers this seems to come from having achieved higher educational qualifications.

### Barriers to social mobility

The Performance and Innovation Unit mentioned the following barriers to social mobility: (i) educational attainment; (ii) childhood poverty and linked psychological and behavioural development; (iii) the family and the way they support the children – not just money but values that affect access to opportunities; (iv) attitudes, expectations and aspirations, including aversion to risk; (v) economic and other barriers by which some groups limit access to high status professions, such as law.

This suggests policy makers need to find ways to raise educational achievement, e.g. (i) tackling family poverty, (ii) raising expectations and aspirations, (iii) removing barriers to entry into high status jobs,

---

**Checkpoint 1**

Give a definition and an example of social mobility.

---

**Example**

Earnings mobility reflects the likelihood of a person getting a significant pay rise – it is suggested that workers are now less likely to get the big promotion or the giant leap forward in salary.

---

**Link**

See also page 203: Is the determination of youth to be different a true catalyst for change?

---

**Example**

DfES figures published in Nov 2003 show that while 48% of initial applicants aged 18–19 to degree courses in 2000 came from social classes 1, 2 and 3, only 18% of initial applicants from the same age group came from social classes 4, 5 and 6.

(iv) greater disclosure of firms' recruitment practices and (v) clearer progression routes to the top. The aversion to risk and the hatred of debt by working-class families were cited by opponents of top-up fees and loans for HE students (rather than grants) as being major flaws in policy if the government's goals to achieve equality of opportunity were to be realised.

## The moving workplace  ●●●

→ *Jobs for life* are a thing of the past. People now often work on short contracts, allowing them to gain experience and have career breaks as they wish.

→ Higher educational qualifications give people greater self-confidence to operate like this, either as employees or setting up their own business.

→ As the numbers employed in manufacturing and agriculture have declined in the UK, the service or tertiary sector has grown.

→ Many people now work in tourism or finance or help people access services through call centres (though UK firms such as HSBC and Prudential have decided to move their call centres overseas).

→ The European Union provides substantial subsidies to encourage the growth of new jobs in the UK in areas of high unemployment or where restructuring is needed, such as Wales, the north east and Cornwall.

→ In recent years the government has moved government agencies to all parts of the UK, so government-funded jobs are available in all regions, not just London.

## Equality and inequality  ●●●

→ Between 1971 and 2001, household weekly disposable incomes of £100, £240 and £310 rose to £150, £430 and £600 respectively.

→ Gender inequality is reducing slowly – women's pay is now about 80% of what men receive and more women are being appointed to senior positions, but the *glass ceiling* has not totally gone.

→ However, as direct tax rates (such as income tax) have declined and indirect tax rates (such as VAT) increased, the tax system has become less progressive and more regressive – leading to greater inequality.

→ During the early 1990s, the income distribution appeared to stabilise, but more recently there has been a further small increase in inequality.

→ *The Institute for Fiscal Studies* found that growth in self-employment and unemployment also led to increased inequality. But the growth in one-person households was a less important reason than labour market changes.

---

**Exam preparation**                              answers: pages 112–113

1 Give and explain one reason why further investment in the education system is desirable.  (5 minutes)

2 Give and explain three ways in which UK employment patterns have changed since the 1950s.  (15 minutes)

3 Evaluate the view that 'it is equality we want, not equality of opportunity'.
(30 minutes)

**Checkpoint 2**

Give three examples of service jobs.

**Checkpoint 3**

Why would the EU offer subsidies to remote regions in the UK?

**Example**

Include: Central Science Laboratory, York; Defence Evaluation and Research, Farnborough; Ordnance Survey, Southampton; DoE Buying Agency, Liverpool; Patent Office, Newport, Gwent; Driver and Vehicle Licensing Agency, Swansea; Child Support Agency, Dudley; Social Security Contributions, Newcastle-on-Tyne.

**Checkpoint 4**

Do these figures suggest inequality has increased or decreased?

**Check the net**

See the ONS website www.statistics.gov.uk to find details of pay levels for women and men.

**Checkpoint 5**

What is the difference between a direct and an indirect tax? Why is an increase in indirect taxation regressive rather than progressive?

**Checkpoint 6**

What is inflation? If inflation is 5% and a pay rise is 3% for some and 7% for others, is this good or bad? Why do we need to adjust for inflation when considering equality and inequality?

# The changing family

The structure of the family has changed and so has its function in society, as marriage has declined. More women now enjoy equality in the workplace, making parenthood less attractive than careers. While the birth rate falls, many children are brought up by working single parents, often in poor economic circumstances and quite often missing out on the socialisation the nuclear family used to provide.

## Extended, nuclear and fragmented families

The **extended** family of the 19th century (in which brothers, sisters, aunts, uncles, parents and grand-parents lived near to and supported each other) was largely replaced by the **nuclear** family in the 20th century. This **nuclear** family typically comprised a married mother and father and two dependent children; the children learned values and were socialised by the parents – often the nuclear family chose to move away from the larger family unit for work or choice. While men worked and earned money, many women stayed at home to look after the house and children, perhaps having a part-time job as the children grew older. As the 21st century neared, it was clear that the nuclear family was **fragmenting**; many marriages broke up, more people preferred cohabitation to marriage, the birth rate fell as more women focused on careers and single parenthood increased – though now the single parent had to work to support themselves and the children, thus providing less socialisation and support for the children.

## Marriage, divorce, remarriage, cohabitation and single parenthood

→ The types of families in which people live today are increasingly varied.

→ Some leave their parental home, form partnerships, marry, and have children.

→ But many will then experience separation, divorce, single parenthood and the formation of new partnerships, leading to new households and second families, which also quite often break down.

→ More people now spend time living alone, whether before or instead of marriage or cohabitation, or because of divorce or a failed relationship. Between 1971 and 2002, the number of one-person households rose from 18% to 29%, two-person units from 23% to 35%, but the numbers in all other household sizes fell from 50% to 37% and the average number of people per household declined from 2.9 to 2.4.

## Mean, median and mode

*Size of household, by frequency*

| Type | Frequency of households | Number of occupants |
| --- | --- | --- |
| 1 person | 20 | 20 |
| 2 person | 8 | 16 |
| 3 person | 8 | 24 |

**Link**

See also page 202: The relationship between science, equality and family values.

**Action point**

Talk to your friends and family. Look for examples among your own family or the families of your friends of extended, nuclear and fragmented families.

**Checkpoint 1**

Identify three differences between extended, nuclear and 21st-century families.

**Watch out!**

Often we can understand statistics best by using *mean, median* and *mode*. Are you clear on how **mean**, **median** and **mode** are calculated and why they are each important? See table opposite.

| Type | Frequency of households | Number of occupants |
|---|---|---|
| 4 person | 7 | 28 |
| 5 person | 4 | 20 |
| 6 person | 4 | 24 |
| 7 person | 4 | 28 |

1 To calculate the **mean** size of household in the table, divide the total number of people (160) by the total number of households (55), giving a mean of 2.9. *In this case this is reasonable but if there had been a very high value for one household type this could have given a misleading impression.*

2 To find the **median** size of household, place the seven different values in ascending order and select the middle value – the fourth – so there are three numbers higher and three lower: 4-4-4-7-8-8-20, so the middle value is therefore 7, telling us that the median size of household is 4 persons. *This avoids giving undue weight to a value which would distort the whole picture.*

3 The **mode** is the value which occurs most frequently. This is 4 (occurs three times and refers to 5-, 6- and 7-person families). *The frequency of values is very important in quality assurance activities where it is particularly helpful.*

## The family, work and society ●●●

→ Since 1961 the average age at which people first marry has increased from 25.6 for men and 23.1 for females to 30.5 and 28.2 respectively, suggesting people now see careers as more important than establishing families. As more women get full-time jobs, more men take on the roles of househusbands and child carers.

→ The number of marriages has gone from 408 000 in 1950, reaching a peak of 472 000 in 1972, to 306 000 first marriages and remarriages in 2000.

→ Following the Divorce Reform Act 1969, which introduced the single reason of *irretrievable breakdown*, the number of divorces went from a low of 30 000 in 1960 to a peak of about 180 000 in 1993 and 150 000 in 2000 – like marriage, divorce has recently declined, perhaps explaining the attraction of cohabitation, which doesn't usually come with an expensive ceremony.

**Watch out!**

Candidates sometimes think 'households' means 'houses'; this is a mistake – a household is a family unit – as more people live alone there are more single-person households and the average number of people in each household has dropped.

**Checkpoint 2**

Suggest a reason why the number of divorces dropped between 1993 and 2000.

**Watch out!**

Don't assume that because two sets of numbers correlate, there is a cause and effect relationship, e.g. the more oranges grown in an area, the fewer clothes people wear – the wearing of clothes and the number of oranges have nothing to do with each other – it is the variable of the climate and prevailing temperature which decides both!

**Example**

The trends outlined here have been accompanied by more deviant, antisocial or criminal behaviour by the young, many from fragmented families – the peak ages for offending in 2001 were 18 for males and 15 for females.

**Exam preparation**                    answers: page 113

1 Give an example of when it might be most useful to use a mean, a median or a mode. (5 minutes)

2 Why might some young people have been less successfully socialised in 2002 than earlier generations? (10 minutes)

3 Identify two facts and two opinions on this page and the immediately preceding page. (10 minutes)

4 How far do you agree that 'society changes because the family changes'? (30 minutes)

# Answers
## Objectivity in the social sciences 1: society

## The mobile society

### Checkpoints

1 The mode of travel in which the percentage change was greatest was air travel – going from 1 billion passenger kilometres (bpk) to 8bpk – a rise of 800% – even though the distances travelled in this way are still relatively small compared to the rise in travel by cars, vans and taxis, which rose by only about 400%. The percentage increase was greatest for air travel but the actual increase in bpks for cars, vans and taxis (from 157 to 624) was much greater.

2 Close to this checkpoint, we are given a **fact** that the London congestion charge is £5 for each vehicle entering a central area and the **opinion** that 'averages may be misleading since a few people may travel hundreds of miles while many others may travel less than a mile'.

3 90 400 more Britons left than arrived. If these movements are not counted, the inflow would have been 418 200 and the outflow 174 400, increasing the net inflow from 153 500 to 243 800 (418 200 – 174 400).

### Exam preparation

1 Increase in inflow is 195 000 from 317 800 in 1996 to 512 800 in 2002. The percentage is therefore found by calculating 195 000/317 800 × 100 = 61.36%.

2 Three reasons for the increase in travel could be (i) more people owning cars; (ii) greater wealth means more people travel more in their leisure activities; (iii) many more people live further from work and therefore commuting distances are greater.

### Examiner's secrets

Always check you calculate using data from the correct year – many candidates lose marks by using the wrong set of numbers when under pressure in the exam room.

3 It is true that the UK is more densely populated than other parts of Europe, though many areas within the UK still have very low populations. There is, however, no reason why more people could not come to live here so, strictly, it would be a mistake to say the UK is *full*. Many UK residents believe the reasons why people wish to come here are very important. People fleeing persecution have always been welcomed regardless of their ethnicity – e.g. those fleeing Robert Mugabe's dictatorship in Zimbabwe. The present age structure of our population also suggests the arrival of young economic migrants could be beneficial. The idea that the country is full can be a coded way of discriminating or showing opposition to the arrival of asylum seekers or economic migrants. *Whichever view you believe to be the stronger needs to be backed up by evidence and argument, not by assertion alone.*

## Pressures for social change

### Checkpoints

1 Social mobility involves an individual or family moving from one social class to another – a school groundsman who gets a degree, trains to become a teacher and perhaps a head teacher experiences upward social mobility; the sons of a judge who choose to work as farm labourers would be examples of downward social mobility.

2 Three examples of service jobs could be (i) working in a bank, (ii) working as a bus driver, (iii) working in a call centre.

3 The EU is committed to strengthening the economies of the more outlying parts of the EU and to encourage the people in those regions to take up the opportunities offered by EU programmes – this is an attempt to reverse depopulation in such areas, to discourage more and more people from moving to overcrowded towns.

4 The average income of low-paid people is now a quarter of that of high earners; previously the average income of the low paid was about a third of high earners – this suggests inequality has increased.

5 We pay a direct tax on income whereas an indirect tax is collected if we decide to spend our money – e.g. an airport tax if we decide to travel by air or an excise tax if we decide to buy a bottle of whisky. *Progressive* taxation means the higher the income, the greater the share of the income is paid in tax; regressive taxation is the reverse – if an airport tax of £20 is paid by someone earning £200 per week, it amounts to 10% of weekly income but for someone on £1 000 per week it will amount to only 2%. Those who want to achieve greater equality prefer direct to indirect taxes.

6 Inflation is simply *rising prices*. If inflation is 5% and a payrise is 3%, the real purchasing power of the individual has fallen by 2% (bad); when inflation is 5% and a payrise is 7%, the individual's purchasing power increases by 2% (good). If a highly paid person was given the 3% pay rise and a low-income person 7%, this could be justified as a way of reducing inequality.

### Exam preparation

1 Further investment in education is desirable to help more children achieve qualifications, thus making a real contribution to social mobility; educational attainment is the main reason for upward mobility.

2 Three ways in which UK employment patterns have changed since the 1950s could be that (i) people no longer expect to occupy one job for life; (ii) many more people now work in service industries and (iii) many fewer men and women now work in agriculture or manufacturing.

3 Those who believe in a meritocracy argue that there will always be some who turn out to be more hard-working or able than others. As long as everyone has an equal chance to gain the education and qualifications needed to get to

# and application of number

the top without race, gender or age discrimination, they argue that this is as far as society can be expected to go. But others feel equality should be our goal – we acknowledge that everyone has the same human and legal rights so is it fair that those with higher IQs or rich parents should have higher wages or better homes or more comfortable lifestyles? If government focused on equality rather than equality of opportunity, inheritance tax and other taxes on better-off people would have to be raised substantially. But meritocrats argue that such an approach would damage the country by killing off incentives.

## The changing family

### Checkpoints

1 Three differences between extended, nuclear and 21st-century families could be (i) in extended families a large number of family members live in close proximity – this is not as likely to be the case for the nuclear family or the 21st-century family; (ii) nuclear families involving a married mother and father and an average of two children perhaps living far from other family members differ from 21st-century families in which the birth rate is now much lower; (iii) in 21st-century families, 40% of children are born to unmarried parents and many children are brought up by single parents as a result of divorce.

2 The number of divorces may have dropped between 1993 and 2000 because the rate of marriages has fallen significantly since 1970.

### Exam preparation

1 If two groups of pupils take a test in a subject – say, General Studies – it is perfectly reasonable to compare the *mean* mark of the two groups. However, if the classes are of mixed abilities and one group has more high-ability children and the other more low-ability children, a *median* may be a good measure since it avoids the disproportionately high or low scores of the most or least able mean or a median or a mode. If we wish to compare an individual pupil's performance across a number of subjects, the *mode* may be useful. If one pupil has mostly A grades this would be shown up in contrast to a pupil who achieved mainly Es.

2 Fewer pupils are brought up in two-parent households and this may have a big impact on their socialisation – also many more mothers now work than previously so children may be more influenced by peers than parents.

3 (i) Two facts – from the 'Marriage, divorce, remarriage, cohabitation and single parenthood' section – 'more people now spend more time living alone' and 'the average number of people per household has declined from 2.9 to 2.4' – both based on research for *Social Trends*.
(ii) Two opinions – from 'The family, work and society' section – 'people now see careers as more important than establishing families' and 'perhaps explaining the attraction of cohabitation, which doesn't usually come with an expensive ceremony'.

4 This is a truly 'chicken and egg' type of proposition – as with many of the changes to society – declining marriage, more cohabitation, falling birthrate have arisen as more women have overcome the discrimination of the past and are now able to secure senior positions in employment – it could be that the family has changed because of such social changes but it could also be that society has had to adapt because of changes in the family – if there are no longer two parents at home to provide primary socialisation for the children then Citizenship needs to be added to the national curriculum. In recent years our very expectations for what a family is have changed, with many more children being brought up by single or gay parents – in this sense society has accommodated to the changes in the family.

# Databank

**commuting** – long distance travel to work; workers often wish to reside some distance from work and therefore may travel dozens or hundreds of miles per day or week by car, rail or air. Sometimes (e.g. if they work in London) they may commute because they cannot afford to pay typical housing costs in London. Many jobs are now seen as relatively short term (i.e. *not* jobs for life) so people do not see the need to move home when they move job.

**congestion** – traffic costs millions of pounds per week because it lengthens journey times for movement of freight and for workers if this involves travelling to meetings or to see clients.

**direct/indirect tax** – a direct tax is a tax levied on an individual or organisation (e.g. income tax) while an indirect tax is a tax on a good or service such as VAT on goods we purchase.

**Divorce Reform Act 1969** – made divorce easier to obtain and has led to an increase in remarriages, though a very high proportion of these appear to fail.

**glass ceiling** – the transparent barrier which seemed to keep most women in the lower levels of the promotion ladder in business and the professions; when *The Times* reported in December 2003 that Canon June Osborne had been appointed Dean of Salisbury to become the most senior woman in the Church of England, it did so with the headline: *Woman breaks Church's stained-glass ceiling*. Slowly the glass ceiling seems to be rising but the low numbers of women judges or company directors suggest that it has not gone completely.

**household** – family unit (nothing to do with houses); the average size of households has fallen in recent years.

**international division of labour** – increasingly raw materials are gathered in one part of the world, used in a manufacturing process elsewhere and sold in other areas – multinational companies locate manufacturing in low-cost areas but they can only do this in countries with economic and political stability and where the workforce has or can acquire the skills needed – e.g. the use of graduates in India to operate call centres previously operated in the UK by workers receiving very much higher rates of pay.

**location of industry** – since the 1930s the UK has tried to reverse the decline of areas with high unemployment by operating regional policies to move work to people rather than vice versa – such efforts have met only limited success and often depend on the proximity of the area to skilled labour, raw materials, markets and the adequacy of road or rail links. Improvements in technology make it much more possible for many government and commercial functions to be undertaken far away from London or other major centres.

**property-owning democracy** – the past 25 years have seen a major increase in property ownership – not just houses but also shares and financial products such as personal (or stakeholder) pensions and endowment policies.

**social economy** – there is growing interest in the development of cooperative networks; the social economy involves the participation of millions of members in (i) the Cooperative movement, (ii) the ownership of mutual building societies such as Nationwide or the Portman Building Society or (iii) mutual assurance companies such as Standard Life or (iv) involvement in share ownership schemes at big employers such as Waitrose and the John Lewis Partnership and (v) employee buyouts in many smaller businesses such as Loch Fyne Oyster Company.

# Revision checklist
*helps you check what you still need to do*

## By the end of this chapter you should be able to:

| | | | |
|---|---|---|---|
| 1 | Use all the information in Databank, above, with confidence | Confident | Not confident. **Revise** page 114 |
| 2 | Explain the causes of commuting and congestion | Confident | Not confident. **Revise** pages 106, 107 |
| 3 | Show how migration patterns of people from different countries have changed | Confident | Not confident. **Revise** page 107 |
| 4 | Consider the extent of social mobility in UK society | Confident | Not confident. **Revise** pages 108, 109, 112 |
| 5 | Understand the changing patterns of work in the UK | Confident | Not confident. **Revise** page 109 |
| 6 | Consider how far social engineering has (or has not) contributed to greater equality and reduced inequality | Confident | Not confident. **Revise** pages 108, 109 |
| 7 | Explain changing patterns of birth, marriage, cohabitation, divorce and increased longevity and their significance | Confident | Not confident. **Revise** pages 110, 111 |
| 8 | Demonstrate an understanding of the differences between facts, opinions and beliefs | Confident | Not confident. **Revise** page 112 |
| 9 | Apply number skills to social science tasks involving addition, subtraction, multiplication and division | Confident | Not confident. **Revise** pages 106, 107 |
| 10 | Undertake calculations of percentages and identify means, medians and modes – and why they are significant | Confident | Not confident. **Revise** pages 111, 113 |

# Objectivity in the social sciences 2: the economy and application of number

Once we recognise how social scientists examine and analyse information, it is only a short step to considering the theories that have been formulated and tested and the conclusions or explanations that are reached. We know that economists ask different questions from sociologists or psychologists – yet even within the study of economics, people disagree about the value or emphasis to be given to certain factors. An example of such a difference is the debate between Keynes's view that public policy should focus on the management of demand in contrast to the New Right view that it is the supply side that requires most attention in the making of public policy.

So how do social scientists in general and economists in particular use and present data for estimation and prediction – and how reliable are such predictions?

## Exam themes

→ Producers and consumers

→ Supply and demand

→ Prices and markets

→ Work and leisure

→ Free trade and fair trade

→ Protecting the planet

→ Markets, democracy and war

→ Representing data – drawing or interpreting graphs or charts

→ Estimation, explanations and predictions

## Topic checklist

○ AS  ● A2

| | AQA A | AQA B | EDEXCEL | OCR |
|---|---|---|---|---|
| Producers and consumers | ○● | ○● | ○● | ○● |
| The domestic economy: work and leisure | ○● | ○● | ○● | ○● |
| The global economy | ○● | ○● | ○● | ○● |

# Producers and consumers

Prices and quantities of goods or services on sale are decided by the supplies offered in a market by producers and the demands of consumers. Our expenditure depends on our income. At one time markets were quite small, yet today the EU gives us access to a market of 500 million consumers and, via the Internet, we can buy and sell worldwide.

## Producers and supply

→ The supply of goods depends on producers covering their costs (wages, raw materials, marketing, etc.) and selling the goods profitably.

→ The amount of a product available for purchase will be decided largely by the producers' costs – it will also depend on the intensity of the competition.

## Consumers and demand

→ The demand for goods depends on people having enough money to buy them. Credit cards and personal loans often mean people can buy things they cannot really afford, sometimes at high rates of interest – a £300 TV set bought on credit may cost £3 000 once all the interest charges have been paid.

→ Choosing a particular product depends not only on whether we need it but also whether we like it – fashion, taste and style are important. Most supermarkets now sell cheap trainers, jeans and T-shirts but many consumers prefer to pay more for similar products with brand names and style.

→ Generally, the lower the price of a commodity, the more will be demanded. A shop selling strawberries will sell far more at 50p a tub than £5 a tub.

## Supply and demand

The price of a product is set where the amount sellers wish to sell equals the amount consumers wish to buy in a given market. We often show supply and demand curves on a diagram (see opposite). The supply and demand for a book is set out below:

| Price | Quantity demanded | Quantity supplied | Quantity supplied if £5 tax is added |
|---|---|---|---|
| £30 | 100 000 | 500 000 | 400 000 |
| £25 | 200 000 | 400 000 | 300 000 |
| £20 | 300 000 | 300 000 | 250 000 |
| £15 | 600 000 | 250 000 | 100 000 |
| £10 | 1 000 000 | 100 000 | 20 000 |
| £5 | 1 500 000 | 10 000 | 1 000 |

→ Prices may change because costs – e.g. labour or fuel costs or currency exchange rates – change. Or, if a particular product becomes scarce, sellers will feel they can push up prices. Rising prices is termed *inflation* – whether because of extra costs (cost or wage inflation) or increasing demand/scarcity (demand inflation).

### Checkpoint 1

How would you define a market?

### Example

If there is just one bread shop selling a loaf of bread for £1 (even if it only costs 50 p to make), consumers will lack choice and probably pay up. But if three shops open offering bread at 50 p, the shop charging £1 must cut prices or make people believe its bread is better – healthier, fresher, tastes better.

### Links

See also page 202: The relationship between science, equality and family values.

### Checkpoint 2

Give two reasons why people may be willing to pay more for one pair of jeans or trainers than another.

### Example

If there is no tax, 300 000 books will be supplied and demanded at £20 per book, but if a £5 tax is added, price and quantity will change – look at the diagram below and you will see the price rises from £20 to 'b' when a tax is imposed – and the quantity purchased falls from 300 to 'a'.

Line graph to show demand and supply of a book

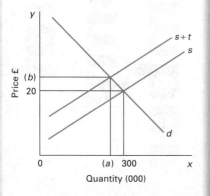

### Example

Note there is a title, the vertical axis (*y* axis) and horizontal axis (*x* axis) are both labelled, the type of diagram is indicated and the information from the table is drawn with care.

## Measuring price rises: why do they differ? ●●●

Prices for goods and services we buy will not all increase by the same amount.

We work out the effect of price changes by calculating the Retail Prices Index (RPI) – the cost of a basket of goods consumed by a typical family.

Look at the cost of the goods in each year, set the index figure for Year 1 at 100 and calculate all the other figures as percentages from that:

| Year | Price of goods | RPI – price as % of Year 1 price | Annual inflation (%) |
|---|---|---|---|
| 1 | £150 | 100.0 | – |
| 2 | £160 | 106.6 | 6.6 |
| 3 | £163 | 108.6 | 2.0 |
| 4 | £170 | 113.3 | 4.7 |
| 5 | £172 | 114.6 | 1.3 |

We could plot the changes in annual inflation as a *bar chart* or as a *line graph*. But to compare our competitive position with other countries we must look at *cumulative* inflation (all years added together) as well as *annual* inflation.

### Patterns of expenditure

Household expenditure of full-time employees and the unemployed, 2001/2: UK £ per week

| Expenditure | Full-time employees % | Unemployed % |
|---|---|---|
| 1 Transport | 15% | 11% |
| 2 Housing, water & fuel | 8% | 13% |
| 3 Food, restaurants, alcohol & tobacco | 21% | 28% |
| 4 Household goods, clothing & footwear | 13% | 13% |
| 5 Education, communication & health | 5% | 5% |
| 6 Recreation, culture, miscellaneous & other | 38% | 30% |
| Total weekly income | **£516.40** | **£225.40** |

Expenditure by full-time employees

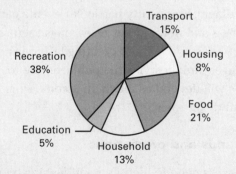

Transport 15%
Recreation 38%
Housing 8%
Food 21%
Education 5%
Household 13%

answers: page 122

### Exam preparation

1  Represent the information relating to unemployed people in a pie chart and indicate how you would calculate the segment for expenditure on transport.   (10 minutes)

2  What is the difference between supply and demand?   (5 minutes)

3  What is the difference between cost inflation and demand inflation?   (5 minutes)

4  'A pair of jeans or trainers are worth whatever people are willing to pay for them.' How far do you agree?   (30 minutes)

### Example

Petrol may cost more because the government adds tax or there are shortages – but go down when the reverse occurs. Vegetables may cost more in winter because supply is short if they are frozen in the ground. Cinema prices may go up because many people want to see a blockbuster release.

Bar chart representation of annual and cumulative inflation (years 1–5)

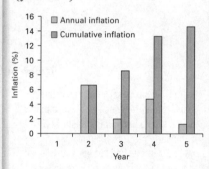

Line graph representation of annual and cumulative inflation (years 1–5)

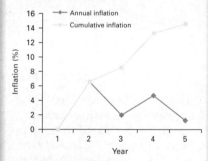

### Checkpoint 3

What would be the average rate of inflation in Years 1–5 – would this be a better measure than annual inflation or cumulative inflation?

### Examiner's secrets

Always label diagrams accurately. You may be asked to draw a diagram or interpret one. You should get used to interpreting diagrams such as those at www.statistics.gov.uk/.

### Checkpoint 4

Suggest reasons for any two differences in shares of expenditure by employed and unemployed, as revealed in the table above.

117

# The domestic economy: work and leisure

People in the UK are often considered *workaholics* because we work more hours per week than workers in other countries and often take on several jobs. To remain healthy, we need to keep a clear *work–life balance*, so we should take leisure as seriously as work. Leisure industries and activities are now very important to the UK economy.

## Trends, predictions, policy and targets

Often expectations for the future are included in data presented in *Social Trends*. Government then plans public expenditure and sets the targets it hopes to achieve as a result of its policies – if the birth rate is rising, more schools and more schoolteachers will be required; if people live longer, we shall need more doctors, retirement homes and healthcare facilities.

> Projections suggest that the number of people aged 65 and over will exceed those aged under 16 by 2014. By 2025 there will be more than 1.6 million more people over the age of 65 than people under 16. The increase in the number of pensioners has policy implications, placing greater demands on health, social services and social security arrangements. As a response, the state pension age (currently 65 for men and 60 for women) will be increased between 2010 and 2020 to 65 for both sexes.
>
> *Social Trends*, 33.

### Market research

→ Private businesses also need such information – if they watch the pattern of changing cinema attendances or television viewing or attendances at swimming pools and leisure centres in recent years, they can predict leisure patterns and opportunities in coming years and plan accordingly. Frequently particular events can change our expectations – and new market research is then required.

→ Market research is as much about creating fashions as it is recognising images and lifestyles the public aspire to. Often the income of clubs will depend as much on income from merchandising clothing as from ticket sales.

### Representing trends and predictions

→ Often policy makers need to identify relationships between different factors and what happened previously can sometimes help our understanding.

→ If we look at the relationship between *unemployment* and *inflation* in an island, patterns are established so we could make a good guess at how things may occur in future. We can work from a table of figures or it may be easier to show the information on a *scatter diagram* and then produce a line of best fit:

*Unemployment and inflation, Island A*

| Year | Unemployment (%) | Inflation (%) |
|------|------------------|---------------|
| 1 | 10 | 2 |
| 2 | 9 | 3 |
| 3 | 8 | 4 |
| 4 | 8 | 5 |
| 5 | 7 | 6 |
| 6 | 5 | 14 |
| 7 | 3 | 16 |
| 8 | 3 | 17 |
| 9 | 2 | 18 |
| 10 | 1 | 20 |

## Changing patterns of work ●●●

→ The Health and Safety Executive (HSE) says stress now accounts for 11% of all sickness absence. Perhaps this is an argument to limit the hours people work for health reasons.

## Changing patterns of leisure ●●●

Leisure activities can be educational for children and provide a fulfilling diversion from work for most adults. But people disagree whether they should be provided by government, councils, lotto-funded organisations or the private sector.

→ With the development of modern shopping centres, three-quarters of women now say they enjoy non-food shopping, compared with less than half of men.
→ Walking/hiking and swimming were the two sporting activities with the highest participation rates in the UK, of around 20% and 15% respectively in 2000–01, with many more people now seeking exercise – e.g. running marathons.
→ In 2001, the most popular holiday destinations visited by UK residents were Spain and France, accounting for 28% and 18% of holidays.

Internet usage for work and leisure is rising, though few rural areas can yet access broadband. UK adults aged 16 and over averaged nearly 20 hours a week (just under 3 hours a day) watching television in 2000–01. About 7 books per person were borrowed from public libraries in 2000/01, though borrowing is declining.

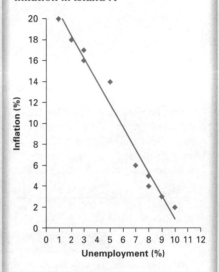

Scatter diagram and line of best fit to show Unemployment and Inflation in Island A

**Example**

If we wanted to estimate the level of unemployment if inflation settled at 8%, the line of best fit suggests around 6% – but of course the prediction depends on economic circumstances remaining the same and is only as good as the assumptions on which it is based.

**Checkpoint 2**

What are GDP and GNP and what is the difference between them?

**Check the net**

Short-term contract working and the anti-trade union attitudes have reduced union memberships from 13 million in 1979 to barely half this in 2000. Most employees no longer belong – union membership is now strongest among professional groups such as teachers. Look at http://www.tuc.org.uk to find the current position.

**Action point**

You and your friends could organise a formal or informal survey to see how far these national trends are evident in the way your families spend their time.

**Checkpoint 3**

Identify the main ways in which the expansion of leisure has increased job opportunities.

**Exam preparation**                                    answers: pages 122–123

1   Suggest two ways in which the expected population projections for 2025 may have an impact on jobs.   (5 minutes)
2   Identify and explain two ways in which a firm might undertake market research to decide whether to invest in a new leisure facility.   (15 minutes)
3   'Leisure and leisure facilities are so important that they should be provided by local councils or the government.' How far do you agree?   (30 minutes)

# The global economy

The food we eat, the clothes we wear, the services we take for granted, the goods we buy will mostly, if not totally, depend on an economic division of labour and coordination stretching across the whole world.

## Stages of economic development

→ W.W. Rostow's theory of economic development is generally accepted. He believed all economies go through a number of stages on the journey from being a less economically developed country (LEDC) to a more economically developed country (MEDC):
(i) traditional society (barter is common, agriculture is important);
(ii) meets pre-conditions for self-sustaining growth (rising savings);
(iii) take-off stage (economic growth occurs); (iv) drive to maturity;
(v) mass consumption (citizens enjoy high consumption levels).

→ Once all countries reach stage (v), the potential for trade is maximised – the richer a country is, the more it can afford to trade with other countries. But the greater the economic potential of a country, the more vulnerable it will be to attack either by (i) other countries which covet its wealth or influence or (ii) people within the country who resent the wealth of the ruling elite.

## Multinationals and the global economy

Multinational companies (e.g. McDonald's, Ford Motor Company, Shell Oil, HSBC, Microsoft) roaming the world in search of profits are courted by governments since they can provide jobs for local populations – sometimes the multinationals will be attracted to a country by (i) their geography (e.g. closeness or access to rich markets), (ii) natural resources (oil, gas, gold, platinum, iron, coal), (iii) skills or temperament of the local population, (iv) stability of systems of government, (v) willingness and ability to embrace new technologies.

The trainers, jeans, T-shirts, computers, calculators or TV sets (for producing which an Asian worker may receive in a week what a European worker would accept for an hour) nonetheless make the Asian worker better off than she or he would otherwise be, yet many feel that the capitalist ethic could be more generous to these workers while still achieving good profits paid to Western investors.

### Aid or trade?

Nobody doubts the importance of providing short-term humanitarian aid for any country in the face of emergencies such as earthquakes, failed harvests or floods. Increasingly, though, it is believed that (i) *cancelling debts* and (ii) *giving access to markets* provides a better chance for an LEDC to develop economically.

## International co-operation: rich world, poor world

→ The UN campaigns to deal with problems such as global warming, free trade, barriers to fair trade and the challenge of HIV/AIDS to find worldwide solutions.

### Check the net

See the websites for the United Nations – http://www.un.org – and the Department for International Development (DfID) – http://dfid.gov.uk – and look for countries whose economic development is at these stages.

### Checkpoint 1

What reasons other than wealth and resources might cause a country to go to war?

### Checkpoint 2

Identify one example of a multinational company taking each of these factors into account.

### Action point

Find out what role the UK has played in promoting moves to *cancel the debts* of poor countries.

→ The International Monetary Fund (IMF) and the World Bank play a big part in promoting economic development. At Rio de Janeiro (1992) an international agreement was made to use sustainable development to manage the environment both short term and long term.

→ The conflicting interests of rich and poor worlds were seen at the Johannesburg Earth Summit (2002) when little progress was made – with targets being set far in the future (e.g. reducing numbers without sanitation in 12 years' time).

→ In 2003 at the World Trade Organisation (WTO) conference in Cancun, LEDCs wanted access to and fair prices in rich markets while MEDCs wanted access to cheap labour and raw materials, often damaging poor countries by dumping subsidised exports on them, ruining their home markets and production cycles.

## Markets, democracy and conflict ●●●

Amy Chua's 2003 book *World On Fire: How Exporting Free Market Democracy Breeds Ethnic Hatred and Global Instability* has caused people to reconsider relationships between markets, democracy and conflict. Chua focuses on *market-dominant minority groups*, arguing that they control hugely disproportionate percentages of their countries' resources. Her argument is that in countries with much poverty and a market-dominant minority, there is a deep tension between democracy and markets which has repeatedly provoked ethnic conflict. The arrival of democracy does not transform voters into open-minded co-citizens in a national community but, rather, the competition for votes sees hatred whipped up against the resented minority with demands that the country's wealth and identity be reclaimed by the *true owners of the nation*, leading to deep hatreds and instability.

### Reflecting on social science explanations

Chua's analysis brings together ideas we do not often associate. It goes a long way to explaining many civil wars which have occurred. Like most good social scientist explanations she has (i) undertaken *observations*, (ii) developed a *theory* or *simple model*, (iii) tested it *factually* against recent history in the Middle East, Africa and countries such as the former Yugoslavia – and perhaps removed some simplifying assumptions, (iv) made strong use of clearly defined *concepts*, (v) but by no stretch of the imagination is her explanation *value-free*. Values are often an important part of social science explanations and need to be explicitly identified as such.

**Checkpoint 3**

What is the difference between fair trade and free trade?

**Example**

In 2001 the US rejected the Kyoto agreement's goals of reducing energy consumption – probably because the USA is the world's largest consumer of energy with 5% of the world's population, yet its profligate use of energy means that it produces 25% of world greenhouse emissions.

**Example**

In Nairobi (2003), the US resisted demands to ban methyl bromide (the most dangerous ozone-depleting chemical still in widespread use, and also a cause of prostate cancer), wanting to be allowed to *increase* its use because it said it needed more time to find new fumigants for crops such as tomatoes, peppers and strawberries.

**Example**

(i) Filipino-Chinese comprise just 2% of the Philippines' population, but control all the major supermarkets, fast-food restaurants and large department stores and all but one of the nation's banks; (ii) Lebanese dominate the economies in Sierra Leone and the Gambia.

**Action point**

Now look at any other social science theories of which you are aware and see if you can recognise the same stages – observation, theory, testing, using concepts – are the conclusions value free?

---

**Exam preparation**                                          answers: page 123

1   Give two reasons why a country may not provide a suitable location for a multinational company. (5 minutes)

2   Give one reason for and one reason against the view that the best way to help LEDCs is through aid not trade. (15 minutes)

3   'Spreading democracy throughout the world must always be our foremost aim.' How far do you agree? (30 minutes)

# Answers
## Objectivity in the social sciences 2:

### Producers and consumers

**Checkpoints**

1 A market is any area over which buyers and sellers are in communication. It could be as small as a village square or it could be an auction organised over the Internet.

2 People may be willing to pay more for one pair of jeans or trainers than another if they think (a) the quality is superior or (b) the product's brand name or style improves their image.

3 The average rate of inflation in Years 1–5, i.e. from the end of Yr 1 to the end of Yr 5, was (6.6 + 2.0 + 4.7 + 1.3 = 14.6)/4 = 3.65%. Average inflation is often easier to understand than annual or cumulative inflation – especially if discussion is about the average rate rising or falling. If we know the current rate is above or below the present average, we can see how the trend is moving.

4 Spending by full-time employed and unemployed people differed markedly over transport, with the employed devoting a higher proportion of household spending to commuting, business journeys and travel for leisure purposes, while the unemployed do not commute or make business journeys and would be less able to afford spending on recreational travel. Housing, water and fuel, being essentials, account for a higher proportion of expenditure for unemployed households compared to full-time employed households.

**Exam preparation**

1 To calculate the number of degrees in each segment of each circle or *pie* we need to multiply each percentage by 3.6. So the segment for transport expenditure by full-time employees will be 10.6% × 3.6 = 39.6°.

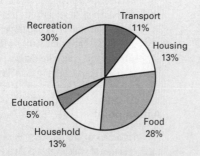

2 Supply indicates the decisions of producers as to how much of a good or service they will provide in a given market at a particular price; demand indicates the decisions of consumers as to how much of a good or service they will purchase in a given market at a particular price.

3 Any kind of inflation involves rising prices. Price rises caused by increasing labour or perhaps fuel costs are known as cost inflation while price rises caused by an *auction effect* arising through scarcity are termed demand inflation.

4 The question is asking us to focus on the difference between *cost* and *price* and *value*. If the labour cost,

raw materials costs, transport and marketing costs of a product amount to £20, few people would think it unreasonable for the producer to charge, say, £25 (i.e. £20 cost + £5 profit) for putting the production process together.

But what if the shop put a designer label on the product and asked £100? A person to whom a designer label matters might buy the product even though the price is now five times the cost. Alternatively, auctions are held every day in which objects are sold for the highest price – this suggests that value is in the eye of the beholder, so a discarded toy may be worth nothing to a child who has outgrown it but may be worth hundreds of pounds to a collector.

### The domestic economy: work and leisure

**Checkpoints**

1 Many people have suggested that the *clean* image of rugby may win supporters if the scandals involving soccer players continue – the cleaner the image of rugby and the less acceptable the image of other sports, the more the rugby boom is likely to continue. Equally though, one possible factor which could kill off such a boom straight away would be any suggestions of drug taking by players or financial manipulation by club owners or managers.

2 GDP is Gross Domestic Product; it is the market value of all goods or services physically made in the UK. GNP is Gross National Product – it includes the goods and services made by British companies in America, Australia or Asian countries but not any production by overseas countries in the UK.

3 The main ways in which the expansion of leisure has increased job opportunities include the following:
- selling lotto tickets and distributing lotto funds to 'good causes'
- the leisure industries including cinemas, theatres, pubs, hotels and restaurants
- betting and gaming
- travel firms which arrange package holidays
- train, coach and bus firms
- heritage tourism
- pop concerts and the recording industry
- making and transmitting radio and television programmes
- spectator and participant sports events and the sportswear market.

**Exam preparation**

1 If as expected there are 5 million more dependent elderly people in the UK and the birth rate does not significantly change, a shrinking proportion of existing workers will have to pay taxes to support the needs of many more dependents, unless retirement ages are increased to, say, 70.

# the economy and application of number

**2** Two ways a firm might undertake market research to decide whether to invest in a new leisure facility could be (i) to undertake a survey of existing provision, e.g. of council-run swimming pools, leisure centres, etc. and how cost-effectively they are run; (ii) to ascertain how fully such facilities are used and whether existing users are satisfied.

**3** If we buy other services, why should we not pay to use local gyms, swimming pools or training facilities? Private management is likely to provide well-run services, utilising the enterprise ethics of the private sector.

However, if leisure activities and facilities are important for education and health then, even though they are expensive to organise (investment costs of a new leisure centre will easily amount to £5 m or even £10 m and running costs will be substantial), it is better they are provided by government or councils since in that way all will have access to them at minimal cost. If such services are provided privately, only those who can afford them will be able to use them – especially since many private leisure centres aim for social exclusiveness.

## The global economy

### Checkpoints

**1** Reasons other than wealth and resources which might cause a country to go to war could be ideology or religion.

**2** Examples of multinational companies could be:
*Geography* – e.g. Japanese car manufacturers such as Nissan and Toyota locating in the UK to be inside the European Union.
*Natural Resources* – oil companies such as BP undertaking oil exploration in Russia.
*Skills or temperament of the local population* – Prudential, HSBC and some telephone enquiries firms locating call centres in India and other Asian countries.
*Stability of systems of government* would make Zimbabwe, Sri Lanka or Iraq less likely locations than Indonesia, where many Nike and Adidas products are made.
*Willingness and ability to embrace new technologies* has brought the US firm Arrow Electronics to Hong Kong and Malaysia.

**3** Free trade is trade between countries undertaken without taxes being added to imports which help to protect home producers from competition. By contrast, fair trade is practised by the Co-op and Starbucks to ensure producers in LEDCs get a fair return for their produce.

### Exam preparation

**1** A country is not a suitable location for a multinational company if its legal framework is unreliable or if it is in a region prone to disasters, e.g. earthquakes or flooding.

**2** A reason for the view that the best way to help LEDCs is through aid not trade could be that aid – maybe in the form of training for key personnel at UK universities or support from business or from the UK Department for International Development – could ensure the country builds up an infrastructure for business in an orderly way.

An example against such a view could be that agreeing to produce goods to agreed quality standards at agreed prices within agreed timescales is an important discipline and learning process for any company and if a developing country once gets a good reputation, the demand for their products will quickly grow, allowing them, not others, to keep ownership of the development process.

**3** Many people might argue that there are far more worthwhile things to do than spreading democracy – conquering AIDS, reversing global warming, improving literacy and living standards for all, sharing the benefits of technology, taking human rights seriously. Democracy may be less attractive to an uneducated, hungry or sick person than to an affluent member of an MEDC. The dangers of majority rule threatening the successful economic base in a country, as suggested by Amy Chua, seem to give a compelling argument against pushing democracy as an essential. The same sort of argument has been advanced by Robert Kaplan, who has long argued that 'the Western wish to export democracy to countries without the institutions to support it is naive and often dangerous, fostering demagogues and communal hatreds'. The importance of democracy and self-determination could be advanced by those who support human rights – yet the work of Mary Robinson, when United Nations High Commissioner for Human Rights, suggests that in many parts of the world, the idea of human rights for all is seen as a Western cultural imperative and in some places may be resisted for that reason alone.

# Databank

**Cancun** – WTO conference in 2003 at which developing countries found a voice.

**demographic trends** – changing population patterns – increased longevity, changing sizes of households, rise of cohabitation, remarriages and divorce, decline in marriage and birth rates.

**fair trade** – trade which gives a fair return to producers in LEDCs.

**free trade** – trade in which importer countries do not impose tariffs to protect home producers (as the USA did to protect the US steel industry in 2002/03 until ordered to desist by the WTO).

**G8** – the eight most economically advanced countries – UK, USA, Canada, France, Russia, Germany, Italy and Japan (with EU representation also) – whose meetings often provoke protests from anti capitalist activists.

**Kyoto** (1997) – conference at which many governments agreed to targets to cut harmful $CO_2$ emissions by 2008 – in 2001 the US rejected the Kyoto agreement's goals of reducing energy consumption and in 2004 Russia still had not signed up.

**monopoly** – when a good or service is available from one seller only; this may lead to prices being higher than they would be if competitors existed.

**multinational company** – worldwide company which often locates itself in countries where costs are low and opportunities for making profits are high; many multinational companies take full advantage of new technologies which allow fast communication to sell goods cheaply produced in developing countries to rich markets in the West.

**Lotto** – The first ever National Lottery draw took place in November 1994. Over £12 bn in funds has gone to 'good causes' including many sporting and cultural landmarks, e.g. the British Museum. Total ticket sales exceeded £40 billion by 2004. The average size of a grant during 2000/01 was around £50 000, down from a peak of over £270 000 in 1995/96.

**product differentiation** – use of brand names and designer labels to make products appear different, making consumers more willing to pay higher prices.

**ruling elite** – an elite is a minority which exercises much greater power than its numbers might lead us to expect; it may be based on education, wealth or privilege.

**values/social science explanations** – explanations offered by social scientists based on facts, theories or models and values; so an explanation offered by a Marxist would differ from a conservative perspective.

**WTO** – World Trade Organisation, seeks to reduce protective tariffs which push up prices of imports to shield home producers from competition by cheaper/more efficient producers overseas.

# Revision checklist
*helps you check what you still need to do*

## By the end of this chapter you should be able to:

| | | |
|---|---|---|
| 1 Use all the information in Databank, above, with confidence | Confident | Not confident. **Revise** page 124 |
| 2 Explain the roles of producers and consumers | Confident | Not confident. **Revise** pages 116, 117, 190 |
| 3 Show how supply and demand lead to the setting of prices in markets | Confident | Not confident. **Revise** pages 116, 117 |
| 4 Consider the changing patterns of work and leisure in UK society | Confident | Not confident. **Revise** pages 118, 119 |
| 5 Understand the differences between and significance of free trade and fair trade | Confident | Not confident. **Revise** pages 123, 124 |
| 6 Examine the differences and disagreements over how the planet should be protected | Confident | Not confident. **Revise** pages 120, 121 |
| 7 Consider relationship between markets, democracy and war – and their implications | Confident | Not confident. **Revise** page 121 |
| 8 Apply number skills to represent data – drawing or interpreting graphs or charts | Confident | Not confident. **Revise** pages 116, 119, 122 |
| 9 Recognise the reliability and nature of estimation, explanations and predictions in the social sciences | Confident | Not confident. **Revise** page 121 |

# The nature and importance of culture

Culture is a broad term with several different but related meanings. It is central to our identity as individuals, but at the same time helps to place us in society, and to locate our own society in relationship to others. Culture, then, enables us to belong. Consequently, we need to understand our own culture and appreciate and respect others.

Central to any culture is language, for through language we communicate ideas, express emotions and describe experience. Language distinguishes us from other groups or societies. Through language we can think and solve problems.

We should remember that culture, in whatever sense we use the term, is created by society. Because it is the product of people, it is constantly evolving. Any culture that is static and inflexible must inevitably decline and eventually disappear. History repeatedly shows that only those cultures able and willing to grow or change can survive. This openness to change has been perhaps a key feature of Western culture during the last 1000 years.

## Exam themes

→ The nature of culture: national cultures; Western culture; minority cultures

→ Popular and high culture; is one preferable to the other?

→ The relationship between cultures and between culture and society

→ Cultural values, prejudices and stereotypes; how values develop or change

→ Differences and similarities between peoples and cultures; the importance of culture to individuals; cultural diversity and multi-culture and mono-culture

→ How cultural values and norms are transmitted; the role of government in the arts

→ Examples of artistic achievement from a range of cultures and times

## Topic checklist

| ○ AS ● A2 | AQA A | AQA B | EDEXCEL | OCR |
|---|---|---|---|---|
| The nature and importance of culture | ○● | ○● | ○● | ○ |
| Culture as art | ○● | ○● | ○● | ○ |
| Judging cultures | ○● | ○● | ○● | ○ |

# The nature and importance of culture

## Watch out!

Make sure you are clear which meaning of culture is being used in any question you are asked!

## Checkpoint 1

Why is a word linked to growing things used to describe different human societies or cultures?

> *"The highest possible stage in moral culture is when we recognise that we ought to control our thoughts."*
>
> Charles Darwin, *The Descent of Man*

## Link

See The changing culture, page 65.

## Checkpoint 2

Why is a small-scale society more likely to have fewer cultural differences than one which is larger scale?

## Jargon

Homogeneous: of the same kind; sharing the same characteristics.
Heterogeneous: diverse in character or content.

Culture can be understood in several different ways. Associated with cultivation, it originally just meant 'a cultivated piece of land' and related to farming, as in agriculture. Today scientists use it to describe growing bacteria or tissues. Sociologists use culture to define different social groups. Another important use describes 'the Arts' and other forms of intellectual achievement.

## Culture meaning society

Sociologists who talk about culture have a very broad understanding of the term. It has been explained as 'common ways of behaving in a society'. So culture is about everything to do with a society:

→ The total way of life
→ The entire range of its material objects
→ The ideas and attitudes that members of the society have created
→ Changes made over time to improve people's collective life
→ Language and symbols
→ Beliefs, values and norms

These different criteria make it easy to identify different cultures, distinguish between them and discover similarities and differences. It has become quite common to talk about Western culture, or Eastern culture, or European culture. Since we are aware of the different criteria that are used to make a classification, the terms are generally easily understood by most people.

## Divisions within cultures

You would expect most people in a culture to share the same cultural characteristics. Unless a society consists of a very small group of people, it is likely that there will be almost as many differences between people as there are similarities. In the same way as we can distinguish between different cultures, we can distinguish different subgroups within a society. These subgroups, or subcultures, are distinguished from the mainstream culture in some distinctive way.

A subculture may be based on location, economic position, social status (class), education, religion, ethnicity or even disability. Though retaining many mainstream features of a culture, a subculture will develop its own way of 'doing things'. This may take the form of a distinctive style, value system, expectations, language or behaviour. Subcultures may be distinguished by differences in occupation, religion or ethnic origin. One of the main types of subculture is that associated with differences in age. A feature of the last 50 years has been the emergence of a very distinctive youth culture. This has resulted not only in what is often referred to as 'the generation gap' but it has also led to challenges to authority, traditional standards and values and the emergence of distinctive styles of entertainment, clothing and even language.

## Culture, symbols and language ●○○

Every culture has its own set of symbols. A symbol, which carries a particular meaning unique to the members of a society, is an important method of cultural communication. Different cultures may use similar symbols but give them totally different meanings. Individuals who do not know the meaning are effectively placed outside the culture. Misuse, or simply ignorance of meaning, can lead to isolation or some form of sanction.

Languages are major symbols found in every culture. Even societies lacking a written language have a form of spoken language. Words are structured symbols with agreed meanings. They allow easy communication between people who share a language, but are a barrier to those who do not. Each society applies its own, often arbitrary, meaning to the sounds which shape our understanding of the world. A similar sound can have totally different meaning in different cultures. We sometimes think we are communicating when in fact we are conveying totally different ideas. An individual wanting to belong to a culture must understand the language of that culture.

## Culture, religion and history ●●○

Cultures change and develop over time. Experience shapes and directs change. Each culture has its own unique history, although, inevitably, from time to time contact with other societies affects developments. At any given time a culture is the product of its own history and tradition.

Religion is another major influence. Some sociologists claim religion is a product of society but others say it shapes society, or emphasise that it can be a force for oppression and social control. Ultimately, many see religion as a source of conflict. Through religion, a culture can explain, establish and transmit values, make sense of human experience. It has provided authority for rules and morals, answered questions about the purpose and meaning of life and created social cohesion. Equally, it can create conflict and division at the same time that it establishes identity.

## Culture, science and technology ●●○

Science and technology are major formative influences on modern Western society, although in the past some societies have limited the influence of science. In Medieval Europe scientific experiment was restricted and scientific theories had to conform to religious teachings. As late as the early 18th century in Britain, the development of canals was forbidden because it was believed to be contrary to the will of God who, it was believed, had created a perfect world.

**Links**

See page 149: The symbolism of religious belief.

**Example**

In Western societies white is often associated with purity, joy and rejoicing. In some cultures it is associated with death and mourning.

**Checkpoint 3**

Why is language important in the development of a culture?

**Watch out!**

It is very easy if you have strong views about religion (whether for or against) to allow your ideas to distort your answers.

**Example**

In 1633 the Catholic Church forced Galileo to deny his earlier claim that the Earth went round the sun, because it contradicted the teaching of the Bible.

**Links**

For more about culture, science and technology see pages 5 and 86.

**Exam preparation**                          answer: page 132

When we talk about different cultures we are really describing differences in historical experience rather than differences in the way that societies are organised. To what extent is this true?   (40 minutes)

# Culture as art

Some people use culture to describe different types of human activity. One view includes every aspect of human behaviour. Another, much narrower definition, given by Matthew Arnold in 1873, claims culture is 'the best that has been said and thought in the world'. This is sometimes called high culture. Activities not meeting his criteria are often dismissed as inferior.

**Watch out!**

Is the term culture being used in its broad (societal) or narrow (artistic) sense?

**Checkpoint 1**

Why should only certain activities be described as high culture?

## High culture

High culture is traditionally associated with wealthy people and governing classes and is said to embody all that is best in European civilisation. It has been claimed that only people with educated or 'cultivated' tastes can appreciate it. Criteria used to decide whether an activity should count as high culture include:

Expense
Restricted accessibility and availability
Longevity
Use of specialist language or jargon

Some people say it reflects the values and standards of the ruling class, who define what it is, and use their influence to keep it exclusive.

Activities often regarded as representing high culture include:

**Watch out!**

Some people treat high culture as though it is based only on social class and miss other criteria that distinguish it from other forms of activity.

| | |
|---|---|
| Classical music | Opera |
| Ballet | Great literature |
| Poetry | Theatre |
| Serious film | Painting and sculpture |

Some critics claim that these art forms are different from others since they speak about human values and the nature and purpose of life.

## Popular or mass culture

→ Refers to activities appealing to the majority of the population.
→ Belittles activities, suggesting they lack quality.
→ Imply no special skill is required to appreciate or understand them.
→ Includes activities that exist for short-term pleasure.
→ Does not make any demands of participants.
→ Assumed to be cheap and easily accessible to all.
→ Generally mass produced with emphasis on quality not quantity.
→ Examples are largely indistinguishable from each other.

**Checkpoint 2**

What do people mean when they say you have to be taught to appreciate high culture?

Each high culture activity has a matching example in popular culture.

Activities usually classed as popular culture include:

**Links**

See page 159 for the influence of the mass media, pages 178–179 on criteria for aesthetic evaluation, and page 200 for high culture.

| | |
|---|---|
| Popular music | Clubbing |
| Popular literature | Magazines |
| Television programmes (e.g. BBC1 and ITV) | |
| Tabloid newspapers | Spectator sports (e.g. football) |
| Cinema | Art reproductions |

Popular culture is produced for the masses rather than by them. Is it the way the ruling classes keep them in their place in society? Or is it simply the type of entertainment that most people enjoy?

## Folk culture ○○○

This differs from popular culture since it is produced by the people rather than for them. Folk culture includes the artistic forms and activities of ordinary people. It is usually associated with earlier times and linked to small local communities. Significant differences could exist in similar activities performed by neighbouring communities. Today much folk culture has been rediscovered and absorbed into popular culture or has been revived by middle-class enthusiasts. It has lost its former unique quality.

Activities that can be described as folk culture include:

Folk dancing                    Morris dancing
Folk singing                    Well dressing
Local costume                   Wood carving
Local foods

## National cultures ○○○

Each society has a unique culture, based on language, history and tradition, religious beliefs and values. This may lead to stereotyping; sometimes this is simply descriptive but often it is culturally and socially damaging. Neighbouring countries or societies may have similar cultures since they share or borrow cultural features. Differences may let you identify separate English, Welsh and Scottish cultures but you can also think of a shared British culture. The same is true about Europe. France, Spain, Germany and Italy all have distinctive cultures but have much in common with their neighbours. We can therefore talk about Western culture.

## Key features of western culture ○○○

Key features of modern Western culture include:

→ Christianity has significantly influenced law, morality and customs.
→ Legal systems are based on the Roman Empire.
→ Similarities in language (e.g. window = fenêtre in French; fenestra in Welsh; fenestration in English).
→ Concern for individual rights and freedoms.
→ Equal opportunities.
→ State provision for those in need (the poor, the sick and the old).
→ Belief in democracy and the political process.
→ Similar lifestyle and individual expectations.
→ Common traditions in the arts (music, painting, literature, etc.).
→ Shared media experiences.
→ Common literary experience.

You might think that many of these features are not unique to Western societies. Many of them may be found in some form in most cultures.

---

> "Television is the first truly democratic culture – the first culture available to everybody and entirely governed by what the people want."
>
> Clive Barnes

**Links**

See page 126: Culture meaning society.

**Checkpoint 3**

In Western societies it is quite usual for governments to subsidise certain forms of high culture, but popular culture is left to market forces. Can this approach to subsidy be justified?

**Examiner's secrets**

A key idea in this question is 'better'. Don't ignore comparison or value words. They are put in the question to help you.

---

**Exam preparation**                                    answer: page 132–133

Is it better to go to the opera than to a pop concert? Give reasons to support your answer.   (20 minutes)

# Judging cultures

At one time most people were largely unaware of different cultures, regarding their own culture as definitive of what is best in human society. Today this ignorance rarely exists in the Western world. You are certain to be aware and have experience of different cultures and practices. This may be because:

→ greater affluence allows you to enjoy foreign travel;
→ relatively high levels of migration bring different groups together;
→ the media show us how different groups of people live;
→ you come into contact daily with different cultural groups at home, school, college or work and in the street.

## Multi-culture or mono-culture?

All British governments are committed to a multi-cultural society. We are encouraged to value diversity, recognising that we live in a pluralist society, containing several equal but different cultures.

Britain has a long history of ethnic and cultural diversity. Some people want minority cultures to be fully integrated into the dominant British culture. A mono-culture exists where minority cultures are actively discouraged in favour of a single dominant culture.

Other people claim our culture is extended and enriched by borrowing from other cultures (for example, in language, food, music, fashion). They argue that this always happens in all societies. Throughout history there has been so much exchange of cultural ideas and influences that it is impossible to identify a pure form of any culture.

Whichever view is taken, we cannot ignore the influence of other cultures on British society. At the same time, other cultures have been influenced by British culture. This process seems to be increasing as a result of globalisation.

## Minority cultures

Minority groups exist in any society. At first you might think of different racial or ethnic groups. These groups are most easily distinguished when their culture, dress, religion or skin colour significantly differs from the majority population. In Britain people are often more immediately aware of people originating from Asia, Africa or the Caribbean than they are of groups coming from Europe or the USA. However, any group seen as different or receiving special treatment may be regarded with suspicion. This can lead to prejudice, stereotyping and discrimination.

There are many minority groups in any society made up by:

age
education
religion
social class
sporting activities
special interest groups (like steam railway enthusiasts).

**Links**

See pages 158–159 for the power and influence of the media.

**Watch out!**

It is easy to confuse multi-cultural and multi-racial. Be careful to recognise the difference between these two terms.

**Checkpoint 1**

What steps have British governments taken since 1965 to ensure that Britain becomes a true multi-cultural society?

**Links**

See pages 64–65 for more on multi-culturalism.

**Example**

Norman Tebbit, a Conservative politician, suggested that all migrants should take the 'cricket test'. In other words, they should support the English team rather than their country of birth if they wanted to be classed as British. Home Secretary David Blunkett has introduced new citizenship rules, including learning English and taking part in a citizenship ceremony, to encourage greater integration and as a test of 'Britishness'.

## Why is culture important to individuals?

Culture, whether defined in a broad social sense or in the more specific artistic sense, is of critical importance to most individuals. It helps to:

→ create a sense of belonging and identity;
→ distinguish a single person or a group of people from others;
→ define a person's beliefs, values and behaviour;
→ embrace a distinctive historical experience and tradition;
→ provide a context and justification for laws, the legal system, political and social structures and moral and religious values.

Most people take pride in their cultural identity, but some can adopt a narrow, extreme viewpoint. They may believe their own culture superior to all others. They can be intolerant of other groups and cultures, especially those from a totally different tradition. It can lead to the type of patriotism associated with 'my country right or wrong'. More extreme forms can be seen in political organisations and pressure groups such as the Ku Klux Klan, or the British National Movement. Extremists may regard minority cultural groups as inferior. These views may lead to violent demonstrations or forms of discrimination directed against minorities. The alleged purpose is the preservation of 'cultural purity'.

## Is cultural diversity enriching?

Access to travel, modern technology and the media (such as the Internet, television and video filming) mean that, for the first time in history, we can become immediately aware of anything that occurs in any part of the world. Consequently, we are all more aware of and influenced by different types of culture.

Some people welcome cultural diversity, claiming that a culture must be enriched by contact with others. But many fear that the technologies associated with globalisation may destroy other cultures rather than enriching them. It is often claimed that we are in danger of establishing a single worldwide Americanised culture in place of the rich diversity that once existed. This process is called cultural imperialism.

## Is cultural diversity class based

Social scientists talk about subcultures. Do such subgroups have their own distinctive culture? You might be tempted to believe high culture is the exclusive preserve of the rich and powerful in society, while popular culture is restricted to ordinary people. Views like this can lead to forms of snobbery. The truth, in the Arts or other forms of culture, is that individuals have different tastes and interests. Major influences on what you like are education, home background or experience.

---

**Checkpoint 2**

Give three different reasons why cultural differences may lead to hatred and/or intolerance.

---

**Example**

In recent history racial hatred and intolerance have been seen in attempts to achieve racial and ethnic cleansing in Nazi Germany, the former Yugoslavia and parts of central Africa.

---

*"I do not want my house to be walled in on all sides and my windows to be stuffed. I want the cultures of all the lands to be blown about my house as freely as possible. But I refuse to be blown off my feet by any."*

Mahatma Gandhi

---

**Jargon**

Globalisation is the spreading of common values on a worldwide scale, largely through the media. It can mean the development of a single common worldwide culture.

---

**Examiner's secrets**

Make sure the conflict you describe does have a real cultural element to it and is not just social or political conflict.

---

**Exam preparation**                                    answer: page 133

Identify one area of the United Kingdom where there is or has recently been cultural conflict. What were the causes of this conflict? How do you think the conflict might be resolved?   (30 minutes)

131

# Answers
## The nature and importance of culture

### The nature and importance of culture

#### Checkpoints

1 Societies are all different. None are static; they must either grow or decline/die. 'Cultured' people are those who have learned/developed/been taught the values of society.

2 Small-scale societies contain fewer people and so they have a common shared experience and history. They are likely to be interdependent and will share values. The group will be homogeneous, may have a simple authority structure. Because of size they may resist new values, but be better able to absorb them when they are accepted.

   Large-scale societies consist of many people with vastly different experiences; they are less likely to be totally interdependent and may contain conflicting or contrasting value systems. Different groups will accept new values at different rates. This may lead to conflict and dissent. Society will be heterogeneous, with members having different expectations.

3 Language is used to express and formulate meanings (especially abstract meanings). It allows communication to enable shared experience and is a means of transmitting, receiving and recording ideas, values and traditions.

#### Exam preparation

You might start by explaining what you understand by a culture and asking how cultures differ. You could then describe some characteristics that help define a culture (language, traditions, religion, food, legal and government systems, clothing, social structure, moral and social values, patterns of behaviour, occupations, social organisation, economic structure etc.).

   You could then show that though details differ, these features are common to all societies. Differences are being reduced by globalisation, technology and the mass media; other factors are travel and migration. Cultures borrow from each other and absorb various features. The UK consists of four different distinctive cultures but they share a common language, history, style of government, legal system etc.

   Rivalries between cultures are often linked to national identity, patriotism and pride. These encourage us to see differences rather than similarities. Many cultures developed in isolation (e.g. China or Japan), excluding 'barbarians' to preserve a pure culture. Some, such as the Amazonian tribes or Australian Aborigines, developed in total isolation from the Western world until relatively recently. As a result they each developed their own distinctive culture, history and tradition. Encounters with other cultures came through conflict. Victory for a dominant culture reinforces ideas of superiority and inferiority. Cultural imperialism occurs if a dominant culture 'colonises' another culture by imposing its own values. This could be seen in the impact of Britain on Indian culture in the 18th and 19th centuries.

   The nations of Western Europe began as independent warring tribes. They were united under the Roman Empire, which imposed a common culture (language, system of government, law, religion). When Rome collapsed, fragmentation occurred, leading to the development of separate nation states. Gradually the common culture diverged as each added its own distinctive features. Rivalry, conflict, war and invasion added to individual cultures but also created barriers of fear and suspicion. From this arose a range of cultural stereotypes (e.g. Scots are misers, the Spanish are lazy, Italians are cowards and Germans are super-efficient).

   You could conclude by pointing out that what we see today as a culture is the result of historical interaction rather than of intrinsic organisational difference.

### Culture as art

#### Checkpoints

1 Snobbery; tradition; longevity; people must be 'trained' to appreciate them; expense; funding; accessibility; aesthetic qualities; content; government; it's the culture of the ruling classes; require thought and involvement not passive enjoyment; limited audience. 'All that is best . . .' (M. Arnold)

2 Appreciation is an acquired taste; and takes time; can be appreciated on a variety of levels; will have qualities of depth and detail; appreciation builds on previous experience; appeals to intellect as well as emotions. What does 'appreciate' mean? Fear of the unknown; we need to be shown how to appreciate.

3 High culture expensive to produce; limited audience appeal (and therefore income); good art is worth preserving; it embodies the values of society. Without subsidy would die and be lost. Government has a responsibility to preserve. Subsidy increases accessibility for ordinary people. Popular culture is transient and has little of lasting worth. Good popular culture is self-financing and relatively cheap to stage. It attracts larger audiences. The best will survive and become 'high culture'.

   But whose money should be used to subsidise? We ought to pay for what we want. Why should the poor subsidise the rich? 'Good' popular culture may not attract large enough audiences. High culture is only done for prestige/elitism. Popular culture does get subsidy through tax breaks.

#### Exam preparation

You must pay attention to the term 'better'. Too often people who deal with this type of question simply give their own opinion on the issue without considering the importance of qualifying or 'value judgement' words.

   Supplementary questions to consider include better 'for whom?' and 'under what circumstances?' You will have to show that 'better' is about taste and depends on preference in music, availability or accessibility.

   You might argue that opera is a cultural experience and is relatively rare outside London. It is a passive form of entertainment, may attract an older age group, generates prejudice among non-lovers of opera, and makes demands on the audience (plot, language, characters etc.). It may last for long periods of time, is often expensive but can involve great performers.

A pop concert is likely to attract younger people, may be more expensive than opera but can involve the audience more actively. It is likely to make limited intellectual demands but will involve the emotions. There may be outstanding performers, and opportunities, certainly outside London, may be limited. Those who attend are likely to get a 'buzz' from the experience, may attend with a group of friends, and will certainly have much to discuss afterwards.

## Judging cultures

### Checkpoints

1 Race Relations Acts (e.g. 1965 set up Race Relations Board; 1968 discrimination in housing, work and commercial services prohibited; Community Relations Committee; discriminatory practices limited; Commission for Racial Equality). 1981 Scarman Report: need for anti-discrimination laws.

Other laws affecting race relations: 1976 Immigration Act; 1981 British Nationality Act; 1991 Asylum Act.

**Examiner's tip**: *note the date. Do not include laws passed pre-1965. Question asks for steps taken by the government. Do not include other institutions.*

2 Ignorance; fear of differences; conflicting ideas or practices; different styles or behaviour leads to misunderstanding or misinterpretation; ridicule and mockery of differences; media-based stereotypes.

### Exam preparation

Possible issues to consider are either Northern Ireland, race riots in various towns or football rivalry. You should start by explaining what you mean by cultural conflict and explain why your chosen topic is relevant. This answer focuses on Ireland.

You could outline the causes of conflict as: history and tradition; different perceptions of the role of England/Britain in Ireland; religious differences – are they a cause or a symptom of conflict? Economic exploitation and hardship experienced more by some groups than others; inequitable treatment of Ireland by the British and regional governments. Political differences including Home Rule, republicanism, Eire, independence and Unionism and the emergence of open conflict due to the civil rights movement of the 1960s. The inevitable escalation of conflict in reply to rival violence and the emergence of rival extremism and the role of the churches are key features.

You should then outline ways in which you think the conflict might be resolved. These need to be developed and explained, not simply listed. You might consider any of the following.

- The acceptance of an agreed power-sharing agreement that satisfactorily safeguards the interests of all sections of the community.
- The enforcement of partition that separates the rival factions giving independence to either or both, or allowing/compelling the Republican section to unite with Eire while letting Unionists remain in the UK.
- Total reunification of the whole of Ireland, making the Protestants a minority. This would require guarantees and safeguards.
- Repatriation to Britain of Unionists who refused to accept reunification (or of Republicans to Eire if they refused to remain in the UK) could remove individuals who are causes of conflict. This is a form of ethnic cleansing and would require the willingness of the minority population. It would require a considerable financial outlay by the various governments involved.
- The majority of peaceful citizens continue to put pressure on the extremists. This could isolate and eventually drive out extremism. This should result in the establishment of a democratic government since the majority are tired of violence.
- A renewal of oppressive British military rule could impose peace by force. (This has failed over the last century.)
- Pressure and involvement from external agencies (such as the USA, UN or EU) could negotiate or enforce a settlement.
- Growing prosperity and continued moves to a more egalitarian treatment of the whole population might remove the underlying causes of conflict.

You might be able to use illustrations from other areas of the world where cultural conflict has been successfully resolved to support your answer.

# Databank

## Key components of culture

**Culture** is generally taken to mean the total way of life of a society. It also includes the complete range of objects, ideas and attitudes developed by members of a society to allow them to conduct a collective life.

**Symbol** refers to all things that convey meaning for members of a culture. They are therefore 'message carriers' that allow cultural communication.

**Language** is one of the most significant symbols. It is a structured system with commonly agreed meanings that permit communication between people. All societies have a spoken language; development of a written language is regarded as a measure of civilization. It is the principle medium for cultural transmission, helps us to shape the reality of our world, and develops as society progresses.

**Values** are attitudes or standards of behaviour seen as desirable in a society. In addition to societal values individuals develop their own personal values. Value inconsistency occurs if two value systems differ due to certain criteria such as age, sex, race or religion. If an individual's values are opposed to social values there will be value conflict.

**Norms** are rules that guide an individual's behaviour within society. These may be formal, written rules, as in law, or they may be informal as in traditions and customs. Norms both define acceptable behaviour, (such as standing for the National Anthem), and prescribe unacceptable conduct (such as theft or drunkenness).

**Sanctions** (a system of rewards and punishment) are meant to promote compliance with normative conduct. They may be formal (e.g. prizes or fines) or informal (verbal praise or criticism) and are a significant part of a culture's system of social control.

**Mores** refer to norms having great moral worth and often relate to respect for people and property. They may include prohibitions such as restrictions on sexual behaviour, or may prescribe required conduct, such as wearing clothes in public. There are usually strong sanctions for breaking these norms.

**Cultural diversity** exists in all societies. No culture is totally uniform, but varies according to social class, geographical location, predominant race, average age, religion, educational standard, or tradition.

**Subcultures** refer to groups that differ significantly from some aspects of the cultural life of the dominant mainstream culture. They may have their own beliefs, dress code, language or values. Subcultures exhibit distinctive features in some ways, though conforming in the main to dominant practice.

**Countercultures** (or contracultures) are subcultures that are strongly opposed to the dominant culture and challenge mainstream morality or values. They are often associated with youth movements (e.g. hippies in the 1960s) or the politically disaffected (e.g. anti-war groups and the IRA). They often develop distinctive 'uniforms', appearance, language and values.

**Ethnocentrism** occurs if you judge other cultures by the standards of your own culture. In many ways this is probably inevitable, because we understand the social world in terms of our own cultural experience.

**Cultural relativism** is when we judge a culture by its own standards. This is only possible if we understand the norms and values of the culture we are judging.

**Cultural deprivation** is when an individual or group lack appropriate cultural resources, such as language or knowledge. Some say the reason some subcultures experience difficulty in meeting the norms of society is because of cultural deprivation.

**Cultural imperialism** refers to the process by which aspects of one culture are exported to other cultures in order to replace aspects of the original culture.

**Cultural transmission** is how awareness of cultural expectations is passed on between generations. This is traditionally an aspect of socialisation associated with family, education and religion.

# Revision checklist
*helps you check what you still need to do*

## By the end of this chapter you should be able to:

| | | | |
|---|---|---|---|
| 1 | Use the information in Databank, above, with confidence | Confident | Not confident. **Revise** page 134 |
| 2 | Understand the nature and meaning of culture | Confident | Not confident. **Revise** pages 126–7, 134 |
| 3 | Explain why there are divisions between cultures | Confident | Not confident. **Revise** pages 126–7 |
| 4 | Show the relationship of language, religion, history and science in the development of culture | Confident | Not confident. **Revise** pages 127, 204 |
| 5 | Identify advantages of multi-culture and mono-culture | Confident | Not confident. **Revise** page 130 |
| 6 | Show awareness of different types of minority culture | Confident | Not confident. **Revise** page 130 |
| 7 | Explain why culture is important to individuals | Confident | Not confident. **Revise** page 131 |
| 8 | Appreciate the qualities of cultural diversity | Confident | Not confident. **Revise** page 131 |
| 9 | Distinguish between popular, folk and high culture | Confident | Not confident. **Revise** pages 128–129 |
| 10 | Identify the key features of Western culture | Confident | Not confident. **Revise** page 129 |
| 11 | Appreciate different factors influencing change | Confident | Not confident. **Revise** pages 189, 202, 203 |

# Beliefs, values and moral reasoning

Every society develops its own system of values. Most members of society conform to accepted norms, transmitted through different institutions, such as family, religion and education. Some behavioural norms are embodied in the law; others less clearly defined are generally understood by most of society. Some behavioural norms, dealing with questions of right and wrong, are called moral values.

New issues often emerge which are not clearly dealt with by the existing value system, so that it is necessary to develop new values. This process is called moral reasoning. However, some people believe there are moral absolutes, which should apply under all conditions to all people. They are often linked to strong religious beliefs.

You should be able to identify the principle values of your own society and contemporary moral issues. Some specifications require you to identify formative influences that have helped develop moral values. You should be able to describe different methods of moral reasoning and apply them to contemporary issues. You will find sections of the Science and Society units deal with different aspects of moral and social values.

## Exam themes

→ Formative influences in the development of moral reasoning and value judgements

→ Moral absolutes and different types of moral reasoning

→ The relationship of moral reasoning to contemporary moral issues

→ Matters of tolerance, conscience and public morality

→ Knowledge, belief and unbelief

→ The role and importance of value systems

→ The transmission of beliefs and social values

→ The process of changing and developing morality

→ The relationship between the individual and society

## Topic checklist

| ○ AS  ● A2 | AQA A | AQA B | EDEXCEL | OCR |
|---|---|---|---|---|
| Beliefs and moral values | ○● | ○● | ○● | ○ |
| Contemporary moral issues | ○● | ○● | ○● | ○ |
| The basis of moral reasoning | ○● | ○● | ○● | ○ |

# Beliefs and moral values

If you claim to 'know' something, you can mean several different things. You might refer to something that is generally accepted as true, such as 'the moon goes round the Earth'. This is a fact. You may refer to something that you are convinced is true, but which others are certain is false, such as 'there is life on Mars'. This is an opinion.

## Where does knowledge come from?

Factual knowledge is the body of information that is accepted as true at any given time in history. As new knowledge is discovered, 'facts' may change. The body of knowledge is steadily increasing.

Knowledge can be gained in several different ways. We can:

→ be taught things that other people know;
→ discover things by applying logic and reason;
→ learn through personal experience;
→ find things out by experiment.

Knowledge discovered by experiment is sometimes called scientific or empirical knowledge. Some people claim that we are born with certain knowledge. This is called innate or intuitive knowledge.

## What are beliefs?

Beliefs are a particular type of opinion. They may not be accepted by other people, and it may not be easy to verify them. But to a believer they are true. Beliefs are based on personal conviction.

You might say, 'I know God created the Earth'. You really mean, 'I believe God created the earth'. Although you may be convinced it is true, others may prefer different ways to explain the origin of life. Belief depends on faith or trust in something that cannot be verified empirically. To a believer this would count as knowledge, but to a non-believer it would be considered an opinion. A belief is very personal, whereas factual knowledge is impersonal.

## Where do beliefs come from?

Throughout our lives we are exposed to many different influences which help us to develop our beliefs and values.

→ In our early years the most significant influences are our families. We usually learn by copying our parents.
→ Later, friends and people we meet and mix with influence us.
→ Education and work can affect our attitudes and beliefs.
→ We can be influenced by our neighbourhood.
→ The media and entertainment can shape our thinking and so help us to develop and fix our beliefs.

Most people in a community share a common system of beliefs and values, although there will be some variation between individuals. A person whose value system is totally different to the majority is likely to be treated as deviant or may become an outcast from society.

---

**Example**

Once, men 'knew' that the sun circled the Earth. Scientific discoveries in the seventeenth century showed this to be false. Today, 'new' facts show that the Earth circles the sun.

**Link**

See page 201 for the difference between knowledge and belief.

**Checkpoint 1**

Why do some beliefs lead to conflict between members of the same society?

**Checkpoint 2**

How can either education or work influence our beliefs?

**Links**

See pages 145–154 on religious belief.

## Moral values and moral codes

When we talk about morality we are thinking about particular types of belief. Morality concerns what is believed to be right and wrong. It deals with how individuals, as members of a group, should conduct their lives towards each other. It also deals with the responsibility of the group to individuals. Moral values can refer to the rules guiding the behaviour of a whole society or can refer to the beliefs of an individual.

Moral values may be expressed formally as written rules or laws or may simply be accepted and taken for granted as a result of custom and practice. In any society it should be possible to identify a set of generally accepted moral principles. These are described as a moral code. Societies develop a moral code in order to regulate behaviour between individuals. We need to understand how other people are likely to react to our actions and we need a way to control our own self-interest so that our actions do not conflict with the interests of others.

In some societies a single shared value system exists. In most modern societies there are differences of opinion, especially concerning moral questions. This can lead to unrest and sometimes to conflict. For example, in Britain, although abortion has been legal since 1967, not everyone accepts that it is morally right. Some groups have protested against this law on grounds of morality.

## Where do moral values come from?

Is morality innate? Can human beings automatically distinguish between right and wrong? Is morally correct behaviour instinctive and do people behave towards others as they ought because their conscience tells them to? These views imply that people who don't live according to generally accepted moral values are in a sense 'abnormal'.

Are we taught moral values? This could be indoctrination, meaning that we are persuaded or made to accept what other people want us to believe. It implies the loss of our right to free choice.

Do we develop our views of right and wrong through personal experience? In other words do we discover the difference between right and wrong through interaction with others?

Are there absolute moral principles? Some claim these are contained in the teachings of the major religions and have been revealed to us by a superior power, often called 'God'.

Can each individual discover what is right and wrong for themselves simply by the use of reason?

There is probably no single answer to 'where do moral values come from?'. Most answers will depend on an individual's own perspective on life. Contemporary moral values are the product of a combination of different factors.

**Jargon**

Values are beliefs or opinions which an individual or group consider to be of central importance to life.

**Example**

One of the best-known examples of a written moral code is the Ten Commandments. It is contained in the Old Testament of the Bible and forms a statement of principles not only for members of the Jewish and Christian religions but also for many people who don't claim a particular religious belief.

**Checkpoint 3**

List three different moral values that might be regarded as innate. Choose one of them and explain whether you believe it is innate or taught.

**Checkpoint 4**

Which individuals or organisations might indoctrinate other human beings?

**Exam preparation**                          answer: page 142

How far do you believe it is necessary to teach people the difference between right and wrong?   (15 minutes)

# Contemporary moral issues

## Watch out!

It is easy to confuse a question about morality (right and wrong) with one that simply asks for a descriptive account.

## Checkpoint 1

Why do scientific developments sometimes lead to moral dilemmas?

## Links

Look at pages 15, 22, 36 and 37 to find more about genetic modification.

## Action point

You may have strong views on these and other scientific and technological moral questions. Think carefully about why people might hold different opinions to your own. Apply the different styles of moral reasoning (explained on pages 140–141) to these issues to discover different views.

## Links

See pages 34, 36, 38 and 194 for more on science and morality.

Scientific and technological change and the collapse of traditional values have created a new range of moral questions. As society has become more complex and less authoritarian we are forced to make up our own minds about issues for which in the past a central authority might have provided answers. These would often not have been open to debate or question. Now, when faced with moral dilemmas, we demand the freedom to make up our own minds. Moral questions can be divisive.

## Scientific and technological change

The rate of increase in scientific knowledge is now greater than ever. Once discoveries are made, they must be applied to serve humanity. Very often discoveries can be beneficial or harmful, depending on how they are used. This raises a major moral dilemma. Who should decide what work scientists do and the use to which their discoveries should be put? We must remember scientists are people who have the same moral commitment, feelings and emotions as any other individual. Can scientists be genuinely objective in their work?

Many scientists claim that their role is simply to develop new knowledge and not make moral judgements about the use to which their discoveries are put. Others argue that scientists must work in an ethical way, taking care that their work should contribute only to human good.

Contemporary moral issues relating to science which you could consider include: genetic modification; new scientific farming methods; cloning; developing and using new expensive medical treatments; use of animal organs in humans; organ transplants; nuclear power; designer babies; identification and termination of potentially damaged foetuses.

Medical progress is an area of scientific development that must impact on all our lives. Few would argue against the idea that medicine's main purpose is to preserve and improve the quality of life. The media often report on the financial problems of the National Health Service, the need for extra costly resources, a lack of expensive medicines in some areas; and the difficulties patients face while waiting months or years for treatment. At the same time, we often hear of exciting new treatments developed at great expense to combat previously untreatable illnesses.

This presents society with a moral dilemma. Is it right to spend vast amounts of money to treat a few people with rare complaints, or would it be better to divert the money to relieve the suffering of large numbers? Linked to this is a similar issue concerning elderly patients. It has been claimed that some old patients, who could have been revived, are allowed to die because of the cost of treating and caring for them. Some scientists say that the application of discoveries is not their responsibility. Their job is to extend knowledge but society must decide how that knowledge is used. How many hip replacements are worth a single heart transplant? How might social contract theory or a utilitarianism resolve these moral dilemmas?

## Social and political issues ●●●

Moral dilemmas about social issues are as complex as scientific ones. Most people feel they are easier to discuss since there are no obvious 'experts' involved. However, most of us tend to feel that our own opinions are right and contradictory opinions are wrong. You could think about different moral answers to questions about: abortion on demand; the rights of fathers; the rights of children; legal limits on family size; the right to disobey bad laws; freedom of conscience for soldiers in war time; the rights of the unemployed; taxation as a way to redistribute wealth; the right to protest; euthanasia; the purpose of punishment; victims' rights.

Euthanasia literally means 'a good death' and usually describes 'mercy killing'. Recently there has been discussion in the media about whether it should be legalised in this country. At present it is illegal to assist another person to take their own life. Moral arguments used to oppose a change in the law are usually based on the sanctity of human life. It is claimed that it is impossible to draw up adequate safeguards to protect the elderly or terminally ill against unscrupulous relatives. It is said to be a small step from legalising euthanasia to allowing the killing of the unwanted. Some say our trust in doctors would be damaged if, as they are sworn to preserve life, they were involved in ending it. People who suffer great pain through illness one day may think they want to die, but the next change their mind and wish to live.

On the other hand, people say that mature human beings should have the right to choose what to do with their own lives. If life becomes unbearable, why should the law enforce continued suffering? Supporting the terminally ill is expensive and resources could be better used to help those who could recover to enjoy a better quality of life.

Increased longevity and the prospect of greater numbers of old people in the population will make the issue of euthanasia a continuing dilemma. What do you think now? How might your views change by age 70?

## Cultural questions ●●●

There are many moral issues linked to the arts and culture. These areas affect us all. We may think that what interests us is important, but things that don't affect us are unimportant. Some issues lead to vigorous, and at times violent, discussion. They concern a conflict between personal freedom and the rights of the public. Questions to consider include: racial discrimination; subsidy of some art forms but not others; artistic freedom of expression; environmental issues; justification for some forms of censorship; racial integration; sexual orientation; and the role and responsibility of religious leaders.

**Checkpoint 2**

Give three different moral reasons to support or challenge the view that all women should be entitled to abortion on demand.

*"I disapprove of what you say, but I will defend to the death your right to say it."*

Attributed to Voltaire

**Checkpoint 3**

What do you understand by 'freedom of expression'? Why might it not be a good thing in the Arts?

**Examiner's secrets**

When answering questions about moral issues be careful not to become emotionally involved in your answer.

---

**Exam preparation**                                    answer: pages 142–143

Identify and comment on two different moral issues associated with medicine in the 21st century.   (10 minutes)

# The basis of moral reasoning

### Examiner's secrets

It is easy to confuse morality with moral reasoning. Check the question carefully to be sure which you are asked to write about.

### Checkpoint 1

To which religious groups do each of these Holy books belong? (Bible, Torah, Qu'ran, Upanishads, Granth Sahib, Vedas, Tripitaka)

### Links

Find out more about religious belief from pages 145–154.

### Checkpoint 2

How might the attitude of a Christian follower of natural law theory differ from that of a social contract theorist with regard to cohabitation (living together without being legally married)?

### Jargon

An absolute value is one that must apply in all circumstances and conditions, at all times and in every society without modification. A universal value is one which applies to every society or individual.

Moral values help us make judgements about simple and straightforward issues. Most people can decide fairly easily whether it is right to steal or to lie. Sometimes problems are complicated and not obviously covered by our moral code. We have to work out what is right and what is wrong. This process is called moral reasoning. There are different ways of discovering moral answers.

## Religious morality

Many religious people believe their religion defines a moral code to direct their life and behaviour. Faced with a difficult moral problem their aim is to find out 'what God wants them to do'. This may be done by:

→ reading a holy book, such as the Bible, Qur'an, Vedas or Tripitaka;
→ consulting a religious leader or teacher, such as a vicar, guru or rabbi;
→ prayer and meditation.

This approach is more concerned with obedience to a higher authority than with the consequences of particular actions. Behaviour is often influenced by the prospect of future reward or punishment.

## Natural law

Some people believe in 'natural' laws that govern behaviour, which can be discovered by studying society and human beings. These laws, once discovered, make it possible to say which behaviours are right and which are wrong. Natural law is taught by some religious people who believe that God has decided these laws. It is also followed by non-religious people who believe that 'right' conduct is behaviour needed if humanity is to survive. This moral approach claims that if everyone adopted a natural form of behaviour, a perfect society would exist.

## Social contract

This view claims that moral codes are invented by society to make life better. People agree to obey moral principles and in return expect society to protect them. The contract is ended if either party breaks it. Moral conduct is based on self-interest and fear of sanctions. Followers of social contract theory believe an action is right if it is beneficial to society, but is wrong if it unfairly restricts an individual's freedom of choice and action.

## Duty or self-interest?

Kant argued that people know, on the basis of reason, what is right or wrong. Instinct tells us to perform certain actions even if we gain no personal advantage. Similarly, we know that certain acts are wrong, even if we could perform them without being discovered. Such moral values are universal, objective and absolute. The criterion for judging an action is 'what would happen if everybody else did this?' The theory assumes that every individual is a rational person, able to act in a rational way.

## Consequentialism and utilitarianism

Some forms of moral reasoning called 'consequentialist' judge whether an action is right or wrong by its effects or consequences. Consequentialism claims that actions are neither good nor bad of themselves, but that every action has a measurable consequence. The best known form of consequentialism is utilitarianism. It argues that, where a person has a choice of actions, the correct or right action is the one that brings about the greatest amount of human happiness or least amount of suffering. As a universal theory it considers the sum total of human happiness and not just people directly concerned. It is criticised because it ignores the concept of justice and is impracticable in most everyday circumstances. If applied, it could generate more unhappiness than would exist if a decision were taken on more practical grounds.

## The decline of authority

Until the 1950s Britain had a well-established respect for authority based on broadly Christian principles. Rules, laws and moral values were clearly understood and generally accepted. There was generally respect for police, teachers and even politicians. People respected the wisdom of age and experience. Parents were usually seen as figures of authority to be listened to and obeyed. Religion was clearly in decline but its teachings still influenced many aspects of life and social values. Britain was a well-ordered hierarchic society in which everyone knew and accepted their proper place.

Since then attitudes have changed radically. Authority is increasingly challenged. Traditional values are questioned. As youth culture has emerged, so respect for age and authority has decreased. Moral issues, which once had clear and accepted answers, are increasingly questioned. Moral certainties have become moral doubts.

Today, few accept or believe in moral absolutes. Many claim 'right' is what you are comfortable with and want to do, while 'wrong' is anything you are uncomfortable with. Changes in attitude have been matched by changes in law. Activities once forbidden are now allowed. Tolerance of the opinions and behaviour of others is a key feature of modern society.

## Rights and responsibilities

In the past, social behaviour was conducted according to a sense of duty and responsibility to others. Today, greater emphasis is put on individual rights and entitlement. The last 50 years have seen human rights given legal protection and definition. In 1948 the United Nations issued the Declaration of Human Rights. The European Convention on Human Rights was ratified by Britain in 1951 but did not become law until 1998.

---

### Exam preparation

answer: page 143

To what extent do you agree that when we judge the behaviour of other people we should 'live and let live'? (30 minutes)

---

**Checkpoint 3**

What issues might a utilitarian need to consider when assessing whether a change in the law is needed? (For example, in forbidding drinking in public, or allowing topless sunbathing in public parks.)

*"The conscience which 'makes cowards of us all' is rather a censor than a guide. Its decrees form a kind of criminal law; it intervenes to deter and punish."*

RW Beardsmore, *Moral Reasoning*, 1969

**Jargon**

Hierarchic – any organisational structure in which different grades of responsibility or importance are recognised.

**Checkpoint 4**

Name four different laws passed since 1965 that have helped change attitudes about moral issues.

**Links**

See pages 33–42 for moral responsibility in science and pages 96–97 for Morality, deviance and rights.

# Answers
## Beliefs, values and moral reasoning

## Beliefs and moral values

### Checkpoints

1 More complex societies are not homogeneous. Therefore, in any society various belief systems exist alongside each other, often harmoniously. Diversity may increase where a society consists of people from different cultural backgrounds. Beliefs are firmly held convictions and it is impossible to believe something you know to be false. People holding different views to your own must, almost by definition, be wrong. Normally where tolerance exists such differences are unimportant. Tolerance is usually found when people do not feel threatened. Threats may have many causes.

 Differences of religious belief over the nature of God, salvation, the afterlife, organisation, leadership and authority have led to conflict; for example, in the Middle East, Northern Ireland and the former Yugoslavia.

 Political differences have led to terrorism, revolution or civil war, as in Northern Ireland, Haiti or Zimbabwe.

 Moral differences over abortion, euthanasia, genetic modification or road building have resulted in demonstrations and sometimes violence or even death.

2 **Education** influences our beliefs through lesson content, school rules and regulations, sanctions and rewards and the hidden curriculum. A principle reason for collective worship is to reinforce accepted beliefs.

 **Work** can influence people similarly. It establishes a sense of corporate identity and responsibility, fosters the work ethic, rewards desired attitudes and conduct and provides us with role models.

3 Innate moral values are values that we are born with, rather than ones that are learned and taught. Examples might be the sacredness of life, honesty, concern for others and faith within relationships.

 You can defend either point of view but could show that these are all regarded as natural and are found in all societies. Equally, they exist in most legal codes as a statement of desirable behaviours.

4 The list is almost endless. Consider: politicians, teachers, priests, parents, journalists, friends, writers, colleagues, employers or managers, school, family, government, church, army, work, police, media, etc.

### Exam preparation

This question is really asking you whether beliefs are innate or need to be learned. It is like Checkpoint 3. You need to explain what the terms right and wrong mean to you. Are there any forms of behaviour that we know instinctively? You could point out that children rarely appreciate differences until told or unless they learn by experience. There would be little need for sanctions if we naturally know about right and wrong. You could show that not all societies hold similar views. Some cultures accepted that unwanted children could be exposed to die; punishments in some cultures use execution or maiming, but others banned prison; some religions do not allow divorce or abortion but others allow several wives at a time.

You could consider if it is necessary for all people to have the same ideas of right and wrong. Who decides what should be taught (family, church or state); how ought conflicting differences between belief systems to be resolved? Who should undertake the teaching?

## Contemporary moral issues

### Checkpoints

1 See the unit on moral responsibility in the science section, pages 34, 36 and 38.

 Your answer should deal with the idea that morality concerns what is right and wrong and therefore, as far as science is concerned, the issue is about application rather than discovery. You should consider the nature of scientific research as well as morality. The issue is how far scientists simply ought to extend knowledge, leaving to others the responsibility to decide if it is right to make use of such knowledge. You should show that many discoveries might have various applications. Few developments are intrinsically evil; even fewer are designed to be harmful. Very often scientists may not be aware of possible results or use of discoveries. You should illustrate your response with scientific illustrations like the dilemmas created by discoveries such as nuclear power or genetic modification.

2 Note the requirement to give moral (not social or scientific) reasons. You may support or challenge the view and do not have to justify abortion, only examine the labels attached to it. Your answer might include:
 • it is wrong to bring into the world an unwanted child;
 • a mother's needs should be of primary concern;
 • every woman should have rights over her body;
 • it is always wrong to take life;
 • fathers should have the same rights as mothers;
 • existing rules stop abortion becoming an alternative to contraception;
 • many women would welcome the chance to adopt;
 • the unborn child has rights;
 • abortion on demand could encourage irresponsibility.

3 This is the right to say or do what you want without restriction or limit, implying that all thoughts and ideas are of the same worth and should not be censored.

 Total freedom of artistic expression may not be a good thing since it could be a licence to offend or be outrageous. Artists have a responsibility to their audiences, since art is a form of communication. We all share the right not to be upset. Artistic freedom may lead to pornography and obscenity. It is better to have clear restrictions before an event rather than go to law afterwards. Restriction of freedom implies that somebody must define what is and is not acceptable.

### Exam preparation

You could suggest a range of possible answers:
 • Should cloning be permitted?
 • Is genetic modification of humans acceptable?

- To what extent should people with private health insurance be allowed preferential treatment?
- Should the 'post-code' lottery influence treatment?
- Should the NHS pay to use private medical provision to reduce waiting times for hospital treatment?
- Should animal organs be used in human transplants?
- Is it right to provide expensive treatments for a few patients rather than cheaper operations for many?
- Should third world countries be deprived of medicines on grounds of cost?

Your comments ought to state the nature of the issue and say why it poses a moral dilemma. This means you should comment on different viewpoints.

## The basis of moral reasoning

### Checkpoints

1 Bible – Christianity and Judaism; Torah – Judaism; Qur'an – Islam; Upanishads or Vedas – Hinduism; Granth Sahib – Sikhism; the Tripitaka – Buddhism.

2 Natural law claims that laws, once discovered, are binding; Christians believe God has revealed natural law in the Bible. The Bible teaches life-long marriage and so cohabiting would be morally wrong.

Social contract theory claims moral codes are defined by society and so can be changed. In modern society, many laws do not distinguish between marriage and cohabiting. Since society benefits more from lasting rather than casual relationships, cohabiting is morally acceptable.

3 Utilitarians consider effects rather than actions. In asking if a law needs changing they would check how it might affect all of society. Ideally they would review all possible effects, both short and long term. Benefits to individuals would be balanced with possible costs to society. Utilitarians might conclude that legalising topless sunbathing could benefit the few people who wish to practice it, but might offend many more. If the number upset exceeded those pleased, utilitarians would reject change. Utilitarian beliefs are described as 'the greatest happiness of the greatest number'.

4 There are many, but note the laws must relate to changes in moral attitudes and not just social reform. In questions of this type you should state the moral values your example concerns. Choose from: 1965, Race Relations; Capital Punishment; 1967, Sexual Offences; 1969, Divorce; Abortion; 1970, Equal Pay; Capital Punishment; 1975, Sex Discrimination; Race Relations; 1984, Matrimonial Property; 1986, Animal Research; 1989, Children; 1990, Disability; 1992, Human Fertilization; 1995, Disability; 1996, Divorce; 1998, Human Rights; 2000, Carers and Disabled Children; Race Relations; 2001, Disability; 2002, Genetically Modified Organisms; Abortion.

### Exam preparation

The key issue is toleration. Note the question is about behaviour, not just moral values. You are expected to evaluate arguments to reach a conclusion. The title implies there may be times when adverse judgements are justified. Consider the views of those who argue for universal standards of behaviour as well as those who believe in the right of each individual to behave as they wish. You should include practical examples.

Explain what you understand by the term 'live and let live'. It means that we ought to get on with our lives at the same time as other people are entitled to live life as they choose without interference.

Arguments supporting a less tolerant attitude might include religious teachings, legislation including the Human Rights Act, and ideas about social solidarity and cohesion.

The opposite viewpoint should pay more attention to the rights and freedom of individuals in a democratic society. Again, you might make use of Human Rights legislation, but a key aspect of your answer should deal with circumstances and conditions. Perhaps the context in which behaviour occurs is as important as the nature of the behaviour itself.

In your answer you should consider the way different types of moral reasoning might be used to help you reach a conclusion. Utilitarians would be concerned with the consequences of actions but social contract arguments would be concerned with the effect of actions on society. Remember there are some people or institutions that have a duty to make judgements about behaviour (parents, judges, policemen, priests or teachers). Similarly, you may feel entitled to make judgements about behaviour by which you are personally involved or affected.

# Databank
## Moral dilemmas – database

### Some contemporary dilemmas

**Abortion** was illegal in the United Kingdom until 1967 when it was allowed under strictly defined rules. Now, every year, thousands of abortions take place.

Some people claim that the law should be changed to give women even greater rights to choose whether to terminate a pregnancy. Some say that fathers should have rights, while others say only the mother should take the decision. On the other hand, many believe that abortion is totally wrong under all circumstances and should never be allowed. Some religious groups forbid abortion since they believe life is sacred, while others take a more liberal attitude. In the USA one person was killed by an anti-abortion campaigner.

**Contraception** is now widely available, advertised in the media and the subject of lessons in schools. Until the end of the Second World War the principles of contraception were not taught in any British medical school and before the 1920s people who gave advice about contraception could be jailed. Some people say that the use of the contraceptive pill since the 1960s has contributed to changing sexual behaviour and declining moral standards. Roman Catholics are told not to use contraception, but most religious groups let members decide for themselves. The law forbids sex before 16 but some doctors feel responsible for the physical health of their patients rather than for their morals.

**Designer babies** have become a realistic possibility as a result of developments in genetic science. It is now quite common for parents to know the sex of their unborn child. Screening in the womb for a range of diseases is possible. If abnormalities are detected, parents may have the choice to end a pregnancy. Some people find this morally unacceptable. However, others say that parents ought to be able to choose not only the sex of their child, but also the characteristics and features it should have. It may be that this could favour wealthy parents able to pay for the necessary treatment. It might also lead to discrimination against children who lack fashionable or desired qualities.

**Euthanasia** (or mercy killing) is illegal in almost all countries. Attempts to legalise it in the UK have failed because it is difficult to draw up adequate safeguards to protect the vulnerable from exploitation by relatives or doctors. Some people say the terminally ill should have the right to end their own life, if necessary, with the help of others. However, the right to euthanasia is opposed on both religious and moral grounds since life is sacred and no one has the right to end it. It is wrong for doctors to help end a life since they swear to preserve it. Undoubtedly many terminally ill people are allowed to die by the withholding of treatment. Does this make euthanasia more or less justifiable? Scientific and medical changes have made this moral issue more difficult than ever before.

**Welfare benefits** have existed for those in need since the early 20th century. The aim of the National Health Service, set up in 1947, was to provide healthcare for all without charge. Costs were to be paid from taxation. Since then, new treatments and drugs have increased costs. Recently politicians have debated the future of the Health Service. Some claim that provision should be free at the point of service. Others say we cannot afford the high costs and people should take out their own private insurance to cover their needs. How far is the state morally responsible for individual needs?

*Check the web to research other moral dilemmas.*

# Revision checklist
### *helps you check what you still need to do*

### By the end of this chapter you should be able to:

| | | |
|---|---|---|
| 1 Use the information in Databank, above, with confidence | Confident | Not confident. **Revise** page 144 |
| 2 Explain differences between knowledge and belief | Confident | Not confident. **Revise** pages 136, 201 |
| 3 Understand how we develop our beliefs and moral values | Confident | Not confident. **Revise** page 136 |
| 4 Explain the meaning of moral values and moral codes | Confident | Not confident. **Revise** page 137 |
| 5 Identify different types of moral reasoning | Confident | Not confident. **Revise** pages 140–141 |
| 6 Discuss reasons for changing patterns of authority | Confident | Not confident. **Revise** page 141 |
| 7 Distinguish between rights and responsibilities | Confident | Not confident. **Revise** page 141 |
| 8 Show how scientific and technological developments have contributed to the increase of moral dilemmas | Confident | Not confident. **Revise** page 138 |
| 9 Identify a range of contemporary moral dilemmas | Confident | Not confident. **Revise** pages 138–139 |
| 10 Explain some of the pressures that are helping to influence and change social values | Confident | Not confident. **Revise** page 139 |

# Religious beliefs

There are many different types of religion and religious belief. Definitions of religion range from the restricted idea of belief in the supernatural to the broader concept of any belief system that attracts an individual's devotion, such as football or pop stars. Religion takes various forms, but there are six major world religions. Recently some people have argued that we should include paganism or satanism.

Religion has been significant in many aspects of life, although its influence today has declined. Believers may look to religion for guidance in daily living. In Western Europe it has been the basis for much of the legal system. Many systems of values and moral codes are derived from religion, even in modern secular societies.

In some areas of the world religious belief remains a powerful force. However, Christianity, the dominant religion in the Western world, has faced challenges from science and the emergence of a secular society. Relatively few people are practising believers, and some argue that Religious Education should no longer be compulsory in our schools.

## Exam themes

→ The role and importance of religion

→ Features and beliefs of the major world religions; their impact on daily living

→ The nature of religious belief; differences of opinion about beliefs and values; alternatives to religion

→ Why people have religious belief: the need for purpose in life

→ Tolerance and religious controversy; issues relating to a multi-faith society

→ Religion and secularism: science; the relationship between religion and the state

→ Religious and secular sides of moral arguments

→ Spiritual experience and religious belief

→ The power and influence of religious beliefs and leaders in society

→ The symbolism of religion

## Topic checklist

○ AS  ● A2

| | AQA A | AQA B | EDEXCEL | OCR |
|---|---|---|---|---|
| The major world religions | ○● | ○● | ○● | ● |
| The importance of religious belief | ○● | ○● | ○● | ● |
| Religion and conflict | ○● | ○● | ○● | ● |

# The major world religions

Religion is usually understood to be about belief in and worship of a superhuman controlling power. From this it is used more broadly to mean a particular system of faith and worship. In the broadest sense it can refer to any pursuit or interest that is followed with commitment and devotion. Almost all societies have developed their own religious systems. Six religions have spread from a local to a worldwide context. Generally they can be classed as either monotheistic or polytheistic.

**Jargon**

Monotheistic: belief in one god.
polytheistic: belief in many gods.
Deist: belief in a supreme power or creator who does not interfere in human experience.
Theist: belief in a supreme power or creator who does interfere in human experience.

## Buddhism

→ Started in India by Siddhartha Guatama (the Buddha) about 2500 years ago.
→ Mainly found in China and the Far East.
→ Main teachings (in the Tripitaka) are 'The Four Noble Truths' and 'The Eightfold Path'.
→ Full understanding leads to peace, happiness and enlightenment.
→ Humans are repeatedly reborn (reincarnation) to experience suffering.
→ Meditation and obedience to Buddha can lead to nirvana (paradise).
→ Does not necessarily involve belief in a God, the soul or worship.

**Checkpoint 1**

Should Buddhism be classed as a religion?

## Christianity

→ Founded 2000 years ago by followers of Jesus of Nazareth.
→ A development of the much older religion of Judaism.
→ It is based on the belief that Jesus is the son of God.
→ Its teachings are contained in a holy book, the Bible, part of which is shared with Judaism.
→ Some believe the Bible is literal truth. This conflicts with science.
→ Christians believe that obedience to God will result in everlasting life in God's Kingdom or in heaven.
→ It teaches one God, but most Christians are Trinitarian.
→ The main worship (Communion or the Eucharist – bread and wine) is a commemoration of the death and resurrection of Jesus.
→ People join the Christian community through the rite of baptism.

**Watch out!**

Many students get into difficulties when writing about religion because they allow their personal emotions and beliefs too much influence in what they say.

## Hinduism

→ Developed in India about 3500 years ago.
→ Main beliefs are reincarnation and karma (law of cause and effect).
→ It is a way of life governing social, moral and political behaviour.
→ Moral duty varies from person to person, according to situation.
→ Code of conduct stresses truth, non-violence and honesty.
→ Worship is mainly home based, but there is communal worship.
→ Aim of life is to escape to nirvana – freedom from rebirth.
→ Belief in a universal spirit (Brahman) seen in many different forms.
→ Is it polytheistic or monotheistic?
→ Teachings found in the Vedas and other holy books.
→ There are many festivals, most notably Divali.

**Checkpoint 2**

Explain the terms Trinity, Ramadan, Sabbath and Communion.

## Islam

→ Islam means 'submission to God'.
→ Founded in AD 622 by Mohammed in Mecca (Saudi Arabia).
→ Muslims believe in one God, Allah.
→ The holy book, the Qur'an, was revealed to Mohammed by Allah.
→ Most Muslims want to make a pilgrimage (hajj) to Mecca.
→ Worship takes place in a mosque.
→ The way of life is based on the Five Pillars of Wisdom.
→ Islamic laws (the Shari'ah) influence all aspects of daily life.
→ There are many similarities with Judaism and Christianity.

## Judaism

→ Founded about 3500 years ago in the Middle East.
→ Strictly monotheistic, it claims a special relationship with God.
→ Teachings are contained in the Old Testament of the Bible.
→ God's law is contained in the Torah (first part of the Bible).
→ The Ten Commandments form the key part of the law.
→ Judaism has a strict attitude to personal morality.
→ Worship takes place in the synagogue or the home.
→ They believe God gave Israel to their ancestor Abraham for ever.
→ Saturday (the Sabbath) is a special day when God rested.

## Sikhism

→ Founded in India about 500 years ago.
→ Beliefs are based on the teaching of ten Gurus.
→ All males are named Singh (Lion) and women Kaur (princess).
→ All Sikhs observe the 5 Ks.
→ They believe that God is one, the only eternal reality and is present in all creation and every human being.
→ Sikhism has no priests and worship takes place in the gurdwara.
→ Emphasis is placed on caring, service to others and equality.
→ Sikh teachings are found in the Guru Granth Sahib.
→ It combines aspects of both the Hindu and Muslim religions.

## Religious divisions

Most world religions are split into rival groups. Divisions, based on different interpretations of laws and beliefs, often lead to conflict. The conflict in Northern Ireland is an example of this. Christians are divided into Catholics and Protestants, but there are many different Protestant groups. Most religions believe in a purpose in life and that obedience to religious rules will win a believer the promised reward.

---

**Checkpoint 3**

What do you understand by the terms monotheist, polytheist, pantheist and theism?

*"There are only two forces in the world, the sword and the spirit. In the long run the sword will always be conquered by the spirit."*

Napoleon Bonaparte

**Links**

For more information on conflict, see pages 150–151, 188.

**Examiner's secrets**

Make sure if you are asked to name something that you do so before going on to answer other parts of a question. You may lose all the marks if you have ignored this instruction.

---

**Exam preparation**                                   answer: page 152

Name a religion you have studied. (a) List three key aspects of its beliefs which are shared with some but not all world religions. (b) Give two of its key beliefs which are shared with most other religions.   (15 minutes)

# The importance of religious belief

Religious belief is very personal. To believers it is inescapable and brings commitment and responsibilities. Alternatives seem improbable and may be ignored or explained away. A key feature of belief is faith, or trust in a supreme power or idea. To a non-believer, faith may seem illogical and implausible. Most of us find it difficult to understand how others can rely absolutely on the truth of ideas that do not convince us.

## Why do people have religious beliefs?

If you say a person is 'religious' you may mean a person who:

→ believes in a supernatural power, but does not live a religious life;
→ accepts religious teaching but does not join in organised worship;
→ regularly attends organised worship, and lives by religious rules;
→ lives entirely according to religious teaching.

People hold religious beliefs for many different reasons:

→ a religious experience which converted them;
→ reading a religious book, which convinces them of 'truth';
→ family background and tradition;
→ hope of future reward or fear of future punishment;
→ it answers questions about things they don't understand;
→ because it gives comfort and consolation following loss.

Most people need to have a purpose in life. For many people this need can be satisfied through religious belief and practice. Some people find reassurance in the belief that human affairs are controlled by a greater power than themselves, which knows what is going to happen.

## Other reasons for religious belief

Sociologists who study religion claim that religion is created by society rather than by a supreme supernatural being. They say it reflects the values and culture of society. Religious people generally accept the religion associated with the culture that they grow up in. They suggest that religious belief is important because it:

→ creates social solidarity through a shared value system;
→ gives people a respect for the values of their society;
→ draws people together after a crisis which might destroy society;
→ helps people to handle different life crises;
→ develops a sense of tradition and continuity;
→ provides an external authority for rules, regulations and moral codes.

## What is religious belief?

There are different views about what religious belief is. Believers will often claim that, although beliefs cannot be verified, they should count as knowledge since they are based on revealed truth. Others say belief is no more than opinion, often based on very flimsy grounds. A third view is that religious belief is based on authority, whether of a religious leader such as the Pope or Buddha, or on the evidence of miracles.

**Links**

See pages 136, 198 and 201 for more about the nature of belief.

**Example**

In the Bible, the Apostle Paul was converted to Christianity when he had a vision of Jesus Christ on the road to Damascus (Acts 9, verses 1–13).

**Action point**

Make a list of the possible future rewards offered by the six main world religions

**Link**

See also page 198: Can citizens of the world 'walk by on the other side'?

**Checkpoint 1**

List four different life crises that religious belief might help people to handle.

## The symbolism of religious belief

Major religions have holy books to guide believers. These often claim to be divine revelations, containing a mixture of teachings (doctrines) and moral instruction to control behaviour. Worship usually involves rituals and prayer.

Symbols help believers to understand and express intangible aspects of their faith. These may be special language, buildings, writings or objects. Symbols, with special religious meanings, are usually based on particular religious experiences. The key to understand a symbol's meaning is to identify the truth or reality expressed. Symbols can be easily understood by non-believers, but may have a deeper 'secret' meaning for initiates.

## The effects of belief on behaviour

Religious belief generates different levels of commitment. For some, with fairly conventional belief, it may have little real impact. People of strong belief are likely to be greatly influenced and will try to build their lives around the teachings of their faith. All religions have ethical codes to say how believers should conduct themselves. Belief will influence all aspects of daily life: life at home; relations with fellow believers; conduct towards non-believers; and attitude to authorities.

Many Western European law codes are based on Christian teachings. In this sense, whether you are a believer or not, your behaviour is influenced by religion, but not necessarily by religious belief.

A key moral principle, present in some form in most religions, is 'love your neighbour'. Society has a strong sense of responsibility to the needs of disadvantaged people. It forms the basis of much charitable and voluntary work.

Most religions specify some actions that believers should fulfil. These may concern the rituals of worship; requirements to fast, pray at specified times, wear certain clothes, or not eat certain foods. Obedience to these instructions will depend on individual commitment and how important the rules are believed to be.

## Religion and education

People with religious faith often wish to spread their beliefs. This is done by teaching children at home or in religious school. Some faiths try to gain converts, often using different forms of the media. In England the earliest schools were founded by religious groups. Since 1870 'broadly Christian' religious education has been compulsory in state schools. Some faith schools exist to teach their own beliefs. Many people say religious belief and teaching should not be part of education.

---

**Link**

See page 140 for more about religion and morality.

**Checkpoint 2**

Name three different religious symbols. Explain what meaning the symbols would have to a believer.

> *"The trouble with some of us is that we have been inoculated with small doses of Christianity which keep us from catching the real thing."*
>
> Leslie Dixon Weatherhead

**Checkpoint 3**

What reasons can be used to justify compulsory religious education in school in the 21st century?

**Examiner's secrets**

You will find it helpful if you know the principle beliefs of at least one major world religion.

---

**Exam preparation**                              answer: page 153

Why do many people think that there should be a close relationship between religious belief and moral behaviour?   (10 minutes)

# Religion and conflict

**Checkpoint 1**

What different conflicts taking place today have religion as one of their causes?

**Links**

See the nature of belief, pages 136, 201.

**Jargon**

Tolerance: in the context of religion the willingness to accept that different people may hold different views or beliefs.

**Checkpoint 2**

Name three ideas that you would expect to find in some form in most of the major religions.

You would think that religion would be a great force for world peace and harmony between different people. Too often the reverse is true. Religion has often been the cause or excuse for disputes between neighbours and wars between nations. The reason is an almost inevitable consequence of conflicting beliefs.

## Differences of opinion about belief

Where two different belief systems exist it is almost certain there will be disagreement. The nature of belief means that if one view is right, others must be wrong. Some people can be very tolerant of conflicting views. Others find it very difficult to accept alternatives and may seek to defend and enforce their views vigorously. Inevitably this leads to opposition.

It was once unusual for more than one religion to be allowed in a country. This is still true in some countries, especially in the Middle East. The approved religion may be closely linked to the government. In return for political and often financial support, organised religion would give divine approval and authority to the government.

This was the case in England. Before 1533 everybody was required to obey the Catholic Church. When Henry VIII wanted a divorce he changed the religion of the whole country. Everybody was expected to belong to the Church of England. Those who refused were punished by law. It was not until 1689 that tolerance of other religions was allowed in England. However, the tolerance of the law has not always been carried out in practice. Today, the Church of England is still the official church of the country, but people are no longer compelled to obey it. In fact, today, people are allowed to follow any religion they wish.

## Differences between religions

Although major religions have some features in common, they also have many differences in beliefs, practices, teaching, history and traditions. Immigration in the twentieth century gave many people a first experience of other world religions. Confronted with obvious differences it is easy to become afraid through ignorance. Fear of what is different can breed prejudice and intolerance, leading to conflict.

Religion is closely associated with culture. In the 1950s and 1960s large-scale migration from India and Pakistan settled large numbers of Sikhs and Hindus in many British inner-city areas. The racial tensions that developed contained some elements of religious intolerance.

Religious difference has contributed to a number of conflicts. The Crusades of the Middle Ages arose from a dispute between Christians and Muslims over control of the Holy Land. Conflict in the Balkans has, for over five hundred years, been based on religious as well as political disagreements. Since the State of Israel was set up in 1948, Arab and Jewish conflict has had religious as well as territorial overtones. Some claim September 11 and the subsequent War on Terror organised by the USA have religious as well as political foundations.

## Conflict within religions

Bitter disputes can develop within religions. Most religions have divisions based on different interpretations of doctrines. This is particularly true of Christianity. There are today three major Christian traditions. Throughout history there has been conflict between these traditions, often resulting in persecution of minorities and even war. The oldest is the Orthodox, which is found mainly in Eastern Europe and Russia. The Catholic Church was dominant in Western Europe and, as a result of exploration, was introduced into South America. The youngest tradition, Protestantism, began about 500 years ago as an attempt to reform the Catholic Church. The Protestant movement has splintered into many hundreds of smaller communities. In some areas the hatred between different Protestant groups is almost as violent as between Catholics and Protestants or Jews and Arabs, or Muslims and Hindus in India and Pakistan. The conflict in Northern Ireland, which has been continuing in its present form since 1967, is an example of a conflict with its roots based in religious disagreement.

## Fundamentalism

Religious leaders can have considerable power and influence. Because they claim to be able to interpret the real meaning of religious belief, by implication they claim to have a special relationship with the God whom they worship. The Pope, as Head of the Catholic Church, claims divine authority when speaking about matters of doctrine. Most Catholics are happy to accept this authority.

Problems can develop with the emergence of charismatic leaders. These, through force of personality, may develop almost total control over the lives of their followers. In some of the worst cases such leadership has resulted in mass suicide pacts. When combined with fundamentalism such leadership can become very dangerous and even a threat to world peace.

Islamic fundamentalism has become a powerful force in the last 30 years. In 1979 it contributed to the overthrow of the Shah of Iran. The literal imposition of Islamic law caused the destruction of a Westernised society and the restoration of a traditional Islamic social structure. This had very adverse effects on the place of women in society. In Afghanistan the Taliban established an Islamic theocracy and ruled with extraordinary severity and intolerance to other religions.

*"At the heart of racism is the religious assertion that God made a creative mistake when he brought some people into being."*

Friedrich Otto Hertz

**Links**

See pages 188, 198 for religious belief and responsibility.

**Remember!**

Religion affects all aspects of life. It can have an influence on culture, law, education, government, art, sculpture and music. Influence is not always positive or for the benefit of society.

**Link**

See also page 188: How do religious and secular beliefs affect world peace and stability?

**Checkpoint 3**

Name two different social changes which were reversed when the Taliban took control in Afghanistan? Which group of people suffered most as a result of these changes?

**Link**

See page 188 for more on fundamentalism.

**Exam preparation** answer: page 153

The last 30 years have seen the growth of religious intolerance in many countries throughout the world. Choose one example of a country that has experienced changes due to religious intolerance in the last 10 years. Explain why these changes have taken place and what effects they have had on society. (45 minutes)

# Answers
## Religious beliefs

## The major world religions

### Checkpoints

1 You should define what you mean by religion, and compare the characteristics of Buddhism with the criteria in your definition. If your explanation is based on belief in the supernatural, you will probably say it is not a religion; however, if you define religion simply as a belief system, with no reference to the supernatural, then Buddhism will count as a religion. Key features of Buddhism are: belief in a God unnecessary; need to live a good life; reincarnation; nirvana; meditation.

2 **Trinity** is a belief associated with Christianity. It is that the single godhead has three separate persons, the Father, the Son and the Holy Spirit, who are a unity but appear in three forms.

   **Communion** (or Eucharist) is a Christian celebration in wine and bread of Jesus' death. Some Christians believe it simply shows his death. Others believe its nature is changed to become his flesh and blood.

   **Ramadan** is the ninth Islamic month. A daily fast is observed between daybreak and sunset to mark Allah's first revelation of the Qur'an to Mohammed.

   Jews observe the **Sabbath** (Friday evening to Saturday evening) as a time of rest without any form of work. It commemorates God's rest after creation.

3 **Monotheism** is belief in a single God (as in Islam Judaism, or Christianity). **Polytheism** is belief in many gods, as in Hinduism. **Pantheism** is the belief that god is everything and everything is god. Sometimes it is associated with the worship of all gods. **Theism** is belief in the existence of a god revealed to mankind supernaturally and sustaining a personal relationship with his creation. **Deism** is the belief in the existence of a god but without accepting revelation to humanity.

### Exam preparation

You may choose any religion. The example chosen here is Buddhism.

**(a)** These key aspects may not be totally unique to Buddhism. Focus is on personal spiritual growth and the attainment of deep insight into the true nature of life and is not centred on a relationship between God and humanity. Buddhists have no concept of a saviour or of a heaven or hell. It does not demand blind faith or belief but claims people should test teachings against personal experience. Karma: actions have consequences, so our lives are conditioned by past actions. Rebirth: consciousness continues after death and finds expression in a future life. Following the Buddha's path can escape the cycle of karma; the Four Noble Truths and Eightfold Path. Enlightenment, a state of existance beyond suffering, is the chief goal of life. Dharma (duty): the teachings of Buddha. Nirvana. Belief that all life is interconnected.

**(b)** Pilgrimage to sacred sites to foster spiritual growth. Venerating and making gifts to images of the Buddha.

Gifts of alms to others, especially monks. Emphasis on moral life. Worship at home or the temple. Prayer and chanting. Religious festivals (Wesak) are times of colour, gaiety and celebration.

## The importance of religious belief

### Checkpoints

1 Birth, death and bereavement, marriage, old age, loneliness, illness, poverty, unemployment, effects of war or famine, homelessness, deformity.

2 Symbols are a form of representation used in all religions as a type of shorthand to convey meanings and messages. They may be understood at a simple level by believers and non-believers alike, but also have a deeper meaning for believers that depend on their understanding of the teaching and traditions of their religion. Some religions use similar symbols but give them different meanings.

   You have a wide choice of symbols to choose from. A key part of this question is the second part that asks you to explain what your symbol means to a believer. You might use:

   A **Mandala** is used in Buddhism. It is a circle made up of different coloured sands. Each colour has a distinct meaning (white represents purity, blue the vastness and truth of doctrine, red is warmth and compassion). The circle shape shows the continuity of life; spaces represent divinities and the centre is a focal point of meditation.

   In Islam the **star and crescent moon** represent light and guidance. Originally Muslim people were desert nomads, dependent on the stars and moon for light at night. The teachings of Islam provide guidance and light in a dark world.

   **Khanda** is a Sikh symbol. In the centre the two-edged sword represents God's concern for truth and justice. The two swords (kirpans) represent his temporal and spiritual power and the circle (chapra) shows the unity of God, the continuity of life and the equality of all.

   The Jewish **ner tamid** (lamp of perpetual light) burns continually in front of the ark in a synagogue, to show the continuity of Jewish tradition and God's presence.

   **Om** (or Aum) is a sacred symbol constantly repeated in Hindu worship. It represents Brahman, the ultimate reality who is beyond human expression. In addition it symbolises the whole world, past, present and future.

3 The influence of organised religion has declined significantly over the last hundred years. Only a small proportion of the population attends religious activities or has a serious commitment to religious belief. Many of our values and moral beliefs have developed from the religious teachings and traditions of the past.

   Since 1870 a daily act of collective worship and RE have been compulsory parts of every state school's curriculum. Recent attempts to remove this rule have failed. Some people believe that there is no need for religious education in state schools, but others say it is necessary because of the growth of secular ideas.

The1988 Education Reform Act states that a school should 'promote the spiritual, moral and cultural . . .' growth of all pupils and 'prepare pupils for the opportunities, responsibilities and experiences of adult life'.

These aims are met in part by compulsory RE. Pupils are taught according to an agreed syllabus about the moral values traditional in the UK. They learn some of the history, tradition and teachings of Christianity. In a multi-cultural society, where there are many different religious traditions, they learn about other faiths. In a sense RE in schools helps transmit the standards and values seen as important in this country. As a result, it contributes to social continuity and stability.

Some people say it is wrong for schools to teach this type of moral and cultural conformity. However, others choose to send their children to faith schools because they want their children to learn about specific beliefs.

### Exam preparation

Note this question does not ask whether there is a link between religious belief and moral behaviour but whether there ought to be such a link.

You need to start by explaining what you understand by the two terms. In your introduction you could show briefly that there is a link between the two. Be careful not to write too much on this because time is limited and you are only expected to produce a brief answer.

You might make the following points:
- People with a religious conviction believe their God has defined rules for how people should live.
- Religion provides an external authority to support a moral code.
- Many of our modern values are based on religion.
- Most of the religions of the world have very similar moral codes, which suggests that there are some values regarded as important in most societies.
- Religious morality developed in response to real social problems and so offers a practical guide to conduct when faced with new problems.
- Our legal system, which defines right and wrong behaviour, is based on religious values.

## Religion and conflict

### Checkpoints

1 The most obvious answers are the conflict in Northern Ireland, the Middle East and the campaign of the USA against Islamic terrorists. Other conflicts include the civil wars fought in Iraq and Afghanistan or some of the tribal conflicts in Africa and the war in the former Yugoslavia.

2 There is a vast choice. You could consider:
- Why are we here?
- Where did we (life) and the universe come from?
- Is there a God?
- How should God be approached/worshipped?
- Is there a purpose in life?
- Does it matter what we believe or do?
- What happens after death?

3 The main ones were education and the liberation or equality of women. Religious toleration and dress are other possible answers.

The answer to the second part is women.

### Exam preparation

You could choose any of the countries in the Middle East or eastern Africa that have seen an upsurge of Islamic Fundamentalism (such as Iraq, Iran, Afghanistan, Somalia) or even in parts of the Bible Belt in the USA. Note that the changes do not have to be the result of political upheaval.

Your answer to why changes have occurred should focus on religious fundamentalism. Belief in the total inspiration of a holy book is often linked to certainty that only those in power have a correct understanding of 'truth'. Such people may believe they have a divine duty to make others accept their interpretation. This can be done either by persuasion or coercion. It is likely that government will be an absolute dictatorship and the holy book will be accepted as sole authority. Fundamentalists often come to power as a reaction against corrupt dictatorial regimes. As such they aim to create a pure society. Westernisation is often seen as a major threat.

The changes reflect this. Traditional law is reinstated (to modern Western society this is often presented as harsh and inhumane). Religious teaching is the sole authority for this law and the punishments linked to it. The role of women is usually heavily restricted and freedoms previously granted are reversed. Education is often restricted in content and availability. Often the rule of law is maintained by force and fear. Religious intolerance is intensified and society is severely restricted. Oppression of minorities can be extended into the fields of the arts and thought. Opposition groups may be banned or persecuted.

# Databank

## Founders of religion

**Judaism:** Abraham and Moses, about 1800 BC
**Hinduism:** No particular founder, about 1500 BC
**Buddhism:** Guatama Buddha about 530 BC
**Christianity:** Jesus Christ and St Paul, about AD 30
**Islam:** Muhammad, about AD 600
**Sikhism:** Guru Nanak, about AD 1500

## Holy books and divinities

**Judaism:** The Bible (Old Testament). Jehovah
**Hinduism:** Vedas. Brahman, Shiva, Vishnu
**Buddhism:** Tripitaka. No gods
**Christianity:** The Bible (New Testament). God
**Islam:** Koran. Allah
**Sikhism:** Guru Granth Sahib. Akal Parkh

## Religious symbols and their meanings

**Judaism:** Menorah, Star of David
**Hinduism:** Om or Aum
**Buddhism:** The wheel of the law, Mandala
**Christianity:** the cross, bread and wine (Eucharist)
**Islam:** The star and the moon
**Sikhism:** Khanda
*Check the web to find out details of what these symbols represent to believers and the festivals celebrated by each community.*

## Beliefs about death

**Judaism:** immortal soul, but no explanation of what it will be like; used to believe in Sheol (hell) where the ghosts of the dead awaited bodily resurrection. Some look for a Messiah and the Day of Judgement (reward and punishment) following bodily resurrection.

**Hinduism:** death separates soul and body. The soul cannot die or be killed. Individuals must work out their destiny during several lifetimes, since one experience would be unfair as the basis for eternal judgement. A soul moves from one body to another (reincarnation). The new body is determined by the quality of life lived in the previous existence. If a soul finds its 'real self', it will become part of the godhead and so gain release.

**Buddhism:** teaches reincarnation but, unlike Hindus, the cycle of reincarnation ends with the achievement of nirvana. This is reached when all wrong or selfish thoughts are overcome. The individual alone is able to overcome this continuous process of rebirth.

**Christianity:** sees death as the gateway to eternal life in heaven and teaches belief in an immortal soul. Some believe in a Day of Judgement following bodily resurrection and resulting in everlasting life on earth. Believers are promised God's gift of eternal life, but the wicked will be punished in hell. Humans have one chance at life. Failure to please God results in eternal consequences. The key is the death of Jesus Christ.

**Islam:** death is the end of the present life. Believers are granted eternal life at the Day of Judgement when they must give an account of their life. The wicked are thrown into hell but the righteous cross into paradise.

**Sikhism:** people consist of body and soul. Bodies die but the soul is part of the spiritual universe, which is God. Individuals are repeatedly reincarnated until the soul is united with God. Man is not inherently wicked. A person's deeds in life follow the soul like a shadow. The individual has control over immortal destiny. The wicked are condemned to endless reincarnation until they repent and earn God's grace.
*Check the web to research other important beliefs.*

# Revision checklist
*helps you check what you still need to do*

## By the end of this chapter you should be able to:

| | | | |
|---|---|---|---|
| 1 | Use the information in Databank, above, with confidence | Confident | Not confident. **Revise** page 154 |
| 2 | Identify some aspects of major world religions | Confident | Not confident. **Revise** pages 146–147 |
| 3 | Explain why religious belief can lead to conflict both within and between different religions | Confident | Not confident. **Revise** pages 150–151, 188 |
| 4 | Understand the nature of religious belief and explain why it is important to some people but not to others | Confident | Not confident. **Revise** pages 148–149 |
| 5 | Name religious symbols and explain their meaning | Confident | Not confident. **Revise** page 149 |
| 6 | Understand how religious belief can affect behaviour | Confident | Not confident. **Revise** page 149 |
| 7 | Show how religious fundamentalism can be a problem | Confident | Not confident. **Revise** page 151 |
| 8 | Give reasons to explain religion's loss of influence in some parts of the world | Confident | Not confident. **Revise** page 188 |
| 9 | Describe belief systems that are alternatives to religion | Confident | Not confident. **Revise** page 188 |
| 10 | Show how religious belief can threaten world peace and national security | Confident | Not confident. **Revise** pages 150–151, 188 |

# Media and communication

In the modern world it is almost impossible to escape from the intrusive nature of the media. At one time, for most people communication was limited to direct personal interaction. Since many people could not read, there was no quick and easy method of mass communication.

The development of printing in the 15th century speeded up the process of mass communication, but was still restricted to those who could afford and read books. In the late 19th century better education and literacy created new markets. The mass media started in the form of inexpensive mass circulation newspapers. Subsequent technological changes have created various new forms of mass communication.

Consequently people are better informed and entertained but, according to some, they have become open to influence and manipulation. Censorship can limit the availability of information, while editorial control determines how information is presented. A major debate is whether the media exercises too much control and influence over individuals or whether individuals, through the application of market forces, shape and influence the media.

## Exam themes

→ Processes and effects of the media and communication industries

→ Similarities and differences between various media

→ Ownership, control and censorship of the media

→ How the media influence opinion and people's lives; the power of language and images

→ The creation of wealth and exercise of power in the media and communication industries

→ Moral issues arising from the activity of the media

→ Current developments within media and communications

→ The influence of market forces on the media

→ The impact of global broadcasting and journalism

## Topic checklist

○ AS  ● A2

| | AQA A | AQA B | EDEXCEL | OCR |
|---|---|---|---|---|
| The nature of the media | ○● | ○● | ○● | ○ |
| The power and influence of the media | ○● | ○● | ○● | ○ |
| Ownership and control of the media | ○● | ○● | ○● | ○ |

# The nature of the media

Communication occurs when information is exchanged or imparted to other people. This may be through direct face-to-face speech, or may make use of an agent. Such agents are called media (a single agent is called a medium) and can use verbal, written or visual forms of expression. Technological advances, starting with the development of printing in about 1450, allow us to communicate with a mass audience all at the same time. These agents are often called mass media.

## Different mass media forms

The major forms of mass media include:

| | | |
|---|---|---|
| Newspapers | Books | Film |
| Magazines | Radio | Videos |
| Periodicals | Television | Internet |
| Video games | CD/DVDs | Mobile phones |

In Western society these are all readily available and have become a normal part of everyday life. They are becoming increasingly available in other parts of the world. The nature and function of most forms of mass media are constantly changing. Most have been criticised for what is believed to be their impact on society; some are seen as a health hazard; others are regarded as a moral threat. It is, however, certain that they will continue to exist and their use and functions will grow.

## Current developments within media

Driving forces behind the mass media are technology and profit. Media owners want to maximise profit and so must use the latest techniques if they are to attract and hold audiences. As new forms of media develop, older forms must adapt or fall out of use. The media always respond to technical change. The development of radio and television, which could give immediate news, forced national newspapers to find new roles as commentators rather than simply reporters. The new local radio stations of the 1960s challenged the existence of the local press, making it focus more on advertising than news. Local radio also led to a completely new style of national broadcasting, with Radio 1. New technologies continue to face the existing media with new challenges.

## The press

This includes newspapers, magazines and periodicals. Newspapers can be local, regional or national. Most national papers are daily morning papers; many regional papers are published in the evening; local papers are usually weekly and concentrate on local news and advertising.

Newspapers began before 1700, but most modern papers started in the 19th century. Many of the more popular modern papers were set up after 1870 for the new educated working class. Until broadcasting developed, the press was the main source of information for the population. Key features of today's press are the development of 'free' advertising papers and of specialist magazines aimed at niche markets.

---

**Checkpoint 1**

What similarities and differences are there between these different media forms?

**Links**

See pages 56, 191 and 198 for more information about globalisation.

**Checkpoint 2**

How have new high-technology forms of media affected shopping?

---

*"News is that which comes from the North, East, West and South. If it comes from only one point on the compass, then it is a social class publication and not news."*

Benjamin Disraeli

## National newspapers  ○○○

The national press consists of 'popular' and 'quality' newspapers. The quality press, or broadsheets, are usually aimed at an educated, middle-class, professional market, contain a considerable amount of print and cover world and national news in depth.

The popular press, or tabloids, dominate daily sales. Stories are short and well illustrated, with an undemanding reading level. They deal with 'human interest' rather than news. *The Daily Mail* and *Daily Express* are tabloids but aim at a better-educated market than other tabloids. They fall somewhere between the quality and popular press.

**Example**

The quality press includes: *The Times, The Guardian, The Independent, The Daily Telegraph* and *The Financial Times*.
The popular press includes: *The Sun, The Daily Mirror* and *The Daily Star*.

## Broadcasting  ○○○

**Radio**, the original form of broadcasting, began under government sponsorship in the 1920s. Both local and national radio exist today. BBC funds radio as a public service from licence money, but independent companies are funded from advertising revenue and run for profit. Radio's popularity declined in the 1950s, as television became available, but has recovered in recent years, thanks to the broadcasting of popular music and chat shows. The main development today is digital radio. Legally, in Britain, radio stations need a licence to operate, but cheap technology has allowed the growth of illegal pirate radio stations. The government can ultimately decide whether a radio station will retain its licence.

**Television**, invented in the 1930s, only came into general use in the 1950s. At first, like radio, it was a BBC monopoly. Independent commercial television, funded by advertising, was set up to compete with the BBC in 1954. In the 1990s the introduction of satellite and cable television started a broadcasting revolution. Viewers were given greater choice than was offered on the older terrestrial channels. Since then, digital television, which offers even greater choice, has been introduced, but subscription levels have been disappointing. Television is probably the most criticised form of the media because of the quality of programmes, the effect of competition for market share and the influence it is said to have on viewers.

**Checkpoint 3**

What are the advantages and disadvantages of digital radio or television compared to traditional broadcasting?

## A question of taste?  ○○○

Do the media have a responsibility to consumers? Some critics claim the media simply give the audience what it wants, but others say they shape people's tastes. A major discussion point is whether some parts of the media have a dumbing down effect on public taste. It is often claimed that the press and broadcasters cater for two distinct audiences, described as having mass and minority tastes.

**Links**

See pages 128, 129 and 200 for more on popular and 'high' culture.

**Examiner's secrets**

If you are asked to select one form of the media, be careful not to refer to others, unless you can make what you say relevant to the question.

**Exam preparation**                                        answer: page 162

Choose any one form of the mass media that has experienced technological change in the last ten years and consider the extent to which 'new' means 'better' in this context.   (40 minutes)

# The power and influence of the media

The media play a significant part in our daily lives. Fo most of us they are the main source of information about our world. Some claim the media help to create our opinions and shape our behaviour. Importan questions are:

→ How and why do the media influence us?
→ Do the ruling class use the media to shape ou thoughts?
→ Do the media work for the capitalist economi system?
→ Do the media simply respond to what we want?

Some critics blame the media for declining social an moral standards and an increase in violent behaviour

## How do the media influence us?

People who claim we are influenced in our thinking and lifestyle by the media say they achieve it in several ways. For example, news reporters:

→ shape our world-view by selecting what news to present;
→ influence our opinions by the emphasis given to news stories;
→ allow editorial bias to distort stories;
→ use language and images to create and reinforce desired ideas;
→ create a sense of the relative importance of news stories by the order in which they appear;
→ use celebrity presenters, such as Jeremy Paxman, to persuade us of the reliability and accuracy of stories.

Entertainment, such as films, videos and television or radio shows, can also influence the way we think and behave. It has been claimed that the media have adversely affected sexual habits, lifestyle and violent behaviour. Some critics claim that the media simply reflect rather than create social attitudes. Remember that not all media influence is harmful. Some abuses are only uncovered by investigative journalism.

## Does advertising influence us?

Advertising is not a medium, but it uses the various media as an agent. The media, apart from the BBC, depend on advertising for a large part of their income. In fact, local 'free' newspapers exist mainly as vehicles for advertising. Broadsheet newspapers and commercial broadcasters could not survive economically if they relied only on sales.

Advertising is designed to influence behaviour. It aims to persuade consumers to buy or use one product rather than another. Advertisers may use blanket advertising, a very inefficient form, to promote cheap essential goods, but will target specific audiences and media for more expensive items. In order to attract advertisers, media producers need to provide large audiences. Consequently, programme content is often designed for this purpose. A major criticism of the media is that the quality of output is reduced in order to attract large audiences. You need to be aware of different types of image used by advertisers to attract and influence customers. You should also consider which are the most effective forms of advertising, and why they are effective. Do you think we suffer from too much advertising?

**Links**

See pages 157, 160 and 161 on ownership and control of the media.

**Example**

We were shown almost everything that happened before and during the 2003 Iraq War. We are left in almost total ignorance of other contemporary wars, which editors choose not to broadcast because 'they are of little interest to people in Britain'.

**Checkpoint 1**

How might watching films or TV shows influence or change our behaviour and attitudes?

**Checkpoint 2**

List five different types of image used by advertisers. Which do you consider to be most effective? Give and explain reasons for your decisions.

## The place of soap operas ●●●

Soap operas are the most popular form of entertainment on television, attracting daily audiences of up to 14 million. The original American soap got its name from being a vehicle to advertise a soap company. Today, major companies sponsor some of the more popular soaps.

Soaps are serial dramas, screened several times a week at peak viewing times and aimed at a largely female audience. Producers feel if they can attract large audiences to watch soaps, audience inertia will allow them to retain large numbers of viewers for the remainder of the evening.

The key structure of a soap is a series of concurrent, interlocking story lines running over several weeks, with exciting and dramatic plots. These are designed to attract and retain viewer loyalty. Many British soaps are said to reflect real life, and viewers can become totally absorbed with the characters, often forgetting they are fictional. Many story lines address important social issues, raising awareness and giving important information. Issues dealt with recently have included:

→ Sexual issues, such as lesbianism and teenage pregnancy.
→ Health issues, such as testicular cancer, AIDS and breast cancer.
→ Social issues, such as drug addiction, adoption and euthanasia.

The BBC set up *The Archers*, the earliest and longest running radio soap, to convey important farming information.

**Example**

Cadbury sponsor the most popular British soap, *Coronation Street*, while Heinz salad cream has sponsored *Emmerdale*.

**Example**

In the 1960s the broadcasting time for *Crossroads* was changed. This led to a strike of female workers in Devon, because they were no longer able to watch it.

## Media bias and moral issues ●●●

It is often said that most forms of media are biased. Most newspapers and magazines follow their own editorial policy, often determined by the owner or editor. This will influence the slant that is given to stories. It is seen particularly in political stories. The owner of the *Sun* claims that a change of political support to Labour from Conservative in 1996 influenced the outcome of the 1997 General Election. The BBC is often attacked for unfair political bias. In 2003 this caused a major row with the government over issues relating to the war with Iraq.

Questions you should consider include:

→ Does the exercise of bias allow the media an unfair advantage?
→ Should the media be neutral and objective on important issues?
→ Do some interviewers and journalists have too much power?
→ Does the press have power without responsibility?

It has been claimed that the media have used their power to create 'moral panics' by publicising and exaggerating certain events. This was shown recently by a newspaper campaign directed against paedophiles, which resulted in outbreaks of violence. However, the media have used their position to raise awareness of moral issues. Key examples can be seen in the development of Childline, Comic Relief and LiveAid. It is likely that these activities would not have succeeded without media support.

**Jargon**

Bias is a prejudiced view. Media bias is when one side is given an unfair share of coverage or the use of language and images creates an unbalanced picture. For example, the terms 'terrorist' and 'freedom fighter' can be used to describe the same activities but create totally different ideas in the minds of an audience.

**Checkpoint 3**

Why do people remain loyal to one newspaper or television station?

**Examiner's secrets**

Remember there are positive aspects of the media as well as negative. Don't forget the good things the media can do.

---

**Exam preparation**                                      answer: page 163

To what extent does the press shape, rather than simply reflect, public opinion?   (10 minutes)

# Ownership and control of the media

The BBC is a state-owned broadcasting company. One of its major roles is to provide a public service. It is funded through a combination of licence fee and sales. Until the 1950s it had monopoly control of broadcasting in the UK. All other forms of media are commercially owned and the majority operate for profit.

## Who owns the media? ●●●

Private sector ownership of the media is divided into distinct groups in Britain. A large number of relatively small and localised groups exist in each of the media. These are 'independents'. They are often recently formed, have a limited range of staff and resources and take advantage of new technologies, which allow the production of fairly cheap quality products. If successful, they are likely to be absorbed by larger groups. A small number of these larger groups, called conglomerates, dominate almost 90% of output in each of the media. Sometimes a conglomerate may be international, having holdings in several countries. They often have interests in more than one of the media. Their size and dominance of market share give such companies a powerful position.

## Why do people want to control the media? ●●●

There are two main reasons. Profit is a major factor. Possibly a more significant reason is power. The media allow owners great power and the opportunity to influence people and events. Owners of newspapers or broadcasting companies can dictate editorial policy, determine the appointment of staff, and use their position to support political groups or lead campaigns for change. It is often said that owners such as Murdoch can manipulate public opinion and even challenge governments. Some people say the media have given too much power to too few people.

## Regulation of media owners ●●●

Although individuals can have considerable power and influence, there are a number of restrictions designed to limit their opportunities.

→ **The Monopolies Act** lets the government investigate and restrict ownership if a group or individual has too large a market share.
→ **Licensing and franchises** control the establishment of radio and television broadcasting. Licences can be withdrawn.
→ Government **regulations** control media output.
→ Government **funds** parts of the British film industry.
→ **Ofcom** was set up in 2003 as a single independent regulatory body, replacing bodies that previously dealt with different sections of the media. Its aim is to protect the interest of citizens in all matters of communication and, where appropriate, encourage competition.
→ **Laws** restrict slander, libel and obscenity.

These limitations raise the question of who really controls the media. Is it the owners or the government? Alternatively, do customers have real control since, if they won't buy the media, they will be bankrupted.

---

**Example**

Some conglomerates are dominated by a single figure, such as Rupert Murdoch, who owns News International, or Richard Desmond, who controls Northern and Shell and Express Newspapers.

**Links**

See pages 158–159 for more information about the influence of the media.

**Checkpoint 1**

Has the development of the Internet made it harder or easier for media owners to manipulate public opinion?

## Do we need censorship?

Traditionally censorship of the media was only associated with totalitarian regimes. However, it can exist in any society, and is often justified as protecting individuals or the security of the state. The US constitution guarantees freedom of speech. In Britain some people think of censorship in the context of wartime. The truth is that a form of censorship can exist in most states.

Parents very often impose a form of censorship when they control what their children can see or read. They justify this because they feel that exposure to violence or overt sexuality can have a corrupting effect.

The British press is not officially censored, but governments can limit sensitive information. There are three main forms of censorship:

→ The Official Secrets Act and D notices can be used to prevent the publication of information harmful to state security.
→ The Obscene Publications Act can be used to prosecute anyone who publishes anything of an obscene nature. This is after the event.
→ The Defamation of Character Act permits the prosecution of anyone who libels or slanders another person. Damages can be very high.

Television programmes are subject to the same laws as the press. In addition, output is subject to the oversight of regulatory bodies that forbid the publication of anything that will 'offend decency and good taste'. Furthermore, there is self-censorship through the 9.00 p.m. watershed, which restricts earlier programmes to having 'a family nature'. Both the BBC and ITV issue their own guidelines to producers.

Until the 1970s the theatre was subjected to the censorship of the Lord Chamberlain. The same laws that limit the freedom of broadcasting and the press apply to other art forms. Films are given an appropriate age category by the British Board of Film Classification. It can require unacceptable scenes to be cut, or can forbid cinemas to show films that are unacceptable. It justifies these actions as giving guidance to parents and cinema owners and no longer to 'preserve public decency'.

## Do we need privacy laws?

There is great concern that the tabloid press and sometimes television journalism has become too intrusive. Many feel this is because of the continuing competition to attract readers by feeding them on a diet of celebrity lives and activities. It has been claimed that Princess Diana's death was a direct result of press intrusion. Some claim that people in the public eye have no right to privacy and the press should be entitled to publish anything it wishes. Others say we need privacy laws like those in France to protect the individual, since press self-restraint and regulation are inadequate. They argue that the press and television are so concerned with meeting the pressures of the market that they are willing to ignore issues of good taste.

**Exam preparation**                              answer: page 163

Outline arguments for and against a free press. What restrictions, if any, should be placed on journalism?   (45 minutes)

**Jargon**

Censorship is the restriction of free expression of ideas. It can be used either by governments or individuals.

**Checkpoint 2**

What do you understand by censorship? Do we need censorship today? Give two different examples of government-imposed censorship.

*"Taste cannot be controlled by law."*

Thomas Jefferson

**Examiner's secrets**

You can use the same information to answer questions about censorship in the arts as you use in discussing television or press censorship

# Answers
## Media and communication

## The nature of the media

### Checkpoints

1 They are all forms of communication; recipients are passive; audiences are willing participants; editors or producers have control over presentation, content and opinion; recipients can do little to influence them; they are opinion formers; they exist mainly for profit, they compete for a limited market share.

 Differences include: the technology used; ownership; some are verbal, others are visual; costs; some are influential for a very short time, others for a long time; speed of production (some take months, others a day); target audiences; some inform, others entertain.

2 Note the question is not simply about the impact of technology, but its impact in a particular context. The main focus should be Internet shopping, including both advertising and purchasing; speed and convenience of purchases; telephone shopping; impact on costs. Remember: use of bar codes to speed point of sale and stock-check; TV shopping channels.

3 Quality and quantity of output; greater efficiency; interference-free reception; wide-screen programmes; interactive and online services; access to websites.

 Cost; availability of decoders; analogue equipment becomes redundant; high cost of developing and selling services; popular programmes no longer available to traditional viewers/listeners.

### Exam preparation

You could select any of the mass media, but the most likely are broadcasting, newspapers or cinema. You should outline the technological changes your chosen medium has experienced and explain how you think they have affected it. Remember you are asked about changes over the last decade. You may interpret this fairly generously, but be careful that you don't ignore the time period completely and deal with changes that occurred a long time ago.

If you choose broadcasting, you might include: digital, satellite and cable broadcasting; digital filming; news gathering and transmitting methods; videotext; video links; phone-ins and chat shows; computer graphics; television and the Internet; interactive broadcasting; greater immediacy; amateur footage; DVDs and CDs.

It is important to show how technology has influenced your chosen medium. Don't simply list technology and don't mention technology that has not in some way affected your chosen medium.

Most of your answer should deal with whether new always means better. Your answer must be related to your chosen medium and should not be a generalised approach to the question. Use specific examples.

You could show that extra outlets made possible by new technology have not always been beneficial to viewers or listeners. For example, increased demand for product may mean either a considerable number of repeated programmes, a decrease in standard of production to save costs or a reduction in the quality of material in an attempt to attract and retain a large audience share. The result could be over-competitive programming, an excessive number of game shows, imported programmes or the current craze, reality TV.

Second, technology is expensive and a desire to be modern and up to date may lead to overspending on equipment and underfunding of programme making.

A third major point could focus on the idea of 'better'. You should ask 'better than what?' You could argue that technology may not always improve on what was done previously. Programme making might be faster and slicker, but may not achieve an improved output. However, you should also point out that young people in particular like technology and may find programmes made with older technology dull and uninspiring.

Remember that you are asked to assess the extent to which 'new' means 'better'. Your answer must include evaluation of the evidence you provide so that you can reach a balanced conclusion.

## The power and influence of the media

### Checkpoints

1 This is a very disputed topic. Some writers believe that films and television have a major influence; some claim that only people who want to be influenced will be; some say that we are so used to the media that they don't influence most people at all.

 Media students have developed a number of different models to explain the influence of the media. These models include the hypodermic syringe, the two-step flow, and uses and gratification. There is evidence to support each viewpoint.

 Points you could make include: constant repetition of ideas persuades us to accept them; sanitised images of sex and violence make them seem acceptable and normal; producers select the information we receive; visual images shape our vision of the world; they help shape our opinions; they do all of our thinking for us; they distort stories to make them present the view they want us to receive; celebrities are turned into authority figures whose word we can trust; our expectations are raised. We usually think that media influence is harmful, but there are occasions when it can serve a positive purpose. Think of the way news broadcasts have raised our awareness of suffering and encouraged charitable donations (Red Nose Day, Children in Need, *Blue Peter* collections), but they may also lead to 'compassion overload'.

2 Happy families; stereotypical roles; reverse stereotypes (like a man cleaning a kitchen); animals as humans; holidays; sex ideals; manliness; success. The choice is almost unlimited. The important part of this activity is to identify the reasons you think one image is more effective than another. Reasons might include: it is amusing (tango adverts); it's easy to identify with; it is easy to remember (a memorable slogan or jingle) etc.

If you are asked to explain a reason, you must note the need to give a developed answer. For example, it is not enough to say an image makes you laugh; you must say what it is about the image that strikes you as funny or amusing. It helps to link the image to a particular advert and not give a generalised answer.

3 Habit, familiarity, inertia, it says what they want to hear, easy availability, cost, all their friends buy it or watch it, they like the style (shape, contributors, size, content), image (would anything else make you feel like a snob or a yob?).

### Exam preparation

Notice once again this question asks you to make an assessment and not just provide information.

Shaping opinion would include selection of stories; how stories are presented; choice of headlines; use of language; selection of supporting images; editorials and feature articles; carefully chosen letters to the editor; sustained campaigns.

Reflecting opinion could include: newspapers must sell, so they give audiences what they want; hostile reaction from readers leads to loss of sales and new directions from the editors; placement of articles can be changed according to public reaction.

## Ownership and control of the media

### Checkpoints

1 Media owners such as Rupert Murdoch or Richard Desmond own a variety of media outlets and have often been accused of having too much power and influence. For example, Murdoch's News International controls the *Sun*, *The Times* and B-Sky-B, and many other media outlets in different countries. This means that he has access to a wide variety of people whose opinions he might influence. However, he doesn't have monopoly control, since there are other broadcasters and newspapers that take a different line to his. Even without the Internet we have free choice and can use whatever news source we like. Usually people buy a newspaper or watch the television programmes that reflect their own opinions or interests. This suggests that media owners' influence is already limited. The value of the Internet is that it gives greater freedom to find sources of information. However, people who are likely to search the Internet for news are also likely to be selective in the programmes or newspapers they watch. Media owners may be able to shape the ideas of large numbers of the public who are committed already to their influence. These people are the target of newspaper campaigns and are less likely to take advantage of the Internet.

2 You need to define censorship as the suppression of information that might harm individuals or threaten security. Individuals (teachers or parents), institutions (e.g. the BBC or ITV) or the government can impose censorship. You do not have to say if we need it, but should give examples of government censorship. You might suggest: D notices, the Official Secrets Act; the 30-year rule for official documents; laws against obscenity and defamation of character.

### Exam preparation

Define what a free press means. Don't confuse it with the local free advertising papers. In this sense free is not about cost but about control.

Arguments in favour of a free press could include: our right to freedom of information; the press has often uncovered scandals which could not happen if it was controlled; dictators can control the press in order to manipulate public opinion; in a democracy we should be fully and properly informed before we decide about important issues or vote; a free press is the best way to prevent the government becoming too powerful.

Arguments against a free press include: it is needed to protect people from intrusive journalism; it is better to prevent unfair publication than to deal with the damage it causes after the event; in time of war there are secrets that could help an enemy; freedom of the press could allow the publication of obscene, harmful or offensive material; too much freedom could lead to damaging 'cheque book' journalism.

In the second part of your answer you might refer to the need for privacy laws; heavier punishments for breaches of the law; stronger external regulation. Remember, it is not enough to name restrictions; you should be able to justify them.

# Databank

## Explanations of media influence

**Hypodermic syringe model** (or stimulus-response) was once the most popular explanation of how media influenced audiences. It assumed that we are all the same and impartially received anything 'injected' into us by the media. People who claim that young people particularly are corrupted by the media use this theory to support calls for television and cinema censorship.

**The two-step flow model** was popular in the 1950s but has been criticised as impossible to test. It claims that audiences are made up of different groups with 'opinion leaders' helping to shape their ideas. Media focus on these 'opinion leaders', who in turn transmit the ideas they receive. Thus, the media are important in shaping the ideas of a select few, who decide what to pass on to others. This theory is used to explain why different groups can respond in varied ways to the same stimulus material.

**The use and gratification model** is built on the belief that people use and enjoy the media in different ways. It accepts that modern audiences are not all the same and have a variety of interests. People use the media for different reasons subject to circumstance, interest, inclination and time of day. Because audiences often identify with favoured characters or stories, reality and illusion can merge. As a result, certain audiences may be vulnerable to media influence.

**The cultural effects model** says the media build up influence over time. Newspapers and broadcasters reinforce cultural stereotypes. Images received by different groups are related to individual situations as they are encountered in real life. Media messages are therefore linked to the general culture of society. The long-term effect is to translate media images into new realities and so reshape social and cultural values. It assumes that audiences are vulnerable and supports demands for more censorship and control.

## Some media terminology

**Audience** should not simply refer to those who are involved in the process of 'hearing'. It refers to any individual or group receiving communication whether verbal or visual. Some people prefer to use the term 'readers', although this implies the perusal of text.

**Cultural discount** is the idea that programmes based in one culture will be attractive in that environment but will have less appeal to other audiences who will find it difficult to identify with the issues involved.

**Cultural reproduction** refers to the maintenance and perpetuation of a society's norms, values and thought processes. It describes the way some people think the mass media support a dominant ideology.

**Intrapersonal communication** is within the self and includes thought processes and reminders, like notes or diaries that are used to help personal reflection.

**Interpersonal communication** between people is usually face to face. As well as written and spoken communication it includes non-verbal interaction.

**Group communication** involves clearly identifiable groups of individuals, or between different groups.

**Mass communication** usually refers to the role of the mass media and should involve a mass audience who receive a universal message.

**Extrapersonal communication** takes place without direct human involvement (as between machines) or between humans and machines.

**Monosemy** is about the meaning that is conveyed by a message. It implies that there is only one possible way of interpreting it.

**Polysemy** implies that a text can be interpreted or read in a number of different ways.

**Semiotics** is the study of the social production of meanings from signs in art, language and the mass media. Signs evoke ideas that must be interpreted.

*Check the web to research other aspects of media.*

# Revision checklist
*helps you check what you still need to do*

## By the end of this chapter you should be able to:

| |  |  |
|---|---|---|
| 1 Use the information in Databank, above, with confidence | Confident | Not confident. **Revise** page 164 |
| 2 Identify different forms of media | Confident | Not confident. **Revise** pages 156–157 |
| 3 Be aware of some current media developments | Confident | Not confident. **Revise** pages 156–157 |
| 4 Understand how media can influence you | Confident | Not confident. **Revise** pages 158–159 |
| 5 Show how soap operas and advertising influence us | Confident | Not confident. **Revise** page 159 |
| 6 Explain the problem of media bias | Confident | Not confident. **Revise** page 159 |
| 7 Identify different types of media ownership | Confident | Not confident. **Revise** pages 160–161 |
| 8 Be aware of how media are regulated | Confident | Not confident. **Revise** page 160 |
| 9 Explain the nature and purpose of censorship | Confident | Not confident. **Revise** page 161 |
| 10 Discuss the benefits of privacy laws | Confident | Not confident. **Revise** page 161 |
| 11 Show how mass media have led to globalisation | Confident | Not confident. **Revise** page 189 |
| 12 Examine possible threats from globalisation and multinational companies to different cultures | Confident | Not confident. **Revise** page 189 |

# Creativity and innovation

The creative urge is one of the most fundamental human characteristics. It is a natural response to the ability to feel and to think. Most of us experience pleasure and achievement after making something, even if it is of poor quality. We see the creative urge in children at play, in the preparation of food, or cultivating a garden. We all desire praise and approval from others.

Creativity is perhaps best seen in the different art forms. Artistic work may be produced solely for the creator's pleasure or for a wider audience. Inevitably, creativity leads to criticism, evaluation and comparison. The nature of creativity changes according to circumstance, tradition, expectation and the resources available.

As part of the creative process some people can demonstrate originality of thought and technique. This may result in individuality or, if adopted by others, may lead to new styles or genres. Sometimes, in societies such as Stalin's USSR or Nazi Germany, the creative process may be controlled by the state for political purposes. This raises serious questions about creative independence and artistic freedom.

## Exam themes

→ To be aware of the creative process in the development of various artistic areas

→ Appreciation that creativity is in part a response to the context of social structures and traditions within which it takes place

→ Understanding that innovation is a continuous process within the creative process, involving both talent and genius

→ The role of artists and their contribution to society

→ The place and value of the arts in education and of participation in the arts

→ Art works and major practitioners of major artistic movements

→ Why people are creative

→ The influence of religion and technology on the arts

→ The structure of art forms and genres and how their meaning is communicated

→ The role and responsibility of critics, patrons, sponsors and governments

## Topic checklist

| ○ AS ● A2 | AQA A | AQA B | EDEXCEL | OCR |
|---|---|---|---|---|
| The nature of creativity and innovation | ○● | ○● | ○● | ● |
| Creativity and the role of artists | ○● | ○● | ○● | ● |
| The development of artistic style | ○● | ○● | ○● | ● |

# The nature of creativity and innovation

Creativity and innovation exist in all aspects of life. We may think they are qualities associated with science or technology but they are also essential features of the arts. You are not expected to have detailed knowledge about all of them but you should know something about two or three of them. You should choose from:

Architecture
Fashion
Painting, photography or sculpture
Drama, film, literature or music

## Creativity and innovation ●●●

Some people say all of us are creative. If we make anything, decorate a room, cook or even work in the garden, we are being creative. Literally, create means to bring into existence. It often refers to activities that use imagination or original ideas. In this sense the production of any work of art, using any art form, is a creative act. It doesn't matter whether the work is original or copied or whether or not it is of good quality.

Innovation is rather different. It is creative, but it must also be original. To be innovative a work must in some way be different to what has been done previously. Innovation may refer to new ideas, the use of new or different materials or techniques, a new understanding or simply a new insight into old problems. Innovation may lead to imitation or perhaps improvement. In the arts, innovation is often linked to the development of a new style or form.

## Artistic style and the creative process ●●●

Most of the arts are classed as either performing or visual. The main exceptions are literature and architecture. It is usual to subdivide each group or type according to style. Sometimes the terms 'form' or 'genre' are used instead of style. These terms may be used in several different ways to describe:

→ works of art that share similar characteristics
→ the nature of a specific performance
→ the particular way in which an artist works or performs
→ a specific appearance, design or arrangement
→ the quality or sophistication of a performance.

These all refer to the way in which the work of art is 'done'. For your chosen categories of art you need to be able to identify different 'styles'. In particular you should be able to:

→ name different artistic styles
→ identify key characteristics that distinguish different styles
→ name examples of artists who are associated with each style
→ name examples of different works associated with each style
→ identify factors contributing to developments in each style.

Architecture is probably the easiest art form to use when studying style because it has distinctive features that are easy to categorise and compare.

**Links**

You must read this section and the section on aesthetics together as they offer two separate approaches to the same issues.

**Watch out!**

Take care that you don't treat these two terms as though they are interchangeable. It is possible to be creative without being innovative.

**Checkpoint 1**

What do critics mean when they talk about 'artistic style'?

**Examiner's secrets**

If you are asked to write about artistic style, you may find that your knowledge of modern music will give you an advantage over most examiners, who may not be as well informed as you are.

## The creative process in different artistic areas

Critics find it helpful to label different artistic styles. This lets them put different works into categories, so that they can be compared. Very few artists probably thought of their work as belonging to any specific style. The labels given to each of the major art forms roughly correspond and can be linked to historical periods. The labels are fairly broad and there is overlap between different styles. Some artists are linked to more than one style, and sub-divisions are found within some styles. Modern art includes, among others, post-impressionism, expressionism, cubism, surrealism, Dadaism, and pop art. The table lists examples of artists, architects or composers associated with each major style or period.

| Name | Period | Art | Music | Architecture |
|---|---|---|---|---|
| Renaissance | c.1400–1600 | Leonardo Raphael | Palestrina Byrd | Palladio Smythson |
| Classical | c.1600–1700 | Poussin Lorrain | Monteverdi Lully | Inigo Jones Wren |
| Baroque/Rococo | c.1650–1750 | Bernini Rubens | Bach Handel | Talman Vanbrugh |
| Classical/Palladian | c.1750–1820 | Canaletto Stubbs | Mozart Beethoven | Adam Holland |
| Romantic | c.1780–1900 | Goya Rosetti | Brahms Tchaikovsky | Wyatt Pugin |
| Impressionist | c.1880–1920 | Monet Degas | Debussy Ravel | Morris |
| Modern | 1900– | Picasso Warhol | Britten Berio | Le Corbusier Venturi |

Within each style and art form there are different types of work. Classical music, for example, can be divided between:

→ choral, orchestral or instrumental;
→ religious or secular;
→ ensemble or solo;
→ cantata, concerto, symphony, sonata, opera.

In modern music the divisions are considerable and ever changing.

For literature it is easier to think of the main divisions of poetry, prose and drama rather than to think of styles linked to historical periods. We do talk about Elizabethan, Jacobean or Victorian literature, and poetry may be described as Romantic or war poetry. Prose is often categorised as detective, crime, historical, adventure, Western, science fiction or romance, according to subject matter. Film is also most often grouped in this way, although different styles can be identified.

### Exam preparation
answer: page 172

How true is it to say that there is no such thing as artistic style, merely individual works of art? In your answer you should refer to at least one of the major art forms (art, music, literature, architecture, film).   (40 minutes)

**Action point**

(i)  Find and give examples of artists linked with each of the styles of modern art named in the text.

(ii)  List as many different styles of contemporary popular music as you can and name a performer associated with each.

**Checkpoint 2**

What must an artist (or composer or writer) do to be original?

**Checkpoint 3**

How would you decide whether a single work of art should be classed as belonging to one particular artistic style rather than another?

**Examiner's secrets**

Read the question carefully. If you are asked to refer to 'at least one', you should refer to a range of examples if you can; if you are asked to refer to 'one example' then you will not get credit if you give several different examples.

# Creativity and the role of artists

The term 'art' is usually applied to things that are man made. Natural objects, however beautiful or pleasing, do not count as art since they are not the result of human creativity. There are, in whichever art form is considered, two main purposes in creativity. First, creativity explores ideas, developing and using the structures and materials of a chosen art form. Second, it is about self-expression and communication. Art works are effective when they establish a dialogue between artist and audience. Unless a work engages and involves the audience in some way, it will fail to justify its existence.

**Checkpoint 1**

Should natural objects count as works of art?

**Watch out!**

If you are asked to write about any art form, you must make specific reference to examples and not simply generalise.

**Checkpoint 2**

Is photography an art form?

**Watch out!**

When writing critically about any of the arts be careful not to use words such as 'great' or 'brilliant'. Make sure that you support and justify your opinions.

## Why people are creative

**The visual arts** were among the first art forms to develop. Cave paintings may have been a combination of information, religious worship and decoration. Photography, the latest of the visual arts to develop, radically affected the others. Until photography was invented in the 1820s, painting and sculpture could represent reality. Art was expected to be realistic and true to life, whether showing human images or nature. Many painters used symbols to convey messages, but still had to show what their patrons wanted to see.

Photography gave a more accurate picture than a painting. As a result, artists were encouraged to seek new forms of expression. This led to the development of more abstract styles of painting and sculpture in the 20th century. At first photography was not regarded as an art form, but technological improvements let photographers become more creative. Different photographic styles evolved like those of painting. The label 'visual arts' recognises the way these forms appeal primarily to the eye.

**Architecture** is more than just about buildings and depend more than any of the other arts on the skills of technology and science. It is about applying scientific principles, creativity and design to create pleasing structures from raw materials. Architects as artists must appreciate the:

→ qualities of the materials used
→ context of the built and natural environments within which it is to be constructed
→ relationship of design to space
→ purpose and function of the building
→ limitations of cost
→ requirements of the purchaser
→ cultural context and relevant architectural traditions.

Architects are subject to the changing influence of fashion and taste and must adapt creativity to new materials and engineering techniques. Differing styles reflect the changing values and needs of society.

**Music** is perhaps as old as painting. It takes many forms but is always about communication through sound. As with the other arts, it must be both created and experienced. Some musical forms, such as the operas of Mozart or the symphonies of Beethoven, have survived for long periods of time, but most music is transitory and reflects the values of its composer and first audience. Styles, especially in recent years, have changed rapidly in a quest for novelty. However, music is subject to both tradition and fashion. Some critics say that music can create moods and emotions, but most reject this view. They claim that when we listen to music we are moved not by sound but by association of sounds with events. Over the centuries music has developed a type of language. We tend to associate some sounds or instruments with particular meanings. We may link certain types of music with particular lifestyles or images. This is true especially of pop music. We may like some styles of music because we like and want to identify with its associated image. In this way music can help give us a sense of identity and belonging.

**Literature and drama** rely on the written or spoken word. You should know something about novels, poetry and plays from English Literature lessons. Today not many people read a great deal and visiting theatres can be very expensive. Most people experience great literature through film or television adaptations. Some critics feel this does not do justice to literature, but others say it introduces audiences to some of the great literature of the past and may encourage people to 'read the book' after they have seen the film.

## Religion through the arts ●●●

Each of the arts has been used to express religious belief. Architecture is one of the best examples of this. Religious buildings, which dominate the landscape, create the character of Britain's towns and countryside. Giant cathedrals and humble parish churches demonstrate the various qualities of architecture. Many took several lifetimes to build. Not only do they illustrate different architectural styles and features but they also testify to the faith of their builders. This is true for all world religions. Many of the world's greatest buildings have religious associations.

Painting and sculpture have a long association with religion, apart from Judaism and Islam. The Middle Ages was a largely illiterate society, so paintings and stained glass pictures were used to teach religious stories. Many of the great works painted during the Renaissance used religious themes, such as Leonardo's wall painting of *The Last Supper*. In a similar way music also has very close links with religion. It is a central part of church worship. Many of the great musical compositions are inspired by religious belief, such as Handel's *Messiah* or Messiaen's *Méditations sur le mystère de la Sainte Trinité*.

In all societies the arts are seen as a way to express and foster spiritual ideas, to bring people closer to their gods, to teach, as an act of worship and to encourage contemplation of religious values.

> **Example**
>
> Many people feel that 'Song to Athene' by John Taverner evokes feelings of sorrow. This is not due to the musical sounds, but because we associate the piece with the funeral of Princess Diana.

> **Checkpoint 3**
>
> What are the advantages and disadvantages of making a famous work of literature (play or novel) into a film?

> **Example**
>
> Some of the world's greatest buildings have religious links:
> the Parthenon in Athens was the temple of the goddess Athene, built in the 5th century BC.
> The Pyramids of ancient Egypt were meant to house their builders for eternity.
> The Taj Mahal is an Islamic tomb, built by Shah Jehan for his wife 1630–1648.
> Angkor Wat is a complex of over 100 Hindu temples in Cambodia, built in c. AD 1000.

> **Examiner's secrets**
>
> Be prepared to make use of your knowledge of English Literature from GCSE. The books you read should give you useful information to help answer General Studies questions.

### Exam preparation                                 answer: page 173

How true is it to say that religion can inspire rather than limit artists? Illustrate your answer with reference to a variety of art forms and/or artists.

(40 minutes)

# The development of artistic style

If you accept that we can identify different artistic styles then you should ask how and why new styles develop. A crucial issue is whether style creates artists or whether artists create style. This is a significant aspect of creativity and innovation. Several different factors need to be taken into account.

## Talent or genius?

It is often claimed that we are all creative. It is also claimed that people involved in creative activity can better appreciate artistic creativity than passive observers. This is one reason why the arts, such as painting, music, drama and creative writing, are so important in the school curriculum. A second reason is that many creative people might not show their real ability if they were not taught necessary skills and techniques. However, some critics say teaching children about the arts can damage creativity.

Relatively few of us have the talent needed to produce work suited to a public audience. Some people have real flair and aptitude that separates them from the majority. As a result of the work they produce they are often associated with particular artistic styles.

Gifted people with originality as well as talent may look for new ways to do things. They may produce something that is mocked and ignored, or others may see their work as innovative. If other artists apply their own creative talents to build on the innovation, a new style may emerge. A style is often linked to the individual believed to have significantly contributed to its development. Since creativity and innovation are interdependent they lead to a continuous process of change.

## Technological changes

Innovation is often linked to the development and use of new materials or equipment. Technological changes can enable artists to do what was previously impossible. Inventions and discoveries have influenced all of the major art forms, often leading to new styles or forms:

→ The paintings of the Renaissance were made possible by the perfecting of an oil-based medium and varnish by Jan Van Eyck.
→ Modern art has benefited from the invention of acrylic paints.
→ In the 15th century Brunelleschi's counter-weighted crane made possible the construction of buildings with large domed roofs.
→ In the 1890s Otis invented the lift. This, together with the use of steel frames, made possible the construction of ever-taller buildings.
→ Eastman's invention of plastic film in the 1890s made possible the development of continuous photography, leading to the cinema.
→ In 1926 the invention of the synchronised music track made possible the development of 'talking' films.
→ Electronic synthesisers transformed both popular and 'classical' music in the 1950s and 1960s.

However, technological change on its own will not produce innovation. Innovation in the arts can only occur if an artist has a new idea, or sees a way to use new technologies to achieve different effects.

---

*"Genius does what it must, talent does what it can."*

Edward Bulwer-Lytton

**Example**

Monet's name is always associated with the impressionist style of painting, while Andy Warhol is always linked with pop art. In music, Schoenberg is associated with atonality.

**Links**

See page 186 for creativity in science and technology.

**Checkpoint 1**

How far do materials determine style?

## Social structures and traditions

If we are to properly appreciate any work of art or artistic style, we need to understand the age in which it was created. Each work of art, like its creator, is a product of its time. A major question is how far an artist or work of art is influenced by the circumstances of the time. We must ask also to what extent a work shapes or reflects the society for which it is created. Factors to take into consideration might include:

→ No creative person lives in total isolation from society.
→ We all absorb the values of our own society.
→ Artists must use the language and resources of their own time.
→ Most creative work is produced for an audience or customer.
→ Customers and audiences are generally conservative in their tastes.
→ Economic demands encourage creative conformity, not experiment.
→ Before about 1900 most art was representational rather than abstract and was expected to show life as it was understood to be.
→ The ideas of innovators are only likely to be taken up by others if they seem to be commercially successful.
→ Traditionally there were clearly understood rules governing most art forms. If these were ignored, critics might condemn works as inferior.

Remember social attitudes can change. At times a society may be more conservative, looking back to a so-called 'golden age'. In such periods the arts may adopt more traditional styles and values. At other times society may be more liberal, ready to accept experiment and change. In these periods true innovation is more likely to take place. It is said that a major formative influence on pop music and fashion is the need to be different to gain commercial success. This may explain why extremes of music and fashion are popular with the young and the media.

## The role of sponsorship and patronage

Sponsorship and patronage have always been important in the arts. In particular this is true of expensive art forms such as sculpture, architecture, painting and music. In earlier times gifted artists were often patronised by private individuals. Today, state funds are used to sponsor the arts. In the UK a proportion of Lotto profits are allocated to the arts through the Lotto Heritage Fund. There is considerable criticism of the way that these funds seem to help activities based in London and favoured by the wealthy (such as opera and theatre).

Some countries give more generous subsidies than Britain. Some major companies, especially in the United States, are patrons of the arts. It is said that sponsors have too much influence on their employee's output. Consequently poor quality art, pleasing to a patron, may be produced, while higher quality work, lacking financial support, may fail.

---

**Example**

The late 18th century was a time when new ideas developed. There was a new interest in nature and the nobility of human nature. It was in this context that Romantic poets such as Wordsworth and Coleridge developed a new form of poetry.
In the 19th century French art was strictly controlled by the Academy. Monet rejected traditional training and rules. He was committed to finding new approaches to painting. From his experiments and rejection of tradition developed the new movement of impressionism.

**Checkpoint 2**

What makes a building a work of art?

**Example**

Bach and Mozart were both employed as court musicians.
From 1482 to 1499 the Dukes of Milan were patrons of Leonardo da Vinci.
Lord Burlington sponsored the work of the architects Kent and Campbell in the early 18th century.

**Checkpoint 3**

What are the functions of public works of art (such as sculptures or buildings)?

---

**Exam preparation**                                    answer: page 173

Discuss the advantages and disadvantages of public sponsorship of some art forms (e.g. opera and theatre) rather than of others (e.g. pop music festivals or street carnivals).   (15 minutes)

# Answers
## Creativity and innovation

### The nature of creativity and innovation

#### Checkpoints

1 'Style' is about how things are done, rather than content. Critics often analyse one piece or the work of a single artist, but artistic style helps if they want to compare different work of artists.

   Most painters, composers or writers are probably not concerned about belonging to a particular 'style'. They may be influenced by, or consciously imitate, the work or technique of others but most would claim to have their own style.

   Critics developed the idea of artistic style to classify artists working in a similar way, with similar materials, ideas and resources, to achieve similar results. The style labels of today often developed long after the 'style' ceased to be fashionable or popular. This can be illustrated with the term Baroque. It was first used derisively in the 18th century of work failing to match classical standards. Later it was applied to anything odd or grotesque. By the early 20th century it was applied to the style of work from the late 17th century.

   'Style' should not be confused with 'school'. Artists belonging to a particular school are trained by, or deliberately use the technique of, a more famous artist. To some the copyist's work may be confused with the work of the founder of the 'school'.

2 Originality is doing what is completely new, never done before. Newness may in itself be minor. Originality may be seen in any aspect of artistic work. An artist may:
   → have a new idea or way of looking at things;
   → develop a new technique;
   → use new materials, equipment or resources;
   → make new demands on the audience;
   → challenge traditional methods;
   → see things as they have never been seen before.

3 Identify key features of different styles and compare the characteristics of your chosen work with the criteria you have identified. Allocate your chosen work to the style that best fits.

#### Exam preparation

Often this type of question needs a general answer, but because you are told to refer to at least one art form you must show you can apply your knowledge.

Creativity is unique, since artists want to express their own ideas and vision of the world. Artists may use similar methods to other artists, but their work should be distinctive. If a work is copied many times, each copy is different, possessing its own unique quality. This is true whoever the copyist is. For example, many versions of the *Mona Lisa* exist; a number of galleries claim to own the original; many are of excellent quality; but no one really knows which Leonardo painted.

   Impressionist painters all showed light in a similar way, depicting exactly what they saw. All recognised the influence of Monet, but some later critics argue about whether they all really were impressionists. Even Monet used traditional styles in some paintings. If expert critics disagree about the style a painting belongs to, how can ordinary people know?

   An artist's work can share features with others yet still be individual. Some say Mozart's music is easy to identify, considering him the greatest, most innovative of all musicians. A comparison of his early and later works shows how his ideas developed, but apart from his earliest work which sounds like Haydn, his music is distinctive and clearly by him. In this sense, artists definitely have a style.

   But do artists belong to a style? We can identify shared characteristics in art. Classical architects, such as Burlington, Kent, Campbell or the Smiths of Warwick, designed distinctive buildings. Each used key features such as symmetry, columns, pediments, cornices and porticos which helps distinguish their work from the Baroque. But should they all be categorised as classical just because they meet the same criteria?

   Artistic style is a convenient way to categorise art to allow meaningful comparisons but saying a work belongs to a specific style should not remove creativity.

### Creativity and the role of artists

#### Checkpoints

1 Some artists say any object, natural or man made, can contain aesthetic potential, and if exhibited these so-called 'objets trouvés' should count as art. Some Surrealists favoured this approach. Other artists say only the products of human creativity are art.

2 Distinguish between photography that is simply taking pictures and that which involves the creative processes. Photography combines functional and creative use of technology. It depends on the skill and artistic flair of the photographer. Photographers, like artists, are concerned with changes in light and shade, colour, composition, shape and the creation of effects. They need to be perceptive to compose pictures, which are more than simply records of reality. Since developing in the 19th century, photography has passed through similar movements or styles as painting. Cinema special effects show photography as art.

3 Some people criticise film versions of literature, saying:
   • it 'dumbs down' when it should challenge;
   • the director not the reader does all of the work since the story is seen through his eyes;
   • films use different ideas to the author;
   • large sections of text are omitted;
   • rich language is replaced by visual images or simple dialogue;
   • characters are oversimplified;
   • there is no active audience involvement.
   Others say film can:
   • bring new audiences to major texts;
   • persuade viewers to read the book;

- retain or rework classic ideas for new audiences;
- appeal to the senses better than some books;
- adapt classic texts easily as many were written in instalments;
- encourage authors to write specifically for cinema;
- engage emotions as easily as a novel;
- say something new.

## Exam preparation

Religion has always influenced the arts. Early cave paintings had religious significance. Greek and Roman sculptures show pagan gods. Religion was the dominant influence in the Middle Ages in music, painting, sculpture, literature and architecture. Renaissance art often resulted from religious patronage. Baroque arts were encouraged by the Catholic Church to stimulate faith and express religious ideas. Secularism and lay patronage became more influential in the late 17th century. Today religion still influences artistic output.

Religion can be restrictive. All religions use the arts to bring people to God. Christianity used them to teach doctrine and shape thought. Stained-glass windows and church wall paintings created obedience through fear, depicting images of hell and everlasting punishment. Religious moral codes limited ideas, freedom of expression and experiment. In Judaism and Islam certain art forms using human images are forbidden. Religious leaders are often among the most vocal critics of new art forms, often condemning them as decadent and degenerate.

## The development of artistic style

### Checkpoints

1 Resources and materials restrict artists' output. Great Medieval cathedrals were made possible by the invention of the flying buttress. Oil painting was transformed in Flanders in the 15th century, making possible the great Renaissance paintings. In the 17th and 18th centuries new instruments let composers extend musical style almost as dramatically as the synthesiser did in the 20th century. Steel frames, reinforced concrete and lifts have made possible modern skyscrapers. Computer graphics have transformed film-making.

2 Most buildings are functional but some are works of art. Architects use scientific, mathematical and design skills, but they are also creative. Buildings as art should be aesthetically pleasing, possessing qualities such as physical appearance, use of available space, beauty, and suitable materials, unity of form and concept, contribution to the environment, and have a message for audiences.

3 To celebrate great individuals or events; honour success; give identity to a locality; make a statement; allow public patronage of artists; provide employment; be a status symbol, an investment or an experiment.

Examples: Nelson's Column; Blenheim Palace; Angel of the North; a Victorian Town Hall; the Dome; Oban's Coliseum; Trafalgar Square's fourth plinth.

## Exam preparation

Deal with two issues: public subsidy of the arts; should subsidy be selective?

Arguments for: it preserves cultural heritage; other states do it; it helps some art forms survive, making them more widely available and accessible; it gives a sense of identity and of being civilised; it cuts prices and costs but permits the use of world-class figures; it supports tourism and increases income; it encourages talent and experiment; it trains artists for more popular and commercially successful art forms; the arts won't need to rely on economic success; lack of money may lead to a rapid decline in standards; selectivity is an efficient use of resources; any cultural organisation or group can apply for a subsidy; many obscure or small art forms are subsidised.

Arguments against: it is unfair as people should pay the true costs of their entertainment; it is elitist, subsidising a wealthy minority; criteria for subsidies are secret and unclear; it discourages private subsidy; it is not a government's job to support the arts; waste and inefficiency are encouraged; prestigious London projects get too much and insufficient goes to other areas; costs and wages which market forces should control are inflated; subsidy from Lotto and taxes should go to what the public want; the arts should be accountable to the public, not government agencies; it makes artificial divisions between art forms; money could be better spent to benefit the public; only economically viable activities should survive; it gives the ruling class what they want on the cheap.

# Databank

## Some innovative works of art

### Gothic

**Architecture:** Chartres Cathedral (France), 12th century. The invention of flying buttresses
**Literature:** Chaucer, *The Canterbury Tales*, c. 1400. The first great poem in English
**Music:** de Vitry motet from *Roman de Fauvel – Garrit gallus*, c. 1330. Ars nova and isorhythmic tenor
**Painting:** Giotto, *Scrovegni dedicating the Arena chapel*, 1304. One of the first realistic portraits
**Sculpture:** Pisano, pulpit panel at Pisanoi, c. 1330. Use of drama in sculpture

### Renaissance

**Architecture:** Michelangelo, St Peter's, Rome, c.1550. Created a unified scheme from others' work
**Literature:** Erasmus, *The Praise of Folly*, 1511. A new-style satire on contemporary institutions
**Music:** Josquin des Prez motet *Absalon fili mi*, 1497. An early example of suiting the music to the words
**Painting:** Raphael, *The School of Athens*, St Peter's, Rome, 1513. Composition and character
**Sculpture:** Michelangelo, *The Pieta*, in St Peter's, Rome, 1499. Accuracy of anatomical detail

### Mannerism

**Literature:** Montaigne, *Essais*, c. 1590. A sceptical approach to religion and a desire to 'tell the truth'
**Music:** Thomas Tallis, *Lamentations*, c. 1580. Melodies have an essentially vocal quality
**Painting:** Giulio Romano, *The fall of the Giants*, 1532. Exaggeration of facial expressions and gestures

### Baroque

**Architecture:** Vanbrugh, Castle Howard, Yorkshire, c. 1700. Monumental grandeur, courtyards and dome

**Music:** Pergolesi, *Stabat Mater*. Combines fragile texture, balanced phrasing with sentimental tone
**Painting:** Rubens, *The Adoration of the Kings*, 1634. Use of colour, composition and energy.
**Sculpture:** Bernini, *David*, 1623. Combines art with sculpture; uses fluid movement, not static shape

### Roccoco

**Architecture:** Poppelmann, *Pavilion of the Zwinger*, Dresden, 1717. Joins gaiety and lack of pomposity
**Music:** Handel, oratorio *Saul*, 1739. Used a new-style orchestra and was cheaper than opera
**Painting:** Watteau, *Embarkation for the island of Cythera*, 1712. Light and delicate joined with drama
**Sculpture:** Lemoyne, *Portrait bust of Voltaire*, 1745. Simple relaxed outline combined with sensuousness

### (Neo)classical

**Architecture:** Gabriel, the Petit Trianon, 1760s. Straight lines, simplicity and pure classical principles
**Music:** Mozart, opera *The Magic Flute*, 1791. Joined German singspiel with Italian operatic form
**Painting:** David, *The Oath of the Horatii*, 1785. Uses a classical theme; simple, severe and precise
**Sculpture:** Falconet, *Baigneuse*, c. 1770. Simple classical outline but with warmth and softness

### Romantic

**Architecture:** Nash, The Royal Pavilion, Brighton, 1825. Exotic and elaborate Oriental decoration
**Literature:** Keats, *Endymion*, 1817. Great passion, power and emotion based on personal experience
**Music:** Beethoven, symphony No. 3, *The Eroica*, 1803. Size, orchestration, passion and discord
**Painting:** Delacroix, *The massacre at Scios*, 1824. Use of colour and contemporary events
*Check the web to research details of these and other works. Check the web to research details of 20th century of works and styles.*

# Revision checklist
## helps you check what you still need to do

### By the end of this chapter you should be able to:

| | | | |
|---|---|---|---|
| 1 | Use the information in Databank, above, with confidence | Confident | Not confident. **Revise** page 174 |
| 2 | Explain the meaning of and relationship between creativity and innovation | Confident | Not confident. **Revise** page 166 |
| 3 | Explain what is meant by artistic style | Confident | Not confident. **Revise** page 166 |
| 4 | Be aware of the creative process in some artistic areas | Confident | Not confident. **Revise** pages 166–167, 170 |
| 5 | Appreciate why people are creative | Confident | Not confident. **Revise** pages 168–169, 170 |
| 6 | Explain how religion has influenced art forms | Confident | Not confident. **Revise** page 169 |
| 7 | Show the effect of technology on the arts | Confident | Not confident. **Revise** page 170 |
| 8 | Understand the effect of social structure and tradition | Confident | Not confident. **Revise** page 171 |
| 9 | Discuss the role of sponsorship, patronage and government | Confident | Not confident. **Revise** page 171 |
| 10 | Show relationships between reality and representation (see page 192) | Confident | Not confident. **Revise** page 192 |
| 11 | Understand the contribution of art to society | Confident | Not confident. **Revise** page 192 |

Aesthetic evaluation is a term to describe the evaluation of the qualities of works of art. It asks whether we must assess art subjectively or whether the use of objective criteria would allow a more consistent approach. If we only judge art from a subjective perspective it means that all creative work will possess the same value. However, if we apply universally agreed criteria to different works, we can make effective comparisons.

You will need to apply the skills of aesthetic evaluation to the knowledge base from the creativity and innovation unit. You may be asked to write essays, provide short answers, respond to structured questions or use textual material. This unit may be the basis of coursework in AQA B.

You should understand 'aesthetic evaluation', be able to apply the criteria in evaluation, and discuss the relative merits of objective and subjective approaches to judging art. You should have some knowledge of individual works of art through which to demonstrate your ability in aesthetic evaluation.

## Exam themes

→ Principles of aesthetic evaluation

→ Key characteristics of different artistic styles

→ Subjectivity and universal standards – how do you judge art and use the language of criticism?

→ Personal response to the arts; their effect on the individual and society

→ Should the arts have a practical message?

→ The relationship of the arts to reality

→ What do artists hope to achieve or express?

→ Art in context

## Topic checklist

| ○ AS ● A2 | AQA A | AQA B | EDEXCEL | OCR |
|---|---|---|---|---|
| Aesthetic evaluation | ○● | ○● | ○● | ● |
| Aesthetic criteria | ○● | ○● | ○● | ● |
| Subjective approaches to the arts | ○● | ○● | ○● | ● |

# Aesthetic evaluation

What is beauty and what makes an object beautiful? We may all have views about these questions. More crucially, each of us will have different answers which could well change according to circumstance – where we are, what we are doing, whom we are with and what we are considering. This is shown by the type of comments made about beauty:

→ beauty is only skin deep;
→ beauty is in the eye of the beholder;
→ a thing of beauty is a joy forever.

## Aesthetic theory

It is usually fairly easy for people to agree on what is or is not beautiful or pleasing in the natural world. We may find there is more discussion and disagreement about man-made objects. Most of us are fairly certain about what we like or dislike. Difficulties may come if we try to explain our feelings. Aesthetics is about the study and appreciation of beauty. It attempts to define criteria by which different works of art can be judged and compared, and also tries to identify principles underlying the work of individuals or artistic movements. Some claim, once identified and understood, these principles can be used and applied to any work of art.

People have always attempted to assess the value or beauty of works of art, but aesthetic theory was not developed until the 18th century. Prior to this, art criticism was usually expressed in broad general terms concerning an artist's moral purpose and high ideals. 'Aesthetics' was used first in the 1730s to show that paintings, music, sculpture and literature could be appreciated by the senses as well as the intellect. In 1757 Edmund Burke distinguished between works that were merely beautiful and art that was sublime (so excellent as to inspire great admiration and awe).

At this time it was believed that art itself was a form of knowledge that could be unlocked with the proper use of analytical tools. The aesthetic process continued during the 19th and 20th centuries. In the 1880s in England an artistic movement developed devoted to the idea of 'art for art's sake'. This rejected ideas that art should have any moral or social purpose, claiming it should be judged solely in its own terms.

## Aesthetic evaluation

Aesthetics has now reached a stage where many feel we can evaluate a work of art or artistic movement with a set of agreed principles. In 1988 Barrett, an art critic, said aesthetics considers three distinct ideas:

→ sensual perception (or pleasure)
→ beauty (or value)
→ superior taste.

The first two are constant and unchanging, but taste is open to external influences and responds to changes in fashion. Until recently fashion changed relatively slowly. Now, the media, electronic communication and commercial pressures cause rapid change. As a result it seems that aesthetic evaluation deals with transitory rather than absolute values.

**Watch out!**

We can talk about a painting being beautiful but we may need to use different words to describe similar qualities in music, literature, drama or buildings. This is often done by talking about things being 'aesthetically pleasing'.

**Checkpoint 1**

'Beauty' may not always be the most appropriate word to use when discussing aesthetics. Suggest other words that could be used in aesthetic evaluation when discussing other art forms.

**Watch out!**

It is not enough, if you are asked to give an opinion about any work of art, simply to say, 'I like it,' or 'I don't like it'. If your opinion is to have any value you must be able to give reasons to justify what you say.

**Checkpoint 2**

How can art be a form of knowledge?

**Links**

See page 197 for more information on the way tastes and fashions change.

## Art for art's sake ●●●

Some art critics say we are mistaken if we try to agree about what is or is not beautiful. They claim that every individual response to a work of art is unique. Your own response can vary from total involvement to complete indifference, depending on a range of factors. They also claim aesthetic appreciation is not an automatic feature of every response. You may react spontaneously to one item but approach another analytically. Attitude of mind is just as vital as aesthetic criteria when judging beauty.

In the early 19th century a critic said beauty could exist for its own sake, needing no other justification. This means we can enjoy art purely and simply because it gives us pleasure and not because it meets approved 'rules'. Some critics argue that any work of art, having aesthetic value, must give pleasure or satisfaction. However, we get pleasure from many things which are not works of art and have no obvious aesthetic value.

The German philosopher Kant said aesthetic response should be based on 'disinterested contemplation', a view that does not require pleasure to depend solely on satisfying desire. Human beings ought to enjoy any experience just for pleasure since pleasure should be an end in itself and not simply a means to a different end. He thought we could enjoy works of art because we like them, and not because they met certain criteria.

## How much should we pay for art? ●●●

You may enjoy the arts as a passive observer. It is easy to visit galleries, museums or concerts and we can all buy reproductions, videos or CDs. However, some people can buy original works. This raises the important issue of what makes art valuable. Aesthetic criteria can help determine artistic quality but may not always determine price, which can respond to the number of people who want to buy. Other factors may include:

→ Fashion. Some painters or musicians are more 'fashionable' than others. Prices will increase or decrease as fashions change.
→ Fame or notoriety. Works with a high public profile may seem more collectable than others, which are just as good but are relatively unknown.
→ Investment. Some people buy artworks for an anticipated increase in value rather than because they like the work or its creator.
→ Media hype. The media may raise awareness of particular artists or works and by increasing desirability may raise prices.
→ History and tradition. The price of art work can be increased if it is associated with particular events or people.
→ Topicality. Items which achieve a topical association with an event or individual may become desirable and collectable. Artists who win prizes, e.g. the Turner, attract attention and become collectable.

**Exam preparation**                                     answer: page 182

'Great art need only appeal to our emotions. It does not have to make us think.' To what extent do you agree with this opinion?   (40 minutes)

---

*"I never saw an ugly thing in my life: for let the form of an object be what it may — light, shade, and perspective will always make it beautiful."*

John Constable (1776–1837)

**Links**

See pages 165–174 for information about creativity and innovation.

**Checkpoint 3**

Should all art galleries and museums be free to the public?

**Example**

Many people became aware of the work of Vermeer as a result of the 2004 film *Girl with a pearl earring*.

**Examiner's secrets**

Whenever you get a question containing a value judgement (e.g. great), be prepared to explain what you understand by the term in the context of the question.

# Aesthetic criteria

## Checkpoint 1

Are 'experts' the only people who can properly appreciate works of art?

*"Criticism comes easier than craftsmanship."*

Zeueis (*c.* 400 BC), quoted by Pliny

## Links

Look at pages 165–174 for information about creativity and innovation.

## Checkpoint 2

Is it true to say that everyone is creative even though most people are not original?

## Watch out!

When using aesthetic criteria to evaluate a work of art you should look for a 'best fit' rather than a 'perfect fit'.

Critics are often asked whether a work is good or bad; or if one work is better or worse than another. Most people will make judgements based on personal taste. Some, especially critics, are more likely to give opinions based on aesthetic criteria. There are three main features of a work of art that can be examined using aesthetic criteria:

→ Form
→ Longevity
→ Content.

These can best be understood through the use of a series of questions. The questions are relevant whenever we examine the work of any artist or art form.

## Form

Form concerns the method of production used to create a work of art. There are several different questions we can ask about form.

*Does the work conform to the generally accepted rules associated with the particular style to which it belongs?*

If the artist has ignored or misinterpreted the rules for no good reason, or combined different styles, the work may be less aesthetically pleasing than a work that correctly observes accepted principles.

*Does the work demonstrate originality?*

In some ways this may contradict the first point. Most works of art are creative, but not necessarily original or innovative. A work of art that is original will contain features or ideas that have not existed previously. This may relate to content, style, technique or materials used. It may be original because the artist has discovered new rules. In this case a work may be regarded as more noteworthy than perfectly 'good' works that lack a spark of originality.

*Does the work contain a high level of skill and craftsmanship?*

A work may be creative or original but be executed poorly by the artist. Poor craftsmanship can detract from the value of a piece, whereas work showing a high degree of technical skill, even though otherwise fairly ordinary, will have value. Similarly, works that require a relatively low level of skill to complete may not be considered as of similar worth to one that could only be produced if the artist had considerable expertise.

*Does the work have unity of form?*

Complex works will contain many disparate elements. Here the skill of the artist is most apparent and crucial. A critic must ask how expertly the different elements are drawn together to form the whole. A work in which the artist has integrated the parts into a complete unity, where each part contributes to and does not detract from the whole, will have value. However, where the viewer is more aware of the different parts than of the entire work, some of the value of the work will be reduced, whatever other qualities it may possess.

## Longevity

*Is a work of art old?*

Some assume this to mean that objects that are old are naturally better than anything that is new. It is a belief that has contributed to the view that there is a difference between 'high' and 'popular' culture and that 'popular' is inferior to 'high'. Age alone does not automatically mean that an artefact is of value. There are many reasons, mostly accidental, to explain why some old objects survive and others disappear.

*Does a work continue to impress over a period of time?*

This is a more important question. It raises the issue of whether a work makes a positive contribution to our culture and heritage. Some works may simply be 'nice', but contribute little else besides their age. Others seem to have something to say to viewers or audiences of all times.

## Content

This is about how a work affects an audience and the creator's purpose.

*Does the work have anything to say to us?*

If we seek to analyse a work of art we should ask whether the artist has anything to say or whether it is simply decorative. Some critics say we can only know what a work is meant to say if the artist has written or explained his purpose. Others say we should deduce from great work what the artist wished to say. Therefore, works with a message may be more valuable than those without. However, great works can still have meaning for us even if we have no idea of an artist's creative purpose.

*How does a work of art affect an individual?*

Some critics say that art can only be experienced. This means that no single work is better than any other. Others say a way to test a work for greatness is to assess its effect on people. Should great art challenge, provoke, shock, or even change the lives of people who experience it?

*Does a work of art possess any moral content?*

A work may satisfy all the criteria relating to style and yet not be great. If an artist creates a work that is evil, that contradicts the moral values of the age, or which encourages or celebrates undesirable conduct then, however attractive it may be, it will not be aesthetically pleasing.

*Does a work of art comment on the human condition?*

If the purpose of art is to communicate then clearly a great work of art must have something to say about society and humanity. Any work that does not help increase our knowledge and understanding of life has limitations, and therefore should not count as great.

Aesthetic criteria can be used to compare one piece of art with another. In this sense, you may decide that one work is better than another.

**Jargon**

Longevity literally means having a long life. It is a relative term when used to assess art. The Beatles song 'Yesterday' has longevity when compared to most popular songs, but is a relative newcomer when compared to the work of JS Bach. Nevertheless, it should still count as a great piece of music.

**Example**

In recent years there has been public discussion about the future of the *Madonna of the Pinks*, a painting allegedly by Raphael. For 150 years it was left in obscurity. It was not 'identified' as a masterpiece until 1991.

**Example**

Mozart and Salieri both lived and composed at the same time. The music of both is still available. However, Mozart's work is still regularly performed and considered outstanding. In contrast, Salieri's is seen as pleasant, occasionally performed, but not thought remarkable.

**Checkpoint 3**

Why is it important for a work of art to have a meaning or a message?

---

**Exam preparation**  answer: page 183

Briefly explain what you understand by the term 'aesthetic evaluation'.

(10 minutes)

**Examiner's secrets**

If a question uses a word like 'better', make sure that you qualify its meaning to you in your answer.

# Subjective approaches to the arts

An important aspect of aesthetic evaluation is that it helps us identify and apply constant principles to the assessment of works of art. This lets us compare different works or styles to decide which are 'good' and which are 'poor'. Aesthetic evaluation is an attempt to evaluate art objectively. Some critics, however, say that true art is an appeal to the senses and not just an intellectual exercise. They argue that the only valid judgement of a work of art is subjectivity.

## Are we all critics?

Most of us know if we like something. Whether we do or not, our decision is usually based on an emotional rather than an intellectual response. This is as true when we admire a country view, choose clothes, select a holiday or react to other people. Our judgement is personal, based on our own tastes. What I think is wonderful, you may reject as valueless. One of our greatest strengths as human beings is that we all have different tastes. We use the same methods to judge architecture, ballet, music, painting, literature, fashion, theatre or film. We assume that what pleases us is, by definition, 'good', and certainly 'better' than what fails to give us pleasure.

Although most of us are fairly tolerant of other people's views, problems can arise if we are asked to justify our opinion. If we make an objective judgement, we can easily say how far a work meets agreed criteria. But there can never be one correct answer with subjectivity, since all judgements are personal. Does this mean every work of art, artist or style is just as good (or as bad) as any other?

## Are we elitist about the arts?

If judgements about the value of art are personal then there can be no universal standard for judgement. Does this mean a work popular with a majority audience is 'better' than art that appeals to a minority? This is central to the 'high' versus 'popular' culture debate. How far is:

→ classical music 'better' than popular or pop music
→ opera 'better' than musicals (e.g. *Cats* or *Les Misérables*)
→ theatre (e.g. Shakespeare) 'better' than film
→ ballet 'better' than disco dancing
→ paintings (e.g. *Mona Lisa*) 'better' than graffiti
→ literature 'better' than modern novels (e.g. *Harry Potter*)?

Society has developed contradictory values. We like to be entertained but often put greater value on 'the arts' than on more popular activities. This has two results:

→ governments subsidise the arts but leave more popular entertainments to market forces;
→ many people believe you have to be trained to appreciate the arts.

---

**Jargon**

An artefact is an object made by a human being as opposed to an object produced by nature. A derivative of the term is artificial (as opposed to natural).

**Checkpoint 1**

Are expensive works of art better than cheaper ones?

**Links**

See page 128 for more information about high and popular culture.

**Checkpoint 2**

Are we too elitist in our attitude to the arts?

## Are forgeries a problem?

Sometimes a picture is said to be 'from the school of' and not 'by' a particular artist. A painting by a famous artist may not be entirely his own work, but completed by pupils or employees. Some artists copy the style or work of more famous artists. These do not create a problem if properly identified. Sometimes copies are passed off as if painted by a celebrated artist. Forgery has occurred since people began to collect art but it creates a serious problem. Accident or war increases opportunities for forgery. During disturbances art collections can be broken up and paintings be lost or looted. In such circumstances able artists can easily paint new works, claiming them as rediscovered masterpieces. Collectors, eager to obtain famous paintings, may accept their authenticity, especially when supported by false provenance.

Does this matter? As far as a work itself is concerned, probably not. If you like a painting, does it matter who painted it? If aesthetic evaluation is a matter of personal judgement or taste then all that matters is whether a work gives pleasure to the owner. From an economic perspective, however, forgery is significant because we would expect to pay more for a famous artist's work than for a copy. Forgery is cheating and intended to deceive.

## Morality, law and the arts

You might argue that art is about personal expression. That is to say, art is a way for artists to explore and develop perspectives and ideas. So, should artists be limited in what they are free to 'say'? How ought restrictions to be enforced? In Britain several institutions share enforcement. At first, religion, through the Church, imposed universal standards. When religion lost influence, parliament passed laws to uphold standards and protect the public from artistic excess. In practice laws can only be effective and enforced if an offence has been committed. The law courts are responsible for maintaining good taste. In the theatre, a public official, the Lord Chamberlain, was the official censor of plays. Perhaps artists only exercise restraint through fear of the law. Recently certain private individuals have tried to monitor artistic activity 'to protect the public'.

Is this type of external protection desirable or necessary? Is it morally justifiable that artists may not say what they want? Is it right that, as individuals, we are not free to see or hear what we want? Should appreciation of what is right or acceptable in the arts be defined collectively rather than by individual choice?

**Exam preparation**                                   answer: page 183

Is the purpose of the arts only to entertain or do they have other values for the public? Illustrate your answer with examples from any of the art forms.

(15 minutes)

**Examples**

In 1946 Han van Meegeren was imprisoned for forging 6 paintings in the style of the 17th century artist Vermeer. His forgeries were so good that they were bought by the Nazi leader Goering. Tom Keating, who died in 1986, was one of the most successful 20th century forgers. He specialised in the work of Samuel Palmer, an obscure 19th century artist.

**Check the net**

Look up other famous forgers:
Reinhold Vasters
Alfred Andre
John Myatt (see 'genuine fakes').

**Jargon**

Provenance refers to the origin of a work of art. It is the pedigree or record of ownership.

**Checkpoint 3**

Should artists be morally responsible?

**Links**

For more information on freedom of expression, see pages 142, 161–168.

**Examples**

In 1963 Mrs Mary Whitehouse set up the National Viewers' and Listeners' Association because she claimed the relaxation of controls over the media had led to declining moral standards.

**Examiner's secrets**

When writing about the arts, don't be afraid to express your own opinions – but you must be able to support them with evidence.

# Answers
## Aesthetic evaluation

### Checkpoints

1 Aesthetic pleasure; awe; wonder; opulence; joy; bliss; enjoyment; grandeur; excitement; fascination; stimulation; exhilaration; splendour; magnificence.

2 Knowledge, quite simply, is 'what is known', as opposed to what is thought or believed. Many artists claim they explore experience and emotions through their art. It is an expression of experiences, feelings and emotions discovered about themselves and their world. The arts are communication between artist and audience. Any work of art is a statement of what the artist knows or has learnt. Some art is meant to instruct or convey facts, knowledge or information (e.g. paintings of hell or the Crucifixion, or Milton's *Paradise Lost*). Some say paintings, sculptures or photographs showing realistic images, of people or places, present knowledge in a tangible way.

3 Distinguish between private and public owners. Democratic societies recognise private property. Few think owners should be forced to open their collections to the public free of charge. However, many benefactors have done this. Private collectors are entitled to impose charges. Many private galleries and museums exist in towns, villages and houses.

   The real issue concerns publicly owned collections. Entrance charges were imposed to raise revenue for maintaining and extending buildings and collections. The original aim was to transfer costs to the public from government. They said it was fair to charge people for using the galleries, but unfair to make the entire population pay through taxes, since few visited them. Attendances and income fell in fee-charging institutions. In 2001 the government abolished fees for many publicly owned galleries and museums.

   Arguments supporting free entry are that exhibits were often bought with public money or left as gifts to the nation. Since we have already paid for them they should be freely accessible. Objects in museums and art galleries are part of our cultural heritage and exist for our good. Charges deny access to our heritage.

   Should charges be made for special exhibitions, like the 2004 Turner exhibitions? These are gathered from public and private sources. Many feel that people who choose to visit special exhibitions should pay an entrance fee.

### Exam preparation

The key issue is the purpose of art. You should show what you understand by great art, emotions and how art can make us think. Remember to assess the evidence used to support alternative views so that you can reach a justified conclusion.

Great art appeals to our emotions or feelings, but so does much poor or second-rate art. Art that fails to appeal to our senses is not likely to affect us at all. Key words in the first sentence are 'only' and 'great'. You must pay attention to both words, showing that an appeal to the emotions alone is not enough to justify the use of the term 'great'. You might support your answer with examples of art that though technically inferior can appeal to the emotions. You might compare emotions evoked by 'patriotic' songs sung at major international sporting events (e.g. 'Swing Low Sweet Chariot' or 'Delilah') with those considered as famous classical pieces such as 'Land of Hope and Glory' or *Messiah*. All can create great feeling, but some depend for effect on context or circumstance.

You should examine what makes one item a great work while another is simply 'pleasing'. You could apply the criteria of aesthetic evaluation (e.g. content, longevity, unity of form and message). Don't just name examples of great or famous works. You must show how your chosen examples demonstrate aspects of aesthetic evaluation.

Finally, address the issue of whether it is necessary for a great work to make us think. How you explain this term is critical if your answer is to be convincing. You should show that great art could make people think in many different ways. It can:
- introduce us to ideas or concepts we have never met before;
- make us challenge the accuracy of former ideas;
- revive our awareness of feelings and sufferings against which familiarity has inured us;
- help us empathise with the experience of others;
- simply encourage us to deeper contemplation and meditation.

As with earlier sections, you should illustrate your answer with appropriate examples.

Don't forget to reach a reasoned conclusion.

## Aesthetic criteria

### Checkpoints

1 The key issue is your understanding of appreciate. If you just mean 'like' or 'enjoy' then you won't require any special skill or training.

   If you mean you are moved emotionally by an artistic experience then you don't need to be expert.

   If it means you can apply agreed criteria to judge the merits of a work of art then you must understand the criteria and know about similar work so that you can compare the way different works meet the criteria.

   You can apply criteria clinically without experiencing any feelings or involvement for the work.

2 Creativity means making something; originality is the ability to make something new or different that has never been done precisely that way before. Very few, including some professional or trained artists, are really original but most of us can create things; for example, amateur gardeners or cooks are creative.

3 Some people claim art works are valuable for their own sake and do not need to 'say' anything to an audience. Others say the arts are communication between artist and audience and so should have a message. Aesthetic criteria include content and message. A work without a message may have little real worth. Messages, taking various forms, can:

- evoke feelings and emotions (pity, pleasure, anger, joy);
- appeal to the intellect, challenging our ideas;
- make us think;
- appeal to our senses (visual, tactile or auditory).

If a work of art has value, the viewer or audience should be changed in some way as a result of the encounter.

### Exam preparation

Aesthetic evaluation is the process used to assess the worth of a work of art, or to compare one work with another. It attempts to apply objective standards to what is often regarded as a subjective process. A number of criteria have been established and are used by critics. These are explained on pages 176, 178 and 179.

## Subjective approaches to the arts

### Checkpoints

1 Value and cost are different. Cost, or price, is what a buyer will pay for the production or purchase of a work. Several factors influence cost:
   - an artist's reputation;
   - the rarity of a piece;
   - the time taken to make it;
   - the cost of materials used;
   - its availability;
   - the number of potential customers;
   - media influence;
   - any special qualities or associations it has.

   Value is different. It depends on qualities possessed by a work. These are usually determined through aesthetic evaluation. A great work may attract a high price, but so may inferior works in demand. Similarly, an unknown or unwanted masterpiece may fetch a low price, but the quality of a work is unchanging in spite of variable market values which influence price.

2 Elitism is the superior attitude or behaviour linked to an elite or exclusive group. It implies that some art forms are thought better and preferable to others. Some people say a false distinction is drawn between popular and high culture, claiming, for example, that the Beatles wrote music just as good as great classical composers. Others show contempt for more popular art forms, suggesting that only the 'great masters' are worthy of respect. Claims like this are based on prejudice rather than sound comparison and valid criteria.

3 Some people say artists should have total freedom to explore ideas in any way they choose, without legal restriction or moral control. This implies there is no such thing as obscenity or pornography. The creator does not have a duty to decide how his work should affect audiences. If a person is offended by art then it is the fault of the individual and not of the art or artist. Another view is that artists, as members of society, should observe the values and rules of their society. People who believe the arts influence the thoughts and attitudes of audiences may extend this view further. The real issue is the nature and function of the arts. Should they inspire us with high ideals or challenge traditional beliefs and values?

### Exam preparation

This question relates to the value of the arts for the public but does not concern the purpose of art for the artist. Remember, to gain full marks you must use examples from at least one art form. Your response will be shaped largely by the examples you use.

You might challenge the theory that the purpose of art is to entertain. Many conceptual artists might say their work has little to do with entertainment. Most films are primarily about entertainment, but some are designed to inform, instruct or even challenge ideas. Public art, e.g. buildings or statues, is often intended to celebrate success or achievement or make a statement. Some art can be functional, such as the Millennium Bridge, while other works are meant to create a sense of eternity, or at least longevity. Some art can encourage audiences to become participants in exploring their own feelings. Art can be a historical record, preserving memory of past events for future generations (as with museums, films such as *All Quiet on the Western Front*, paintings such as *Guernica*, sculptures such as Churchill in the House of Commons lobby, or classic recordings of musicians performing their own work).

# Databank

## Characteristics of styles

**Gothic** describes the art and architecture of the late Middle Ages (c.1300–1500). The name was used in the Renaissance to describe what was seen as non-classical ugliness. Subjects were typically religious. Churches had distinctive arched designs, high roofs, decorated ribs and tall columns. Paintings appear stiff and simple. Sculptures adorned church walls or graves usually showing saints, the holy family or devils.

**Renaissance** (or rebirth) describes radical changes which affected culture in the 15th and 16th centuries. People were aware of a cultural revival inspired by the arts of ancient Greece and Rome. Works of art were created simply as objects of ideal beauty. Artists dealt with the real world and the senses. Key features were secular values, individualism, scientific enquiry and realism. The use of light and shade, variety in content and form, classical principles, innovation, anatomical accuracy and secular content were common. Domes, columns and symmetry were features of architecture, while mathematical principles provided a basis for proportion and perspective.

**Mannerism** followed the High Renaissance. Key features were complexity of design, great technical accomplishment and muscular, elongated figures in complex poses. Stress was placed on theatricality. Mannerist art demonstrates little passion or feeling and is formulaic rather than original. Art was meant to show grandeur and not natural realism.

**Baroque** (c. 1600–1740) was a term of contempt applied in the 19th century to painting, architecture or music. A key feature of Baroque art is the appeal to the senses. It is stylistically complex, dramatic and emotional but often austere. Works reflect grandeur, sensuous richness of colour, movement, tension and exuberance. Baroque artists were multi-talented.

**Roccoco** (c. 1715 to 1750) was a climax to Baroque. It achieved elegance with decorative trimmings, curves, bands and lines. Key features were the combination of fantasy shapes with elegance. It stressed lightness and the picturesque. Instead of rigidly following rules and principles, artists felt free to be imaginative.

**(Neo)classicism** (c. 1750–1810) was a reaction to the extreme energy of the Baroque and Roccoco. It stressed reason and order, clarity of expression and strict aesthetic ideals. Individuality was discouraged since the arts should appeal to the intellect and not the emotions. Stress was placed on 'proper' subject matter with detail subordinated to design. Concepts such as symmetry, unity, grace, proportion and harmony were vital as were correct form and craftsmanship.

**Romanticism** (1790s to c. 1900) was a rejection of the calm, harmony and balance of classicism. It emphasised individualism and was often subjective, imaginative and irrational. Feelings, sensitivity and emotion were more vital than reason or intellect. Key ideas were the beauties of nature, the self and human personality with its inner struggle. Artists were seen as individual creators whose creative spirit was more important than formal rules. Romantics were often inspired by the Medieval period, folk culture and tradition. This could lead to the weird or monstrous.

Check the web for modern movements such as: *impressionism; art nouveau; symbolism; cubism; the Pre-Raphaelites, arts and crafts movement, Dada; etc.*

# Revision checklist

*helps you check what you still need to do*

## By the end of this chapter you should be able to:

| | | | |
|---|---|---|---|
| 1 | Use the information in Databank, above, with confidence | Confident | Not confident. **Revise** page 184 |
| 2 | Understand and explain aesthetic theory | Confident | Not confident. **Revise** pages 176, 197 |
| 3 | Recognise key characteristics of artistic styles | Confident | Not confident. **Revise** pages 167, 184 |
| 4 | Discuss whether art should have a deeper purpose (practical message) or should exist for its own sake | Confident | Not confident. **Revise** page 177 |
| 5 | Be aware of some of the reasons why some art works are expensive (personal response to the arts) | Confident | Not confident. **Revise** page 177 |
| 6 | Understand different principles of aesthetic evaluation (aesthetic criteria) | Confident | Not confident. **Revise** pages 176, 178–179 |
| 7 | Be able to apply some of the aesthetic criteria to specific art works | Confident | Not confident. **Revise** pages 180–181 |
| 8 | Distinguish between taste and aesthetic evaluation (subjectivity versus objectivity or universal standards) | Confident | Not confident. **Revise** pages 176, 180, 197 |
| 9 | Consider if society is elitist about some art forms | Confident | Not confident. **Revise** page 180 |
| 10 | Show awareness of why art forgeries are a problem | Confident | Not confident. **Revise** page 181 |
| 11 | Appreciate the role of law and morality in the arts | Confident | Not confident. **Revise** page 181 |

Much of General Studies is about bringing together ideas and controversies from different disciplines or perspectives and, through argument and evidence, to reach a justified conclusion. The issues below require you to bring together ideas from culture, science and society. Each is explained more fully on the following pages.

## Topic checklist

| ○ AS  ● A2 | AQA A | AQA B | EDEXCEL | OCR |
|---|---|---|---|---|
| In what ways does science have an impact on society? | ○● | ● | ● | ● |
| Do markets meet the needs of society? | ○● | ○● | ○● | ○● |
| How do religious and secular beliefs affect world peace and stability? | ○● | ○● | ○● | ● |
| Proud cultures and globalisation | ● | ○● | ● | ○● |
| Who makes what, and why? | ○● | ○● | ○● | ○● |
| Is environmentalism a scientific or a political issue? | ○● | ○● | ○● | ● |
| The relationship between values, representation and reality | ● | ○● | ● | ● |
| The relationship between needs, interests and opinions | ○● | ○● | ○● | ○● |
| Should society control the development of science and technology? | | | | |
| When and how should people be punished? | ○● | ○● | ○● | ○● |
| What is progress? | | ● | ○● | |
| How and why do our perceptions of beauty change over time? | ○● | ○● | ○● | ● |
| Can citizens of the world 'walk by on the other side'? | ○● | ○● | ○● | ○● |
| How does history represent events and reputations? | ○● | ○● | ○● | ○● |
| Aren't developments in science and technology more important than spending money on historic buildings, ballet and opera? | ● | ● | ● | ● |
| What is the difference between belief and knowledge? | ○● | | ○● | ○● |
| The relationship between science, equality and family values | ○● | ○● | ● | ○ |
| Is the determination of youth to be different a true catalyst for change? | ● | ○● | ○● | ○● |
| Foreign languages | ● | | | |

# In what ways does science have an impact on society?

## What is society?

Society is taken to mean the whole of human culture. Therefore, it covers many different structures or societies and we may be able to show how science affects different **societies.** Common features and beliefs unite a society. For example, a society might be defined by its **religious** beliefs, its **economic** system, its **political** system, or its **culture**. Since science is a method of approaching problems, it could affect societies with different belief systems in different ways.

Science, in the Western philosophical tradition, is a way of doing things and thinking about the universe, such that it satisfies human curiosity. We seek scientific explanations for phenomena (scientific theories). We believe that these theories should be as simple as possible and as powerful as possible. There are scientists who believe, perhaps somewhat ambitiously, that there is a scientific theory that provides an explanation of everything in the universe. Most importantly, most scientists think that scientific theories are not, or should not be, dependent on your beliefs.

Other scientific traditions exist. International societies exist to further 'Islamic science' and 'Chinese science'. It is perfectly in order to describe the history and priorities of aspects of science that have developed in a particular society, but to imply that the way in which science is carried out is, or should be, different in these traditions is very controversial. As far as we know there is only one way to do science – theorise, predict and test – and this is independent of the religious, social or cultural beliefs of the scientist. This notion is important if we are to consider how science can affect society.

Science affects society in more direct ways, by the changes in technology it brings about. These can affect the working lives of citizens – think of all the changes introduced in the wake of the Industrial Revolution of the 18th and 19th centuries. The future growth of any society is dependent on the activities of its scientists and technologists. However, we could just as well ask, 'How does society try to influence science?'

## What is the relationship between science and religion?

Science and religion have sometimes been presented as systems in opposition, but they deal with the world in very different ways. When the control of society was primarily religious, leaders were (and are!) resistant to change. If religion is based on revelation, then an activity like science, which sets out to question all explanations in order to discover better ones, may be seen as a threat. This is well illustrated in the 14th and 15th centuries, when the Christian Church, whose view of the Universe was **geocentric**, did not take kindly to the **heliocentric** views of Copernicus, Brahe and Galileo. However, once a better model of the solar system became accepted, simply because it was manifestly a better picture, the Church had to adopt and adapt to it. A similar problem arose in relation to evolution after Darwin proposed his theory of evolution. A consequence of this theory was the realisation that Man might be subject to evolutionary change and, even worse, might have arisen through evolutionary processes from animals. This is still a problem for some people today, with the result that there are many people whose faith is a direct contradiction of evolutionary ideas. However, there are many Christians and followers of other faiths who find that evolution does not cause them to doubt their beliefs.

## What is the relationship between science and politics?

Science and technology can become the tools of politics, or for those who wish to wield political power, and we could show how politics has often tried to direct science in particular ways. A good example is that of Stalin and Lysenko in communist Russia before the Second World War. Lysenko carried out experiments on cereals, which were intended to show that plants could be changed genetically by the conditions under which they grow, in direct opposition to the developments in genetics brought about by Mendel. It fitted the political ideals of the Russian regime at the time, and resulted in the imprisonment and sometimes death of biologists who expressed doubts.

## What is the relationship between science and economics?

Science, particularly evolutionary biology, has influenced politics through notions of 'survival of the fittest' and natural selection. Ironically, Darwin was influenced by the work of the economist Thomas Malthus, who first identified the blocks to population increase through limitations of food supply. This in turn was used to support the 'laissez-faire' economics of the 19th century.

## What is the relationship between science and culture?

Science affects some forms of culture through its content – for example, the literary genre of science fiction. It provides ways for doing things – arguably computers have opened up more ways for people to express themselves and, more importantly, to show the results to many others. It may have changed the boundaries between high and popular culture, for example by making performances more widely available and affordable. It provides more media, hence greater scope for artistic creativity. It provides thought-provoking ideas, particularly ethical and moral questions and hence the material for artists to work with.

# Do markets meet the needs of society?

## What is the issue here?

'The battle begins,' according to Giovanni Sartori, 'where the *visible hand* of the state enters on a course of collision with the invisible hand of the market.' His point was that during the 20th century our political system developed the state more and more into a 'do everything state'.

The New Right criticised the welfare state for creating a 'nanny state', which lacked incentives, with people paying as little tax as possible and wanting everything in return – a *dependency culture* in which individuals no longer expected to provide for themselves. The New Right focussed on *market forces* as a means of lowering expectations and with the election of Margaret Thatcher as PM in 1979, the UK took a sharp right turn: (i) people should own their own homes, not expect councils to provide them; (ii) they should buy their own private pensions, not expect the state to give them everything; (iii) state-owned businesses were sold off to be sharpened up in the *real* world where the fit survive and others wither away.

## Do internal markets and outsourcing work?

Conservative governments (1979–1997) shared the New Right belief in market forces – so a doctor referring a sick patient to hospital became a matter of competition and contracts (an *internal market*) as hospitals had to compete for work from GPs; similarly, hospitals contracted out work such as cleaning, laundry services and catering, with outside firms winning the contracts. The same approach was applied to the railways, with control of the track and the infrastructure separated from the running of trains by multiple franchise holders such as Thames Trains and Virgin. Much of the track work was *outsourced* to private firms. The Blair government rejected the idea of an internal market in the NHS and reduced the numbers of rail franchisers – with a new body, Network Rail, taking in-house much of the track maintenance work.

## Do markets adequately reflect social costs?

If a firm establishes a quarry, it won't be long before people complain as the quarry becomes increasingly unsightly or many trucks and lorries start trundling through the village, slowing traffic times, creating noise and perhaps polluting the environment. These *social costs* diminish the quality of people's lives, which is why council officials get involved. Some people argue business must be encouraged because it employs people and if quarries didn't produce sand and gravel, roads and houses could not be built. But people's lives and property mustn't be blighted, so maybe taxes should be levied on lorries or noise to maximise environmental protection.

## So what about wants and needs?

Markets do not work if people don't have money to buy things. Few people believe that a homeless person without any money should be left to live in a cardboard box; we accept people have a right to health and education too – so society provides at least a basic safety net which deals with **needs** – identifying such needs can prove subjective. But if we want a bigger house or a nicer car or to live an affluent lifestyle, these are **wants** we must provide for ourselves – without state handouts.

## So what about markets and equality?

The more we allocate through markets, e.g. healthcare (private hospitals), education (private schools), housing (home ownership), legal services (much less legal aid now available), the more likely are better-off people to be able to afford to buy better services than poorer people – e.g. if people had to pay for law enforcement directly rather than through taxation, the homes of the wealthy would be well guarded but poor people might not be able to afford protection by police officers or security guards.

## But what about subsidies for the arts?

Opera, ballet, theatre, orchestras and similar upmarket cultural activities are subsidised through government funding to bodies such as the Arts Council and grants from the National Lottery. Even so, ticket prices are often high. If all costs had to be met by those attending performances, ticket prices might be higher and the numbers able to see performances might drop. Would it be right for *high culture* to be available only to the rich – or are they the only people who want to see it anyway?

## Should sport on TV go to the highest bidder?

Once satellite TV won the rights to show Premier Football matches live, those who could not afford or did not choose to subscribe to Sky Sports were denied the opportunity to see live matches on television. For matches to be seen on public service broadcasting, it means the BBC must make the highest offer when such rights are auctioned. The case for TV companies paying so much is that the soccer clubs depend on this income.

## On balance . . .

Perhaps David Beetham was right in thinking that not all social life can be carried on by means of market relations. In modern economies, the market has to be supplemented by government.

# How do religious and secular beliefs affect world peace and stability?

Since the mid 18th century, religion's dominant position in the 'Christian' world has been challenged. A declining proportion of people, notably among the young, claim religious belief and fewer still practice it.

## Is the power of religion in decline?

Religious leaders have always tried to control people's thoughts and actions. In the past religious leaders in the Christian world had almost absolute power over individuals because of the belief that:

- they alone had access to the mind of God;
- only they could interpret revealed truth and define knowledge;
- they controlled reward and punishment in the afterlife;
- they were supported by the secular authorities.

Their God was an all-powerful, all-knowing creator who had revealed all knowledge in the Bible. People who taught any other knowledge were persecuted. It is similar today in some fundamentalist Islamic states such as Iran or, until recently, Afghanistan.

Challenges to religion have come from rationalism, empirical science, the rejection of authority and the emergence of democracy. The theory of evolution, published in 1858, has challenged religious truth by undermining belief in a creator. Many political thinkers, scientists and sociologists say that religion has served its purpose and is no longer needed.

## Are there alternatives to religion?

Alternative belief systems have emerged as religious belief has declined:

**Atheists** are people who reject belief in any god.

**Agnostics** doubt the existence of a God.

**Humanists** believe:

- there is no superior power to mankind;
- in the ultimate dignity and value of the individual who only has one life;
- that life should be lived well;
- good actions are those which promote the happiness of others;
- that people are rational beings able to accept responsibility for their own actions.

**Hedonists** believe mankind's only aim is the pursuit of pleasure. Some stress the happiness of society as a whole (altruists); others seek personal satisfaction (egoists). Utilitarians have many links with hedonism.

**Nationalists** put national well-being and identity above all else. They may or may not hold strong religious beliefs. Nationalism has cultural and political influence but is not an alternative to religious belief. In extreme forms, nationalism can lead to conflict.

## Does religion encourage conflict?

Nationalism, a powerful force affecting and often reshaping all parts of the world, is often linked to religion. It can generate considerable violence, hatred and polarisation of views or 'ethnic cleansing'.

**The Holocaust** combined both of these features. Racial purity was a key principle of Hitler's Nazi party. He said all non-Aryan races, especially Slavs and Semites, were inferior and should serve the Aryan or German race. He persecuted many different races but directed his greatest hatred against Jews. He tried to destroy them completely through the 'Final Solution'. He did this because of his absolute power in Germany where his opponents were jailed or killed. He justified his actions by blaming the Jews for German suffering after the First World War. Over 6 million Jews were killed but he could not destroy them totally. Jewish nationalism was encouraged and resulted in the state of Israel, set up in 1948. A number of Christian groups supported his anti-semitic policies.

The **Arab-Israeli conflict** is a key feature of Middle East politics in the 20th century. This is strange since Arabs and Jews are descendants of Abraham and have similar religions. For much of history Arab states tolerated Jews when other people persecuted them. The conflict concerns justification for the state of Israel; who should own Palestine; and the rights of Palestinian refugees. Israel's main enemies, the Palestinians, are supported by many Islamic states. The USA traditionally supports Israel. Several factors contribute to the conflict including economics, history, religion, nationalism and politics. It is as far from resolution today as ever and threatens to lead the world into a third major war.

**September 11** was the most devastating terrorist act in a series of incidents that have brought the Arab and Western world into conflict. The West sees its origins in a complex mix of Islamic fundamentalism and Arab nationalism. Terrorist groups say the attack on the USA was a response to US support for Israel. The USA and other Western powers are seen as imperialists and enemies of religion and culture. Terrorist acts are justified on grounds of religious belief.

**March 11 2004** saw over 200 people killed and another 1400 seriously injured by bomb explosions on the Madrid railway. At first Basque separatists, trying to influence the general election, were blamed. Within hours Al Qaeda was accused, and shortly afterwards accepted responsibility for Europe's worst ever terrorist attack. The reason given was that Spain had helped the USA in the war against Iraq.

Do religious fanatics, political extremists or dominant Western powers intent on exploiting less well-developed countries threaten world peace today?

# Proud cultures and globalisation

## Media globalisation

One effect of the emergence of new technology in the late 20th century has been a move towards 'one world'. The reach and extent of the media have been revolutionised. Before the technological revolution the speed and extent of communication was limited. Now we can maintain almost instantaneous contact with all parts of the world. Events occurring in remote parts of Africa or Asia were once ignored and unknown. Most people were only aware of and interested in events happening in their own immediate community. Events in other parts of their country, let alone continent, were outside their experience. Satellite communication now lets us see events as they happen. International news agencies such as Reuters are a major news source about distant parts of the world. These agencies are owned and controlled by Americans or Europeans. Western people know more about other parts of the world than ever before. The expansion of the media worldwide is only one aspect of globalisation. Since the 1950s the pace of economic globalisation has greatly increased. A real concern is that this has not led to 'one world' in which all peoples and nations have an equal share. It has been said that globalisation is Western economic imperialism.

## Cultural globalisation

Western capitalism has created markets for Western products in all parts of the developing world. Initially this was said to be beneficial to poorer, less developed countries. Often unwanted machines were sold cheaply to these areas to help them set up their own industries. Such sales were often tied to maintenance agreements that made the developing industries dependant on the West. Some companies, such as News International, became multinational, setting up centres in several different countries to increase their economic power and influence.

Media corporations from France, Britain, America and Germany competed to equip developing countries with broadcasting equipment. Instead of allowing the development of a home-based industry it made them dependant on the West for the supply of programmes and equipment. Therefore, much profit from the new media provision was siphoned off from the developing nations, to increase the wealth of Western companies.

A more serious issue is that the programmes that are broadcast are made and set in the West. They show Western culture and lifestyle as an ideal to be striven for. The potential effect of this is to destroy, or at least marginalise, native cultures and replace them with a single worldwide Westernised culture. In both cultural and economic terms the worldwide spread of media is of greatest benefit to the West.

## Are cultural values at risk?

Some people feel that a global media is a good thing. They say that easier access to world news makes us more tolerant, caring and involved. It has been said that the rapid development of the Internet has turned us into 'netizens', or citizens of the World Wide Web. If we own a computer we can have immediate contact with people in any part of the world.

Our awareness of **disease and famine** in Africa and other developing countries has been raised, thanks entirely to the media. Consequently, ordinary people have been encouraged to contribute to charitable aid more than ever before. Unfortunately, while such aid has relieved some suffering, it has failed to alter the political systems or corrupt governments, which have often contributed to the suffering in the first place. The media have shown the Western world the severity of the AIDS epidemic in parts of Africa. As a direct result of media campaigns multinational medical firms have changed their policy about the supply of cheap drugs to help the poorer areas of the world.

The media inform us about **tragedies** like war, ethnic cleansing, and environmental disasters such as earthquakes, hurricanes and volcanic activity. Without the immediacy of news reports and pictures we would be ignorant of the sufferings of many of our fellow human beings. Thanks to media coverage, international aid has been mobilised to deal with environmental disasters and international intervention has occasionally been mounted to resolve political conflict.

**Cultural transfer** is a two-way process thanks to the global reach of the media. Just as Western cultural practices and values are introduced to the developing world, the influence of other cultures is experienced in the West. It is claimed that the media help to develop a one-world culture. While the dominant influence is Western, much that is good in the culture of other peoples has been made known to and absorbed by the West. This is a result not only of migration but also of media coverage and increased travel opportunities.

## Multinational companies

The late 20th century saw the growth of multinational companies. These were often leaders of globalisation. It is said they exist only to make profit for their owners or investors. Some critics claim they are not interested in the prosperity or well-being of the countries in which they invest. Consequently it is said they pose a serious threat to the economic survival of poorer countries. Some multinationals may favour undeveloped economies or totalitarian regimes in order to negotiate beneficial trading concessions. In this way they are at liberty to exploit the resources of the poorer countries of the world for their own profit.

# Who makes what, and why?

## Is everything now a commodity?●●●

People used to grow food largely to feed themselves and their families and bartered any surpluses with others – yet today most people work for money, which they use to buy houses, food, clothes, cars, banking services, holidays or whatever. There are very few things that are not bought or sold, so there are now very few things that are not commodities.

## How do natural resources and technology determine location of industry patterns?

There is no point setting up a gold or coal mine in areas where there is no gold or coal or searching for oil if there isn't any there. Initially, power for textile mills came from water. Once electricity was in use, such mills didn't depend for power on fast-flowing rivers and streams. Once refrigeration was understood, meat, fish and perishable goods could be shipped from one side of the world to the other.

How electricity is produced is also important – using fossil fuels such as coal and oil can only add to global warming, yet poorer countries will need support if they are to rely instead on *sustainable* forms of energy production such as wind power or solar energy.

More recently, computers, satellite technologies and the growth of the Internet mean there is no reason for work to be fixed in a particular location. Many teleworkers can now keep as closely in touch with their colleagues or their office from home. Multinationals such as banks, insurance companies, software developers and car makers are just a few mouse-clicks away from billions of consumers.

## What else influences location of industry?

- The closer *production* is to its raw materials, the lower its transport costs are likely to be – e.g. an iron and steel production plant will have lower costs if it is built close to a coalfield (e.g. in South Wales) than if coal has to be brought in from miles away.
- A *skilled workforce* is important; although people can be trained, there are benefits if firms doing the same type of work are located close to each other, e.g. china producers in Stoke-on-Trent or IT workers in Silicon Valley. But if the industry goes into decline, this makes the area vulnerable.
- Levels of *regulation* may be a factor. If a firm knows there are high ethical standards and many health and safety rules in a country, they may set themselves up in an area where they will be less pressured by unions or regulated by the authorities.
- *Climate* can also be a big determinant. At present champagne is produced from grapes grown in France, but as *global warming* occurs, other areas with similar soils may be better placed to provide its ideal climate. France

will no doubt claim that only wine it produces is *real* champagne, yet in future the areas from which the *best* champagne is produced might be in Kent, Sussex, Oxfordshire or the Cotswolds.
- Nearness to *markets* used to be important but, now freight costs are cheap, firms such as Nissan and Toyota try to produce in areas where *labour costs* are low and assemble their cars near the point of sale and within the EU to benefit from the *Single European Market*.

## What links exist between culture and work?●●●

- As people commute to work between the UK and France via Eurotunnel and more UK residents choose to live in France or Spain, distinctive national cultures are declining.
- Migration within and across borders is more likely to occur due to the free movement of people within the EU. Although the UK is keen to reduce the numbers of asylum seekers in the country, it has decided to welcome young, educated economic migrants to arrest the imbalance between working and dependent populations.
- Satellite television helps call centre workers in India and China to understand the worlds in which their American or European customers live – it tells them about who the chart toppers are, what the weather is like and what David Beckham has done recently, so they can chat to customers who think they are just a couple of miles down the road.
- Many people believe the widespread appeal of worldwide satellite television threatens distinctive individual cultures with their cherished values since it promotes a 'one size fits all' global culture.
- Holidays abroad, foreign travel, more fans following sports teams to overseas events encourage awareness of other religions and lifestyles.
- The food we eat is now more varied – though the experience of balti and chicken tikka masala should alert us to the fact that the dishes eaten in Birmingham or Brighton may not be exactly what is eaten in India or China or Thailand.
- Films such as the *Harry Potter* series based on Alnwick Castle and the cathedrals at Durham and Gloucester or the *Lord of the Rings* with New Zealand locations make a big difference to tourism.

## In conclusion . . .

As capitalist multinational companies scour the world looking for profit-making opportunities, MEDCs are engaging more with poorer countries; it is good that the hopes and achievements of LEDCs are increasing – the richer they become, the more they can trade with the rest of the world and thus reduce inequalities.

# Is environmentalism a scientific or a political issue?

## What is environmentalism?

As with all such questions, you need to define your terms, not least because **environmentalism** has no commonly agreed meaning. It is used in many different contexts. For example, it is used in psychology to describe an approach that assumes that human behaviour is determined by the **environment**, i.e. the way in which a person was brought up and the social conditions in which they live, rather than by **genetics** (the genes passed on to a person from their parents). In a general sense, **environmentalism** is a concern of those who wish to conserve, improve, preserve, protect or save the 'environment'. In the scientific study of **ecology, environment** refers to the surroundings in which an organism lives, on which it depends, or to which it responds. The environment is also a political concept, when it refers to Earth and all the organisms it contains.

## What are the major environmental organisations?

Many local and national groups have the aim of **conservation** – preserving the environment from change. It has its origins in the 'healthy ecology' ideas of Rachel Carson (*Silent Spring*). Her book brought to light the dangers of unrestricted actions, such as spraying with pesticides, on other organisms in food chains.

**Green parties** – political parties that have been formed in many countries, loosely united on policies that aim to prevent the destruction of ecosystems. They operate according to the normal political structures of the respective countries.

**Greenpeace** – a non-governmental organisation with branches in many countries. A small group with the main aim of stopping further nuclear weapons programmes founded it in 1971 in Canada. Since then it has embraced ideals of ecological conservation and pacifism, reflected in its choice of name. It receives money through private donations, and claims that any other form of funding, say from governments, would compromise its ideals and potential for action. It is well known for its active intervention in trying to prevent the movement of nuclear waste materials and nuclear tests in the Pacific.

## Isn't everyone an environmentalist?

Like motherhood and apple-pie, environmentalism is difficult to argue against. At its heart are some diffuse but morally acceptable assertions:

- all nature is relational – the world is structured in such a way that any event will inevitably affect others;
- humans have a moral responsibility to maintain 'nature';
- that ecological and environmental viewpoints are superior to other ways of looking at the world.

Recently, some writers have challenged the underlying claims of environmentalism – notably when they are associated with sectional political campaigns, such as eco-feminism.

Others challenge the evidence by which some environmental groups believe that human activities constitute a global threat to the natural world.

## How does environmentalism affect international politics?

Possibly the most notorious international disagreements have been over global warming and greenhouse gases. Many nations, except the US, agreed to a programme of reduction of emissions at a meeting in Kyoto in 1997, sponsored by the United Nations. There are deep political divisions about what to do, and they are linked to the energy requirements of different countries. Less-developed countries resent being told by others that they should stop burning wood and coal, when this may be their best source of energy. Richer countries perceive threats to their prosperity if they are forced to reduce their consumption of fossil fuels. It is no coincidence that they try to cast doubt on research demonstrating the effect of emissions on climate, and the predictions made from that research.

## Doesn't science support environmentalism?

Many scientists have studied how humans affect the environment, and the concepts are nearly all scientific. A well-known exponent is James Lovelock, whose Gaia hypothesis attributes life-like qualities to the whole planet. His notion that the Earth is like a living organism that is capable of regulating its own activities is controversial. Finding out about the changes taking place in and on the Earth is a totally reputable activity; unfortunately some of the results are uncertain, and we need more time and knowledge to produce more accurate predictions. Some will argue that we should do nothing, and hence reduce the risk of doing something irreversible. This is almost impossible – billions of people are on the planet, making changes without noticing. There are those who think that changes can easily be reversed. Others think that change is inevitable and we should just try to adapt as best we can.

In the long term, nothing is forever, and the Earth has seen dramatic changes in climate and its living inhabitants in the 5 billion years life has been present. None of these historic events can have had anything to do with human activities or beliefs, and distant future events may be just the same.

# The relationship between values, representation and reality

## What do artists do?

Artists produce paintings or books, sculpture or buildings, music or poetry, but should their work have meaning? Should the arts seek to influence, reflect or challenge the values and practices of society?

Answers to these questions change through time. During the Middle Ages attitudes were traditionalistic and authoritarian. The arts had to reflect, not change, society. In Western Europe the Catholic Church was a dominant influence in preserving accepted values and the established social structure. The Church used its power to resist the emergence of new ideas or styles.

The Renaissance offered a complete contrast. Renaissance artists ostensibly aimed to rediscover the glories of the ancient world, but in practice they led the search for new knowledge. They helped challenge and overthrow old value systems and social order. After the Renaissance, the Reformation ended the Catholic Church's dominance over the creative and intellectual life of Western Europe. The arts in the Middle Ages were stylised and two-dimensional but in contrast, particularly in painting and sculpture, Renaissance artists constantly sought greater realism and accuracy. Leonardo is as famous for his scientific studies as for his art.

Throughout the 18th century, Western European society was stable and hierarchic. Most countries had authoritarian governments, social status was fixed by birth and society was patriarchal. Laws favoured the property rights of the rich and powerful.

The arts reflected these values. In the theatre the glories of Shakespearean and Restoration drama were neglected in favour of bland sentimental comedy reflecting a society that audiences wanted to see. Shakespeare's plays were bowdlerised, to remove anything offensive or in poor taste. A similar pattern applied to architecture. After the exuberant excesses of the Baroque came austere formalism. The gentry rebuilt or remodelled houses in a more fashionable Palladian (Classical) style to symbolise their wealth, power and status. They emphasised good taste and observation of architectural 'principles'; landscape gardeners sought to 'improve' on nature; even the organisation and layout of houses reinforced and reflected social values and attitudes.

The Second World War led to economic and social uncertainty. Traditional values, challenged in the 1950s, were rejected in the 1960s. At first the arts continued to use pre-war forms and styles. In 1955 Beckett's 'non-realist' theatre caused a revolution in drama. Popular music was transformed by the development of rock 'n' roll. Warhol used pop art to challenge accepted forms of painting.

## Can the arts influence values?

Some people say that, as well as reflecting the values of an age, the arts can help to shape them. Literature, especially drama and novels, has questioned values and challenged common perceptions of what is right or acceptable. In the 1890s William Morris described an imaginary socialist utopia in *News from Nowhere* as a condemnation of Victorian oppression. Most of Shaw's plays were thinly veiled attacks on the corruption and abuse of contemporary life.

Television drama shows clearly how values can be changed by the arts. In the 1960s the plight of the homeless was exposed in *Cathy Come Home*. Its effect on public opinion was both immediate and long lasting. As well as raising awareness of a problem it led to the establishment of Shelter, a charity still working for the homeless today. *Cathy* . . . probably was more effective in changing the values of a society than any other work of art.

## Should art be representational?

A major issue that faces all artists is how far their work should represent reality. This is a particular challenge for painters and sculptors. Medieval art was intended to be symbolic, but Renaissance artists wanted accurate realism. Paintings and sculptures might be larger than life and show nature with an unreal perfection, but the images were easy to recognise. Realism in art probably reached a peak in the mid 19th century. The invention of photography, which could do realism so much better, removed this purpose from art. Artists were either released from the tyranny of realism or driven to explore new methods of expression. Impressionism was the first movement to look for new approaches to painting. Breaking the link with realism opened the way for abstract art. There has been a flood of new art forms, culminating in conceptual art (e.g. Tracy Emin and Damien Hirst). Today it is often claimed that anything can be art.

## Should we look for meaning in the arts?

We can view paintings, listen to music or read books simply for pleasure. Or we can try to analyse them to discover messages or hidden meanings.

Paintings about religious or spiritual beliefs or events are clearly vehicles teaching spiritual lessons. The use of symbols, like a skull reminding us of mortality, can convey messages from the artist to the discerning viewer. Similarly the use of a particular combination of notes in music, such as the '*Dies Irae*', often used by 19th century composers can, by association, remind informed listeners of doom and the wrath of God. In literature an author's message is often clear. Essentially most artists create art because they want to communicate ideas and thoughts to an audience. We must try to understand these messages.

# The relationship between needs, interests and opinions

## What are needs?

Every human being *needs* food and shelter, though in poor countries millions exist at near starvation levels and with only the simplest shelters. In the richer world, people claim a much wider set of needs including access to democracy, rights such as health, education, information and culture (e.g. radio or TV). This should remind us that needs can be seen either in *absolute* (one standard for everyone) or *relative* terms (changing perceptions as wealth improves).

## What are interests?

*Interests* may be financial, personal, scientific or social. They represent situations, policies, events and relationships which work to the advantage of a person or group. Marx believed individuals did not recognise their true interests, claiming most people lived in a state of *false consciousness* in which they failed to recognise they were oppressed by bosses (capitalists). Sometimes interests may conflict – an owner of a petrol station may be pleased in the short term if the passing traffic increases because he will sell more petrol and make more profit, but in the long term the extra traffic may cause more pollution, leading to health problems. Interests may look different from various standpoints – so, raising retirement ages may then make it more difficult for other younger workers to win promotion.

## What are opinions?

Opinions are subjective views; they lack certainty, may not be based on hard evidence, often contain value judgments and sometimes arise from analogy (reasoning from one possibly parallel case to another). A pupil who finds literacy difficult may say there are too many lessons (opinion) but to be successful in the subject, her interests or needs suggest she should have *more* literacy lessons! The analogy 'my mum knows I hate meat and we don't have meat any more; so if I don't like literacy, why should I have so many lessons?' isn't exact and the argument fails – whether or not we eat meat is less important than learning to become literate.

## What can we learn from the Kyoto Protocol?

The Protocol, agreed in Kyoto in 1997, was an effort by the world community to meet the **need** to reduce global warming through the build-up of greenhouse gases. We may see the Kyoto Protocol as one of the proudest achievements of the green movement internationally – this is an **opinion**.

It committed countries to curbing levels of six gases which contribute to global warming, such as carbon dioxide and methane, using emissions in 1990 as a baseline and setting targets for 2010. The goal is set in the Protocol, so this is **fact** – but it will not take effect without the support of countries producing 55% of the world's emissions (**fact**).

The US never liked the treaty, knowing their big cars and cheap petrol would make meeting the targets painful (short-term **interests**, while support for the Protocol would probably have been in their long-term **interests**), so George Bush rejected the Protocol. Russia has not endorsed the Protocol either and though EU countries back it, many of them are unlikely to meet the target of cutting emissions in 2010 to 8% below 1990 levels. Britain and Sweden are on target but other EU countries such as Denmark, Germany and Spain are not. Perhaps this is because **interests** obstructed progress or perhaps local populations' **opinions** (i.e. **public opinion**, as measured through polls) did not realise the seriousness of scientists' fears and the **need** to achieve sustainability.

## What do the Booker and Turner Prizes teach us about needs, interests and opinions?

The *Booker Prize* is the premier British award for fiction. Launched in 1969, recent winners have been: 2001 – Peter Carey: *True History Of the Kelly Gang*; 2002 – Yann Martel: *Life of Pi*; 2003 – DBC Pierre: *Vernon God Little*. The interest generated makes it a focus for debate about new writing, given the interest of the media. By their controversial decisions, the judges meet the **need** for debates about culture and morality – enhancing interest in literature. The *Booker Prize* works to the benefit of publishers and writers (**interests**) by causing people to buy the books. Many people openly discuss their differing feelings about the rival books (**opinions**).

The *Turner Prize* judges often provoke stronger opinions. The *Turner Prize*, sponsored by Channel 4 and organised by the Tate Gallery, puts art on the map – paying £20,000 to a British artist under 50 for an outstanding exhibition or other work in the past year. Recent winners were: 2001 – Martin Creed; 2002 – Keith Tyson; 2003 – Grayson Perry. In his lifetime, Turner, whose works now change hands for £millions, was considered a fraud, yet his contemporaries were wrong and guilty of massive misunderstanding. Today the work of *Turner Prize* exhibitors can provoke **opinions** which are just as strong. Culture Minister Kim Howells described a recent winning entry as 'cold, mechanical conceptual bullshit', thus reopening the debate as to what truly counts as art.

# Should society control the development of science and technology?

It is pretty obvious that changes in society and science are not independent; all human activities can affect others. In history, many political leaders have tried to control science and technology. In the case of dictators such as Hitler or Stalin, the results were awful. In the Nazi regime sufficient scientists cooperated to produce the means of mass destruction of millions of people, carried out experiments on human guinea pigs and set up human breeding programmes.

## What controls should be placed on the work of scientists?

- If science is an inquiring mental activity, solely intended to explain the workings of the universe, some take the view that there should be no control of it.
- Weapons research is a classic case where there are conflicts between ethical beliefs, political expectations and scientific development.
- Science can be very newsworthy – such as cloning human embryos – and some scientists would like the fame of discovery. Controls are necessary because of the ethical complications and risks of such work.

## How is scientific work affected by the beliefs of other members of society?

- Society, particularly in democratic countries, allows the formation of pressure groups. Many are directed at scientific work.
- The anti-vivisection movement has a long history, with the object of preventing cruelty to laboratory animals. Britain has a regulatory system that controls the use of animals in research and product testing. This is not enough for some campaigners and the last 20 years have seen the rise of a philosophical belief that all animals have rights, akin to human rights.
- Members of some religious groups, such as Christian Scientists and Jehovah's Witnesses, object to particular medical procedures.
- Some religious groups, such as the RC Church, object to some aspects of scientific work on reproduction.
- Representatives of many groups object to the idea of cloning organisms and especially humans.
- Various groups of environmentalists and others object to the introduction of genetically modified (GM) crops.
- Whatever view one takes of groups who wish to oppose or limit particular scientific activities, there may be 'hidden' groups at work, for example with financial interests in the development of GM techniques or cloning.
- It is also easy to be swept into conspiracy theories about scientific activities (or indeed anything), and one needs to keep a critical and open mind about any pressure group.

## How should scientific activity be controlled?

- Since the dawn of technology and science, society and the scientists themselves have adopted ethical codes – the Hippocratic oath of doctors is a classic example.
- Codes and laws ensure that society has control over some scientific activities. For example, the regulation of all reproductive science research in the UK by the Human Fertilisation and Embryology Authority (HFEA).
- Political oversight and control of science and technology is applied through funding – research councils decide whether proposals receive financial support. This mostly affects academic research, but financial considerations affect businesses and large companies in research with commercial implications.
- Research that might give a competitive edge is likely to be concealed by businesses. This leads to suspicion that some research is not generally known about, and the growth of yet more conspiracy theories.

## Is it desirable that non-scientists should have the final say on what scientists do?

- It is difficult to see how anyone without some scientific understanding would be able to make a serious assessment of the **scientific** worth of any research.
- On the other hand, ethical, social and political issues may be understood by anyone. Therefore, the public may judge outcomes of research. The real problem is where the nature of the research has a direct bearing on the ethical issue. For example, what are the **scientific** risks in cloning a human baby? If we are unable to understand the risks then it is difficult to judge whether our concerns are real or not. It is therefore important that scientists are able to communicate their work to the general public, and that the public should make serious attempts to understand the science.

## How can society make science produce results that are beneficial to society?

- This is a really difficult question to answer because scientists themselves cannot be certain about the outcomes of their work.
- It is often clear what society wants – science is presented with a never-ending series of human problems. It isn't always clear how science should go about producing answers, and often the answers generate more problems (for example, use of fossil fuels and global warming).
- One aspect of science is about understanding ourselves, and trying to explain our behaviour in scientific terms.

## How practical is it to attempt to control scientific developments?

- Science is what it is – and theoretically there are no limits or frontiers to what it can and should do.
- Should scientists be allowed the benefit of their own ethical beliefs, and trusted to make sure that these are in line with the wishes of society?
- Should technologically advanced nations be forced to share their knowledge with other, less-developed countries? There are obvious global benefits to doing so, but can we trust the government of every country to use, for example, knowledge of nuclear power for peaceful purposes?

# When and how should people be punished?

## Why do views of right and wrong differ?

- *Right* and *wrong* depend on culture and morality, law and religious belief. Drinking alcohol in Saudi Arabia is forbidden but accepted in the UK. Most people feel moral standards are *absolute* – yet if they differ, they represent *relative* values.
- *Culture* is the values and beliefs commonly held in a society; where there are groups – perhaps defined by age or ethnicity – with a subset of values and beliefs, they are known as a *subculture*.
- *Morality* is closely linked to culture – often the moral judgments about what behaviour is right or wrong will relate to *religious* observance and belief.
- So where cultures, morality and religions (or sense of secularity) differ, no wonder if *laws* differ because societies differ in their view of what is just.
- In Western countries, human and legal rights are seen as important, so *freedom of speech* is valued in the UK but considered dangerous in some African countries; there are differences between Western countries too – *freedom of information* is valued in the USA – but there is more secrecy in the UK.
- Killing rare birds or animals to use their body parts for medicines or cosmetics is opposed in the UK but accepted in China – reflecting different attitudes to animal welfare or loss of rare species.

## What can utilitarianism contribute to debates about behaviour and punishment?

A utilitarian perspective comes from men such as Jeremy Bentham who saw it as *enlightened self-interest*. In moral judgements, the utilitarian seeks *the greatest balance of pleasure over pain*. So a utilitarian might justify punishment by referring to:

- *Deterrence*, where a fear of punishment stops other people from committing the crime.
- *Rehabilitation* – punishment which trains the punished to live honestly, avoiding crime.
- *Incapacitation* – society imprisoning criminals so they cannot commit more crime.

## What can social contract theory contribute to debates about behaviour and punishment?

In the 1600s Hobbes argued that to lead people out of a 'state of nature', they gave their rights to their ruler in return for protection of life, property and social order – but a ruler who did not rule effectively could be deposed. The social contract requires us to obey the law, so those who disobey must be punished, *not* to deter others or to improve them, but for *retribution* – punishment for its own sake.

## What about moral panics and punishment?

- In the 1970s, Stan Cohen invented the term *moral panic* to refer to eruptions of concern about social problems, often stimulated or provoked by the mass media failing to exercise self-restraint.
- More recently, *moral panics* have arisen over gangs, guns, dangerous dogs, asylum seekers, child abuse and paedophilia – with communities showing *lynch law* tendencies, targeting chosen scapegoats.
- Such hysteria may lead to MPs passing bad laws in response to *pressure group* activism, e.g. 1991 Dangerous Dogs Act.

### But what if the accused are innocent?

There is concern that media intrusion may lead to unfairness. In 2003 police decided Matthew Kelly wouldn't be prosecuted for alleged child sex abuse because there was no evidence to support such a charge, yet once a suspect is named, her or his life is often shattered, regardless of the result. Perhaps the media should exercise self-restraint and the police should take more care to keep matters private unless or until a suspect is proved guilty.

### Do all law breakers deserve punishment?

- *Could a motorist justify breaking a speed limit if he was on a mercy mission carrying an injured person to hospital?* The rule of law would say no, guilty is guilty. But a utilitarian might say such an act was justified and might successfully argue that, guilty as the driver was, no punishment was due.
- *Could a mother without the money to feed her children justify stealing?* The rule of law would say no. If the mother had foolishly spent her money, it would be her fault she could not afford to feed her children, so the blame would be morally hers if she then took to shoplifting. Being a citizen means that to live in a law-abiding society, we have to be law-abiding ourselves. Stealing is not victim-less or excusable and would be rejected by both social contract theorists and most utilitarians.

### But what about degrading punishments?

- The US Constitution protects citizens from *cruel and unusual punishments* and the Human Rights Act 1998 protects UK citizens from *degrading* punishment, yet such guarantees depend on interpretation; the US still uses the death penalty and many see the treatment of those held at Guantanamo Bay as offensive to judicial process.
- *Amnesty International* has noted that many people lack rights taken for granted in the UK. In 2002, Safiya Husseini was sentenced to death by stoning in Nigeria for committing adultery. Her appeal was successful but the case reminds us that death by stoning and amputation of limbs for theft have been introduced there, even though no one had been stoned to death by the end of 2003.

# What is progress?

## Where does the word come from?

- Progress conveys a feeling of getting further: along the road to where we want to be, completing a task or job of work, or improving social conditions. So behind it is a concept of time. Things were different in the past compared with now – things were worse then than they are now, so we have made progress.
- Progress can be made quantitative – it can be set against targets and to a time scale.
- It can also be qualitative – improvement might mean a change in quality of life or conditions, which you **feel** is better.

### Is it better to be modern?

- Salespeople know that you can sell something if it is new or modern. Some believe that progress is measured by the modernity of our life, home, work, whatever.

## Does science make progress?

- Science aims to improve the power of its explanations of how the world works. In many ways this seems to make science more complex.
- This might seem paradoxical, because science achieves better explanations if they are simpler, or more basic, and if simpler models explain more of the world. Newton's ideas on force, motion and gravity are simply expressed in mathematical formulae, but explain far more than the vague and wordy theories that came before.
- It is the hope of some physicists that they will discover a final 'theory of everything', in which all the laws of the universe boil down to a single set of relationships. Others believe this is not possible.

## Is progress always for the better?

- In the 19th century, life in the developed countries seemed to be becoming better in so many ways, and science and technology promised the citizen almost everything. Philosophers, politicians and scientists believed that change in this way was obviously **progress**.
- Ideas about the world were still strongly influenced by the ancient Greek philosophers, notably **Aristotle**. His worldview was on a scale – from 'matter without form' to 'form without matter'. Roughly speaking he thought that the universe graded from a random mess of matter to the purest form represented by the human soul. He believed that nature showed evidence of design – things existed for a purpose. Living things were on a scale from plants to animals to humans, based on their increasing development of abstract 'form'. Scales of nature – some

organisms being 'higher' than others – were very popular in many religious beliefs, Western and Eastern. They also coincided with popular social beliefs – that some kinds of humans had progressed more than others and were therefore better, or more deserving, and could therefore impose their values on others.

- This seemed to be supported by the theory of evolution by natural selection. In Victorian England the idea that progress could come about through competition and 'survival of the fittest' was very popular and matched the mood of the times.
- However, the Darwinian theory did not require the use of progress in the sense that changes were upwards and for a purpose. The real power of Darwinism was that it could explain changes that were apparently purposeful, complex and unseen by a mechanism that was random, simple and observable.

## Do living things progress?

- Herbert Spencer was a Victorian philosopher who was greatly influenced by the Darwinian theory. He believed that evolution was the basis of nature – organisms developed from simple to complex, and that **progress** was a necessity. While his ideas are no longer fashionable, they were popular in their day.
- This should be contrasted with modern views on evolution, which no longer assume a 'scale of nature'. All organisms are subject to evolutionary influences, but these do not have to be part of a grand design in which everything has its place.
- From what we now know about evolution and the history of our planet, the concept of **biological** progress is not a very helpful one.

## Does humanity progress?

- Progress is described here as something which only has meaning in a human sense. Because we are human and subscribe to values that do not necessarily form part of scientific explanations, it is perfectly proper to talk about **human** progress.
- This is because we can have our own aims and objectives, and because our view of the world is **anthropomorphic**, in other words, we see it almost entirely through our own eyes.
- We must be careful, however, not to assume that this is how the world is – it would be a mistake to think a tree feels pain when chopped down, just because we certainly would, and we empathise with the tree. It would also be a mistake to believe that a jellyfish is less worthy than a chimpanzee because it appears to be less complex and we think that it has not evolved as much. **Everything** alive today is the outcome of millions of years' evolution and, in that way, has parity with everything else.

# How and why do our perceptions of beauty change over time?

## What is beauty?

Beauty is defined as 'a combination of qualities that delights the aesthetic senses', or 'an excellent example or attractive feature'. Even if we accept this as our starting point, disagreements would begin as soon as we tried to apply it in practice. Most people accept that beauty exists, but few would agree on the specific qualities of which it consists.

## What counts as art and why?

A similar difficulty is met if we try to define art. Most agree art is the product of human creativity and it was once fairly easy to identify art as paintings, literature, sculpture, music or buildings as products of human creativity. Some say gardens or created landscapes, as the result of human endeavour, are also art. Today it is more difficult. Is modern art, such as Tracy Emin's *My Bed* (1999) or Damien Hirst's *Mother and Child Divided* (1995), really art? Some say such 'conceptual' work simply takes advantage of public credulity. Is it simply designed to shock or does it offer a realistic image of present culture?

## Do ideas of beauty really change?

The growing esteem of modern art can be measured by the success of art galleries such as Tate Modern or the Turner art prize. Is there similar evidence to show that tastes in beauty have changed? The simple answer is yes. The evidence is to be found in the arts and in secondary evidence such as diaries and letters.

Painting and sculpture show clearly how tastes have changed. Beauty, as illustrated in human form, varies considerably over time. Check the web to compare well-known beauties of the past such as Anne Boleyn, Nell Gwynne, the Gunning sisters, or Lillie Langtry with recognised modern beauties.

In the same way, attitudes to nature show constant change. Romanticism was obsessed with nature. Rousseau, the 18th century philosopher, spoke of the 'beauty and innocence of nature'. Wordsworth, one of the greatest nature poets, wrote in 1798, '*I have learned to look on nature . . . hearing oftentimes the still, sad music of humanity*'. In 1808, Beethoven named each movement of his Pastoral Symphony to suggest country scenes. These were, he said, '*expressions of feelings rather than depictions of reality*' and not intended to be taken literally. Earlier, in the 18th century, landscape scenes were often used simply as a background for portraits.

The landscape gardener 'Capability' Brown was famous for reshaping and reconstructing nature to create man-made landscapes, as idealised settings for great houses. At the time, they were thought to be 'sublime', but in 1794 the author of *An Essay on the Picturesque* rejected the work of Brown and Repton, his successor, as contrived, false, dull and lacklustre. He demanded a return to formality, with gaily planted terraces and dense plantings of exotic shrubs near to buildings. This approach became fashionable after Repton died in 1819. In some ways it was a return to the 17th century concept of beauty inspired by Le Notre. His ideal of beauty was of formal gardens with straight lines and elaborate geometrical patterns.

## Is 'beauty' fashion conscious?

We can see similar changes of attitude in each of the arts, but perhaps most clearly in pop music, films and television. Most modern viewers criticise the products of even ten years ago as dated and uninspiring. The fashion industry, where designs change almost daily, illustrates the point even more clearly.

Several reasons help explain why tastes change:

**Fashion** is perhaps the most critical factor today. Our consumer age stresses the importance of being 'up to date'. This can best be achieved with goods that are 'different'. The mass media can foster this attitude by preaching the virtues of what is 'new'. Market forces and fashion can encourage creative artists. Economic forces, combined with fashion, encourage designers to experiment with new styles and techniques in order to be different and to sell. These pressures have always influenced people, and are a significant reason for the frequency with which ancient houses were rebuilt or remodelled, especially in the 18th century.

**Originality** is the aim of many creative artists. The few who are inspired are genuinely innovative, but others are simply 'different'. It has been suggested that the need to be different is an explanation for the rapid and confusing style changes associated with popular music or the more challenging examples of modern art. Is the intention genuinely to explore ideas in new ways or merely to shock?

**Travel** can introduce people to new ideas and to new ways of doing things. Both creative artists and their audiences are open to such influence. In the past the process was fairly slow, but today ease of travel and mass communication have made us more susceptible than ever before to new influences. In addition, migration brings people of different cultures and traditions together more often than ever before.

**Prosperity** is a significant factor in promoting change. If people have money to spend, they are more likely to purchase art than when resources are limited. This may encourage artists to experiment with new forms.

**Styles** can be identified in each art form. This shows that tastes and techniques change. A significant issue to consider is whether art changes taste or does taste change art?

# Can citizens of the world 'walk by on the other side'?

## What is global citizenship?

- Citizenship means we all have rights and responsibilities. Making globalisation work more effectively for the poor is morally essential. It is also in our common interests. Reducing poverty and inequality could help us overcome war and conflict; refugee movements; violations of human rights; international crime and environmental degradation.
- Apart from reducing poverty and inequality, we should be on our guard against those who use their economic strength to impose their own values on the remainder of the world as a sort of cultural imperialism. Would people in all countries see themselves as citizens? Would they recognise the existence of rights matched against responsibilities? The UN is committed to self-determination but is it always right to aim to replace traditional systems of government with democracy, as in Iraq?
- Giving countries a voice helps reduce tensions in the world.

## What is 'walking by on the other side'?

- The biblical story of the Good Samaritan (Luke 10: 25–37) tells of a traveller who is attacked and injured; other travellers looked but did nothing, passing by on the other side of the road, yet a Samaritan helped him, tended his wounds and left money for him to be cared for. This parable was Jesus's answer to 'Who is my neighbour?'
- Not *passing by on the other side* and supporting people in distress has become a global task of the Samaritans, an organisation founded in 1953 by Rev Chad Varah, now providing mainly telephone support in 49 countries.
- Many people who believe governments have a moral duty to support the vulnerable through welfare provision argue that society should not *'walk by on the other side'*.
- In the 1980s, Margaret Thatcher focused on people doing things for themselves – it was said people became thoughtless, greedy and selfish as a result. Margaret Thatcher commented in 1986: *'No one would remember the Good Samaritan if he'd only had good intentions – he had money as well'*. This suggests wealthy countries need to understand their responsibilities to other nations.
- What is the best way to support different nations – peace-keeping, trade, aid, debt cancellation? Aid provided by the UK is now free of any strings.
- Though the USA once largely ignored the rest of the world, they have become more engaged – perhaps because they want to control countries and exploit resources such as oil.
- Export subsidies to producers in the EU allow cheap goods to reach LEDCs but in fact they may be a form of *dumping*, breaking fragile domestic markets in developing countries with artificially cheap goods – doing more harm than good.

## Are the G20 more important than the G8?

- The G8 countries are the richest countries in the world, such as France, UK, Japan, Germany, USA and Russia, which meet regularly with an EU rep also present. They wanted the G20 to be created (in 1999) to promote talks over policy issues among developed countries and emerging markets to strengthen global financial stability.
- The G20 members include Argentina, Australia, Brazil, China, India, Italy, Japan, Mexico, Russia, Saudi Arabia, Turkey, UK, USA, with the EU, IMF and World Bank also represented at meetings.
- According to John Kirton, the G20 was created as a *deliberative* rather than decisional body, but one designed to encourage the formation of *consensus* on international issues with a focus on *longer term* rather than immediate policy issues.
- Dialogue between the G8 and the G20 helps to improve life in developing countries and to increase international cooperation and understanding.

## What are the best ways to help?

- Bodies such as the Organisation for Economic Cooperation and Development, the World Bank and the IMF help and encourage LEDCs to move through the stages of economic growth.
- Membership of bodies such as the EU, the UN and the Commonwealth encourages nations to engage with each other and promote interdependence – working together towards shared goals, such as the UN Millennium Goals 2000.
- Working with others on such goals makes it less likely they will want to go to war with you.
- Aid needs to be seen in different ways. There is no alternative to *humanitarian aid* after harvest failures, earthquakes or floods. But often *trade may be preferable to aid* – free and fair trade and access to markets in MEDCs are better than handouts because money gifts have sometimes been wasted on status symbols rather than improvements such as good road, rail or telecommunications links.
- What cripples many LEDCs is the *interest* payments and *capital* repayments on loans – sometimes countries with hungry people even have to export food to earn money to meet their debt obligations. That is why G8 countries such as the UK argue for debt reduction strategies to write off poor countries' debts if they agree to spend the money saved on improving equality and essential services such as health and education.

# How does history represent events and reputations?

## What is history?

- History is a record of events – an objective list of happenings. It becomes more complex when we try to explain why things turned out as they did, often involving consideration of competing ideologies or values.
- History also involves *conceptualisation* and *classification* to help us understand events.
- With modern computers, history can be better understood as details studied separately in the past, such as the findings of economists or archaeologists, can now be correlated to provide new explanations, long after the events themselves.

## Is history just a record of what happened?

- If we see history as a list of events for which records exist then *a record of what happened* might be a satisfactory description. But if we are trying to explain or interpret things then history becomes much more than a confirmed chronology of events.
- Historians who ask different questions reach different answers. The art historian and the economic historian may reach a different view of events, yet both can also add to the understandings of social historians.
- The danger of a chronological view (i.e. *first* this, *then* that) is that we have to avoid thinking that what comes first must be the cause of what follows – events may be influenced by other factors and may not be related in terms of *cause* and *effect*.

## How does history help us to make sense of large numbers of separate events?

- History develops meanings through *concepts*, e.g. power, authority, justice, democracy. A problem, though, is that these can easily be used by different historians in slightly different ways.
- History also employs *classification,* though this too can sometimes be equally arbitrary, e.g. Max Weber explained *power* relationships, in terms of: (i) traditional systems such as *feudalism* in England or the *caste system* in India; (ii) charismatic leadership by people who attracted enormous loyalty and commitment from their followers – Mahatma Ghandi, Henry Ford, Adolf Hitler, Margaret Thatcher; (iii) those working in *bureaucracies,* who carry out orders from superiors in the hierarchy.
- History often splits up events into distinct periods, covering particular phenomena such as:
  - *The Renaissance* describes the changes (e.g. in science, rhetoric, literature and music) in Western civilisation, during the transition from medieval to modern times in the 15th and 16th centuries.
  - *The Restoration* is the period following the reestablishment of the monarchy after Cromwell's Commonwealth; in English literature the Restoration period is often taken to extend from 1660 to the death of John Dryden in 1700.
  - *The Enlightenment* refers to the principal ideas in 18th-century Europe and America involving a rational and scientific approach to religious, social, political and economic issues leading to a secular perspective of society and a sense of progress.
  - *The Industrial Revolution* describes the social and economic changes in Britain from 1760 to 1850 in which traditional forms of agriculture and commerce were replaced by an industrial society, with most workers living in towns.
  - *The New Deal* in the USA related to the domestic reform programme of the administration of Franklin D Roosevelt which aimed to provide recovery and relief from the Great Depression and included new laws to help working people.
  - *The Cold War* involved the struggle for power between the Western powers and the Communist bloc from the end of the late 1940s until 1989.
  - *War on Terrorism* – conceived after the attack on the World Trade Center in New York on 11 September 2001, saw George W Bush trying to galvanise a worldwide rebuttal of terrorism.

## Where do reputations come from?

- A radical view of history might see it as the story of those who won – the *history of the winners* – because while those who win write the history, those who have lost are excluded or demonised.
- So when Nelson Mandela went to prison for being an ANC activist in 1963, who would have thought he would emerge from prison a hero, praised throughout the world in 1990 to become reborn South Africa's first black president and the 1993 winner of the Nobel Peace Prize?
- Yet reputations change as headlines recede and we take a longer view. Clement Attlee (Labour PM 1945–1951) was a small, diffident and little-known man when he led Labour to its post-war victory over Winston Churchill, so while Churchill will always be remembered for winning the war, Attlee's reputation has grown as the man who won the peace – mainly because his post-war government laid the foundations of a modern Britain without the tensions that often occur after war.

## What is historiography?

- Historiography is the study of how historians deal with the past – while they generally agree on facts such as the names, dates, places and events, they rarely agree on the interpretations.
- While few people complain if historians find and use new data to explain past events, a greater danger is that reputations and events are judged according to criteria which would *not* have applied at the time being studied.
- So, if we apply 21st-century concerns for human rights, equal opportunities and avoidance of discrimination, the reputation of almost every 19th-century leader in Europe or the USA could instantly be regarded as flawed, even though many of them were actually brave and enlightened according to the values of their own time.

# Aren't developments in science and technology more important than spending money on historic buildings, ballet and opera?

## What kind of question is this?

The way it is phrased invites you to agree, and if you don't, implies that you don't know what is important – all indicators of a **rhetorical** question. In one sense it is a non-question, because it is trying to compare unlike things. On the other hand, it is completely justified, because society, which includes you and me, needs to have a say on how limited resources should be deployed, and presumably we want to do that in the way that benefits everyone.

## How important are science and technology?

**Developments in science and technology** are said to be important because they can improve:
- our health
- our work
- our forms of leisure
- our quality of life
- the development of our culture.

Of course, it is possible to take a negative view of science and technology. Some believe that they:
- are the tools of oppression because they enable developments in weapons and anti-personnel devices
- create problems for the environment
- create problems in human health
- can use up huge resources without much apparent benefit
- are too materialistic and ignore the spiritual and aesthetic sides of our nature
- are always taking us into the unknown, without assessing the risks, and storing up problems for the future.

## How important are buildings, ballet and opera?

**Historic buildings, ballet and opera** are collectively part of high culture. If we believe in the idea of a high culture, it is something that:
- contributes to our spiritual development
- contributes to our aesthetic development
- contributes to our sense of continuity with the past
- makes many believe they live in a developed, civilised society
- encourages artistic activity because it is shown to have value in a society.

Negative views of high culture:
- the activities are elitist and encourage divisions in society
- it wastes resources for no purpose
- it is the opposite of popular culture, which is what most people want.

All these are **qualitative** views and relate to the **values** to which we wish our society to subscribe. While it may be important that we retain and support high cultural aims, the distribution of resources might be so weighted on one side or the other that the qualitative aspects ('how important are they?') could be insignificant compared with the **quantitative** ('how much do they cost?').

## How are these activities paid for?

Where do resources for these activities come from?
For science and technology:
- taxpayers, through support for universities and other publicly funded institutions of learning
- taxpayers, through subsidies or tax relief for businesses and industries
- individuals, through charitable donations
- customers who purchase goods and services from science and technology-based business and industries.

For high culture:
- taxpayers, through subsidies or tax relief
- individuals, through charitable donations
- customers, through the purchase of tickets for performances, entrance fees etc.

It is also not easy to put a figure on these sources, but for high culture it is likely to be much less than that for science and technology. The taxpayer has a heavy burden – funding through the UK science research councils in 2003 was £24bn; and the UK Chancellor said that funding for culture, media, sport and tourism would rise from £1.3bn in 2002 to £1.6bn by 2006.

## How do we compare importance?

A possible answer to the question is that there can be no doubt that science and technology are vastly more important, because in practice we spend so much more on them. This is the most **objective** response.

On the other hand, if we consider artistic, aesthetic and ethical values as more important, we could well argue that such a clear-cut conclusion is not justified. Some people believe that high culture:
- sets aesthetic standards
- defines cultural heritage
- promotes national identities
- counters materialism.

So we can regard high culture as the 'gold standard' for a society. By setting cultural standards, which validate high intellectual standards, it could claim to promote scientific and technological development. This argument leads to the conclusion that high culture is **more** important than science and technology.

However, science and technology improve the material conditions of all members of a society, not just the elite. The wealth created is used and may be indispensable for the development of high culture; otherwise, without the advances of science, all human activity is simply the preservation of life. It is also true that science and technology have a set of values, implicit in their activities, which are as important as those of high culture. Following this argument, we also use evidence based on values to support a conclusion that science and technology are more important than high culture. So, in this case, we are forced again to agree with the rhetoric of the statement.

# What is the difference between belief and knowledge?

## Isn't it obvious?

A major reason for studying general studies is to deepen and broaden your understanding of your specialist subjects in relation to the society in which we live. You should be encouraged to think about **thinking**, develop **arguments** and **analyse critically** arguments that are put to you in all aspects of your work. The more you practise these skills, the better you will become at spotting bad arguments and the confidence tricks that are played on the public. Or you might become better at playing the tricks!

Since philosophy was first recognised as an important activity about 2 500 years ago, in the classical Greek/Mediterranean world, philosophers have debated the meaning of '**knowledge**', or 'What sorts of things do we **know**?' We are still grappling with such problems – 'How do we come to know what we know?' **Epistemology** is the branch of philosophy that deals with problems of knowledge. It is not necessary for you to delve deeply into this subject.

## What is belief?

A **belief** is something that may or may not be true, but is clearly believed to be true by somebody.

## What is knowledge?

A belief becomes **knowledge** if it is **true** and if somebody is **justified** in believing it. Knowledge therefore consists of those things that you can verify independently, which you might do **empirically**, through your own observations and senses, and things that can be worked out through logical reasoning. **Empiricism** is a particular kind of philosophy and strict empiricists consider that all knowledge can only be gained through observation and experience. Empiricism implies that there will be lots of new knowledge to be gained by observation and experiment.

## Are there different kinds of knowledge?

Philosophers refer to empirical knowledge as **a posteriori** – it is obtained **after** observation or experience. They use another term – **a priori** – to refer to non-empirical knowledge. So, logical reasoning, exemplified by mathematics, leads you to conclusions and relationships, which, in a sense, have always been 'there', and only need to be revealed by working through chains of reasoning, as in a mathematical theorem. This is called **a priori knowledge**. You can use the **a priori/a posteriori** label when describing arguments and concepts, as well as knowledge.

Knowledge can be divided, of course, on the basis of the subject under discussion – scientific, geographical, historical etc. There is no fundamental difference between these kinds of knowledge, since they will all be extended by observation and experiment. Since the rise of communication and computer technologies, we have come to use the terms **information** and **data**. These are simply technical words for knowledge that may be encoded in forms suitable for **information and computer systems**.

## Are there different kinds of belief?

Since beliefs are not necessarily supported by evidence, anyone can produce or claim them. It might be an astronomer's belief that there is a black hole in the middle of a particular galaxy – his belief will be tested by the use of whatever instruments are available. He might have this belief because there is a theory of black holes that makes this prediction. If the theory has been tested many times, his belief may be strong, but can only become knowledge on the basis of observations. Then there are beliefs that it is impossible to put to a test. Many people believe in an existence after death, but testing for this is so far impossible.

Beliefs can be individual or collective, but the mere fact that many people believe something does not make it knowledge in our observational sense, or true in a logical sense. However, commonly held beliefs are usually the things that define societies and cultures, and are therefore very important for us all.

## What are 'ethics'?

Societies usually have well-developed codes of **ethics**, or formal sets of beliefs which define what citizens may or may not do. The study of these is the domain of **moral philosophy**. This subject includes consideration of belief systems such as **utilitarianism, the social contract** and **hedonism**.

### Can we explain ethics?

In recent years, some biologists, psychologists and sociologists have tried to show that ethical behaviour, particularly towards one's near relatives, can be explained by the improvement in survival that this may give to one's own genes, since they are also possessed in part by your family. There is much interest, too, in developing theories of the brain, and what defines you as an individual. To this extent, science may be able to contribute to understanding the need for beliefs and how they might have arisen, but may have little to say about whether they are true or not.

## How can we justify our beliefs?

**Justification** is the process of giving reasons for believing something. Any belief is justified if reasons for it can be given, but the reasons don't have to be true, and therefore a justified belief may not be true (and hence not knowledge).

### What is meant by 'validity'?

An argument is **valid** if it is
- **deductive**
- the conclusion is **entailed** by the premises – it must be true if the premises are true.

An **inductive** argument therefore cannot be valid, because the conclusion is the **most likely** product of the premises and the argument, rather than the **only** one.

An argument may be valid, but the **conclusion will not be true** if any of the premises are false.

# The relationship between science, equality and family values

## What are family values?

People who speak about family values generally claim that standards of behaviour were better in the past than they are now. It is easy, if we feel that moral and social values have declined, to look for causal factors.

A popular explanation used to be that religion no longer influences and directs the lives of most people. Some people blame lack of discipline, arguing that the return of National Service is the only way to restore traditional values. Others suggest that declining standards result from prosperity. We live in a consumer-driven age in which self-gratification is more important than others' needs.

A view often expressed by politicians is that declining public standards result from the collapse of traditional family values. These are rarely outlined in detail, but it is usually assumed that we understand what is meant.

This view implies that at one time there was a traditional family structure, based on a common set of values, that was passed on to successive generations. The family might be a multi-generation extended family, or a simple nuclear family, but in either case included both parents and dependant children. Fathers were clearly unchallenged heads of the household with the role of provider and protector, while mothers were carers and homemakers. Mothers were expected to subordinate their own interests to those of other family members. Children were expected to accept parental authority without question, and defer to the wisdom of age. This structure (probably mythical) was thought responsible for the perpetuation of patterns of family values and beliefs that created a stable society. They included:

- Respect for age
- Acceptance of authority
- Obedience to the law
- Lifelong commitment
- Mutual support and shared responsibility
- Restraint in sexual behaviour

The last 40 years have seen considerable changes in traditional family structures. Easier divorce has seen an increase in single-parent or reconstituted families. As marriage has declined in popularity there has been an increase in cohabiting. Many children are born outside marriage. The number of single women choosing to raise children on their own is increasing.

Attitudes to sexuality and sexual behaviour are more liberal than they used to be. Some people claim this is because of a collapse in morality, while others say it simply shows a more honest and open society. Those who deplore these changes demand that government action should support the family and so re-establish traditional family values. Those who welcome the social changes suggest that less support should be directed only to traditional families. All forms of family organisation should receive equal assistance.

## Can scientific change affect family values?

In the 20th century scientific and technological change has transformed almost all aspects of society. This is particularly true of family life. It has been claimed that scientific change has contributed to a decline in family values and adversely affected society.

Domestic work has been totally changed as a result of relatively cheap equipment such as dishwashers, washing machines, microwaves and vacuum cleaners (often called 'white goods'), convenience foods and cheap chemical cleaning products. Housework has therefore become less onerous but more effective. As a result, homes are far more comfortable while homemakers have more free time to use as they wish. This has a number of effects, some of which can add to family strain:

- Families may spend longer together, which may impose greater pressure on relationships;
- greater comfort may mean that individual family members spend time apart in different rooms, so becoming isolated;
- consumer expectations may increase financial strain;
- homemakers may seek, or be driven, to work to pay for new consumer products or to fill spare time;
- partners may experience greater independence;
- children may be left to their own devices and miss out on traditional family upbringing and influence.

Scientific advances have also impacted on family life and expectations and have increased pressures:

- improved forms of contraception have given women greater control over their own fertility, resulting in smaller families, later families and older mothers;
- IVF treatments have enabled women previously unable to do so to give birth;
- medical advances preserve the lives of children who might previously not have survived birth;
- medical progress, by improving longevity, has increased care demands on family members;

The possibilities of cloning and designer babies raise many issues relating to the future of the family.

## Do demands for equality threaten families?

A key social feature of the last 50 years has been a demand for greater equality. Historically, females were regarded as inferior to men, a belief often justified on religious and legal grounds. Most men were happy to believe that 'a woman's place is in the home'. From the late 1960s there was growing pressure to change laws and attitudes. Inevitably this affected family life:

- Patterns of employment changed, with increasing numbers of women working full or part time.
- Women were given the legal right to equal pay.
- Women could get a divorce as easily as a man.
- The social stigma of illegitimacy disappeared.
- One-parent, female-headed families increased.
- Welfare benefits for children were increasingly directed to mothers.

# Is the determination of youth to be different a true catalyst for change?

## Why and how do societies change?

Some people claim that most societies are stable and well integrated; that progress is achieved by most of the population working together; and that progress follows a slow, steady pattern, occasionally disturbed by relatively rare periods of dramatic change. A different view is that society is essentially dynamic, subject to rapid change caused by conflict between rival groups.

Whichever view is most correct, a simple comparison of historical periods shows that societies do change. Sometimes the process is rapid, as during the Russian or French Revolutions; at other times, such as the Middle Ages, change appears to be imperceptible and gradual. From this we may conclude that societies are either conservative or radical, depending on prevailing circumstances. Both historians and sociologists are concerned to discover what causal factors bringing about such change.

## What factors may lead to social change?

It is almost certain that most change is brought about by a combination of factors rather than a single event, group or individual. Among possible influences are:

- Environmental factors such as the discovery of new resources (e.g. oil in Iraq) or exhausting old ones (e.g. North Sea fish reserves).
- Challenges to people's confidence in the old order with the emergence of new ideologies or belief systems (e.g. humanism in Renaissance Europe, or Marxism in early 20th-century Russia).
- Scientific discoveries and the development of new technologies (e.g. the theory of evolution in the 19th century or an effective steam engine in the 1780s).
- Contact between cultures bringing new ideas (e.g. Spain's conquest of Mexico in the 16th century).
- Economic change affecting the position of one culture in relation to others (e.g. the Westernisation of Japan in the 1850s) or of one group in society compared to others (e.g. the emergence of wealthy industrialists in Britain in the 19th century and decline in significance of landed aristocrats).
- War can affect the society of both winner and loser (compare the social and economic experience of Britain and Germany after 1945).
- The influence of charismatic leaders (e.g. Mao Tse Tung in China or Nelson Mandela in South Africa).
- Conflict between rival groups within a society (e.g. the Roundheads and Cavaliers in the English Civil War or British miners and the government in 1972).

## Is the phenomenon of youth new?

It has been claimed that a major force for change in modern society is a new youth culture. Biologically there must always be young people, but historically young people have little social importance. This has changed during the last 50 years in Western society. Children used to be totally dependent on their parents and subject to family control. Young people rarely had resources of their own and lacked the freedom to decide how to use what they did have.

Since the 1950s there have been dramatic changes in attitudes to and the circumstances of young people. It has been suggested that 'teenager' as an idea did not exist before then. Now it is understood by many to define a distinctive and socially powerful subgroup in society, often described as a 'youth culture'.

## What is meant by youth culture?

Arguments supporting claims that there is a separate youth culture suggest that young people have more in common with each other than with older generations. This can be seen most clearly in external features such as clothing, hairstyles, preferred forms of entertainment and language. Rejection of traditional attitudes and values are equally real, if less easy to quantify and, some think, more significant. They include: rejection of authority and social hierarchy, a more self-centred, less community-oriented approach to life and short-termism, as young people give more thought to the needs of today rather than long-term planning. It is said that the emergence of this culture was a direct result of greater affluence experienced by the young after the Second World War. As a result of very high levels of employment, young people had, for the first time in history, a significant disposable income. This led to the development of a separate market to meet their demands. It can be seen today in clothes, music, mobile phones, DVDs and CDs, 18–30 holidays and even food. Economically, young people are a potent force. As the post-war generation grew older it helped change the values of society. Changes included more liberal attitudes to sex, less readiness to accept authority, reduced commitment to long-term personal relationships and rejection of traditional family values. Some believe that each succeeding generation of young people has helped to extend the boundaries of acceptable behaviour further.

In contrast, some people say that young people should not be seen as a single homogeneous group, as there are as many differences separating them as there are similarities uniting them. Not every young person can benefit from the consumer society. Education, social class, race, gender and occupation create real differences. In some ways subgroups of young people have more in common with their parents than they do with each other.

## Why are older people conservative?

A major factor that could support the view that young people are not a real threat to social stability is that as we get older, we develop more conservative attitudes. There are several reasons for this, including greater experience of life, increased responsibility and vested interest in maintaining stability and the status quo.

# Foreign languages

A unique feature of the AQA Specification A course at A2 level is that you are required to show your competence in a chosen foreign language. You will be expected to answer 25 questions to test your comprehension of several short passages in a foreign language. This part of the examination carries half the marks in unit 4, 'Culture, Morality, Arts and Humanities', and counts for 7.5% of the total A-level assessment. In the specification, under the section 'understanding and appreciation of the nature and importance of culture', the content is defined as 'nature and use of English and a foreign language'.

## What languages are available?

You may choose to answer questions in any one of three specified languages: Spanish, German and French. Although the passages are in the foreign language, all questions will be in English. AQA state that they will use passages taken from 'authentic sources'. From this you could assume that they will be drawn mainly from popular newspapers or magazines. You will be expected to answer questions based on passages in only one of the three available languages. You must state your choice of language when your examination entry is made.

## What will the passages be about?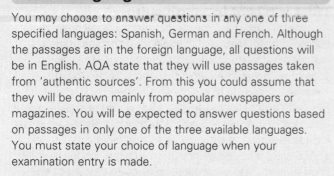

All of the passages are about contemporary issues and the subject content is based on the common Topics and Areas of Experience used in all GCSE Modern Language syllabuses. However, you should not expect that each topic would be given the same coverage in each of the languages in any one examination session. The topics are:
- Everyday activities
- Personal and social life
- The world around us
- The world of work
- The international world.

The language level should be pitched at roughly that expected of GCSE students and will not normally use vocabulary that most students will be unfamiliar with. A guide offered in the specification is the vocabulary list suitable to your chosen language, as contained in the appropriate NEAB GCSE (1997) specified vocabulary lists. You will be provided with a glossary if passages contain words that you must understand in order to answer a question, but with which you might be unfamiliar.

Normally you should expect to have approximately five different sources. Passages will usually vary in length from 100 to 300 words. Sometimes they may contain diagrams or illustrations as well as writing.

## Are all questions based on the passages?

Although most of the questions will be based on the passages, there may be a few questions which are appropriate to each of the languages. These questions will be designed to test how well you understand the structure of language as opposed to whether you comprehend the content of a passage.

## What sort of questions will be asked?

All of the questions will be in English. They will all be objective test (multiple-choice) questions. Most of the questions will present you with four different answers from which you must choose the correct one, based on your reading of the passage. Sometimes you may be given a list of words and asked to match it with an appropriate extract. Very occasionally you may have a multiple-completion question where you must select a correct combination of answers from the choice provided.

You will not be expected to write anything in your chosen language.

## How can I prepare?

It is to be hoped that you studied a modern language to GCSE. Make use of any revision materials you used then. In particular, make sure that you are still familiar with the vocabulary.

Without doubt, the best way to maintain and improve language comprehension is by reading passages in the chosen language.

Your teachers should be able to recommend newspapers or magazines that you could read to improve your comprehension skills. Some schools or colleges may have copies of foreign language newspapers in their libraries. You could search the Internet. Enter French (or Spanish or German) newspapers. This will offer you a variety of sites and will often list local and regional newspapers or magazines that you can consult online. Alternatively you could try either: www.btinternet.com or www.kidon.com or www.tvu.ac.uk. These addresses will all offer you a choice of newspapers to consult.

Try to familiarise yourself with the type of question that is asked. You can do this by practising with past papers. If your school or college can't provide you with examples you can obtain them directly from AQA at: Publications Department, Stag Hill House, Guildford, Surrey GU2 5XJ.

This section is intended to help you develop your study skills as you prepare for AS and A2. It contains useful information and suggestions to improve your exam technique and there is also a handy section covering revision technique.

## Exam board specifications

It is useful to have a copy of your exam specification. You can obtain one from the board's publications department or by downloading the specification from the board's website. The boards also supply copies of past exam papers, updating information and examiners' reports. These reports are incredibly useful as they show how candidates have gained or lost marks in previous years.

AQA (*Assessment and Qualifications Alliance*)
Publications Department, Stag Hill House, Guildford, Surrey
GU2 5XJ – www.aqa.org.uk.

EDEXCEL
One 90 High Holborn, London, WC1V 7BE
(tel: 0870 240 9800) – www.edexcel.org.uk.

OCR (*Oxford, Cambridge and Royal Society of Arts*)
1 Hills Road, Cambridge CB2 1GG – www.ocr.org.uk.

## Topic checklist

| ○ AS  ● A2 | AQA A | AQA B | EDEXCEL | OCR |
|---|---|---|---|---|
| Revision technique | ○● | ○● | ○● | ○● |
| Exam technique | ○● | ○● | ○● | ○● |
| Exam questions | ○● | ○● | ○● | ○● |

# Revision technique

Revising a 'subject' like General Studies in some ways is more difficult than for other subjects, but in other ways it is more straightforward. The amount of knowledge needed is potentially vast, because the specifications state things very broadly. However, you are not tested on the **amount** you know, but on **how you use** the knowledge you have learnt. In most papers you are actually given information. You should not feel despondent if you believe that you have little general knowledge – feel positive that you can revise the skills of thinking and presentation effectively, even in a comparatively short time. It **does** help if you try to keep up with current affairs, though – so read the papers, watch or listen to the news and discuss them with your fellow students.

## Make plans, practise and make perfect ●●●

### Make plans

1 Decide when your revision programme is to start. Don't leave it too late – a month before the exam date should be about right. Don't start too early! This may depend on how hard and effectively you have been working on the General Studies course – if you have been conscientious, you will require less revision time and can start later.

2 Decide how much time you need or can afford. This time should be in reasonable chunks, but **don't** try to have marathon sessions. For each unit you are taking, allow a couple of hours a week. This is total time – therefore include any lectures or tutorials in General Studies, if these are revision orientated.

3 If you have other students with whom you feel able to work, arrange to have some time together – no more than half an hour a week. Each of you should give a 3–5 minute talk on a relevant topic – some facts, an argument and a conclusion.

4 Make a list of topics that you propose to cover each week. Don't be too ambitious, but make sure you cover topics in every main heading in each unit you are taking.

5 Decide on the topics by looking through past papers and selecting about half the topics where you feel you have good knowledge, and half where you feel you know very little. You might identify topic areas which are set often, but don't assume they won't come up again – it may just be that the question is slightly different. Don't choose very recent or 'hot' topics – the exam questions will have been written a year ago or more – although you may be able to bring newer material into an essay.

### Practise

→ **Speed reading a short article** – put it down and list the main points from memory.

---

**Action point**

You can **prepare** a revision programme a long time in advance and then you can make a note as you go along about how much time you need to give individual areas.

**Action point**

Be specific! Note down the details of the topic you are going to revise. *Don't* just write general headings like 'culture'.

**Watch out!**

Simply reading through something does not make it memorable. Doing something with the material will.

- **Making sure you can distinguish** between fact and opinion – is the point something that has been said by somebody? Is there a reference where it can be checked? Is the opinion from an expert or authority?
- **Listing any technical words, ideas and definitions** in your topic. Make sure you know what they mean – don't assume you know; look up the meaning in a dictionary or encyclopaedia and make sure.
- **Picking out the argument** from a short newspaper article on a topic you have chosen – for example, 'binge drinking'. **Use different highlighters** to identify verifiable facts, opinions and conclusions. The leading articles (by the editor and usually in the middle pages) are often brief but clear statements of a point of view. **Explain the argument** to someone else.
- **Listing the main facts** you could use to support an assertion on the topic – for example, 'Drunken drivers who kill should be given life sentences'. Then list **facts** that could be used to oppose it.
- **If you are taking a synoptic paper**, look at the topic from several angles (cultural, scientific and social) – for example, 'Is there such a thing as a "culture" of drinking?' 'What are the effects on health?' 'How does it affect the society we live in?' List all the points for an angle in a bubble, then draw lines between the points in different bubbles which seem to be related.

## Make perfect

1 **Sharpen up your use of English**, since the examiner needs to be able to follow your arguments easily. Write short sentences, and make sure they have verbs in the correct tenses. Try not to repeat yourself.
2 **Write answers to a few questions from an old paper in a set time**. Work out the time to allow yourself by dividing the total marks for the paper by the total number of minutes, to give you the 'marks/minute'. Then calculate the time in which you should complete any particular question from the marks allocated to it. This may have to be modified if you have a passage to read.
3 **Most important** – read and read again the advice on exam technique (see below).

Follow this advice and you won't need good luck!

> **Action point**
>
> Do a brainstorm session occasionally. Before writing any notes, for 2 minutes, just open your mind and list every word that has an association with the topic, or is linked to the key word.

> **Action point**
>
> Take an old essay **of your own**, and read through a long paragraph. Does it make sense? Rewrite every sentence in **half** the words, but meaning the same. Do the same for a friend's essay. Find another friend!

# Exam technique

**Action point**

If your school does not provide them (but ask your teacher of the school/college library first) you can find information about the specification you are studying, past papers and (very useful indeed!) examiners' reports for AQA Specification A or B at http://www.aqa.org.uk, for Edexcel at http://www.edexcel.org.uk, for OCR at http://www.ocr.org.uk.

**Watch out!**

Most General Studies exams carry 50 marks and you are allowed 75 or 90 mins answering time. So you should spend between 1 and 2 mins for every mark a question carries – never spend more than 2 mins on a 1-mark question or less than 25 mins on a 20-mark question! Don't write over a page for just one mark and then have no time left to do well on a 10-mark question!

**Examiner's secrets**

If you write in pale-coloured ink or if your writing is small or if your handwriting is untidy or if you ignore rules for paragraphs, you may lose many marks – not because the examiner wants to punish you but simply because he or she cannot easily read or understand what you have written.

**Jargon**

Always distinguish between facts, opinions (sometimes referred to as objective and subjective statements respectively) and beliefs (e.g. moral standpoints we share or views which come from our faith). A conclusion based on opinion is unlikely to be as strong as one based on facts or moral beliefs. You should indicate this when reaching a conclusion.

**Examiner's secrets**

Sometimes all the questions may be in *multiple-choice* format – or they might be essays – or a mix of the two. If you are given a passage to work on, make sure you know what you are expected to do with it – use it to identify facts, opinions or beliefs – or maybe it is provided as stimulus for you to address issues or to attempt a simple precis.

Candidates often mistakenly fall into the trap of thinking that a General Studies exam simply tests what you know. Look at the assessment objectives and you will quickly find the exam papers test much more than knowledge. Often candidates don't do *exactly* what the examiner asks them to do – and such mistakes may lead to the final grade being much lower than you expected. Always look at a couple of previous, recent papers to remind yourself of the types of question which are set and the skills they test. Always take note of the details – how much time you are allowed, how many questions you have to answer, what equipment you need to bring to the exam, what command words the examiners use.

## Assessment objectives

The assessment objectives for all General Studies AS/A2 exams are as follows:

> Candidates should be able to:

A01 demonstrate relevant knowledge and understanding applied to a range of issues, using skills from different disciplines;

A02 communicate clearly and accurately in a concise, logical and relevant way;

A03 marshal evidence and draw conclusions, select, interpret, evaluate and integrate information, data, concepts and opinions;

A04 demonstrate understanding of different types of knowledge and of the relationship between them, appreciating their limitations.

Sometimes a General Studies exam will aim to assess all these elements through a single set of questions. Even when they do that, remember they will probably be giving as many or more marks to A03 as are given to A01. So even if you give a lot of knowledge and show understanding (A01), you could miss out badly unless you also select relevant and appropriate material and organise it into a coherent framework (A03). Other questions may just test one or two of the assessment objectives – but make sure you know which; that will give you a clue to what skills or abilities each question is testing.

## Command words

Make sure you understand what Assess, Examine, Discuss, Describe, Explain and terms such as 'How far . . .' or 'To what extent . . .' actually mean. **Assess** is asking you to take a critical look at an issue or some evidence and reach a conclusion. **Examine** is asking you to look in detail at something and give the pros and cons. **Discuss** (or critically discuss) means you should look at both sides of an issue or event and reach a justified conclusion. (Remember a justified conclusion is not necessarily the only conclusion which could be reached but it is a conclusion which can logically be reached on the basis of your discussion, arguments and evidence presented.) **Describe** and **Explain** are both more likely to occur at AS than A2 and are asking you to say how something works or why it matters, i.e. show your knowledge of . . . **How far** and **To what**

**extent** both ask you to do some evaluating – you need to look at both sides of an issue – interpret the points you make, showing how and why particular parts of the discussion are or are not important.

## Tools, details and signposts

→ If you know there are likely to be calculations on the paper, always make sure you take a calculator with you into the exam.

→ If there are sometimes questions asking you to draw a diagram, such as a pie chart or a bar chart, make sure you always have a ruler, pencil, pencil sharpener, rubber, protractor and set of compasses.

→ Make sure you have a spare pencil and a pen, preferably with **black** ink.

→ If you are asked to calculate data for a given year from a table, always make sure you work out the answer for the specified year, not one of the other years given.

→ When you complete a calculation, see if the question tells you how many significant figures your answer should be expressed in. If you are told to produce three significant figures and you give two or four, you may be denied some or all of the marks available. Equally, when you give your answer make sure you accurately state the units. If the answer is 516, is it £516 or $516 or 516 million tons or 516 miles? You must always be explicit.

→ Whenever you are writing an essay with more than one point of view, always include a clear **signpost** to the examiner. You could say, 'Now let us examine a different point of view' or 'But some people have argued differently, believing that . . .' Examiners greatly value such signposts and they may earn you extra marks because they make clearer the structure of your answer.

## The *don'ts* are just as important as the *dos*

Every year some very able candidates underperform for the following reasons:

→ They revise too late the night before and don't get enough sleep before the exam – and sometimes just give up half way through a paper through tiredness!

→ Their writing is difficult to read – what an examiner cannot read, she or he cannot give marks to!

→ They don't take General Studies seriously enough, failing to recognise that even universities which don't specify offers in the subject may still give you a place if your General Studies grade is good and compensates for a lower grade than asked for in one of the specified subjects.

→ They lapse into poor or vulgar language and fail to take care with spellings.

→ They disobey the rubric and don't answer the specified number of questions.

→ They seem to think that a powerful or determined assertion will gain marks (unlikely!) when what examiners are seeking are arguments, supported by evidence, rounded off by considered conclusions that answer the question.

→ Remember all these points – and you will do well because you deserve to do so.

**Watch out!**

Always check how many questions you are to answer. Where there are several essays, check whether you are supposed to do one of them or all of them; if you are only supposed to do one, you will not gain marks for any more answers you offer.

**Examiner's secrets**

Always show your working – that way you may get a few marks for applying the correct method even if there is an error in your final answer.

**Examiner's secrets**

If there are good reasons for your poor handwriting, see if you could be allowed to word process your answers or dictate them to an amanuensis. Ask your Exams Office 3 or 4 months before the exam. If you are allowed to dictate your answers, get plenty of dictating practice well before the exam.

# Exam questions

Each exam board uses various types of question. You need to know the sorts of question set in your exams and the types of answer are required. Practise answering questions that ask for a written response before the exam. This will help you judge the correct length of response and the amount of time needed for each type of question.

## Types of question

All three boards use **essays and extended writing** as important parts of their assessment. Their structure will vary, but they all carry a large proportion of marks. Since each board has its own preferred structure the essay is the easiest type of question to prepare for.

**EDEXCEL** offers a choice of essays in all papers, favouring a style which invites argumentative consideration of a controversial statement.

**AQA A** does not use essays in any of the AS papers but does employ them in all three A2 units. Candidates are given a wide choice.

**AQA B** uses a combination of essay questions and extended writing in Units 1 and 2 at AS and structured extended writing in their A2 units.

**OCR** use two-part structured essays in most units, and essays written as responses to stimulus material in A2 units.

**Multiple-choice and multiple-completion** (or objective) questions are used extensively by AQA A, and occasionally by EDEXCEL. They do not appear to be used in AQA B or by OCR. They are often based on a passage and you should select a correct answer from several possible answers provided. These questions can test comprehension or factual recall. Multiple-choice questions are more straightforward since you have to choose between simple answers. Multiple-completion questions offer combinations of answers from which you must choose the correct combination. It is best to eliminate wrong answers before you guess.

**Structured questions** help you by guiding you through the information required. They are often linked to passages to test comprehension, your own opinions or factual recall. Marks at the end of each part give an idea of how much you should write.

All boards use **short answer questions**. These may be free standing or linked to source material and require you to write concisely, avoiding long irrelevant answers. They often carry few marks and test factual recall or understanding.

## Source material

All three boards use source material:

→ to test comprehension and evaluation, as in AQA A;
→ as stimulus material, as in OCR or AQA B;
→ as data for interpretation or analysis, as in EDEXCEL Unit 3 or 5;
→ to test thinking and analytical skills, as in all EDEXCEL section Bs;
→ as pre-release material for a case study, as in AQA A or OCR.

# What makes a good General Studies essay? ●●●

[Ge]t your essay right and you should achieve a good score on the whole [pa]per. In most other subjects that use essays the body of knowledge [yo]u should use is fairly limited and clearly defined. In General Studies, [to]pics are usually broader and designed to allow you much greater [fr]eedom to choose the particular evidence you want to use.

**Deconstruct the title**. Identify the theme and check exactly what is [ex]pected. Look for guidewords. Ask yourself does the question:

- ask you simply to provide information (describe);
- give reasons for particular events or occurrences (explain);
- examine the merits of different views (assess, analyse, evaluate);
- identify different points of view (consider or examine);
- create your own balanced argument (justify);
- reach a conclusion (how far, to what extent)?

**[Pl]an your answer**. It is helpful to include a short plan at the start. [Th]is will help you decide what to include and give you a checklist to [co]ver everything without repetition. A plan will also give the examiner [an] overview of your ideas. If you are constructing an argument, divide [yo]ur plan into 'for' and 'against'. Remember that opinions are usually [in]teresting but have little value unless supported with evidence.

**Select evidence**. Don't just put down all you know about a topic. [Se]lect evidence to support what you say. You don't have to know [ev]erything but should be able to apply, explain and interpret what [yo]u do know. Explain how your evidence helps answer the question.

**Your essay** should have three clear parts. A brief introduction sets [th]e scene and explains what you understand by the title. Define any key [te]rms or important words. This will let you take control of your answer [ra]ther than trust to the examiner sharing your ideas. If you are asked [to] reach a conclusion it is useful to indicate it tentatively at the outset. [M]ake sure you reach the same conclusion at the end of the essay.

The main body of the answer contains evidence and argument. Make [su]re this is relevant, balanced and well organised. It should not be just [a] series of assertions or disjointed 'facts'. Use trigger words to show [w]hen you look at different points of view. Remember to evaluate or ['w]eigh up' the relative merits of the evidence and arguments you use.

[In] your conclusion don't just repeat what you have already said. Make [a] direct reference to the question to show you have addressed it. If you [ar]e asked to reach a conclusion, don't play safe by sitting on the fence.

Finally, check through your answer to see that it:

- says what you intended
- is easy for an examiner to read and understand
- deals with the question you were set.

[D]on't forget that your essay will be marked for qualities of [co]mmunication as well as for your knowledge of the topic.

[S]pecifications give details of the different types of questions used. Use [p]ast papers to practise the type of responses required.

# Index